XML—
the Microsoft Way

XML—the Microsoft Way

Peter G. Aitken

Addison-Wesley

Boston • San Francisco • New York • Toronto • Montreal
London • Munich • Paris • Madrid
Capetown • Sydney • Tokyo • Singapore • Mexico City

The publisher offers discounts on this book when ordered in quantity for special sales. For more information, please contact

Pearson Education Corporate Sales Division
201 W. 103rd Street
Indianapolis, IN 46290
(800) 428-5331
corpsales@pearsoned.com

Visit A-W on the Web: www.aw.com/cseng/

Library of Congress Cataloging-in-Publication Data
Aitken, Peter G.
XML, the Microsoft way / Aitken, Peter G.
p. cm.
Includes bibliographical references and index.
ISBN 0-201-74852-5
1. XML (Document markup language) I. Title.
QA76.76.H94 A47 2001
005.7'2—dc21 2001053629

ISBN 0-201-74852-5
Text printed on recycled paper
1 2 3 4 5 6 7 8 9 10—MA—0504030201
First printing, December 2001

To my wife, Maxine Okazaki,
for her many years of love, support, and friendship
years past and years future

Contents

Introduction

Extensible Markup Language (XML) is quite simple in concept. It is nothing more than a set of rules for providing structure to data. Despite this underlying simplicity—or perhaps partly because of it—XML has become an extremely important technology that is widely used in diverse areas of information processing. Because XML can be used with essentially any kind of data, it has found application in areas as dissimilar as finance, agriculture, law, medicine, and computer programming. Because XML is a public, nonproprietary standard, it can be used by anyone, anywhere. Because XML is platform independent, it is used on Windows PCs, Macintoshes, Linux boxes, mainframes, and just about any other platform you care to mention. What's more, XML permits these various types of computers to exchange data with an ease that was never possible before. More and more applications developers find themselves needing to write XML applications. Given that you are reading this, I suspect you are one of them.

About This Book

This book is intended for software developers who need to learn the fundamentals of XML and its most important related technologies, and who also want to learn how to include XML support in their applications. It is specifically aimed at developers who create applications for the Windows platform using Microsoft development tools. About half of the book's chapters deal with public XML and related standards and would be useful to any XML developer regardless of the platform or development tools being used (although coding examples make use of Microsoft languages). The remaining chapters deal specifically with using XML with Microsoft development and end-user tools:

Visual Basic, Visual C++, Internet Explorer, Active Server Pages, the .NET Framework, and so on.

Readers are assumed to have little or no experience with XML and its related technologies. The XML material is presented "from the ground up" and is suitable for XML beginners as well as those with an intermediate level of knowledge. The programming chapters, on the other hand, assume some prior experience with the specific language or technology in use. For example, Chapter 15 shows you how to manipulate XML from a Visual Basic program, but it does not teach you the fundamentals of using Visual Basic. Chapters on Visual C++ and the new .NET language C# are included as well.

What about Java?

For many XML programmers, Java is the language of choice. There are many good reasons for this preference, not the least of which is the availability of many powerful Java tools for use with XML. However, you'll see that there is no coverage of Java in this book. This is because the book is designed specifically to cover Microsoft tools as they relate to XML, and Microsoft's Java, known as Visual J++, has reached a dead end. As a result of legal settlements, Microsoft has agreed to stop upgrading Visual J++, so the current version of this product (Visual J++ version 6.0) will be the last. Thus, there is no place for Java in a Microsoft-oriented book—much to my dismay, as it is an excellent language.

Yet all is not lost for the Java lover working in a Microsoft shop. The latest Microsoft development tools, collectively known as Visual Studio .NET, include a new language called C# (C sharp). While Microsoft officially denies it, many people see C# as Microsoft's replacement for Java. C# is Java-like in many ways, and I think that any Java programmer will soon feel at home with C#.

About the Listings

Throughout the book, code samples are presented both as code fragments interspersed in the text and as separate numbered listings. For the most part, the numbered listings are complete files—for example, a complete XML file or a complete Visual Basic source code file. In a few cases, a listing is a fragment of a file, such as a section of source code that cannot function on its own but must be part of a larger program. These exceptions are clearly noted.

Source Code and Corrections

You can download all of the code (from the numbered listings) from the book's companion Web page at `http://www.pgacon.com/xml_ms.htm`. The download file is a ZIP archive. When you expand the ZIP file, you will have a separate folder for each of the book's chapters (except those that do not have any listings). This Web page also lists any corrections that have been reported. If you find what you think is an error in the book, please let me know by e-mailing me at `peter@pgacon.com`. I am also delighted to hear from readers with any comments or suggestions regarding the book. Please note, however, that I can respond only to queries that are directly book-related, and I cannot answer any general programming questions you may have.

Peter G. Aitken
Chapel Hill, North Carolina
August 2001

Acknowledgments

While this book lists only a single author, it was in many ways a group effort. My appreciation goes to Mary T. O'Brien, executive editor at Addison-Wesley, for her guidance and oversight throughout the project, and to Alicia Cary, editorial assistant, for handling many of the unavoidable details. This book benefited greatly from thorough technical reviews by Ann Navarro, Robert J. Brunner, Duane Nickull, Robert W. Husted, Dr. Abbas Birjandi, and Steve Heckler. While they caught many errors, I, of course, am responsible for any that remain. Finally, I thank T.E. "Raj" Rajagopal for contributing Chapter 16 when I realized that my C++ skills had become far too rusty to inflict on any readers.

CHAPTER 1

XML: What and Why?

This chapter provides an introduction to the fundamentals and history of XML. You'll learn what XML is, what it is used for, and why it is becoming so important. You'll also learn something about the history of XML and about the standards process. If you already have experience with XML, you may be familiar with some of this material. For XML newcomers, the information presented here will provide an important foundation for the material that is covered in subsequent chapters.

What Is XML?

In a nutshell, XML, or Extensible Markup Language, is a technique for creating structured data. The term "structured" means that the data is organized in a manner that clearly and unambiguously identifies each individual piece of information. XML has not been around all that long. The XML 1.0 specification was released in 1998, but in the brief time since then it has attained an importance in the computer and data processing world that has surprised many observers. This importance is expected to increase even further in the years to come. What's the big deal? There are three factors involved, which I explain in the sections that follow.

XML Is a Markup Language

A *markup language* is a specification for storing structured data—in other words, for storing data along with information about what the data means. Here is a simple example of data that is not marked up:

```
Jane Smith
123 Oak Street
Durham
```

```
NC
27705
```

A person reading this data will be aware of what it means. It is clear that "Jane Smith" is a name, "Durham" is a city, and so on. A computer, however, is not quite as smart. It has no reliable way of knowing what the individual pieces of data represent. A markup language can be used to provide this information, or structure, as shown here:

```
<person>
  <name>Jane Smith</name>
  <address>123 Oak Street</address>
  <city>Durham</city>
  <state>NC</state>
  <zipcode>27705</zipcode>
</person>
```

Once the data has been marked up as in the preceding example, the structure of the data is clear: It comprises an element called "person" that contains subsidiary elements called "name," "address," and so on. A program can unambiguously determine exactly what each piece of information represents. There are many different forms that a markup language can take. The preceding example (which follows the XML standard) adheres to certain rules.

- Text inside brackets <...> is a markup tag. Text outside brackets is data.
- The start of a unit of data, or *element,* is marked by a tag that identifies the data.
- The end of a unit of data is marked by an end tag that is identical to the start tag with the addition of a leading slash (/) character.

In the previous example, you can see that "<address>" is a start tag, "123 Oak Street" is data, and "</address>" is an end tag.

There are a lot more rules of XML, of course, and they will be covered later in the book. For now it is important only to understand the fundamental concept of what XML is and what it is used for. While the concept of a markup language may seem rather simple, it provides an amazing amount of power and flexibility. This is because the structure of an XML document does not place any constraints on what can be done with the data that is in the document. How this works will become clear as you learn more about XML.

There is nothing special about the way XML data is stored: It is kept in standard text files. You can use any text editor, such as the Notepad application that comes with the Windows operating system, to read and edit XML files.

Note, however, that while XML files *can* be read by humans, they rarely if ever are. In most cases, an XML file will be created by a program and then used by other programs without ever being viewed by a person.

XML Is Extensible

The *X* in XML stands for "eXtensible"—in other words, the language can be extended as needed to meet the requirements of a specific situation. Another way of expressing this is to say that, technically speaking, XML is not a language but rather it is a *metalanguage,* a language for defining other languages. In practical terms, this means that you are not limited to a predefined set of tags in creating an XML document—you can create any tags you need for a specific application. The XML standard provides a set of rules that specify some details, such as how to create tags and how an XML document can be structured, but within the XML framework you are free to define and use tags that best suit the data. Whether your XML document contains a mailing list, an auto parts inventory, a Web page, or the annotated sonnets of Shakespeare, you can represent and structure the data with essentially complete freedom.

XML Keeps Data Storage Separate from Data Display

In order to be useful, data usually needs to be displayed in some form that is usable by human beings. The term "display" is used here in the widest possible sense and includes possibilities as diverse as

- A document on a 21-inch computer screen
- A document on the 3-inch display of a personal digital assistant
- A Web page
- Text converted to speech for audio output
- Playback of music
- Output to a typesetter for magazine publication

XML was specifically designed so that the storage of data in an XML document would place absolutely no constraints on the display of the data. When data is stored using the XML specification, you can be confident that there will be no limitations on how the data can be displayed. XML data can be and often is displayed, but as you will see, the display of the data is kept totally separate from the storage of the data.

XML Is a Public and Widely Accepted Standard

The XML standard was created by the World Wide Web Consortium (W3C). This is an open, public organization whose task is to develop technologies and standards for the Internet. In addition to XML, W3C is the force behind standards for Hypertext Markup Language (HTML), Portable Network Graphics (PNG, a graphics file format for Web use), and HyperText Transfer Protocol (HTTP, the standard for information transmission on the Internet), to name a few. W3C and the standards process are explained in more detail later in the chapter. You can learn more at the W3C Web site (`http://www.w3.org/`).

Because the XML standard is public, it is not owned or dominated by any single commercial interest. Many of the current standards for data storage and manipulation were developed by companies such as IBM, Microsoft, and Sun. These so-called proprietary standards may work perfectly well, but because they are controlled by a single company, an outside developer has no assurance that the standard will not be changed without warning, subjected to licensing fees, or dropped altogether. With a public standard such as XML you know these things cannot happen.

The Development of XML

To have a good understanding of XML, you should know something about its development—its origins, precursors, and the motivation for its creation. In the sections that follow, you'll see that the idea for a markup language is nothing new.

Early Markup Languages

Almost 40 years ago, people at IBM were pursuing the idea of a standard method for structuring documents, with the goal of facilitating the exchange and manipulation of data. The result was Generalized Markup Language (GML), which was used internally at IBM to create various kinds of documents. Similar technologies were developed at other organizations, but these were all proprietary and incompatible with each other. There was no worldwide standard.

The first standardized markup language also originated at IBM. Called Standard Generalized Markup Language, or SGML, it was originally created for working with legal documents. SGML was expanded to be suitable as an all-purpose markup standard, and it was soon being used in a wide range of settings. In 1986, SGML was released as an official standard by the

International Organization for Standardization (ISO). SGML is an extremely powerful and flexible technology, which unavoidably entails a great deal of complexity and processing overhead.

Hypertext Markup Language

The next important step in the development of markup languages was motivated by the Internet. Many documents of various types (text, graphics, and so on) were available on the Internet, and Tim Berners-Lee, at the time a software engineer at the European Laboratory for Particle Physics in Switzerland, realized that access to these documents would be vastly improved if they could be linked to one another in a meaningful way that would enable users to move easily between related documents. A method was needed for marking up these documents in order to specify the links between documents and also to specify how a document was to be displayed in the browser. The resulting language was a subset of SGML called Hypertext Markup Language (HTML). With HTML came the birth of the World Wide Web, which consists of the entire web of linked documents. HTML is the standard "language of the Web," and any Web page you view uses HTML.

HTML has been a huge success, but along with that success came some growing pains. As the Web grew, developers wanted to include more and more things on their Web pages—animations, database access, interactivity, and so on. HTML, originally designed as a hyperlink and display markup language, was not really up to the task. A lot of very clever people worked long, hard hours to squeeze the desired results from HTML. The results are clearly impressive, as anyone who surfs the Web knows.

Even so, it was clear that the days were numbered that HTML would continue to meet the needs of Web developers. Something more powerful and flexible was needed. The most serious limitation of HTML is its fixed tag set. You can use the tags defined in HTML and that's all—there is no extensibility. SGML, on the other hand, fully supports custom tags. Yet the complexity and processing overhead of SGML made it unsuitable for general Web use.

SGML for the Web

In 1996, W3C set itself the goal to develop a standard that would provide the power and flexibility of SGML in a form that was suitable for use on the Web. Among the requirements for the new standard was that it include three of SGML's most significant benefits:

- *Extensibility:* The developer can define custom tags as needed for a specific application.
- *Structure:* The language syntax follows a well-defined structure.
- *Validation:* Documents can be validated against a data model.

The W3C committee worked on its task for almost 2 years. In February 1998, it was ready with the first version of the standard for the new language. Known as Extensible Markup Language version 1.0, it remains as of this writing the current XML specification, or in W3C terms, the XML Recommendation.

Optional XML Technologies

The core XML standard provides a set of rules for creating tags and attributes to provide structure for data, and a Document Type Definition (DTD) facility to constrain these structures. Taken by itself, this core standard is sufficient for many purposes. For other data-related applications, however, the tools provided by the core XML standard are not sufficient. To address these other needs, a family of optional technologies has grown up around the core XML standard.

Cascading Style Sheets

Cascading Style Sheets (CSS) is a style sheet language that is used to associate display styles, such as fonts, indentation, line spacing, and colors, with the elements of an XML document. CSS is also used with HTML documents. A display program, such as a browser, will use the information in a CSS to determine how to display the data in an XML document. Keeping the display specification separate from the data provides a great deal of flexibility. When you define different style sheets, the same data can be displayed in various ways as appropriate to a specific situation. Also, if the display of many documents is controlled by a single style sheet, you can easily change the look of *all* your pages by modifying one style sheet.

Extensible Stylesheet Language

Extensible Stylesheet Language (XSL) is a style sheet language that serves essentially the same purpose as CSS: to define how the data in an XML document is to be displayed. XSL is considerably more powerful than CSS, and it is correspondingly more difficult to learn and use. XSL is composed of two parts: XSL Transformation (XSLT) and Formatting Objects (FO). XSLT is used to transform the structure of an original XML document as required by the current display needs. For example, the order and organization of the data can be changed, and new elements, such as a table of contents or index, can be created. The transformation will also add references to Formatting Objects. FO is a class of objects for specifying display intentions, such as font, color, and layout. The transformed file is processed by a *formatter*, a program that uses the FO instructions to create the final output. Typically, FO is used to create printed output while CSS is applied more to Web browser display, although this distinction is far from being absolute.

XSL is not only applicable to the display of data. By using XSLT alone, without reference to FO, it is possible to transform an XML document to a different representation and structure. There are various uses for such transformations, the most common being the transformation of an XML document to an HTML document for display in a Web browser.

XML Schema

XML Schema is a standard for defining the data model for an XML document. A *data model* is a set of rules that the data in a document must follow. Put another way, a data model specifies the tags that are permitted in the document, the relationship between the tags, and the type of data each tag can contain. To illustrate, look again at the XML fragment that was presented earlier in the chapter:

```
<person>
  <name>Jane Smith</name>
  <address>123 Oak Street</address>
  <city>Durham</city>
  <state>NC</state>
  <zipcode>27705</zipcode>
</person>
```

The data model for this XML document would specify the following (among other things):

- The tags `person`, `name`, `address`, `city`, `state`, and `zipcode` are permitted.
- The tags `name`, `address`, `city`, `state`, and `zipcode` must be inside a `person` tag.
- The data in a `state` tag must consist of two letters.

Data models specify what tags are permitted, what tags are required, the relationships between tags, and various other aspects of how an XML document must be structured. Data models are an important aspect of XML because most applications that use data in XML format require that data to be structured in a specific manner. This is accomplished with the *validation* process. During the processing of an XML document, the contents of the document are checked against the document's data model. If the document adheres to the model, it is considered to be valid and can then passed to further processing with confidence that there will be no surprises regarding the type or structure of the data.

The XML Schema standard is one way to create a data model. The other method, Document Type Definition (DTD), is not mentioned separately because, as I mentioned earlier, it is a part of the core XML 1.0 standard rather than being an optional standard. In fact, DTD was the original method of creating a data model, and it is still the most widely used. Note that "schema" is a general term referring to an XML data model, while "XML Schema" is a specific technology for creating schemas. Also, the term "vocabulary" is sometimes used to mean the same thing as a schema. Thus, a schema can be said to define an XML vocabulary.

Well-Formed and Valid XML Documents

An XML document is considered well-formed if it meets the rules of XML syntax. This is a separate matter from a document being valid. There is no DTD or Schema involved in a document being well-formed. A document can be well-formed without being valid. To be valid, however, a document must be well-formed and must also adhere to the data model defined in a DTD or Schema.

XLink and XPointer

The XML Linking Language (Xlink) standard defines a standard way to create a link to an external resource, such as another XML file. The links defined by XLink are similar in concept to the hyperlinks used on the World Wide Web, but with significantly greater flexibility. Thus, XLink uses XML syntax to provide links between resources (files) and provides the capability for bidirectional links and even more complex connections. A related standard, XPointer, provides links within an XML document (from one part of a document to another part).

Document Object Model

The Document Object Model (DOM) is a standardized set of procedures that programs and scripts can use to access and manipulate the content of an XML document. DOM provides access to the data in the document as well as to the structure of the document (its tags). DOM is most often exposed, or made available, by a *parser*, a program that performs the first steps in processing an XML document. You'll learn more about parsing later in this chapter. For now it is sufficient to know that a parser reads an XML file and makes the contents of the file available to a program or a script. The program or script uses DOM to access the information. Specifically, DOM defines a set of programming procedures—referred to collectively as an *application programming interface (API)*—that the program or script calls to access the XML file contents. By writing your program or script to adhere to the DOM API, you can use a DOM-compliant parser. Likewise, if you write your own parser to be DOM-compliant, you know it can be used by any program or script that uses the DOM API.

Simple API for XML

Simple API for XML (SAX) is an application programming interface, or API, that is designed to serve the same purpose as DOM—that is, to provide a programmatic interface to the content of an XML document. While DOM and SAX serve the same basic purpose, they go about it quite differently. The details of how these two technologies work will be presented later in this book. For now it is sufficient to say that SAX is not quite as powerful as DOM (although perfectly adequate for many uses), but it has a lower overhead in terms of memory and processing power. SAX and DOM are not an either/or proposition, and a given application may use both APIs, choosing one or the other as best suited for a particular task.

XML Namespaces

The XML Namespaces standard was developed to permit the creation of compound XML documents. A *compound document* is a document that is composed of two or more fragments that are each based on a different vocabulary (a different DTD or Schema). With two or more vocabularies, there is no guarantee that the same tag name is not used by both vocabularies for different purposes. To prevent such possible confusion, the Namespaces standard provides a method for unambiguously identifying which vocabulary is applicable to each and every part of the document.

The XML Standards Process

The term "standard" has two different but related meanings. Its everyday meaning is a widely accepted agreement about what something means or how something should be done, without implying any official status or approval. This is how I have been using the term up to this point. In other contexts, however, a standard is an official internationally negotiated specification, or document, that is issued by an organization. It is impossible to overstate the importance of standards in almost all areas of modern life. Many everyday things that we take for granted, such as the length of a meter, the volume of a quart, and the duration of a second, have been established as standards.

Standards are equally important in the world of computers and data processing. As an example, consider one of the most important and widely used standards, the American Standard Code for Information Interchange (ASCII, sometimes called the ANSI standard after the American National Standards Institute, the organization that publishes the standard). Because computers work with numbers, it is necessary to represent letters and other symbols by numbers inside a computer. The ASCII standard specifies the codes for the letters, punctuation marks, numerals, and symbols that are used in text documents. A letter saved as a disk file might well start with the values 72 101 108 108 111 but any program that adheres to the ASCII standard will know to interpret those values as "Hello." The ASCII standard is universally accepted, which means that text documents can be freely exchanged between different programs and different computers. You can imagine the problems that would arise if different programs and operating systems used different codes for letters and symbols!

The World Wide Web Consortium

There are numerous organizations in the world that deal with standards (again, using the term in its general sense), but the one that is relevant to the topic of this book is the World Wide Web Consortium, or W3C. This organization was started in 1994 at the Massachusetts Institute of Technology by Tim

Berners-Lee, the inventor of the World Wide Web. Currently, W3C is equally hosted between three institutions: MIT, INRIA (French National Computing Research Center), and Keio University.

Berners-Lee and others realized that the future development and usefulness of the Internet and Web would depend to a great extent on the availability of the appropriate standardized technologies. The most important task of W3C is to design these technologies and to publish public specifications for them.

W3C is composed of over 400 members at the present moment. These members are not individual people, but rather organizations, such as software and hardware vendors, academic institutions, corporations, governmental agencies, and content providers. Any organization that is interested in the activities of W3C can join.

The Standards Process

W3C does not issue standards in the official sense that was described previously. Rather, it issues *Recommendations.* Whatever the terminology, a W3C Recommendation can be considered a standard in the more general sense of the word. The process of creating a Recommendation begins with the identification of a need. For example, the development of the XML Recommendation had its origin in the recognition of a need for a markup language that provided the structure and extensibility of SGML with significantly less complexity and overhead (this was covered in more detail in the section "The Development of XML" earlier in this chapter). When a need has been recognized, W3C creates a Working Group assigned to the specific task. This group consists of members of the W3C technical staff as well as representatives of member organizations. The Working Group is issued a charter specifying the goals or needs it is to address.

As the Working Group develops a preliminary technical specification, it issues Working Drafts that describe the current state of the proposed specification. These Working Drafts are works in progress, and they provide a way for individuals and organizations that are not directly involved with the Working Group to comment on and propose changes to the specification. A Working Group is required by W3C rules to publish a Working Draft at least every 3 months.

When the Working Group agrees that the specification has become stable and meets its charter, it issues a Last Call Working Draft. The Last Call signals the final opportunity for individuals and organizations to comment on the proposal before it moves to the next stage of development. The Last Call Working

Draft period is typically on the order of a month but it can be extended as needed.

When the Last Call has ended and all issues that were brought up have been resolved, the proposed specification is given Candidate Recommendation status. This is an explicit call to the technical community outside W3C to comment on the Candidate Recommendation and also to implement the specification. The main purpose of the Candidate Recommendation stage is related to implementation, as it is sometimes the case that problems with a specification become apparent only when attempts are made to implement it. It is recommended, although not required, that a Candidate Recommendation have two independent and interoperable implementations before moving to the next step: Proposed Recommendation. In some cases, sufficient implementation will have occurred during the Working Draft period to permit the Candidate Recommendation phase to be skipped, with the specification moving directly from Working Draft to Proposed Recommendation.

A Proposed Recommendation is in effect the Working Group saying, "We think this is finished." A Proposed Recommendation must meet the requirements of the Working Group's charter and adequately address dependencies and technical comments from the technical community. Technical issues should all have been resolved at this point. One way to look at a Proposed Recommendation is as a "last chance" for anyone to comment on the specification before it is finalized.

After the review period, a Proposed Recommendation (with any changes) is accorded Recommendation status. A Recommendation is a specification that is published and publicly available, and it is often seen as a de facto standard. The term "recommendation" is used because W3C has no power to enforce its standards on anyone. Its Recommendations are available for anyone to use, however, and because of the open nature of the process by which a Recommendation is created, the resulting specification is almost always acceptable to all concerned parties. Because W3C Recommendations are publicly available to anyone who wants to use them and are not under the control of any commercial interests, they are nonproprietary.

The issuance of a W3C Recommendation is not the end of the story. Despite the extensive development period, errors are sometimes found and will have to be corrected in a revised Recommendation. Furthermore, as people work with the technology, ideas for extensions and improvements will always arise. It's fair to say that as soon as a Recommendation is issued, work on the next one begins—perhaps not officially at W3C, but certainly in the programming community.

Proprietary and Nonproprietary Technologies

A *proprietary technology* is one that is owned and controlled by a company or organization. In and of themselves, there is nothing evil about proprietary technologies. In fact, they are an important driving force behind innovation in many fields. A company is not likely to devote a lot of time and investment to developing a new technology unless they will be able to make a profit from their ideas. This is all well and good, but there are two serious problems that affect outsiders who want to make use of a proprietary technology. First of all, the owner of the technology can charge a licensing fee or can deny permission to use it altogether. Second, the owner can modify the specifications at any time, without warning or public input. These are two powerful arguments for the use of a nonproprietary technology such as XML. Not only is XML freely available to anyone who wants to use it, but you are also guaranteed that any changes or additions to the specification will be made only with timely notification and public input.

Unfortunately, things are not quite as simple as this. It may sound like there is always a clear distinction between what is proprietary and what is not, but this is not always the case. Sometimes a software publisher will be anxious to get a new technology to its customers, so it will release a product that is based on the Working Draft or Proposed Recommendation for the technology, before the details have been finalized by W3C. If the specification undergoes further revisions before being finalized, the software vendor (and its customers, partners, and suppliers) will be stuck with a noncompliant product. If the software publisher's customers have come to rely on this product, the publisher may be unwilling to change its product to meet the final Recommendation. Another scenario has a software vendor waiting until the W3C Recommendation is complete, but then deciding that there are some nifty features that should be added to a product even though they are not part of the specification. In either case, the result is a tool or product that almost but not quite meets a particular specification. The difference may be minor, but it can still "break" software.

History has shown that Microsoft is perhaps the most visible offender in this regard, but given their clout in the development world it is often impossible to ignore them. One goal of this book is to clearly identify those technologies that are nonproprietary specifications, those that are proprietary (particularly with regard to Microsoft), and those that fall into the gray middle ground.

Tools for Working with XML

A common question that is asked by developers just getting started with XML is "What tools do I use to work with XML?" This is not an easy question to answer. Unlike some development technologies, XML does not require any specific software packages. For example, to program in Visual Basic there's no ambiguity: You need the Microsoft Visual Basic program, and that's all you need. Unlike Visual Basic, XML is a nonproprietary technology, so anyone is free to create and distribute tools for working with XML. This situation means there are many tools available for you to choose from, but it also can lead to some confusion about what is available, which tools perform which tasks, and what exactly *you* need for your development projects.

Tools for Creating XML

Because XML files are text, they can be created by any program that can create text files. Any text editor, including the Notepad utility that comes with Windows, is suitable. You should not use a word processing program, such as Microsoft Word, unless you know it can save your files in plain text format. Plain text editors can be cumbersome to use for anything but the simplest XML editing tasks, and you may want to consider one of the many specialized XML editors that are available. These programs automate or simplify many aspects of creating XML, and they make the developer's job a lot easier. Some editors have a parser integrated with them. XML editors are available as commercial software, as shareware, and as freeware. You can locate various editors by performing a Web search on the term "XML editor." Microsoft provides a free XML editor called XML Notepad. You can download this program from `http://msdn.microsoft.com/xml/notepad/intro.asp`.

A Note on URLs

Throughout this book I will be providing you with URLs for accessing various kinds of tools and information. I do not have any association with the organizations or corporations who provide these materials, nor am I implying any endorsement beyond my belief that an XML developer may find this material useful. Remember that URLs sometimes change or disappear, and while this information was current at the time of writing, there are no guarantees that it will still be current by the time you read this.

In many situations, XML is not written directly by a developer but is generated automatically by an application. For example, your company may keep all of its sales data in a Microsoft SQL database. Your job as the resident XML developer might be to create an application that extracts selected data from the database and outputs the data as an XML file for use on a Web page or for transfer to other applications. Almost any programming language can be used for tasks such as these. All that is required is the ability to access the data in its original form and to output the resulting XML as a text file. Any programming language I have ever seen has the text manipulation capabilities that will permit a developer to write the required code. Microsoft Visual Basic is my favorite tool because of its strong database access and text manipulation capabilities, but that's my preference—other development languages such as Java or C++ are equally suitable.

Tools for Browsing XML

One area where use of XML is widespread is the World Wide Web. This means that browser support of XML is increasingly important. To support XML, a browser needs to do two things: display the content of an XML document formatted according to its associated style sheet and parse the XML document to allow access to its contents. The first commercial browser to support XML was Microsoft Internet Explorer version 5.0. This browser is currently in version 5.5, and by the time you read this there may be a newer version available. Internet Explorer supports some XML-related technologies as well, including XML Namespaces and the XML Document Object Model (DOM). Chapter 17 covers the details of using Internet Explorer with XML.

Because this book emphasizes Microsoft tools for XML, I suggest that you use the latest version of Internet Explorer as your XML browser. It is not, however, the only browser to support XML. The Mozilla browser promises complete XML support. This browser is an open source code initiative that is based on the Netscape Communicator browser, and it is being developed with the cooperation of Netscape. You can find additional information at `http://www.mozilla.org/`. Also, W3C has developed its own browser, Amaya. You can use this browser to browse XML documents and also as an XML editor. The editor is designed specifically for creating XML Web pages. You can download Amaya from the W3C Web site (`http://www.w3.org/Amaya/`).

Tools for Parsing XML

The one essential tool for reading and modifying XML files is a *parser*. The terms "parser" and "processor" are sometimes used interchangeably, although technically this is not correct. Any program that takes an XML file as its input and produces some output based on the XML file's content is an XML processor. An XML browser is one example of a processor, as are programs that create typesetting codes, synthesized speech, or HTML pages based on an XML document. A parser is a software component that performs the first steps in processing an XML document. Rarely, if ever, will an XML parser operate on its own. Rather, a parser is almost always used as part of an XML processor.

The most basic task a parser performs is checking the XML document for well-formedness, making sure the document content follows the rules of XML syntax. All XML parsers perform this task. It is essential that no further processing be carried out if the document is not well-formed. XML syntax was carefully designed to ensure that the structure of a document is completely unambiguous. If the syntax is incorrect, the parser will detect it.

Most parsers can also check a document for validity by checking it against its DTD or Schema. While not all XML documents require validation, many do. The processing software that uses the output of the parser is likely to be programmed to expect the document content to follow certain rules as defined in the DTD or Schema. That a document is well-formed is not enough—the data must be structured properly if the processing software is to work correctly.

The final task a parser may perform is to make the content of the document, both the markup and the data, available to the processing software. This is done by means of the SAX API or the DOM API (these were explained earlier in this chapter). Some parsers support both SAX and DOM, permitting the processing software to use one or the other as needs dictate.

Overall, the parser is an essential part of XML document processing. When an XML document has been successfully parsed with no errors, the processing software then

- Knows that the document is free of syntax errors
- Knows that the document follows the data model specified in a DTD or Schema (if one is attached) if validation was performed
- Can access the document content via SAX or DOM calls

XML parsers do not usually exist as stand-alone applications as their usefulness would be compromised. A stand-alone parser could perform the first two tasks in the previous list but not the third. Most parsers are in the form of a software component, or class, that can be used by processing applications. The processing software interacts with the parser, making calls to the parser's properties and methods to perform the needed tasks. You'll see how this is done in later chapters.

The Microsoft XML Parser

There are numerous XML parsers available, but because this book is focused on Microsoft technologies for XML, the material covered will be limited to the Microsoft XML Parser (MSXML). This is a very powerful parser that is currently in version 4.0. It performs syntax checking, does validation, and exposes the document content with both SAX and DOM. It is available at no charge from the Microsoft Web site, and it can be used as a software component from a wide variety of development languages, including Visual Basic, C++, and Java. Unlike previous versions of the MSXML Parser, version 4.0 is (or at least claims to be) in compliance with the W3C standards for XML Schema, and it also supports the earlier Microsoft-specific XDR Schemas (explained in detail in Chapter 4). To download the installation package for the MSXML Parser, go to `http://msdn.microsoft.com/downloads/` and search for "MSXML 4.0 Parser."

The Microsoft XML Software Developer Kit

Another useful tool that is available from Microsoft is the Microsoft XML Software Developer Kit (MSXML SDK). The most important part of the SDK is an online documentation file that provides information on using the Microsoft XML Parser, an XML developer's guide, an XML reference and tutorial, DOM and SAX reference material, and more. It is very useful to have this information at your fingertips while working on your XML projects. The SDK is installed at the same time you install the MSXML Parser.

Summary

This chapter provided an overview of the "XML world." XML is deceptively simple in principle, but it is this very simplicity that is at the root of its tremendous power and flexibility for representing structured data. By being extensible, XML places essentially no limitations on the data structures it can be used to define. By separating data storage from data display, XML lends itself to technological advances that will see data presented in a wide variety of forms, from computer screen and print output to cell phones and speech synthesis. By virtue of being a commonly accepted public standard, XML provides the security of widespread compatibility, a wide selection of tools and utilities, and freedom from the problems that attend proprietary technologies.

CHAPTER 2

The Syntax of XML

Languages such as English and Spanish have a *syntax*, or set of rules, that specifies how the language should be spoken and written. Word order, capitalization, and use of punctuation are some of the areas in which syntax provides guidelines for usage. If someone does not follow the rules perfectly, however, it is usually still possible to figure out what that person said or wrote. Computers are not nearly as smart as humans—at least not yet. For a computer to understand a language, such as XML, the rules of syntax must be very clear and they must be followed precisely. A seemingly trivial error, such as a misplaced punctuation mark, will halt a computer dead in its tracks. XML syntax is not all that complicated, but it must be followed exactly. This chapter covers those aspects of XML syntax that apply to all XML documents. Aspects of syntax that apply only to certain types of XML documents, such as Document Type Definitions (DTDs), will be covered in later chapters.

Syntax Overview

Before I get into the details of XML syntax, I present an overview of the more important elements of syntax. With this broad, if incomplete, view of what an XML document contains and how the syntax works, you will find it easier to place the details that are presented later in this chapter into their proper perspective.

Everything in an XML document is either markup or character data. Markup consists of tags, which are always enclosed in brackets (< >). XML markup is case-sensitive. Character data is usually outside brackets, with the two exceptions being attributes and `CDATA` sections, which are covered later in this chapter. Almost all the rules of XML syntax are concerned with tags. XML has several types of tags to serve various purposes:

- Provide instructions to the XML processor
- Provide references to information that is stored somewhere else
- Organize the data in a meaningful way

The use of tags is illustrated in Listing 2.1 and Listing 2.2, which present an XML document that is split up over two separate files. The document contains an address list. In Listing 2.1, the lines are numbered for easy reference. The function of the individual lines is explained following the listings.

Listing 2.1 Sample XML Document to Illustrate Syntax Elements

```
1. <?xml version="1.0" encoding="UTF-8" ?>
2. <!DOCTYPE addresslist SYSTEM "addresslist.dtd" [
3. <!ENTITY oldlist SYSTEM "oldaddresslist.xml">
4. ]>
5. <addresslist>
6.   <person>
7.     <name>Ann Smith</name>
8.     <address>35 Oak Street</address>
9.     <city>Albany</city>
10.    <state>NY</state>
11.    <zipcode>12345</zipcode>
12.   </person>
13.   <person>
14.     <name>Jose Gomez</name>
15.     <address>12A Western Boulevard</address>
16.     <city>Sacramento</city>
17.     <state>CA</state>
18.     <zipcode>98765</zipcode>
19.   </person>
20.   &oldlist;
21. </addresslist>
```

Listing 2.2 The File oldaddresslist.xml That Is Referenced As an External Entity on Line 3 of Listing 2.1

```
<?xml version="1.0" encoding="UTF-8" ?>
<person>
  <name>Nelson Agee</name>
  <address>1012 Main Street</address>
  <city>St. Louis</city>
  <state>MO</state>
  <zipcode>12321</zipcode>
```

```
</person>
<person>
  <name>Elizabeth Chang</name>
  <address>421 Lakeshore Rd.</address>
  <city>Los Angeles</city>
  <state>CA</state>
  <zipcode>55555</zipcode>
</person>
```

The functions of the tags in Listing 2.1 are as follows:

Line 1: This is a processing instruction that informs the XML processor that the file adheres to XML version 1.0 and that the file uses the character encoding known as UTF-8 (more on character encoding later).

Line 2: This is the start of a multiline `DOCTYPE` tag. This type of tag is used for various purposes, and it often contains other tags. On this line, the tag specifies that the document is of type "addresslist" and that it follows the data model that is defined in the DTD located in the file addresslist.dtd. In this case, the name of the document type and the name of the DTD are the same, but they need not be. Note that the DTD file addresslist.dtd is not presented here; its name is used only to demonstrate the `DOCTYPE` tag.

Line 3: This is an `ENTITY` tag, which is contained within the `DOCTYPE` tag. It declares a reference to an external file. Specifically, it defines the term "oldlist" to refer to the file oldaddresslist.xml.

Line 4: This marks the end of the `DOCTYPE` tag.

Line 5: This tag marks the beginning of the content portion of the document, of type "addresslist." Note that the name of this tag must be the same as the name specified in the `DOCTYPE` tag (line 2). This is the document's root element.

Line 6: This tag marks the beginning of a unit of data called "person."

Lines 7 through 11: These lines contain tags and data that define the information belonging to this "person" unit.

Line 12: This tag marks the end of the "person" unit of data.

Lines 13 through 19: The tags and data on these lines define a second "person" unit of data.

Line 20: This line references the "oldlist" entity that was declared on line 3. It is marked as an entity reference by the leading ampersand (&) and the ending semicolon (;). The effect of this line is the same as if the contents of the file oldaddresslist.xml were cut and pasted into the document at this location.

Line 21: This final tag marks the end of the "addresslist" document.

Processing Instructions

A Processing Instruction, often abbreviated as PI, provides instructions for applications that process the document, such as a parser. PIs can appear anywhere in an XML document and have no bearing on whether or not a document is valid. The format for a PI is as follows:

```
<?target instructions ?>
```

The *target* is a name identifying the application to which the instruction is directed. The target name "XML" in all of its uppercase and lowercase variants is reserved for passing instructions to the processor. The *instructions* are one or more parameter/value pairs in this form:

```
parameter="value"
```

Here's an example PI, which is in fact the only regularly used PI and if present must be the first line of most XML documents:

```
<?XML version="1.0" encoding="UTF-8" ?>
```

This PI instructs the processor to use the syntax rules of XML version 1.0 when processing the file (this is the only version of XML that exists at present, but additional versions will be developed in the future). It also specifies that the XML file is in UTF-8 format. The one other character format that XML processors are required to support is UTF-16.

PIs are meaningful only if the program that is processing the document is looking for them. Otherwise, as long as they follow proper syntax, they have no effect.

> ***Character Encoding***
>
> *The XML Recommendation states that legal characters in XML are those of the Unicode standard. Computers use numbers to represent characters, and character encoding specifies the way in which the Unicode characters are mapped to numbers. There are two Unicode Transformation Formats (UTFs) that XML processors must support. One is UTF-8, in which the ASCII characters (standard English letters, punctuation, and so on) are represented by 1-byte values, and other characters (accented letters, Chinese characters, and so on) are represented by 2- or 3-byte values. The other format, UTF-16, represents each character as either a 2- or a 4-byte value. Please visit* `http://www.unicode.org/unicode/reports/tr20/index.html` *for more information on Unicode and XML.*

Physical and Logical Structure of an XML Document

An XML document has both a physical and a logical structure. The physical structure permits the components of the document, or *entities*, to be named and stored separately, in multiple disk files or other storage units. The logical structure permits the data in the document to be organized and divided into named units and subunits called *elements*.

It is important to remember that the concept of an XML document does not correspond to a single disk file. An XML document is often contained in a single disk file, but it does not have to be.

XML Names

A name in XML is an identifier used for the various syntax elements: tags, entities, attributes, and so on. Names in XML must follow certain rules.

- *The first character must be a letter, a colon (:), or an underscore (_).*
- *Subsequent characters can be letters, digits, or the symbols period (.), hyphen (-), underscore (_), or colon (:). Some additional non-English language characters are permitted as well. Refer to the XML Recommendation document at* `http://www.w3.org/` *for details.*
- *Names are case-sensitive.*
- *There is no length limitation.*
- *Names starting with "XML" in any combination of uppercase and lowercase are reserved.*

The following are legal XML names: "X40_9," "total," ":security-2," and ":::_x." These names are not legal: "interest%," "xmlname," "!name," and "R&D." While not required, it is conventional to use all lowercase without separators for the names of XML elements and attributes—for example, "firstname" rather than "FirstName" or "first_name." Note that the colon, while legal, is best avoided in names because it is used with namespaces.

Entities

An XML document consists of one or more entities. The one required entity is the Document entity. The Document entity may contain the entire document, but it does not have to. The Document entity is the starting point for the XML processor. If the document consists of multiple entities, other entities will be referenced either directly or indirectly in the Document entity.

This concept is not as complex as it may sound. The XML document presented in Listing 2.1 and Listing 2.2 is a good example. The Document (note the uppercase *D*) entity is contained in Listing 2.1. The Document entity references an external entity—namely, the XML file in Listing 2.2. Together, these two entities comprise the entire XML document (lowercase *d*).

You can see that an XML document consists of the Document entity and zero or more other entities. You can think of these other entities as a way to define a name so that it refers to some content. There are various reasons why using entities in this manner is useful.

- The same content is used in multiple locations in a document. Using an entity saves time and reduces the possibility of errors when compared to the alternative of duplicating the content at each location.
- The content is represented differently on different platforms.
- The document is too large to be represented practically by a single entity. A book, for example, could have each chapter represented by a separate entity.
- The content is not in an XML-compatible format, such as binary image data.

All entities are declared inside the document type declaration, or `DOCTYPE` tag. The basic syntax is as follows:

```
<!DOCTYPE MyXMLDocument [
<!ENTITY ...>
]>
```

You can declare as many entities as needed within the `DOCTYPE` tag. Entities fall into three categories with slightly different syntax, as explained in the following sections. A fourth type of entity, the Parameter entity, is used only within DTDs and is covered in Chapter 3.

Declaration versus Definition

Do not confuse the document type declaration *with the document type* definition. *The document type declaration is a tag within an XML document that gives the name of the document element, and optionally contains* ENTITY *declarations and gives the name of the document's Document Type Definition (see line 2 in Listing 2.1). The Document Type Definition is (usually) a separate file that contains the definition of the document's data model.*

Internal Text Entities

An *internal text entity* is an entity defined within the XML document that refers to text data. The syntax of the declaration is as follows:

```
<!ENTITY EntityName "EntityText">
```

`EntityName` is the name that will be used to refer to the entity, and `EntityText` is the replacement text. You can use double quotes, as in the example, or single quotes. If `EntityText` is enclosed in double quotes, it can contain single quote characters, and if `EntityText` is enclosed in single quotes, it can contain double quote characters, as shown here:

```
<!ENTITY LincolnQuote 'Abraham Lincoln said "Four score and seven years
ago..."'>

<!ENTITY ListOfContractions "don't can't won't">
```

External Text Entities

An *external text entity* is declared within an XML document when the replacement text is stored in an external location. The syntax is one of the following:

```
<!ENTITY EntityName SYSTEM "FileIdentifier">
<!ENTITY EntityName PUBLIC "PublicFileIdentifier"
    "FileIdentifier">
```

When the SYSTEM keyword is used, `FileIdentifier` specifies a file on the local system or on the network. The specification must follow the rules for a

Uniform Resource Identifier (URI). This is the name of the external file specified using relative path notation. The path is relative to the location of the XML file that contains the entity declaration. For example, this declaration specifies that the external file is located in the same folder as the XML file:

```
<!ENTITY Name SYSTEM "name.ent">
```

This declaration specifies that the file is located in the entities folder off the root folder:

```
<!ENTITY Name SYSTEM "\entities\name.ent">
```

This declaration specifies that the file is located in the parent folder of the folder where the XML file is located:

```
<!ENTITY Name SYSTEM "..\name.ent">
```

If the external entity file is located on the Internet, the URI specifies the protocol, the location (or URL), and the filename:

```
<!ENTITY Name SYSTEM "http://www.whatever.com/entities/name.ent">
```

It is not required that entity files have the .ent extension; you can use any naming convention you want. This extension is often used, however, as a way to indicate that a given file is intended for use as an entity and not as a standalone XML file.

URIs, URNs, and URLs

Almost everyone knows what a Uniform Resource Locator (URL) is: a string that identifies the location and protocol for a resource on the Web (for example, `http://www.microsoft.com/` *or* `ftp://ftp.usa.gov/`*). But what about URIs and URNs? Uniform Resource Identifier, or URI, is a broad term for any and all strings that identify resources. A URL, therefore, is a type of URI. A Uniform Resource Name, or URN, is a URI that has an institutional commitment to continued availability. A URN may also be a URL. This is admittedly confusing, and you can find detailed information about URIs, URNs, and URLs at* `http://www.w3.org/Addressing/`.

When the `PUBLIC` keyword is used, *`PublicFileIdentifier`* provides information about the location of the external entity file. The XML processor may use this information to generate a URI reference and then retrieve the entity. If the processor does not generate an alternate URI, it will retrieve the entity from the file specified in `FileLocation` (which follows the same rules as described previously for the `SYSTEM` keyword). Here is an example of an entity declaration using the `PUBLIC` keyword:

```
<!ENTITY copyright PUBLIC "-//TextEntities//Text general//EN"
    "text005.ent">
```

When an XML processor encounters a `PUBLIC` entity declaration such as this, it attempts to match the identifier (in this example, `"-//TextEntities//Text general//EN"`) typically by looking it up in a catalog file. If a match is found, the URI associated with the identifier will be used to retrieve the entity. Otherwise, the `SYSTEM` URI is used to retrieve the entity (in this example, `"text005.ent"`).

External Binary Entities

An external binary entity is declared within an XML document to refer to data that is not text, such as an image file. The syntax for declaring external binary entities is essentially the same as described in the previous section for declaring external text entities, including the use of the `SYSTEM` and `PUBLIC` keywords. There is also a requirement to identify the format of the data. This is done by including the `NDATA` (Notational Data) keyword followed by a format identifier, as shown here:

```
<!ENTITY coverphoto SYSTEM "\images\cover.jpg" NDATA JPEG>
```

The `NDATA` keyword tells the XML processor that the data being referenced by the entity will not be parsed. This is in contrast to text entities whose data is parsed. The format identifier (`JPEG` in this example) identifies the format of the data. The XML processor uses the format identifier to determine how to handle the unparsed data. The connection between a specific format identifier and how the data is handled is specified in a Notation. Notations are covered later in this chapter.

Referencing Entities

For internal and external text entities, the syntax for referring to the entity is the entity name preceded by an ampersand (&) and followed by a semicolon (;):

```
&EntityName;
```

Binary entities cannot be referenced in this manner. It makes no sense to insert binary data directly into an XML document. Binary entities are referenced using an attribute of type `ENTITY` or `ENTITIES`. Attributes are covered later in the chapter.

Character Entities

A character entity is used to refer to a character by its numerical code. This type of entity differs from the others that are explained in this chapter in that a character entity does not have to be declared. Rather, it can simply be used wherever it is needed. The format is as follows:

```
&#n;
```

where *n* is the decimal (base 10) code for the desired character. Values of *n* in the range 0 to 255 represent characters from the extended ASCII set (ISO 8859/1). Thus, the reference

```
&#60;
```

inserts the less-than (<) character in the document. Values of *n* between 256 and 65,535 represent characters in the Unicode (ISO 10646) character set.

To specify the character code in hexadecimal (base 16) notation, precede the code by the letter *x*. The hexadecimal value 3C is the same as the decimal value 60. Therefore, the entity reference

```
&#x3C;
```

refers to the less-than (<) character.

> ***Parameter Entities***
>
> *There is an additional type of entity called a* Parameter entity. *This type of entity is used only in DTDs and is covered in Chapter 3.*

Table 2.1 XML Entities for Representing Special Characters

Character	Entity
<	<
>	>
&	&
"	"
'	'

Reserved Character Entities

Certain characters have special meaning to an XML processor. They are ampersand (&), less-than (<), greater-than (>), quote ("), and apostrophe ('). You cannot include these characters in parsed XML data as they will not be interpreted as themselves—they will be interpreted according to their special XML meaning. The less-than (<) character, for example, will be interpreted as the start of a tag. To include these special characters in XML data, you must use the special character sequences, or entities, that are listed in Table 2.1.

Using these entities, the text

```
The report's title is "Annual Sales."
```

would be encoded as follows:

```
The report&apos;s title is &quot;Annual Sales.&quot;
```

As with other parts of XML, the entities are case-sensitive. You do not need to use the entities to represent these characters in character data that is contained in a `<![CDATA[...]]>` tag (this tag is covered later in the chapter).

Why are the codes for these special characters called entities? It is because they are defined outside the XML document in which they are used. Most entities require an explicit declaration in any XML document that will use them, but these five entities are automatically declared and therefore available in every XML document.

Elements

The data in an XML document is contained in *elements*. An element is defined as a start tag, an end tag, and the text those tags enclose. An element may contain one of the following:

- Data (text that is not part of a tag)
- One or more other elements
- A combination of data and elements

Every XML document contains a single root element called the *document element*. The name of the document element identifies the document, and all other elements are contained within the document element. The name of the document element must match the name specified in the `DOCTYPE` tag. Within the document, the amount of "nesting" of elements within other elements is essentially unlimited. Elements must not overlap. In other words, a child element must be completely enclosed by its parent element.

The XML code presented in this section illustrates these principles. It shows the code for the document element only and does not include the various entity tags that would be part of a complete XML document. Looking at this code, you can note the following.

- The document element is named "cookbook" and its beginning and end are marked by `<cookbook>` and `</cookbook>` tags.
- The "recipe" element contains data and other elements. It is referred to as having mixed content. The data is the title of the recipe—in this case, "Toasted cheese sandwich."
- The "category" and "source" elements contain only data. They are referred to as having data content.
- The "ingredientlist" element contains only other elements. It is referred to as having element content. The containing element is called the *parent* element, and the elements it contains are called *children*.
- The "ingredient" element contains only other elements. Note that while the "ingredient" element is child to the "ingredientlist" element, it is parent to the "quantity" and "item" elements.
- The "quantity," "item," and "directions" elements contain only data.

```
<cookbook>
  <recipe>
  Toasted cheese sandwich
  <category>Sandwiches</category>
```

```
  <source>Aunt Edna</source>
  <ingredientlist>
    <ingredient>
      <quantity>2 slices</quantity>
      <item>cheddar cheese</item>
    </ingredient>
    <ingredient>
      <quantity>2 pieces</quantity>
      <item>white bread</item>
    </ingredient>
    <ingredient>
      <quantity>1 tablespoon</quantity>
      <item>butter</item>
    </ingredient>
</ingredientlist>
<directions>
Butter one side of each piece of bread. Place cheese slices between
bread with buttered sides out. Cook in covered fry pan, turning once,
until bread is browned and cheese is melted.
</directions>
</recipe>
<recipe>
...
</recipe>
</cookbook>
```

It is important to remember that while XML syntax permits almost limitless flexibility in creating elements, the nature of the elements that are permitted in a particular XML document will be determined by its data model, as defined in a DTD or XML Schema. A data model specifies the elements a document may contain, what content an element can contain, and the relationship between elements.

Empty Elements

An empty element contains no data or other elements. You can indicate an empty element using the start and end tags, like this:

```
<elementname></elementname>
```

It is preferable to use the shorthand notation for an empty element:

```
<elementname/>
```

In some cases, an empty element may be permitted to contain data (by the data model), but it just happens to be empty in this instance. For example, an XML document for a library catalog will contain an element for Editor, but if a particular book does not have an editor this element will be empty.

In other cases, an element must be empty as defined by the data model and can never contain data. Empty tags can, however, contain attributes, which are covered later in this chapter. Empty tags can also be used to span sections of data in ways that would violate the rule that a child element must be entirely within its parent. Here's an example:

```
<para>The last two words of this paragraph are marked <revisedstart/>as
revised.</para><para>The first two words of this paragraph are marked
<revisedend/>as revised.</para>
```

You could not use `<revised>...</revised>` tags in this case because the resulting element would span two `<para>` elements, which is not permitted.

Attributes

Attributes provide additional information about an element. Attributes are part of an element start tag, as shown in this example:

```
<para keywords="Napoleon, France, history">
...
</para>
```

An attribute has two parts: a name and a value. In this example, the attribute name is "keywords" and the value is "Napoleon, France, history." The name and value are separated by an equal sign (=), and the value is enclosed in double or single quotes. If double quotes are used, the value may contain single quotes, and vice versa.

A tag may contain multiple attributes:

```
<para topic="XML" author="J. Smith" lastrevised="10/30/2000">
```

Attribute names and values are both case-sensitive. Attribute names beginning with "xml:" (in any combination of upper- and lowercase) are reserved by the XML standard.

Languages

The `xml:lang` *attribute is reserved for providing information about the language in use. The value of this attribute is set to a code specifying a language. Four types of codes are possible:*

- *A two-letter language code, such as "en" for English or "de" for German. The codes are defined in the ISO 639 standard.*
- *A two-letter language code followed by a hyphen and a two-letter country subcode, such as "en-US" for American English or "en-GB" for British English. The code follows the ISO 639 standard and the country subcode follows the ISO 3166 standard.*
- *A code following the Internet Assigned Numbers Authority (IANA) format. These codes begin with "i-" or "I-" followed by a language code, such as "i-yi" for Yiddish.*
- *A user-defined code, which must start with "x-" or "X-".*

Declaring Notations

A Notation is used to define the way in which external binary data is to be handled. You saw earlier in this chapter, in the section "External Binary Entities," that the declaration of a binary entity includes information on the data format. Here's an example of such a declaration:

```
<!ENTITY coverphoto SYSTEM "/images/cover.tif" NDATA TIFF>
```

The `NDATA TIFF` part of this entity declaration specifies that the entity refers to nontext data in the TIFF format. However the identifier "TIFF" is meaningless to the XML processor. You must define what "TIFF" means, or to be more precise, you must specify what application should be used to process this data format. This is done using a Notation, with the following format:

```
<!NOTATION FormatName SYSTEM "AppIdentifier">
```

`FormatName` is the name of the format and can be any arbitrary name although it is advisable to use a name that identifies the format, such as BMP

for bitmap images, JPEG for JPEG images, and so on. *AppIdentifier* is either the relative path to the application that will be used to handle the data, or it is helper information that is meaningful to the operating system in terms of specifying an application. For example, this Notation specifies that the application \programs\showtiff.exe will be used to handle binary data that is identified as type "TIFF":

```
<!NOTATION TIFF SYSTEM "/programs/showtiff.exe">
```

This example specifies that whatever application the operating system associates with the name "JPG" should be used for binary data identified as "JPEG":

```
<!NOTATION JPEG SYSTEM "JPG">
```

A Notation can use the `PUBLIC` keyword and specify both a public and a system identifier. Here is an example:

```
<!NOTATION TeX PUBLIC "-//SmithCo//NOTATION TeX HelpFile//EN"
    "\programs\texdisplay.exe">
```

This Notation specifies that for binary data in the TeX format (TeX is a typesetting language), the XML processor will first look for an application name that is associated with the public identifier `"-//SmithCo//NOTATION TeX HelpFile//EN"` and, if found, use that application to process the data. Otherwise, the application \programs\texdisplay.exe will be used.

When no information about a particular format is available, and no application is available to process the format, the format identifier must still be declared using the minimal Notation format, as shown in this example:

```
<!NOTATION ENGR "">
```

This Notation specifies that there is no application available to process binary data in the format identified as "ENGR."

Character Data

XML provides a tag for marking sections of character data that will not be processed by the XML parser. Character data is placed inside a `CDATA` tag, as shown here:

```
<![CDATA[
The character data goes here
]]>
```

CDATA sections can be as long as needed. The XML parser simply ignores all character data. This means that items that normally have a special meaning to XML are treated as plain text. Consider this example:

```
<![CDATA[
<firstname>Alice</firstname>
<lastname>Walker</lastname>
]]>
```

Because they are in a CDATA section, <firstname> and <lastname> are not recognized as XML tags. There are various situations that call for the use of CDATA sections. The two most common are as follows:

- To quote a section of XML code—for example, in an XML tutorial or reference manual
- To enclose VBScript or JavaScript code that may contain characters such as < and & that have special meaning to XML

XML and Scripting

There are at least two situations in which XML documents will contain script code. One is when a Web page is written in XML and the page contains script code. The other is when a desktop script for the Windows Script Host is saved in XML format. In either case, the actual script code is enclosed in one or more CDATA *sections because the code should not be processed by the parser.*

Comments

A comment is not considered part of an XML document in that it is never processed. You create a comment by enclosing text in <!-- ... --> tags. There is no restriction on what may be placed in a comment with one exception: a double hyphen (--). Here's an example of a comment:

```
<!-- This section of code needs some fine-tuning. -->
```

Comments are typically used by the author or editor of an XML document to indicate text that needs further work and for similar purposes. However, you should not use comments if you want them preserved when the document is processed, because some XML processors discard the comments. Rather, it is preferable to define an element, perhaps named "Comment," to contain comment text. Then you can define your style sheet to prevent the comments from appearing in published output.

White Space Issues

The term *white space* refers to those characters that do not have their own visual appearance but have an effect on the formatting of the document. These characters are the space, the tab, the line feed, and the carriage return. The way that white space is handled depends on its location in the XML document. At some locations the handling of white space can be determined by the document's author, while at others it is determined by the processing application. When white space, particularly line feeds and carriage returns, is used by the document author for formatting to improve the readability of the source code, there is the possibility of ambiguities.

Two characters, the Carriage Return (CR, ASCII value = 13) and the Line Feed (LF, ASCII value = 10), are used alone or in combination to mark the end of a line of text. The standard on the Windows system is to use the CR-LF pair to mark the end of a line, whereas Macintosh systems use CR alone and UNIX systems use LF alone.

White Space in Markup

Within markup—that is, inside of tags—all white space is the equivalent of a single space character. These two tags are functionally identical:

```
<para keywords="Napoleon, France, history">

<para              keywords
        =   "Napoleon,
               France,
                   history">
```

The conversion of all white space to single spaces is called *white space normalization*.

White Space in Content

Within content, white space is more problematic. Is it intended to be retained when the document is published or not? The document author can control this by using the `xml:space` attribute. This attribute can be set to the values "preserve" or "default" with the default setting being "default." When `xml:space` is set to "preserve," all white space is passed unchanged to the application. This attribute applies to the element where it appears and to all child elements, unless the attribute has been set to "default" within specific child elements. Here's an example:

```
<chapter xml:space="default">
  <para>...</para>
  <para xml:space="preserve">...</para>
  <para>...</para>
</chapter>
```

The result will be that white space is normalized throughout the entire chapter except for the second paragraph, where it is preserved.

The XML Tree Model

Many things that you do with XML will rely on the fact that any XML document can be represented as a branching tree that is made up of *nodes.* The nodes represent the elements and data in the XML file, and the pattern of the branches represents the parent-child relationships between the elements. The root of any XML is the node representing the document. Below the root node (XML trees are traditionally drawn upside-down, thus the root is at the top) are nodes representing processing instructions, elements, and so on. A node in an XML tree can be one of the following:

- The root
- An element
- An attribute
- A processing instruction
- A comment
- A namespace
- Text

An example will make this structure clearer. Listing 2.3 shows an XML file containing name and phone number data for two people. Figure 2.1 shows the tree representing this file. You can see that the root node has three branches, which represent the XML processing instruction, the comment, and the "people" root element. The root element node has two branches, representing the two "person" child elements. The tree continues to branch until it reaches the ends of the branches (sometimes referred to as a *leaf*), which, in this case, represent the data. If some of the document elements contained attributes, or if there were a namespace declaration, these too would be represented by nodes.

When an XML document is parsed, the output of the parser is this tree, often called the *parse tree.* You never see this tree directly, but it serves as input to later stages of XML processing. For example, when you use XSLT to transform an XML document (covered in Chapter 7), the tree output of the parser is the input to the XSLT processor. Likewise, when you use the Document Object Model (covered in Chapter 10), you are accessing the tree.

> ***Root Node versus Root Element***
>
> *Don't confuse the root node of a document tree with the root element of the document. The root node represents the document itself, and the node representing the root element is a branch off the root node.*

Listing 2.3 A Simple XML Data File

```
<?xml version="1.0"?>
<!-- My imaginary friends -->
<people>
  <person>
    <name>Popeye the Sailor</name>
    <telephone>
      <home>555-1212</home>
      <work>999-1234</work>
    </telephone>
</person>
  <person>
    <name>Betty Boop</name>
    <telephone>
      <home>123-4567</home>
      <work>321-9999</work>
    </telephone>
  </person>
</people>
```

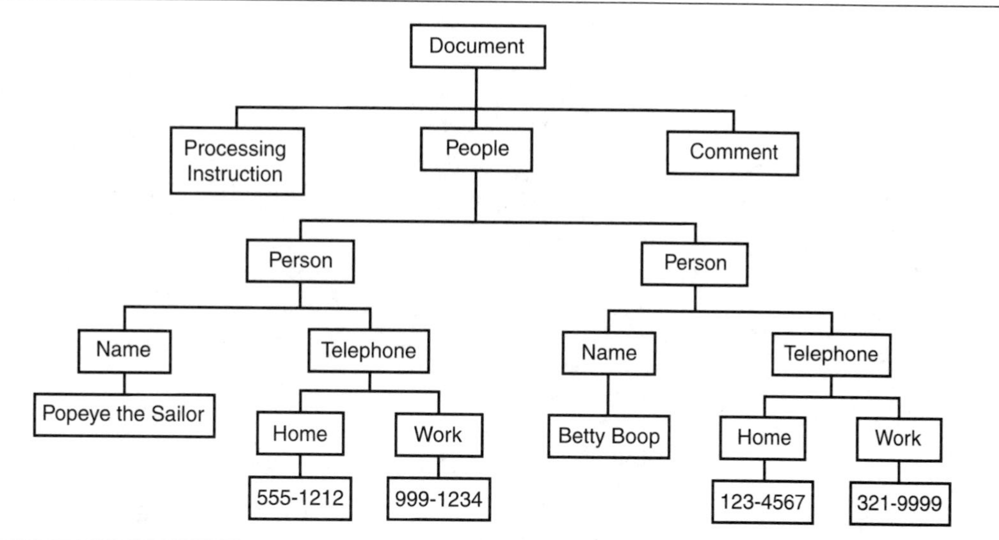

Figure 2.1 The parse tree representing the document in Listing 2.3

Summary

While there are certainly plenty of details to deal with, XML syntax is conceptually quite simple. Anything in an XML document is either markup or character data. The markup, or tags, is delineated by being enclosed in brackets <like this>, and it serves to give structure to the data, provide processing instructions, and provide references to data that is stored elsewhere. Data is organized in elements, an element being defined as a starting tag and an ending tag, with the ending tag being identical to the starting tag with the addition of a forward slash: `<tag>...</tag>`. The actual character data is located between the starting and ending tags. Additional data can be contained in attributes, which are located in the start tag of an element. This seemingly simple structure provides enormous flexibility in structuring data of many different kinds.

CHAPTER 3

Data Modeling with DTDs

A data model, or schema, provides a representation of the logical structure of an XML document. It specifies what elements the document can contain and the permitted relationships among these elements (among other things). Document Type Definitions (DTDs) and XML Schema are the two techniques available for specifying a data model. DTDs are covered in this chapter, and the two varieties of XML Schema are covered in the next two chapters.

Importance of Data Modeling

XML is a language for storing structured information. It is often necessary for the information in a document to adhere to a specific structure. This is done by defining a *schema,* or data model, that describes the structure of a document. Sometimes the term *vocabulary* is used to mean the same thing. An XML document that adheres to a schema is said to be *valid.* XML documents that adhere to the same schema are said to belong to the same class or vocabulary. A schema can specify

- The names of the tags, or elements, that are permitted in the document
- The attributes that can be assigned to each element
- The relationships between the elements—which elements are child elements, which are parents, and the degree of nesting
- What data each element can contain—text, other elements, or a combination of text and elements

The importance of document validity has to do with the various applications that process XML data. Such applications are written to expect the data in the document to be structured in a certain way. A library catalog program, for example, will expect every book to have a title, or in XML terms, will expect every "book" element to contain one and only one "title" element. If the program encounters a "book" element without a "title" element, processing will not be able to continue properly. By validating a document against its schema, a task performed by the XML parser, you ensure that problems such as this will not occur.

The following is an example taken from the Cookbook document in Chapter 2. It provides a structured format for recipe data. Only a single "recipe" element is shown here for the sake of brevity, but there could be more.

```
<cookbook>
<recipe>
Toasted cheese sandwich
  <category>Sandwiches</category>
  <source>Aunt Edna</source>
  <ingredientlist>
    <ingredient>
      <quantity>2 slices</quantity>
      <item>cheddar cheese</item>
    </ingredient>
    <ingredient>
      <quantity>2 pieces</quantity>
      <item>white bread</item>
    </ingredient>
    <ingredient>
      <quantity>1 tablespoon</quantity>
      <item>butter</item>
    </ingredient>
</ingredientlist>
<directions>
Butter one side of each piece of bread. Place cheese slices between
bread with buttered sides out. Cook in covered fry pan, turning once,
until bread is browned and cheese is melted.
</directions>
</recipe>
</cookbook>
```

The schema for this document would specify the following:

- The root "cookbook" element can contain one or more "recipe" elements.
- A "recipe" element can contain text data as well as other elements. It must contain one each of the elements "category," "source," "ingredients," and "directions."

- The “category” element contains text data and it must not be empty.
- The “source” element can contain text data or it can be empty.
- The “ingredientlist” element must contain one or more “ingredient” elements.

This is only a partial list, but it serves to make the point about the things that are specified in a schema. The two methods for defining schemas, DTDs and XML Schema, each have their own syntax for defining a data model.

In this example, you will note that the `<recipe>` element contains both character data and child elements. For reasons that are explained later in the chapter, this type of structure is best avoided, although it is legal in XML. It is included here for illustration purposes. Thus, an element would normally contain child elements or text data, but not both.

Document Type Definitions

DTDs are the original and most widely supported means for defining a schema for XML documents. DTDs are part of the base XML 1.0 specification, and they have their origins in SGML. DTDs use a specialized syntax for describing the structure of an XML document. DTDs come in two types: internal and external. An internal DTD is contained within the body of the XML document it applies to, while an external DTD is contained in a separate file that is referenced from the XML document. An XML document may use either or both types of DTD.

What is the purpose of having both internal and external DTDs? It is primarily a matter of flexibility. When both internal and external DTDs are present, the XML parser gives precedence to the internal DTD. This means that if an external DTD already exists that is almost but not quite right for your XML document, you can use it and make the necessary changes in the internal DTD. Often, an external DTD is used to describe the general document structure for a class of documents, and an internal DTD is used to define those details of structure that are specific to that document.

When designing your own XML documents, you may need to decide between using an internal and an external DTD. Here are some factors to consider:

- An external DTD can be used with multiple documents.
- A document that uses an external DTD is more concise.
- A document that uses only an internal DTD is completely independent and does not depend on any external sources of information.

The format and syntax is the same for both internal and external DTDs—they differ only in their location.

The Document Type Declaration

Within an XML document, both external and internal DTDs are included in the document type declaration (the DOCTYPE tag). The syntax is as follows:

```
<!DOCTYPE rootelement SYSTEM ExternalDTDReference [ InternalDTD ]>
```

ExternalDTDReference is a reference to the file containing the external DTD, and *InternalDTD* is the text of the internal DTD. This DOCTYPE tag has both an internal and an external DTD:

```
<!DOCTYPE AddressBook SYSTEM "addressbook.dtd" [
<!ELEMENT salutation (#PCDATA)> ]>
```

This DOCTYPE tag includes only a reference to an external DTD:

```
<!DOCTYPE AddressBook SYSTEM "addressbook.dtd">
```

Stand-alone Documents

You can specify that an XML document is a stand-alone document that relies on no external information by specifying it as such in the XML declaration. The syntax is as follows:

```
<?xml version="1.0" standalone="yes"?>
```

When a document is declared as being stand-alone in this manner, all external references, including those to external DTDs, are ignored. You can set stand-alone to “no,” but because that is the default value it is not necessary to do so. Declaring an XML document to be stand-alone is rarely if ever of any use, in my experience, but it is mentioned here in case you should run across the declaration.

Declaring Elements

To declare an element in a DTD, use an element declaration. The syntax is as follows:

```
<!ELEMENT name type>
```

Name is the name of the element, and *type* is the content specification. There are four possible settings for *type*:

- Empty: The element contains no data or child elements.
- Element(s) only: The element can contain child elements but no data.
- Mixed: The element can contain data and child elements.
- Any: The element can contain any content permitted by the DTD.

Empty Elements

An empty element contains no content, but it can (and usually does) provide information by means of attributes. This is the syntax to declare an empty element:

```
<!ELEMENT name EMPTY>
```

In the document, an empty element can be represented by a start/end pair of tags with nothing between them:

```
<name></name>
```

More often, the shorthand for an empty tag is used:

```
<name/>
```

This shorthand is preferred because it makes it clear that the tag is declared as an empty tag and is not a mixed content tag that just happens in this instance to be empty. Empty tags are rarely of any use unless they contain one or more attributes, as shown here:

```
<image src="banner.jpg"/>
```

Specifying the attributes that an element can contain is covered later in this chapter.

Element-only Elements

An element-only element can contain child elements but no text data. When an element-only element is declared in a DTD, the declaration includes information about what elements can be contained. The syntax is as follows:

```
<!ELEMENT name contentmodel>
```

Table 3.1 Symbols Used in Element Declaration Content Models

Symbol	Meaning
Asterisk	Indicates that the child element can appear any number of times, or not at all (sometimes called *zero* or *many*)
Comma	Separates element names in a sequence
Parentheses	Encloses sequences or choice lists of element names
Pipe	Separates element names in a choice list
Plus sign	Indicates that the child element must appear one or more times
Question mark	Indicates that the child element must appear zero or one time
(no symbol)	Indicates that the child element must appear exactly once

The `contentmodel` is a combination of child element names and symbols that specifies exactly what can be contained in the element. In the content model, child elements are grouped into sequences or choice groups using parentheses. Child element names in a sequence are separated by commas, while child element names in a choice group are separated by pipes (|). These and other symbols used in content models are described in Table 3.1.

Here are some examples of element-only declarations. The following code declares an element named "cookbook" that can contain one or more child elements named "recipe" and can contain no other child elements and no data:

```
<!ELEMENT cookbook (recipe)+>
```

The next declaration specifies that the element "movie" must contain one child element named "title"; can contain zero, one, or more child elements named "award"; can contain one or more child elements named "actor"; and the child elements must appear in the stated order:

```
<!ELEMENT movie (title, award*, actor+)>
```

This declaration specifies that the element "part" must contain one child element named "partno" followed by one child element named "source" or one child element named "supplier" (but not both), and finally zero or one child element named "comment."

```
<!ELEMENT item (partno, (source | supplier), comment?)>
```

Mixed Elements

A mixed element can contain data and child elements, or it can contain only data. This seems confusing—shouldn't a data-only element have its own category? Perhaps, but that's not the way XML is defined. Mixed elements that are declared to contain only data are informally referred to as data-only or text-only elements, but this is an informal designation and not part of the XML standard. To declare a mixed element that contains only data, use the `PCDATA` (Parsed Character Data) keyword:

```
<!ELEMENT name (#PCDATA)>
```

For example, this element declaration:

```
<!ELEMENT country (#PCDATA)>
```

will define an element that might look like this in the XML document:

```
<country>Japan</country>
```

To declare a mixed element that contains child elements and/or data, use this syntax:

```
<!ELEMENT name ( #PCDATA | ElementList)*>
```

The *`ElementList`* is a list of child element names separated by the pipe symbol (|). The `#PCDATA` keyword can be inserted at additional locations if there will be more than one instance of character data in the element.

Mixed elements have a serious limitation in that the element list only specifies which child elements may appear, but it does not specify how many times they can appear or their order. Another potential problem is that, in the XML document, a mixed element may look like an empty or an element-only element. There will be no way to determine that it is in fact declared as a mixed element without referring to the DTD. For these reasons it is advisable to avoid mixed elements that are declared to contain both data and child elements and to restrict the use of mixed elements to those containing only data. I have yet to see a situation that could not be accommodated with the use of element-only elements, data-only mixed elements, and attributes.

Mixed elements that contain both character data and child elements can cause problems when you are parsing XML using SAX (covered in Chapter 11). For this reason, such mixed elements are best avoided if possible.

ANY Elements

An element declared as type ANY can contain any combination of data and child elements. The syntax is as follows:

```
<!ELEMENT name ANY>
```

Due to their complete lack of structure, ANY elements should be avoided like the plague. They defeat the main purpose of XML documents, which is to provide structured data storage. The most common use of ANY elements is during development when they can be used for prototyping purposes. By the time your DTD is ready for distribution, all ANY elements should have been replaced with more specific element types.

Declaring Attributes

Attributes are used to attach additional information elements. Attributes are assigned a value in the element's start tag:

```
<book author="William Faulkner">Absalom, Absalom!</book>
```

In this example, the element "book" has an attribute whose name is "author" and whose value is "William Faulkner." In keeping with the tightly structured nature of XML, a valid document can use only those attributes that are included in its DTD. You specify what attributes are permitted for a given element using the ATTLIST declaration:

```
<!ATTLIST ElementName AttributeName AttributeType Default>
```

Table 3.2 Possible Values for the Default Entry

Setting	Description
`#REQUIRED`	The attribute is required—it must be defined in every instance of the element.
`#IMPLIED`	The attribute is optional.
`#FIXED`	The attribute has a fixed value that cannot be changed. The fixed value of the attribute follows the `#FIXED` keyword.
`text`	The default value of the attribute is *`text`*. This is the value the attribute will have if it is not assigned another value.

`ElementName` is the name of the element whose attributes you are declaring. *`AttributeName`* is the name of the attribute. *`AttributeType`* specifies the type of the attribute, with the possible settings presented in Table 3.2. *`Default`* is either a keyword specifying the usage of the attribute or a default value that is used when the attribute value is not specified in the element tag.

XML attributes fall into three general categories: string (text), enumerated, and tokenized. Within these three general types there are ten specific types of attributes, as listed in Table 3.3 with more detailed explanations in the text below.

String Attributes

String attributes are the most commonly used type for attributes that contain plain text. A string attribute is indicated by the `CDATA` keyword in the `ATTLIST` tag. Here is an example of declaring a `CDATA` attribute named "author" that must be defined in every "book" tag:

```
<!ATTLIST book author CDATA #REQUIRED>
```

To make the attribute optional, the declaration would be as follows:

```
<!ATTLIST book author CDATA #IMPLIED>
```

Table 3.3 Attribute Types

Type	Description of Attribute
CDATA	Unparsed character data
ENTITIES	A list of multiple external binary entities
ENTITY	An external binary entity
Enumerated	One of a list of string values
ID	A unique identifier
IDREF	A reference to an ID declared elsewhere in the DTD
IDREFS	References to multiple IDs declared elsewhere in the DTD
NMTOKEN	A name consisting of XML token characters
NMTOKENS	Multiple names consisting of XML token characters
NOTATION	A notation defined elsewhere in the DTD

To create a fixed attribute with the name "language" and the value "English," the declaration is as follows:

```
<!ATTLIST book language CDATA #FIXED "English">
```

When an attribute is declared as `FIXED`, you cannot assign a value to the attribute in the element. The preceding declaration would mean that the following is illegal:

```
<book language="French">...</book>
```

Rather, every instance of the element "book" will automatically have the attribute named "language" with the value "English."

Enumerated Attributes

An enumerated attribute is one whose value must be selected from a list of choices. The permitted choices are listed in parentheses and separated by the pipe symbol (|), with the default value (if any) following. While the default value needs to be in quotes, the choices do not. Unless specified otherwise, enumerated attributes are type CDATA, and the CDATA keyword does not need to be included. Here is an example that declares an attribute named "country" with four permitted values and the default value "US":

```
<!ATTLIST person country (US | England | France | Germany) "US">
```

The following line declares a required attribute named "imageformat" with the possible values "jpeg" and "gif":

```
<!ATTLIST image imageformat (jpeg | gif) #REQUIRED>
```

Another type of enumerated attribute is the notation attribute. This type of attribute specifies a list of notations that are defined elsewhere in the DTD. The syntax for defining notations is covered in Chapter 2. The following example declares a required notation enumerated attribute:

```
<!ATTLIST image imageformat NOTATION (jpeg | gif) #REQUIRED>
```

This looks very similar to the previous example, but the NOTATION keyword makes a difference. In the first example, "jpeg" and "gif" are text data, but in the second example, the NOTATION keyword means that "jpeg" and "gif" are references to notations and the actual value of the attribute is determined by the notation definition.

Tokenized Attributes

A tokenized attribute is processed by the XML parser as a token. This means that the attribute value has a special meaning or format. The tokenized attributes are types ENTITY, ENTITIES, ID, IDREF, IDREFS, NMTOKEN, and NMTOKENS.

ENTITY and ENTITIES Attributes

ENTITY type attributes are used to reference entities that are declared elsewhere in the DTD. Defining internal and external entities is covered in Chapter 2. When an attribute is type ENTITY, the value assigned to it must be a valid entity reference. The following declares a required ENTITY type attribute named "source" for the "image" element:

```
<!ATTLIST image source ENTITY #REQUIRED>
```

Assume that an external entity declaration exists as follows:

```
<!ENTITY myface SYSTEM "peter.jpg">
```

Then, the following is a valid use of the attribute:

```
<image source=&myface;>...</image>
```

If, however, no entity named "myface" existed, this would be illegal.

The ENTITIES type attribute is the same as the ENTITY type except that multiple entities can be referenced in the attribute separated by spaces.

ID, IDREF, and IDREFS Attributes

An ID attribute defines a unique identifier. This means that every element that has an ID attribute must have a different value assigned to the attribute. Here's an example:

```
<!ATTLIST part partno ID #REQUIRED>
```

This means that every "part" element must have a "partno" attribute (because of the #REQUIRED keyword) and that the value assigned to the "partno" attribute must be different for every "part" element in the XML file (because of the ID type). Given the preceding ATTLIST, the following would be legal:

```
<part partno="A0123">...</part>
<part partno="B1923">...</part>
<part partno="A0133">...</part>
```

The following would not be legal because the first and third elements have the same value assigned to the "partno" attribute:

```
<part partno="A0123">...</part>
<part partno="B1923">...</part>
<part partno="A0123">...</part>
```

An element can have at most one type ID attribute. An ID type attribute can be required or optional. If the value of an ID attribute is duplicated within the file, the parser will report an error.

An IDREF type attribute provides a reference to an element based on a unique (type ID) attribute. In other words, the data in an IDREF attribute references another element based on the value of its type ID attribute. Because an element can have only one type `ID` attribute, there is no uncertainty. Here is a section of a DTD that declares an element named "person" that has a type `ID` attribute and a type `IDREF` attribute:

```
<!ELEMENT person (lastname, firstname)>
<!ELEMENT lastname (#PCDATA)>
<!ELEMENT firstname (#PCDATA)>
<!ATTLIST person unique_id ID #REQUIRED>
<!ATTLIST person spouse IDREF #IMPLIED)
```

The following is a section of an XML file based on this DTD:

```
<person unique_id="144" spouse="187">
<lastname>Smith</lastname>
<firstname>John</firstname>
</person>
<person unique_id="187" spouse="144">
<lastname>Smith</lastname>
<firstname>Mary</firstname>
</person>
```

The "spouse" value of 187 in John Smith's entry references the entry for Mary Smith based on her "unique_id" value. Likewise, the "spouse" value of 144 in Mary Smith's entry references the entry for John Smith based on his "unique_id" value.

A type `IDREFS` attribute works the same as a type `IDREF` attribute except that it can contain more than one reference separated by spaces. Here is an entry in a DTD for a type `IDREFS` attribute:

```
<!ATTLIST person parent IDREFS #IMPLIED>
```

Continuing with the previous example, the XML file could contain the following entry:

```
<person unique_id="422" parent="144 187">
<lastname>Smith</lastname>
<firstname>Junior</firstname>
</person>
```

The "parent" attribute for this entry references the entries for both John Smith and Mary Smith based on their "unique_id" values.

NMTOKEN and NMTOKENS Attributes

The NMTOKEN attribute type is used primarily to provide information that will be used by the processing application. The reason for using this type rather than the CDATA type is that values for NMTOKEN are constrained to follow certain rules. An NMTOKEN value can contain only letters, numbers, and the characters . - _ and : (period, hyphen, underscore, and colon). No white space is permitted. These restrictions ensure that the value stored in an NMTOKEN attribute will be acceptable to the programming language of the processing application. The following declares a type NMTOKEN attribute:

```
<!ATTLIST sale security NMTOKEN #IMPLIED>
```

The following element would be illegal because the value assigned to the attribute uses an illegal character:

```
<sale security="high!"> ... </sale>
```

The following, however, would be fine:

```
<sale security="high"> ... </sale>
```

The NMTOKENS attribute type is the same as the NMTOKEN type except that multiple tokens can be specified separated by a space:

```
<!ATTLIST sale security NMTOKENS #IMPLIED>
<sale security="high critical eyesonly"> ... </sale>
```

Declaring Multiple Attributes

A single ATTLIST definition can contain the declarations for multiple attributes for a specified element. In fact, it is considered good practice to declare all of an element's attributes in a single ATTLIST tag for the sake of convenience and to make the DTD easier to understand. The syntax requires only that you list the various attributes following the element name using the syntax forms described earlier in this chapter. For clarity, you can put each attribute on its own line, although this is not required. Here's an example for an element named "recording" that is intended to keep data about a collection of records, CDs, and tapes:

```
<!ATTLIST recording media (record | CD | tape) #REQUIRED
    duration CDATA #REQUIRED
    category (jazz | rock | classical | blues | opera) #IMPLIED
```

```
rating (poor | average | excellent) "average" #REQUIRED
comments CDATA #IMPLIED>
```

Parameter Entities

A parameter entity is a type of entity that is used only in external DTDs. They are very similar to the general entity declarations that you learned about in Chapter 2, and they serve the same purpose of permitting a defined name to stand for some other text. A parameter entity can be internal, when the text is located within the DTD, or external, when the text is located in a separate file The syntax for defining an internal parameter entity is as follows:

```
<!ENTITY % EntityName EntityText>
```

EntityName is the name of the entity, and *EntityText* is the text that will replace it in the DTD. Here's a real example of a parameter entity definition:

```
<!ENTITY % size " length, width, height?, weight? ">
```

To reference a parameter entity, use the entity name preceded by a percent sign (%) and followed by a semicolon (;). The entity just defined could be used as follows:

```
<!ELEMENT bakingpan (%size;)>
<!ELEMENT cuttingboard (%size;)>
<!ELEMENT servingtray (%size;)>
```

The end result is the same as if you had not used an entity but had declared the elements like this:

```
<!ELEMENT bakingpan ( length, width, height?, weight? )>
<!ELEMENT cuttingboard ( length, width, height?, weight? )>
<!ELEMENT servingtray ( length, width, height?, weight? )>
```

An external parameter entity is defined with this syntax:

```
<!ENTITY % EntityName SYSTEM FileName>
```

An external entity is referenced in the same way as an internal entity. Where the reference exists, the content of the corresponding file is inserted into the DTD. Obviously, the external file must contain valid DTD content.

Conditional Sections

While you are in the process of developing a DTD, it can be useful to try out different sections of code to see what effects they have. Rather than deleting and entering code as needed, you can use conditional sections in your DTD to mark parts of the code to be ignored or to be included when the DTD is processed. To mark a section of the DTD that is to be ignored, use this syntax:

```
<![IGNORE [
...
DTD code goes here
...
]]>
```

To include the code in the DTD processing, change the opening tag as follows:

```
<![INCLUDE [
...
DTD code goes here
...
]]>
```

An `INCLUDE` section has no effect on the DTD processing—the code is processed as if it were not in an `INCLUDE` block. The only reason for placing `INCLUDE` blocks in your DTD code is that they can be easily changed to `IGNORE` blocks. Conditional sections can only be used in external DTDs. The keywords `INCLUDE` and `IGNORE` cannot be included within markup declarations.

You can enhance the flexibility of this technique by combining it with parameter entities. You can define several entities, as shown here:

```
<!ENTITY % debug1 "INCLUDE">
<!ENTITY % debug2 "IGNORE">
<!ENTITY % debug3 "INCLUDE">
```

Then, write your `INCLUDE/IGNORE` blocks using an entity reference:

```
<![%debug1; [
...
]
<![%debug3; [
...
```

```
]
<![%debug2; [
...
]
<![%debug1; [
...
]
```

With this arrangement, you can change the processing of multiple blocks of code simply by altering the parameter entity definitions.

A DTD Demonstration

The files in Listing 3.1 and Listing 3.2 demonstrate a DTD and an XML file of the class defined in the DTD. This DTD demonstrates many of the things you have learned in this section. You should be able to examine the XML file and then locate in the DTD the declarations that relate to the various XML elements. You'll note that the content of the XML file is indented to make the relationships clear between parent and child elements. This is convenient but not necessary.

Listing 3.1 AddressBook.dtd Defines a Data Model for an Address Book

```
<!ELEMENT addressbook (person)+>
<!ELEMENT person (firstname, lastname, address, birthday?, notes?)>
<!ELEMENT address (street, apartment?, city, state, postalcode,
    country, other?)>
<!ELEMENT firstname (#PCDATA)>
<!ELEMENT lastname (#PCDATA)>
<!ELEMENT street (#PCDATA)>
<!ELEMENT apartment (#PCDATA)>
<!ELEMENT city (#PCDATA)>
<!ELEMENT state (#PCDATA)>
<!ELEMENT postalcode (#PCDATA)>
<!ELEMENT country (#PCDATA)>
<!ELEMENT other (#PCDATA)>
<!ELEMENT birthday (#PCDATA)>
<!ELEMENT notes (#PCDATA)>
<!ATTLIST person category (personal | family | business | other)
          #REQUIRED>
```

Listing 3.2 MyAddresses.xml Is Based on the DTD in Listing 3.1

```
<?xml version="1.0" encoding="UTF-8"?>
<!DOCTYPE addressbook SYSTEM "AddressBook.dtd">
<addressbook>
    <person category="personal">
        <firstname>Arthur</firstname>
        <lastname>Williams</lastname>
        <address>
            <street>5 Oak Street</street>
            <apartment>3B</apartment>
            <city>Anytown</city>
            <state>NC</state>
            <postalcode>23456</postalcode>
            <country>US</country>
        </address>
    </person>
    <person category="family">
        <firstname>Amy</firstname>
        <lastname>Chavez</lastname>
        <address>
            <street>1022 Millbrook Dr.</street>
            <city>Anothertown</city>
            <state>MN</state>
            <postalcode>54321</postalcode>
            <country>US</country>
        </address>
        <birthday>March 5, 1961</birthday>
        <notes>Allergic to chocolate</notes>
    </person>
</addressbook>
```

Validating an XML Document against a DTD

The process of validating an XML document against its DTD is normally performed by the parser (the MSXML Parser, in the Microsoft world). In most scenarios, you will not be performing validation alone—the validation is only the first step in processing the XML file. In later chapters you will learn how to use the parser from various programming languages (Chapter 13 for .NET and the C# language, Chapter 15 for Visual Basic, and Chapter 16 for Visual C++).

If you want just to validate an XML file without performing any other processing, you can use the XMLINT utility that is provided by Microsoft. It is a command-line utility, so it must be used from an MS-DOS prompt. You can download it from the Microsoft Web site (go to `http://msdn.microsoft.com/xml` and search for "XMLINT"). When you unpack the downloaded archive you will have the XMLINT.EXE program plus its C++ source files. You do not need these source files unless you want to modify the utility or see the inner workings of how it was programmed.

To use the utility, open an MS-DOS window. The XMLINT.EXE file must be in the current folder or somewhere on the current path. Then enter the following command:

```
xmlint filename
```

`Filename` is the name of the XML file to validate, including path information if necessary. You can use wildcards. For example, the following command validates all of the XML files in the current folder:

```
xmlint *.xml
```

The utility will check to see if the document is well-formed and, if the XML document has a DTD, it will perform validation. Errors will be displayed onscreen. To perform a check for a well-formed document only, with no validation, use the `-w` option:

```
xmlint -w filename
```

Note that while an XML file with a DTD can be loaded into Internet Explorer 5.*x*, the file will not be validated (although it will be checked for well-formedness).

Summary

A data model, or schema, provides a way to define a set of rules for an XML file. A Document Type Definition, or DTD, is one of the ways you can create a data model. This model can define what elements and attributes are permitted in the XML file, which elements and attributes must be present and which are optional, the kind of data permitted, and other aspects of an XML file's content and structure. A data model is optional for an XML file, but it is an extremely important tool for ensuring that the content of an XML file follows the required structure. An XML file that meets all the requirements of its data model is said to be *valid*. The process of validating an XML file against its data model is performed by the XML parser.

CHAPTER 4

Data Modeling with XDR Schemas

Document Type Definitions (DTDs), as covered in the previous chapter, were the first technique available for defining the data model, or schema, of an XML document. A newer method, XML Schema, offers significant advantages over DTDs in many situations. XML Schema comes in two varieties: XDR Schemas, which are covered in this chapter, and XSD Schemas, which are covered in the next chapter. This chapter starts with an overview of XSD Schemas and also introduces the important concept of namespaces.

XML Schema

XML Schema is the second technology that can be used to define a data model for XML documents (the first being DTDs). XML Schema was developed in response to shortcomings in the DTD technology, and there is no doubt that it offers more power and flexibility than DTDs. The major benefits of XML Schema include the following.

- An XML Schema is an XML document and, unlike DTDs, it does not require a specialized syntax. An XML Schema can be parsed and manipulated like any XML document.
- XML Schema offers an open-ended content model that permits the developer to create new elements and attributes to be used in describing a data model. In contrast, DTDs have a fixed and nonextensible content model.
- XML Schema supports a much wider set of data types than DTDs, such as integers and dates.

- XML Schema supports namespaces, which permits specific parts of the data model to be applied to specific parts of the XML document.

When you are starting an XML project, you are faced with the decision of whether to use a DTD or an XML Schema to define the document's vocabulary. Later in this chapter, in the "DTD or XML Schema: Which to Use?" section, I present information that will assist you in making this decision.

History of XML Schema

The shortcomings of DTDs have been obvious for some time, and the people at W3C have been working on a more powerful data modeling specification for several years. In 1998, W3C issued two notes proposing XML vocabularies for describing document structure. The first is called XML Data and the second is called Document Content Description (DCD). Being just notes, however, these were far from being official specifications (or *Recommendations,* in W3C parlance).

In the interim, Microsoft became impatient. They needed an improved data modeling language for use in their products, and they did not want to wait for the completion of the laborious and time-consuming process for the W3C XML Data and DCD notes to become Recommendations. Microsoft looked at the proposals for both XML Data and DCD and devised a combination of the two that was called XML Schema. The first implementation of XML Schema was in the release of Internet Explorer 5.0.

Will XML Schemas Replace DTDs?

In a word, the answer to the question in this sidebar title is "no." Schemas were not designed to replace DTDs, but rather are intended as a more powerful and flexible data modeling tool to be used in situations where DTDs are not sufficient. Because DTDs are part of the base XML Recommendation, they will be with us for the foreseeable future.

W3C has also gotten into the act and has developed a specification that is also called XML Schema based on XML Data and DCD, with some influence from Microsoft's XML Schema as well. As of this writing, W3C's XML Schema proposal has just achieved Recommendation status.

This sounds promising, but there is a fly in the ointment. Microsoft's XML Schema and W3C's XML Schema may have their names in common (more on names in a bit), but that's about all. The two approaches have the same goals and are similar in the ways they overcome the shortcomings of DTDs, but that's about all. The result is that there are two XML Schema specifications that differ significantly.

The Microsoft version of XML Schema is known as XDR, or XML Data Reduced. This name arose because Microsoft's schema technology was based on a reduced set of the standard proposed in W3C's XML Data note. XDR is very definitely a proprietary specification, but it has fairly widespread adoption because it has been used in many Microsoft products, including:

- The Microsoft BizTalk Framework and server (covered in Chapter 19)
- Microsoft Office 2000
- Microsoft SQL Server 2000
- Microsoft Internet Explorer 5.0 and later

The W3C Recommendation for XML Schema is known as XSD, or XML Schema Definition Language. It is a broader specification than XDR, and it has the undeniable advantage of being nonproprietary. In the Microsoft world, its support is limited to the latest release of the MSXML Parser (which continues to support XDR as well) and the .NET Framework's XML tools. I believe that you will see Microsoft continuing to move away from the proprietary XDR specification for XML Schema and toward the W3C Recommendation, but given the substantial installed base of Microsoft products that adhere to XDR it is likely to be important to many developers for some time to come. The remainder of this chapter covers the XDR specification for XML Schema, while the XSD Recommendation is covered in the next chapter. First, however, you need to learn about namespaces.

Namespace Fundamentals

Names in an XML document are used to identify elements, just like people's names are used to identify individuals. I have a friend named Hector Gomez, and I know perfectly well who he is. However, there are probably dozens if not hundreds of people named Hector Gomez scattered around the world. To precisely identify this particular individual, something more than his name is needed. Using his address is one possibility. If I say "Hector Gomez at 12 Oak Street, San Francisco, California," it clearly identifies one Hector Gomez out of all the Hector Gomezes in the world. You can think of the address as a namespace. Another Hector Gomez might have the address, or namespace, "1022 5th Avenue, New York, New York."

XML Namespaces

Similar problems can arise when working with XML. If an XML document is based on only a single schema, you can be sure that the same element name is not used for different purposes. However, the XML standard permits a document to rely on two or more schemas, and then there is no guarantee that the same name will not be used for different purposes in different schemas. When the name is used in the document, how can the XML processor know which schema to validate the name against?

Here's an example. Suppose that you have designed a schema for an XML document to store information about your music collection. This schema might well include an element named "media" that is expected by the processing software to contain one of the possible values "CD LP MP3 TAPE." Likewise, you have designed a schema for a separate XML file that stores information about your video collection. This schema might well have an element named "media" with possible values "VIDEOCASETTE LASERDISC DVD." Because the two XML files are separate, there can be no confusion between the two different "media" elements.

Now, however, you decide that you want to combine the two XML files so that information about your video and music collections will be stored together in a single file. Do you have to redesign your schemas to prevent possible confusion between the two different "media" elements? No, thanks to namespaces. In a nutshell, here's how it works: You assign a unique namespace to each of the two schemas, and in the XML file you specify which namespace each "media" element belongs to.

Namespace Declarations

There are two types of namespace declarations: default and explicit. Namespace declarations are placed in an XML document as attributes of elements—often the root element—using the reserved `xmlns` keyword. The default declaration has this syntax:

```
xmlns="Namespace"
```

A default namespace can apply to an entire document or to a section of a document. All elements in the document or the document section are considered to belong to the default namespace unless it is specified that they belong to another namespace.

An explicit namespace declaration has this format:

```
xmlns:prefix="Namespace"
```

Prefix is a name that can be used as shorthand to refer to the namespace and to specify that an element belongs to a specific namespace other than the default one.

Here is an example of declaring both a default and an explicit namespace in the root element of an XML document:

```
<addresslist xmlns="x-schema:addresslist.xdr"
    xmlns:old="x-schema:oldaddresslist.xdr"
```

You do not have to declare both—you can declare only a default namespace or only one or more explicit namespaces. Then, within the document

- To have an element belong to an explicitly declared namespace, prefix the element name with the prefix that is associated with that namespace.
- To have an element belong to the default namespace, use the element name as usual (with no prefix).

The following is an example that uses the previous namespaces declarations. This is probably not an example you would run into in real life, but it works for illustration purposes.

```
<person>
    <lastname>Smith</lastname>
    <firstname>William</firstname>
    <address>99 Cedar Crescent</address>
    <city>Peoria</city>
    <state>IL</state>
    <postalcode>55555-1234</postalcode>
</person>
<old:person>
    <old:lastname>Jones</old:lastname>
    <old:firstname>Elizabeth</old:firstname>
    <old:address>11 Charleston Drive</old:address>
    <old:city>Pittsburgh</old:city>
    <old:state>PA</old:state>
    <old:postalcode>44444</old:postalcode>
</old:person>
```

You can see that there are two "person" elements, each with the same set of child elements. The first "person" element and all of its children are in the default "x-schema:addresslist.xdr" namespace and will be validated against the schema located in the file addresslist.xdr. The second "person" element and all of its children are, because of the "old" prefix, in the explicitly declared "x-schema:oldaddresslist.xdr" namespace and will be validated against the schema located in the file oldaddresslist.xdr. In this example, the two schemas differ in that addresslist.xdr requires a 9-digit postal code, while oldaddresslist.xdr requires a 5-digit code.

A Note on Schema Filenames

There are no restrictions regarding the names assigned to XDR Schema files. Because XDR Schemas are XML documents, they can be saved with the .xml extension. It can be helpful, however, to differentiate XDR Schema files from other XML files and from XSD Schema files. Many developers use the .xml extension only for XML files that contain data. XDR Schema files are usually given the .xdr extension and XSD Schema files that follow the W3C XSD Schema vocabulary are given the .xsd extension.

The XDR Vocabulary

As mentioned previously, one of the advantages of XML Schema—XDR, in this case—is that a Schema file is itself an XML document. This means that an XDR Schema can be accessed and modified using any XML techniques—for example, DOM and SAX. However, it opens up the question of how you can know if an XML document containing an XDR Schema is itself valid. You can validate an XML document against a Schema, but if you start validating one Schema against another Schema you end up in a never-ending circular process. The bottom line is that an XDR Schema can only be validated with a DTD.

This may seem to make no sense. If XDR Schema was developed as an improvement on DTDs, why should XDR Schema be dependent on a DTD? It's not as strange as it sounds. Remember that DTDs are part of the core XML specification, and because XDR Schemas are XML documents they must be validated against a DTD. In practical terms, this is not a problem. The XDR Schema DTD is rather simple, and the validation step is not required. In other words, the fact that you want to validate an XML document against an XDR Schema does *not* mean that you need to validate the XDR Schema against its DTD. Even so, it is usually wise to do so, particularly with a new Schema, because a grammar error in the XDR Schema can cause hard-to-find problems.

The XDR Schema DTD is shown in Listing 4.1. You will probably never need to use this DTD, but it is worth examining to see the relatively simple vocabulary of XDR Schema.

Listing 4.1 The XDR Schema DTD

```
<!--
  The possible element datatypes according to
    http://msdn.microsoft.com/xml/schema/reference/datatypes.asp
-->
<!ENTITY % datatypes "(entity | entities | enumeration | id | idref |
    idrefs | nmtoken | nmtokens | notation | string | bin.base64 |
    bin.hex | boolean | char | date | dateTime | dateTime.tz |
    fixed.14.4 | float | int | number | time | time.tz | i1 | i2 |
    i4 | r4 | r8 | ui1 | ui2 | ui4 | uri | uuid)" >

<!ELEMENT datatype  (description)*>
<!ATTLIST datatype
    dt:type %datatypes;  #IMPLIED
    xmlns:dt CDATA #FIXED "urn:schemas-microsoft-com:datatypes">

<!ELEMENT description (#PCDATA) >

<!ELEMENT element  (description)* >
<!ATTLIST element
   type IDREF        #REQUIRED
   minOccurs  CDATA  #IMPLIED
   maxOccurs  CDATA  #IMPLIED>

<!ELEMENT attribute  (description)* >
<!ATTLIST attribute
   type       IDREF    #REQUIRED
   default    CDATA        #IMPLIED
   required   (yes | no)   "no">

<!ELEMENT AttributeType (datatype | description)* >
<!ATTLIST AttributeType
```

```
   name        ID              #REQUIRED
   default     CDATA           #IMPLIED
   dt:type     %datatypes;     #IMPLIED
   dt:values   CDATA           #IMPLIED
   required    (yes | no)      #IMPLIED
   xmlns:dt CDATA #FIXED "urn:schemas-microsoft-com:datatypes">

<!ELEMENT ElementType (datatype | description | AttributeType |
    attribute | element | group)* >
<!ATTLIST ElementType
   name  ID                           #REQUIRED
   model (open | closed)              #IMPLIED
   content (empty | textOnly | eltOnly | mixed) #IMPLIED
   order    (one | seq | many)        #IMPLIED
   dt:type %datatypes;                #IMPLIED
   dt:values  CDATA                   #IMPLIED
   required  (yes | no)               #IMPLIED
   xmlns:dt CDATA #FIXED "urn:schemas-microsoft-com:datatypes">

<!ELEMENT group  (group | element | description)*>
<!ATTLIST group
   minOccurs   CDATA                  #IMPLIED
   maxOccurs   CDATA                  #IMPLIED
   order      (one | seq | many)  #IMPLIED>

<!ELEMENT Schema  (AttributeType | ElementType | description )* >
<!ATTLIST Schema
   name  CDATA #IMPLIED
   xmlns:dt CDATA #FIXED "urn:schemas-microsoft-com:datatypes">
```

While the XDR Schema is fairly simple, it provides for considerable flexibility for describing the data model of XML documents. It consists of only eight elements, which are described briefly here then covered in more detail in the sections that follow.

- Schema: This is the root element for XDR Schema documents.
- datatype: Describes types of data for elements and attributes.
- ElementType: Describes an individual element.
- element: Describes a child element.
- group: Used to group elements for defining order.
- AttributeType: Describes a type of attribute.

- `attribute`: Describes an attribute that can occur within an element.
- `description`: Provides descriptive information for an element or attribute.

XML was designed to be a very flexible standard. This very flexibility, however, has resulted in some problems, one of which is the confusion that could arise when one XML document relies on two or more vocabularies that use the same name for different purposes. The XML Namespaces Recommendation was developed to deal with this potential problem (as covered earlier in this chapter).

The Schema Element

The `Schema` element defines the root element of an XDR Schema. All other schema content is contained within this element. The `Schema` element has two attributes: `name`, which specifies the name of the schema, and `xmlns`, which specifies the schema's namespace. The `name` attribute can be set to whatever value you want (within XML naming rules) and is often the same as the filename of the XDR Schema (but it does not have to be). The `xmlns` attribute must be set to

```
urn:schemas-microsoft-com:xml-data
```

because this is the namespace for the XDR Schema implementation. Here is an example of the `Schema` element in an XML Schema:

```
<Schema name="MySchema" xmlns="urn:schemas-microsoft-com:xml-data">
...
</Schema>
```

The remainder of the schema content is placed between these two tags. While this example is the simplest `Schema` element, it is usually necessary to define another name space for data types. This namespace has the name "xmlns:dt" and the required setting for the XDR data types is "urn:schemas-microsoft-com:datatypes." A more typical `Schema` element would therefore be as follows:

```
<Schema name="MySchema" xmlns="urn:schemas-microsoft-com:xml-data"
   xmlns:dt="urn:schemas-microsoft-com:datatypes">
...
</Schema>
```

The Schema element can contain AttributeType, ElementType, and description child elements, which will be covered soon.

The datatype Element

The datatype element specifies the type of data that an element or attribute contains. A datatype element is placed within an ElementType or AttributeType element. The syntax is as follows:

```
<datatype dt:type="type"/>
```

The datatype element has one attribute, dt:type, whose value specifies the data type. The types of data that can be specified include those types supported by the DTD technology (referred to as *primitive* types) as well as a full range of new types that are supported by XDR but not DTD. The settings that are permitted, and the data types they represent, are listed in Table 4.1 for the data types that you will need most often. Appendix A contains a complete list of the permitted data types. (Note that in Table 4.1, primitive types are marked with an asterisk.)

The following is a datatype element that specifies the date data type:

```
<datatype dt:type="date"/>
```

Additional examples of using the datatype element are presented in the sections on the AttributeType and ElementType elements later in this chapter. Note that the function of this element can be replaced by using the dt:type attribute within the ElementType element.

The ElementType Element

The ElementType element is used to define elements that can be used in an XML document that is based on the schema. This includes the document's root element as well as all child elements. The information about the element is provided by attributes of the ElementType tag as well as by child elements contained within the ElementType tag. The child elements that can be included are described elsewhere in this chapter:

- AttributeType element: Defines a type of attribute local to the element.
- attribute element: Defines an actual attribute local to the element.
- datatype element: Specifies the data type of the element type.
- element element: Specifies a child element for the element type.
- group element: Used to group elements for organizational purposes.

Table 4.1 Settings for the datatype Element's dt:data Attribute for Commonly Needed Data Types

Setting of dt:type	Data Type
date	A date in the format yyyy-mm-dd
entity*	A reference to an entity (same as DTD ENTITY type)
entities*	A reference to multiple entities (same as DTD ENTITIES type)
enumeration*	Same as DTD enumerated type (one of a list of string values)
float	A number with optional sign that can contain a fractional part (for example, "12.0977")
id*	A unique identifier (same as DTD ID type)
idref*, idrefs*	A reference to one or multiple "id" types (same as DTD IDREF and IDREFS types)
int	A number with optional sign and no fractional part (for example, "123")
notation*	A reference to a notation (same as DTD NOTATION type)
string*	Text data (same as DTD #PCDATA type)
time	A time in the format hh:mm:ss
uri	A URI (for example, "urn:schemas-microsoft-com:Office9")

There are five permitted attributes of the ElementType element, which are explained in the following sections.

The name Attribute

The name attribute is required, and it specifies the name of the ElementType. The name must be unique within its scope—in other words, within its namespace.

The model Attribute

The `model` attribute specifies whether the content model is open or closed. An open content model permits additional elements to be defined within the element type beyond those that are declared in the schema. These additional tags can come from the same namespace or a different namespace. If they are in the same namespace, there must be a corresponding `ElementType` or `AttributeType` definition for them in the schema. A closed model permits only those tags defined in the schema. DTDs use a closed model. Set this attribute to the value "closed" or "open." The default, if the attribute is not set, is "open." The use of an open model is appropriate when an XML file *must* contain certain elements (those defined in the model) and *may* contain additional elements not defined in the model.

You may be wondering what purpose is served by an open content model. The closed content model, which is the only type supported by DTDs and is optional in XDR Schema, requires that all elements and attributes used in a document be declared in the document's data model. The open content model permits the data model to be extended by permitting additional elements and/or attributes defined in another data model to be included. The various data models, or schemas, are referenced by means of their namespaces.

There may be times when you do not want to provide the option of extending the data model that is defined by a schema. There can be a variety of reasons why anyone using your schema should be required to stick to its data model. In this case, you need to specify the closed content model in the appropriate locations, because the XML Schema default is for the content model to be open unless specified otherwise.

The content Attribute

The `content` attribute specifies the permitted content of the element type. Possible settings for this attribute are explained in Table 4.2.

These content settings are similar to those permitted in a DTD, with the addition of a "child elements only" setting. When the content model is open, as set by the `model` attribute, the possibility exists of using elements that are not specified in the schema.

The order Attribute

The `order` attribute specifies the order and number of occurrences of the group of child elements contained within the element type. There are three possible settings for this attribute:

Table 4.2 Settings for the `ElementType` Element's `content` Attribute

Value	Description
`empty`	The element cannot contain any content.
`textOnly`	The element can contain text but no child elements. If the `model` attribute is set to "open," the element can contain other unnamed elements in addition to text.
`eltOnly`	The element can contain child elements but no text.
`mixed`	The element can contain both child elements and text. Mixed is the default value of the `content` attribute. If the value of the `content` attribute is mixed, `minOccurs` and `maxOccurs` attributes will not trigger a validation error if the number of child elements is outside the specified boundary.

- `one`: Only one of a set of elements is allowed.
- `seq`: The elements must be in the specified order.
- `many`: No restrictions on the number of occurrences or order.

The following is an example of using the `one` value for the `order` attribute:

```
<ElementType name="vehicle" order="one">
  <element type="automobile" />
  <element type="motorcycle" />
</ElementType>
```

This specifies that the "vehicle" element can contain either an "automobile" child element or a "motorcycle" child element, but not both.

Here is an example of using the `seq` value for the `order` attribute:

```
<ElementType name="person" order="seq">
  <element type="firstname">
  <element type="middlename">
  <element type="lastname">
</ElementType>
```

This specifies that the "person" element must contain exactly one "firstname" element, one "middlename" element, and one "lastname" element, in that order.

The dt:type Attribute

The `dt:type` attribute specifies the type of data contained in the element. It is not relevant for empty or element-only elements. The possible settings for this attribute are the same as for the `datatype` element and were presented earlier in this chapter in Table 4.1 (with a full listing in Appendix A). Use of this attribute is an alternative to using the `datatype` element. The following are two equivalent ways to declare an element that has the `int` data type:

```
<ElementType name="count">
  <datatype dt:type="int" />
</ElementType>

<ElementType name="count" dt:type="int" />
```

Note that the data type of an element does not need to be specified—in other words, the `dt:type` attribute is optional. To achieve the full power of schemas, however, the use of the `dt:type` attribute is recommended.

The element Element

The `element` element is used to specify an occurrence of a particular type of element within the schema. Thus, a type of element is defined by an `ElementType` element, and the placement of elements is defined by the `element` element. There are three attributes associated with the `element` element:

- `type`: The type of the element. This must be an element type defined elsewhere in the Schema using an `ElementType` element. This is a required attribute.
- `minOccurs`: The minimum number of times the element can occur.
- `maxOccurs`: The maximum number of times the element can occur.

The `minOccurs` and `maxOccurs` attributes are optional, and the default value is 1 for both. Table 4.3 explains the use of these attributes.

The following is an example of using the `minOccurs` and `maxOccurs` attributes:

```
<ElementType name="title" content="textOnly" />
<ElementType name="amount" content="textOnly" />
<ElementType name="item" content="textOnly" />
<ElementType name="directions" content="textOnly" />
<ElementType name="comments" content="textOnly" />
```

Table 4.3 Use of the `minOccurs` and `maxOccurs` Attributes

minOccurs	maxOccurs	Times the Element Can Occur
0	1	Zero or one time
1	1	Exactly one time
0	*	Any number of times
1	*	One or more times
n ($n > 0$)	*	At least n times
$> n$	n ($n > 0$)	Zero times
n (any value)	$< n$	Zero times

```
<ElementType name="ingredient" content="eltOnly" order="seq" />
  <element type="amount" />
  <element type="item" />
</ElementType>

<ElementType name="recipe" content="eltOnly">
  <element type="title" />
  <element type="ingredient" minOccurs="0" maxOccurs="*" />
  <element type="directions" minOccurs="1" maxOccurs="1" />
  <element type="comments" minOccurs="0" maxOccurs="1" />
</ElementType>
```

The preceding section of an XDR Schema is interpreted as follows.

- The first five lines declare five text-only elements.
- The next section declares an element-only element named "ingredient." This element contains the two element types: "amount" and "item." Each of these child elements must occur exactly once, because the `minOccurs` and `maxOccurs` attributes were left at their default values of 1. These two child elements must occur in the given order, because the order attribute is set to `seq`.

- The final section declares an element-only element named "recipe" that contains four child elements. The "title" child element must occur exactly once. The "ingredient" child element can occur any number of times. The "directions" child element must occur exactly once; here the values of `minOccurs` and `maxOccurs` are explicitly set rather than depending on their default values. Finally, the "comments" child element can occur zero or one time.

The group Element

The `group` element is used to organize elements into groups, which is required for establishing some complex document content models. Within a group, you can specify the order and frequency of the occurrence of the elements in the same way you can for the `ElementType` element. This is done using the `group` element's `order` attribute. Possible settings for this attribute are as follows:

- `one`: Only one of the listed elements can occur in the group.
- `seq`: The listed elements must occur in the specified order.
- `many`: The elements can occur in any order and frequency.

The use of the `order` attribute with the `group` element is the same as described earlier in this chapter for the order `attribute` of the `ElementType` element.

You can also specify the number of times the group must occur. This is done with the `minOccurs` and `maxOccurs` attributes. These attributes work exactly the same as they do for the `element` element described earlier in this chapter (see Table 4.3).

The following example specifies that only one of the elements listed within the group can occur, and it must occur exactly once (because the `minOccurs` and `maxOccurs` attributes have been left at their default values of 1):

```
<ElementType name="stockitem">
  <group order="one">
    <element type="catalognumber" />
    <element type="partnumber" />
    <element type="itemnumber" />
  </group>
  <element type="description" />
  <element type="quantity" />
</ElementType>
```

The next example defines a group containing two elements: "alternatecontact" and "telephone." The group can occur zero or one time. If it does occur, the two elements must both be present in the specified order.

```
<ElementType name="supplier">
  <element type="contact" />
  <group order="seq" minOccurs="0" maxOccurs="1">
    <element type="alternatecontact" />
    <element type="telephone" />
  </group>
  <element type="address" />
</ElementType>
```

The AttributeType Element

The `AttributeType` element is used to define attributes that can be used in elements. Once you define a type of attribute with the `AttributeType` element, you use the `attribute` element described in the next section to specify the locations where the attribute can be used. The `AttributeType` element has five attributes:

- `name`: The name of the attribute. This must be unique within the namespace of the `AttributeType` element. The `name` attribute is required.
- `dt:type`: The data type of the attribute. Table 4.1 lists the most commonly used data types, and Appendix A presents a full list of permitted types.
- `dt:values`: Specifies a list of permitted values when the `dt:type` attribute is set to "enumerated."
- `default`: Specifies the default value of the attribute—its value if it is not set explicitly.
- `required`: Specifies if the attribute is required, meaning that a value must be assigned to the attribute in every element where it can occur. Settings are "yes" and "no." The default is "no."

The following `AttributeType` declaration specifies a required attribute named "flavor" that is an enumeration, with the permitted values being "chocolate," "vanilla," and "strawberry."

```
<AttributeType name="flavor" dt:type="enumeration" dt:values=
    "chocolate vanilla strawberry" required="yes" />
```

The next `AttributeType` declaration specifies an attribute named "average" that is type `float`, has a default value of 0, and is not required:

```
<AttributeType name="average" dt:type="float" default="0" />
```

You can place `AttributeType` declarations at two locations within an XDR Schema. If placed inside an `ElementType` element, the declared attribute is local to the element being declared; in other words, the attribute can be used only by that element type. If the `AttributeType` declaration is not inside an `ElementType` element, the declared attribute is available throughout the Schema.

> ***Internet Explorer and Attribute Data Types***
>
> *Internet Explorer 5.x supports XDR Schema attributes, but only partially. As of this writing, only the so-called primitive data types are supported.*

The attribute Element

The `attribute` element is used to associate an attribute type with an element type. The attribute type must be defined elsewhere in the schema with an `AttributeType` element. This element has three attributes:

- `type`: The type of the attribute—the value assigned to the `name` attribute in the `AttributeType` element when the attribute type was declared. This attribute is required.
- `default`: The default value of the attribute if no value is explicitly assigned to it. The `default` value specified in an `attribute` tag overrides the `default` value specified in the `AttributeType` tag.
- `required`: Set to the value "yes" or "no" to specify whether the attribute is required. The `required` value specified in an `attribute` tag overrides the `required` value specified in the `AttributeType` tag.

An `attribute` element is placed inside an `ElementType` element to specify an attribute that is permitted (or required) for that element. The following example defines two attributes named "season" and "date." Then it declares an element type named "trip" that has "season" as an optional attribute and "date" as a required attribute.

```
<AttributeType name="season" dt:type="enumeration" dt:values=
    "winter spring summer fall" />
<AttributeType name="date" dt:type="date" />

<ElementType name="trip" content="eltOnly" >
  <attribute type="season" required="no" />
  <attribute type="date" required="yes" />
  <element type="destination" />
</ElementType>
```

The description Element

The `description` element is used to include descriptive text in an XDR Schema document. This element can occur as a child element within the following elements: `Schema`, `AttributeType`, `ElementType`, `attribute`, `element`, and `group`. The format is as follows:

```
<description>Text goes here</description>
```

The text in a `description` element is ignored during validation but is available to XML tools.

Connecting a Document to a Schema

When an XML document is created following a particular schema, it is necessary to include information in the XML file that identifies the schema. This information is necessary for the XML parser to validate the document against the schema. To create the connection, assign the XML document to a namespace that consists of "x-schema:" followed by the name of the file containing the XDR Schema. Here is an example of a root element with a namespace assignment:

```
<addressbook xmlns="x-schema:addressbook.xdr">
...
</addressbook>
```

The XML document containing this root element will be validated against the schema contained in the file addressbook.xdr. In this case, the name of the root element is the same as the name of the Schema file, but this is not required.

Validating Documents against Schemas

The validation of an XML document against its Schema is performed by the parser. As you will see in later chapters, you can use the MSXML Parser with various programming languages to perform validation, which is usually the first in a sequence of XML processing steps. If you want to perform validation alone, you can use Internet Explorer as explained in the next section. Note that you cannot use the XMLINT validation utility (see Chapter 3 for more information) because it supports DTDs only.

An XDR Schema Demonstration

In order to demonstrate the creation and use of an XDR Schema, I have created a Schema that defines a data model that is designed to store information about a collection of audio recordings. The plan for the document is as follows:

- The root element will be called "recordings."
- The root element can contain any number of "recording" elements. Each "recording" element will correspond to one entry in the file; that is, to one item in the collection. The data model is closed.
- Each "recording" element must contain one "title" element and one "performers" element. "Title" is a text-only element. "Performers" can contain one or more "performer" elements. "Performer" is a text-only element.
- Each "recording" element can contain zero or one "comments" element. "Comments" is a text-only element.
- The "recording" element must contain an attribute named "media," which is an enumerated attribute with possible values "CD," "LP," and "tape."
- The "recording" element must also contain an attribute named "quality," which is a type `int` attribute.

The resulting schema is shown in Listing 4.2, and an XML data file based on this schema is shown in Listing 4.3. To view this XML file, you can use Internet Explorer. These are the steps to follow:

1. Open Internet Explorer.
2. Press Ctrl-O or select Open from the File menu to display the Open dialog box.
3. Type in the name, including the path, of the XML file, or click the Browse button to browse for the file. If you use the Browse option, you

have to set the File of Type option to "all files" in order to locate files with the .xml extension.

4. Click OK.

When the XML file is opened, Internet Explorer automatically checks it for well-formedness and also validates it against the XDR Schema. If any syntax or validation errors occur, they will be displayed and you can edit the XML file and/or the Schema file as needed to correct the errors. This is a good opportunity for you to experiment and intentionally insert various kinds of errors to see how the XML parser reacts to them.

If there are no errors, the document will appear as shown in Figure 4.1. You can see that the data and tags in the file are displayed essentially unchanged, with indentation applied to help clarify the logical structure of the document. While not visible in the figure, the display is also color-coded, with various colors used for the data and XML elements.

The way that Internet Explorer displays this document is based on the *default style sheet.* This is the style sheet that is used if there is no other style sheet associated with the document. You'll learn how to create your own customized style sheets later in the book.

Listing 4.2 RecordingSchema.xdr Is an XDR Schema Defining a Data Model for Storing Information about Audio Recordings

```
<?xml version="1.0" encoding="UTF-8"?>
<Schema name="MySchema" xmlns="urn:schemas-microsoft-com:xml-data"
  xmlns:dt="urn:schemas-microsoft-com:datatypes">
  <AttributeType name="media" dt:type="enumeration"
      dt:values="CD LP tape"/>
  <AttributeType name="quality" dt:type="int">
      <description>
          A quality value of 0 means the quality is unknown. Values
          from 1 to 10 reflect a rating from poor to excellent.
      </description>
  </AttributeType>
  <ElementType name="recordings" content="eltOnly" model="closed">
      <element type="recording" minOccurs="0" maxOccurs="*" />
  </ElementType>
  <ElementType name="comments" content="textOnly" />
  <ElementType name="title" content="textOnly"/>
  <ElementType name="performers" content="eltOnly">
      <element type="performer" minOccurs="1" maxOccurs="*" />
  </ElementType>
```

```
    <ElementType name="performer" content="textOnly"/>
    <ElementType name="recording" content="eltOnly">
        <element type="title" />
        <element type="performers" />
        <element type="comments" minOccurs="0" maxOccurs="1" />
        <attribute type="media" required="yes" />
        <attribute type="quality" required="yes" />
    </ElementType>
</Schema>
```

Listing 4.3 Recordings.xml Is Based on the Data Model Defined by the XDR Schema in Listing 4.2

```
<?xml version="1.0" encoding="UTF-8"?>
<recordings xmlns="x-schema:RecordingSchema.xdr">
<recording  media="CD" quality="8">
    <title>
        Pandit Ravi Shankar
    </title>
    <performers>
        <performer>Ravi Shankar</performer>
        <performer>Kumar Bose</performer>
        <performer>Vidya Bataju</performer>
        <performer>Jeevan Govinda</performer>
    </performers>
</recording>
<recording  media="LP" quality="6">
    <title>
        The Little Bach Book
    </title>
    <performers>
        <performer>Glenn Gould</performer>
    </performers>
    <comments>
        There is a scratch at the beginning of side 2.
    </comments>
</recording>
<recording  media="CD" quality="9">
    <title>
        Bach: English Suites
    </title>
    <performers>
        <performer>Murray Perahia</performer>
    </performers>
```

```
        <comments>
            An exceptionally good performance.
        </comments>
    </recording>
    </recordings>
```

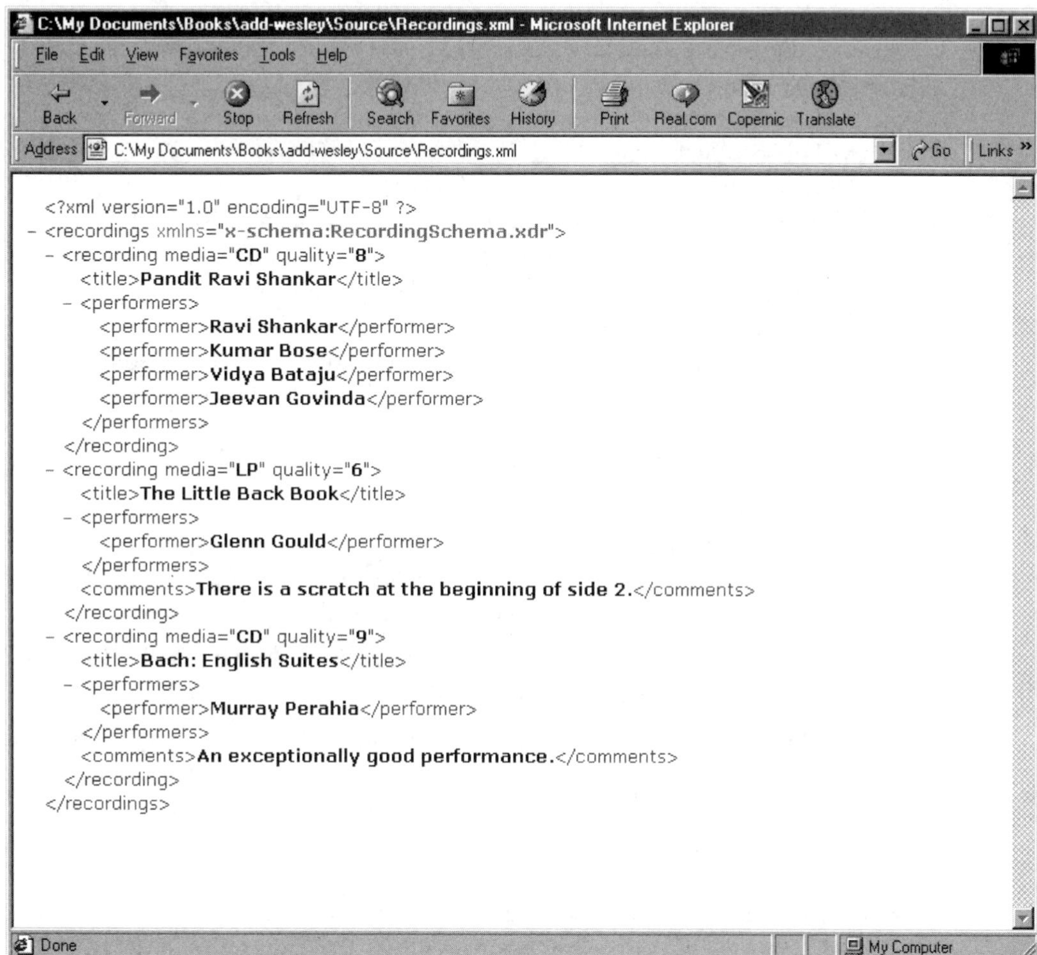

Figure 4.1 The XML file in Listing 4.3 displayed in Internet Explorer

DTD or XML Schema: Which to Use?

When you are starting an XML project that requires document validation, you are faced with the question of whether to use a DTD or a schema. This is not an irrevocable decision, as you can always switch an ongoing project from one to the other, but it is better to make the correct choice at the start and avoid unnecessary effort. I can't give you a step-by-step checklist for this decision, but I can point out the factors you should take into consideration.

The main point in favor of DTDs is that they have been around for a while and therefore enjoy wide support. While support for schemas is certainly on the rise, it will be quite a while before it matches that of DTDs. If you go with schemas, the variety of XML tools you have to choose from is limited, at least for the time being. The wide support for DTDs goes beyond tools to XML vocabularies. If you want to start with an existing and tested XML data model, and use it as-is or with some modifications, you will have a much wider choice of vocabularies that are defined with DTDs.

It's important to remember that DTDs are actually all you need in many situations. Just because schemas are an improvement on DTDs does not mean that the latter is some sort of ancient, crippled technology.

These things being said in favor of DTDs, there is still no doubt that schemas provide the XML developer with a lot more flexibility in defining and applying data models. The most important advantages are as follows:

- Schemas are XML documents and can be parsed and manipulated like any XML document using standard XML tools.
- Schemas offer an open-ended content model that permits the developer to extend a data model without breaking existing documents. In contrast, DTDs have a fixed and nonextensible content model.
- Schemas support a wide set of data types, including integers, Booleans, and dates. DTDs treat all data as strings.
- Schemas support namespace integration, which allows specific parts of the data model to be applied to specific parts of the XML document. DTDs permit only a single association between a document and its data model.

If you do decide to use schemas for your data modeling, you are then faced with the question of which Schema to use: XDR or XSD. This is an easy one to answer. There is no reason to use XDR unless you are working with one of the existing Microsoft products that support only XDR (these were listed earlier in the chapter). Otherwise, the nonproprietary XSD is the clear choice. It probably won't be too long before all Microsoft products support XSD and XDR becomes a relic of history. That time is not with us yet, however.

Summary

An XML Schema is one of two ways to define a data model for an XML file (the other being DTDs, which were covered in the previous chapter). Defining a data model using an XML Schema provides greater flexibility than using a DTD, but is also a more complex process that does not enjoy wide support. Which technique you use will depend on a variety of factors, as explained in this chapter. This chapter covered XDR Schemas, the Microsoft version of XML Schemas. The other version, XSD Schemas, is a W3C Recommendation and is covered in the next chapter. When you want to use an XML Schema in preference to a DTD, you should always use the XSD Schema vocabulary except in those situations (detailed in the chapter) when the Microsoft-specific XDR vocabulary is required.

CHAPTER 5

Data Modeling with XSD Schemas

The XSD Schema specification has been under development for at least a couple of years, and it has just recently achieved W3C Recommendation status. It is a very powerful and flexible specification for defining the data structure of XML documents, and support for it should expand rapidly now that it is a Recommendation. Complete coverage of all the details of the specification would be a major undertaking and is well beyond the scope of this book. This chapter presents the most important aspects of XSD Schema sufficient for the majority of data modeling tasks. You can find complete details on XSD Schema at the W3C Web site (`http://www.w3.org/XML/Schema`).

XSD Schema Overview

The best way to understand XSD Schema is as a hierarchy of data types. At the bottom of the hierarchy are the built-in simple data types that represent the basic units of data that an XML file may contain: strings, integer numbers, floating point numbers, dates, and so on. From these simple data types you can create your own complex data types that are composed of various different simple types in almost any imaginable combination. You then use these data types to define the elements and attributes for your schema. Thus, you would define data types for your XML document's root element, for its child elements, and so on down to the lowest-level elements that hold the document's data. Learning to create XSD Schemas is therefore mainly a process of learning how to define data types.

Software Support

As of this writing, XSD Schema has just achieved W3C Recommendation status. In the world of Microsoft tools, the MSXML Parser has just been upgraded to support this specification, or at least most of it (this is version 4.0 of the parser). In addition, the XML tools in the .NET Framework support XSD Schema. At present, this is the only Microsoft support for XSD Schema. By the time you read this, however, it is very likely that support will have been extended to Internet Explorer. Note that Microsoft provides a free XSD development utility at `http://msdn.microsoft.com/library/dotnet/cptools/cpconxmlschemadefinitiontoolxsdexe.htm`.

XSD Data Types

The concept of data types is central to XSD. Every element and attribute in an XSD Schema is declared as having a specific type. This type determines how the element or attribute can be used. There is a fundamental distinction between *simple* types and *complex* types.

- A complex data type may contain elements and may carry attributes.
- A simple type may not contain elements and may not carry attributes.

The XSD specification contains an assortment of simple data types. In addition, you can define your own data types, both simple and complex, to meet the specific needs of your project. In this section I describe XSD's built-in data types and show how you can define your own complex and simple types.

XSD's Built-in Simple Data Types

The simple data types are used to declare attributes as well as elements that will contain only data—for example, some text or a number. XSD provides a wide range of built-in simple data types. The ones that are used most frequently are described in Table 5.1. These are called *atomic* simple data types because they cannot be broken down any further. The two nonatomic simple data types, the list type and the union type, are described later in this section.

You can find the full list of simple data types on the W3C Web site (`http://www.w3.org/`). In the descriptions in this table, the term "integer" is used to mean a numeric value with no decimal places and "floating point" is used to mean a number that can have decimal places.

Table 5.1 The Most Commonly Used Simple Atomic Data Types in XSD

Data Type	Description	Example
`anyType`	Places no restriction on data type.	
`string`	A string of characters.	This is a string
`byte`	An integer from –128 to 127.	–12, 122
`unsignedByte`	An integer from 0 to 255.	0, 126
`anyURI`*	A URI in either relative or absolute form; can include a fragment identifier.	www.microsoft.com
`integer`	An integer. There is no practical range limit.	–168,112, –11, 0, 1, 16,700,000
`positiveInteger`	An integer with a value of 1 or greater.	1, 12, 40,000
`negativeInteger`	An integer with a value of –1 or less.	–26, –1
`nonNegativeInteger`	An integer with a value of 0 or greater.	0, 1, 12, 780,000
`nonPositiveInteger`	An integer with a value of 0 or less.	–10,000, –2, 0
`int`	An integer from –2,147,483,648 to 2,147,483,648.	–1, 126,789,675
`unsignedInt`	An integer from 0 to 4,294,967,295.	0, 12, 90,010,000
`long`	An integer from –9,223,372,036,854,775,808 to 9,223,372,036,854,775,807.	–12,345, 3,545,300,000
`unsignedLong`	An integer from 0 to 18,446,744,073,709,551,615.	0, 12,678,967,543,233
`short`	An integer from –32,768 to 32,767.	–5, 32,766
`unsignedShort`	An integer from 0 to 65,535.	0, 1, 60,000

(continued)

Table 5.1: *(cont.)*

Data Type	Description	Example
`float`	A floating point value from (approximate) +/– 1.4E-45 to +/– 2E31. Can also take the special values –INF (negative infinity), INF (positive infinity), 0 (positive zero), –0 (negative 0), and "not a number" (NaN).	–INF, –1.1E-12, –0, 0, 2.8E2, 1,200.1, INF, NaN
`boolean`	A Boolean value that can have the literal values true, false, 1, and 0.	true, false 1, 0
`time`	A 24-hour time represented as HH:MM:SS. sss with the fractional seconds being optional. The time can be followed by time zone information represented as a value indicating how far behind or ahead of UTC.	The Eastern time zone in the United States is 5 hours behind (earlier than) UTC. Therefore, 2:30 PM would be represented as 14:30:00-05:00.
`dateTime`	A time and date represented as a date followed by "T" and a time. See the entries for the date and time types.	2001-06-15T14:30:00-05:00
`date`	A date in format YYYY-MM-DD.	2001-06-15

° The MSXML Parser documentation has this simple data type as `uriReference`, but it is `anyURI` in the W3C Recommendation.

The ID Attribute

Any of the elements used in XSD Schemas can contain the optional `ID` *attribute. This is part of the base XML specification and not specifically a part of XSD. Remember that* `ID` *attributes are special in that the value must be unique within the document. Because this optional attribute is essentially universal, it is not mentioned in the context of the specific XSD elements.*

Defining Your Own Simple Data Types

Defining your own simple data types does not mean creating a new atomic type from scratch. Rather, it means building on one of the existing atomic types and customizing it by placing certain types of restrictions on it. For example, suppose your company assigns employee numbers to its workers, from 100,000 to 999,999. You would define a simple data type with these restrictions as follows:

```
<xsd:simpleType name="employeeNumber">
  <xsd:restriction base="xsd:unsignedInt">
    <xsd:minInclusive value="100000"/>
    <xsd:maxInclusive value="999999"/>
  </xsd:restriction>
</xsd:simpleType>
```

This XSD element defines a simple type called "employeeNumber" that is based on the `unsignedInteger` type with a minimum allowed value of 100,000 and a maximum allowed value of 999,999. The `xsd` namespace prefix is typically associated with the default XSD namespace, as will be explained later in the chapter.

If you look at the previous example, you can see that defining a simple type has three parts:

- A `simpleType` element that specifies the name of the new type
- A `restriction` element that specifies the base data type that the new type is derived from
- One or more elements that specify the restrictions on the new data type

The restrictions that can be placed on data types are called *constraining facets,* or more often just *facets.* It is important to note that the built-in simple data types all have facets, so when you define your own simple data type you are really adding your own constraining facets to the base data type's own constraining facets. The facets that are applicable to the simple data types in Table 5.1 are described in Table 5.2.

When using a facet to define a simple type, keep the following rules in mind.

- The type of a value assigned to a facet must be the same as the base type. For example, if you are defining a type that is based on type `date`, if you specify the `minExclusive` facet you must assign a type `date` to the facet.

- Do not assign facets that conflict with the base type's existing constraints. For example, assigning a `minExclusive` of –100,000 to a type that is based on type `positiveInteger` is not allowed because that type already has a `minExclusive` of 0.

Table 5.2 Constraining Facets Used to Define Simple Data Types

Facet	Description	Applicable To
`enumeration`	Constrains the data type to a list of specified values. See the text for more information.	All except `boolean`
`length`	The required number of characters in the data.	`string`, `anyURI`
`minLength`	The minimum number of characters in the data.	`string`, `anyURI`
`maxLength`	The maximum number of characters in the data.	`string`, `anyURI`
`minExclusive`	The data must be greater than this value.	All numeric, date, and time types
`maxExclusive`	The data must be less than this value.	All numeric, date, and time types
`minInclusive`	The data must be greater than or equal to this value.	All numeric, date, and time types
`maxInclusive`	The data must be less than or equal to this value.	All numeric, date, and time types
`pattern`	A regular expression that constrains the data to certain literals. See the text for details.	All types
`totalDigits`	The maximum number of digits in a value.	All integer types
`whiteSpace`	Set to "preserve," "collapse," or "replace." See the text for details.	All types

You saw previously how to create a new numeric data type with a restricted range of values. The following example creates a data type for dates that is restricted to dates in the year 2001:

```
<xsd:simpleType name="year2001">
  <xsd:restriction base="xsd:date">
    <xsd:minInclusive value="2001-01-01"/>
    <xsd:maxInclusive value="2001-12-31"/>
  </xsd:restriction>
</xsd:simpleType>
```

Here's another example—this one creates a type for string data that must contain at least one character:

```
<xsd:simpleType name="nonEmptyString">
  <xsd:restriction base="xsd:string">
    <xsd:minLength value="1"/>
  </xsd:restriction>
</xsd:simpleType>
```

You can base a new data type on another data type you have defined as well as on the built-in types. The following type holds string data between one and five characters in length. It "inherits" the minimum length value of 1 from the type `nonEmptyString`, as defined previously.

```
<xsd:simpleType name="string1to5">
  <xsd:restriction base="nonEmptyString ">
    <xsd:maxLength value="5"/>
  </xsd:restriction>
</xsd:simpleType>
```

Enumerations

An enumeration is a list of permitted values. For example, a list of the names of the 50 states that make up the United States is an enumeration. You can define a data type that is an enumeration and is permitted to take values that are part of the enumeration. You can create an enumeration based on any of XSD's simple types except `boolean`. Use the `enumeration` element to define individual items in the list. Here's an example:

```
<xsd:simpleType name="colors">
  <xsd:restriction base="xsd:string">
    <xsd:enumeration value="red"/>
```

```
    <xsd:enumeration value="green"/>
    <xsd:enumeration value="blue"/>
    <!-- more colors... -->
  </xsd:restriction>
</xsd:simpleType>
```

Here's an enumeration of dates:

```
<xsd:simpleType name="holidaysThisYear">
  <xsd:restriction base="xsd:date">
    <xsd:enumeration value="2001-01-01"/>
    <xsd:enumeration value="2001-12-25"/>
    <!-- more dates... -->
  </xsd:restriction>
</xsd:simpleType>
```

List Types

A *list type* contains a list of two or more individual data types. For example, you could define a list type that consists of a list of integers or of dates. Note that the `restriction` element is not used here. The following is an example of defining a type for a list of dates:

```
<xsd:simpleType name="listOfDates">
    <xsd:list itemType="xsd:date"/>
</xsd:simpleType>
```

The following data element would be a legal instance of this type:

```
<datelist>2001-05-08 1998-12-31 1971-09-21</datelist>
```

You can define a list of strings, but there is a potential problem. An individual string can contain one or more spaces, but within a list a space is used to delineate list elements. Thus, the following list would be considered to have four and not three members:

```
<states>Arizona New York Vermont</states>
```

If your strings do not contain spaces, the use of a list element presents no problems. You can use a pattern that is covered in the next section to define a string data type in which spaces are not permitted.

Once you have defined a list type, you can place further restrictions on it by basing a derived data type on it. The facets `length`, `minLength`, `maxLength`, and `enumeration` can be applied to list types. Using the `listOfDates` type defined previously, the following defines a data type that must be a list of six dates:

```
<xsd:simpleType name="listOfSixDates">
  <xsd:restriction base="listOfDates">
    <xsd:length value="6"/>
  </xsd:restriction>
</xsd:simpleType>
```

Union Types

A *union type* is a data type that combines the restrictions of two or more existing data types. For example, suppose you had defined one data type that was an enumeration of all the countries in South America and another data type that was an enumeration of all the countries in Central America. When you create a union based on these two types, the resulting data type will in effect be an enumeration of both country lists.

The following example creates a data type that is a union of the "listOf-Dates" and the "colors" types that were defined earlier in this chapter:

```
<xsd:simpleType name="dateListOrColor">
  xsd:union memberTypes="listOfDates colors"/>
</xsd:simpleType>
```

The following elements would both be legal instances of this union type:

```
<A>red</A>
<B>2001-12-03 1999-05-12 1998-01-02</B>
```

Using Patterns

The `pattern` facet enables you to define a detailed template for a data type. For example, you could restrict a type to containing strings that consist of a single uppercase letter followed by a dash and three digits. You specify the `pattern` facet as a *regular expression* that has a defined syntax for specifying a pattern. The regular expression language is similar to that used in other contexts, such as Perl. The full language is quite complex, but the fundamentals that are needed for creating most patterns are fairly easy to learn. These important elements are described in Table 5.3.

Table 5.3: Regular Expression Components

<table>
<tr><th>Character(s)</th><th>Description</th><th>Example</th></tr>
<tr><td>(any)</td><td>Matches itself. Use "\(" and "\)" to match parentheses.</td><td>abc matches "abc."</td></tr>
<tr><td>\</td><td>Marks the next character as a special character or a literal.</td><td>\n matches the newline character. \\ matches "\".</td></tr>
<tr><td>^</td><td>Matches the start of text.</td><td>^XML matches "XML" only at the beginning of a string.</td></tr>
<tr><td>$</td><td>Matches the end of text.</td><td>XML$ matches "XML" only at the end of a string.</td></tr>
<tr><td>*</td><td>Matches the preceding character zero or more times.</td><td>to* matches "t" or "to" or "too."</td></tr>
<tr><td>+</td><td>Matches the preceding character one or more times.</td><td>to+ matches "to" or "too."</td></tr>
<tr><td>?</td><td>Matches the preceding character zero or one time.</td><td>to?t matches "tt" and "tot" but not "toot."</td></tr>
<tr><td>. (period)</td><td>Matches any single character except a newline character.</td><td>t.t matches "tat," "tbt," "tct," and so on, but not "toot."</td></tr>
<tr><td>x|y</td><td>Matches either x or y.</td><td>(r|d)ead matches "read" or "dead."</td></tr>
<tr><td>{n}</td><td>Matches exactly n times, where n is an integer greater than zero.</td><td>.o{2}t matches "foot," "boot," and so on.</td></tr>
<tr><td>{n,}</td><td>Matches at least n times, where n is an integer greater than zero.</td><td>be(2,}d matches "beed," "beeed," and so on, but it does not match "bed."</td></tr>
<tr><td>{n,m}</td><td>Matches at least n times and at most m times, where n and m are an integers greater than zero with m>n.</td><td>bo{1,3}k matches "bok," "book," and "boook."</td></tr>
</table>

(continued)

Table 5.3 *(cont.)*

Character(s)	Description	Example
`[`*chars*`]`	Matches any one of the enclosed characters.	b[ae]d matches "bed" or "bad."
`[^`*chars*`]`	Matches any single character except those enclosed.	b[^ae]d matches "bbd," "bcd," and so on, but not "bad" or "bed."
`[a-z]`	Matches any character in the specified range.	[g-m] matches any single character from *g* to *m*.
`[^a-z]`	Matches any character not in the specified range.	[^a-m] matches *n* through *z*.
`\b`	Matches a word boundary.	ed\b matches the "ed" in "tried" but not the "ed" in "tedious."
`\B`	Matches a nonword boundary.	ed\B matches the "ed" in "tedious" but not the "ed" in "tried."
`\d`	Matches any digit character from 0 to 9.	Equivalent to [0-9].
`\D`	Matches any nondigit character.	Equivalent to [^0-9].

Regular Expression and MSXML

At the time of this writing, the latest version of the Microsoft XML Parser, MSXML 4.0, claims to support all of the XSD specification except regular expressions. This support is promised for a later release, and may well be available by the time you read this.

The `pattern` facet is most commonly used with data types based on `string`. The following defines a pattern for a U.S. postal code that consists of five digits followed by a dash and then four digits.

```
<xsd:simpleType name="postalcode">
  <xsd:restriction base="xsd:string">
    <xsd:pattern value="\d{5}-\d{4}"/>
  </xsd:restriction>
</xsd:simpleType>
```

Here is a definition of a data type for part numbers that follow these rules:

- First character is always *X*
- Second character is any uppercase letter
- Third character is a digit from 1 to 5
- Final three characters are digits

```
<xsd:simpleType name="partnumber">
  <xsd:restriction base="xsd:string">
    <xsd:pattern value="X[A-Z][1-5]\d\d\d"/>
  </xsd:restriction>
</xsd:simpleType>
```

The whiteSpace Facet

The `whiteSpace` facet is applicable to the `string` data type and derived types. White space in all other data types is collapsed. For string types you can set the `whiteSpace` facet to one of the following values:

- `preserve`: White space is not normalized or altered in any way.
- `replace`: All occurrences of tabs, line feeds, and carriage returns are replaced with a single space.
- `collapse`: This is the default. The same as `replace` followed by replacing multiple sequential spaces with a single space and the removal of all leading and trailing spaces.

Note that the `whiteSpace` facet differs from other facets in that it does not constrain the data type in any way, but rather specifies how its white space will be handled.

Defining Complex Data Types

A complex data type in XSD is a type that can contain child elements and/or attributes. A complex type is defined within a `complexType` element. The syntax is as follows:

Table 5.4 Elements Used to Define Complex Data Types

Element	Description
`all`	Contains two or more `element` elements, each of which must appear once or not at all, in any order.
`attribute`	Specifies an attribute that the complex type can contain.
`choice`	Contains two or more `element` and/or `group` elements, and specifies that the complex type must contain one of the enclosed items.
`element`	Specifies a child element that the complex type can contain.
`group`	Defines a group of two or more elements that must appear but in no particular order.
`sequence`	Specifies a group of child elements that the complex type must contain in the specified order.

```
<xsd:complexType name="name">
...
</xsd:complexType>
```

The `name` attribute is optional and specifies the name of the type. If you omit the `name` attribute, you are creating what is known as an *anonymous* definition, which is discussed later in the chapter. Within the `complexType` element, you use other XSD elements to define the data type. These are described briefly in Table 5.4 and then explained in detail in the sections that follow.

element

Use the `element` element to identify an element that a complex type may contain. Its `name` attribute specifies the element name, and its `type` attribute specifies the data type (either a built-in type or a type you have defined). The `type` attribute will be omitted if you are using an anonymous definition, which is covered later in the chapter. Here's an example of declaring a complex type called "fullname":

```
<xsd:complexType name="fullname">
  <xsd:element name="firstname" type="xsd:string"/>
  <xsd:element name="lastname" type="xsd:string"/>
</xsd:complexType>
```

Other attributes that can be used with the `element` element are as follows:

- `default`: Specifies the element's default value. Applicable only if the element's content is a simple type.
- `maxOccurs`: The maximum number of times the element can occur within its containing element. Set to any value 1 or greater or to the string "unbounded" for no upper limit on occurrences of the element. The default value is 1.
- `minOccurs`: The minimum number of times the element can occur within its containing element. Set to any value between 0 and the value of `maxOccurs`. The default value is 1.

The `element` element can also be used to refer to an element that is defined elsewhere, by means of the `ref` attribute. The syntax is as follows:

```
<xsd:element ref="elementname"/>
```

`Elementname` is the name of an element that is defined elsewhere. The following example uses this syntax to create the same complex type declaration as in the preceding example:

```
<xsd:element name="firstname" type="xsd:string"/>
<xsd:element name="lastname" type="xsd:string"/>

<xsd:complexType name="fullname">
  <xsd:element ref="firstname"/>
  <xsd:element ref="lastname"/>
</xsd:complexType>
```

This way of using the `element` tag is useful when the same element is used in multiple places in your schema. You can define it once and then refer to it as needed throughout the schema.

group

The `group` element defines a group of elements, permitting the group to be referenced by name for inclusion in complex types. When defining a group, a `group` element may contain one or more `sequence`, `choice`, and/or `all` elements (see the sections in this chapter for these elements for details). The syntax is as follows:

```
<xsd:group name="groupname">
...
</xsd:group>
```

`Groupname` is the name that will be used to refer to the group. Here is an example of defining a group:

```
<xsd:group name="personalinfo">
  <xsd:sequence>
    <xsd:element name="firstname" type="xsd:string"/>
    <xsd:element name="lastname" type="xsd:string"/>
    <xsd:element name="birthyear" type="xsd:unsignedInt"/>
  </xsd:sequence>
</xsd:group>
```

This defines a group that must contain "firstname," "lastname," and "birthyear" elements, in that exact order (because a `sequence` element was used). Once this group is defined, you can use it in a complex type definition as follows:

```
<xsd:complextype name="person">
  <xsd:group ref="personalinfo"/>
  <xsd:attribute name="citizenship" type="xsd:string"/>
  <!-- other elements here as needed -->
</xsd:complextype>
```

The `group` element can occur within the `choice`, `sequence`, `complexType`, and `restriction` elements. It can contain `choice`, `sequence`, `element`, `all`, and `annotation` elements.

sequence

The `sequence` element defines a group of elements that must appear in the specified order. The syntax is as follows:

```
<xsd:sequence minOccurs="min" maxOccurs="max">
...
</xsd:sequence>
```

The `minOccurs` and `maxOccurs` attributes specify the minimum and maximum number of times the sequence can occur. Both are optional, and both have default values of 1. To make the sequence optional, set `minOccurs` to 0. To place no upper limit on the number of times the sequence occurs, set `maxOccurs` to "unbounded."

Here's an example of defining a complex type that uses the `sequence` element. It holds sales data for 12 months, and requires the 12 monthly entries to be in the correct order.

```
<xsd:complexType name="salesbymonth">
  <xsd:sequence>
    <xsd:element name="jansales" type="xsd:float"/>
    <xsd:element name="febsales" type="xsd:float"/>
    <xsd:element name="marsales" type="xsd:float"/>
    <xsd:element name="aprsales" type="xsd:float"/>
    <xsd:element name="maysales" type="xsd:float"/>
    <xsd:element name="junsales" type="xsd:float"/>
    <xsd:element name="julsales" type="xsd:float"/>
    <xsd:element name="augsales" type="xsd:float"/>
    <xsd:element name="sepsales" type="xsd:float"/>
    <xsd:element name="octsales" type="xsd:float"/>
    <xsd:element name="novsales" type="xsd:float"/>
    <xsd:element name="decsales" type="xsd:float"/>
  </xsd:sequence>
</xsd:complexType>
```

The `sequence` element can occur within the `choice`, `group`, `sequence`, `complexType`, and `restriction` elements. It can contain `choice`, `group`, `sequence`, `element`, `any`, and `annotation` elements.

choice

The `choice` element defines a set of elements where any one, but only one, of the contained elements is permitted in the containing element. The syntax is as follows:

```
<xsd:choice minOccurs="min" maxOccurs="max">
...
</xsd:choice>
```

The `minOccurs` and `maxOccurs` attributes specify the minimum and maximum number of times the choice can occur. Both are optional, and both have default values of 1. To make the choice optional, set `minOccurs` to 0. To place no upper limit on the number of times the choice occurs, set `maxOccurs` to "unbounded."

The following example defines a complex type that can contain either the specified sequence or the group "MyGroup" (which is assumed to be defined elsewhere):

```
<xsd:complexType name="MyType">
  <xsd:choice>
    <xsd:sequence>
      <xsd:element ref="firstname"/>
      <xsd:element ref="lastname"/>
    </xsd:sequence>
    <xsd:group ref="MyGroup"/>
  </xsd:choice>
</xsd:complexType>
```

The `choice` element can occur within the `choice`, `group`, `sequence`, `complexType`, and `restriction` elements. It can contain `choice`, `group`, `sequence`, `element`, `any`, and `annotation` elements.

all

The `all` element defines a group of elements that may appear or may not appear, in any order, in the containing element. The syntax is as follows:

```
<xsd:all minOccurs="min" maxOccurs="max">
...
</xsd:all>
```

The `minOccurs` and `maxOccurs` attributes specify the minimum and maximum number of times the element(s) can occur. Both are optional, and both have default values of 1. To make the elements optional, set `minOccurs` to 0. To place no upper limit on the number of times the element(s) occur, set `maxOccurs` to "unbounded." The following is an example of defining a complex type using the `all` element:

```
<xsd:complexType name="AnotherType">
  <xsd:all>
    <xsd:element ref="element1"/>
    <xsd:element ref="element2"/>
    <xsd:element ref="element3"/>
  </xsd:all>
</xsd:complexType>
```

The `all` element can occur within `group`, `restriction`, and `complexType` elements. It can contain `element` and `annotation` elements.

attribute

The `attribute` element defines or references an attribute. To define an attribute, the syntax is as follows:

```
<xsd:attribute name="name" type="type" use="use" value="value">
...
</xsd:attribute>
```

`Name` is the name of the attribute.

`Type` is the data type of the attribute, and it can be a built-in type or a simple type defined in the schema. *`Type`* is optional; if omitted, the type of the attribute will be defined within the body of the `attribute` element.

`Use` specifies the use of the attribute. Possible settings are described in Table 5.5 This attribute is optional.

`Value` is optional and specifies the default or fixed value of the attribute based on the setting of *`use`*.

Table 5.5 Settings for the `attribute` Element's `use` Attribute

Setting	Description
`default`	The attribute has a default value. If the attribute is not specified, it has the value specified by the `attribute` element's `value` attribute.
`fixed`	The attribute has a fixed default value. If the attribute is not specified, it has the value specified by the `attribute` element's `value` attribute. If the attribute is specified, it must be assigned the value that is specified by the `attribute` element's `value` attribute.
`optional`	The attribute is optional. This is the default setting.
`prohibited`	The attribute cannot be used.
`required`	The attribute must appear once. If the `value` attribute is specified, the attribute must have that value. If the `value` attribute is not specified, the attribute can have any value legal for its type.

The simplest way to define an attribute is to use the `attribute` element's attributes. For example, the following defines an optional attribute named "category" that is type `string`:

```
<xsd:attribute name="category" type="xsd:string"/>
```

This example defines a required attribute:

```
<xsd:attribute name="quantity" use="required" type="xsd:integer"/>
```

You have more flexibility in defining attributes if you use a `simpleType` element within the `attribute` element. Specifically, you can place restrictions on the attribute data just like you can for any user-defined simple type. The syntax for specifying restrictions is the same as you learned earlier in the chapter. Here is an example of defining an attribute that is restricted to values between 0 and 100:

```
<xsd:attribute name="percentage">
  <xsd:simpleType>
    <xsd:restriction base="xsd:unsignedByte">
      <xsd:minInclusive value="0"/>
      <xsd:maxInclusive value="100"/>
    </xsd:restriction>
  </xsd:simpleType>
</xsd:attribute>
```

An attribute can be defined directly within a complex type, as shown here:

```
<xsd:complexType name="AnotherType">
  <xsd:element ref="SomeElement"/>
  <xsd:attribute name="quantity" use="required" type="xsd:integer"/>
</xsd:complexType>
```

You can also include an attribute by reference, assuming the attribute has been defined elsewhere:

```
<xsd:complexType name="AnotherType">
  <xsd:element ref="SomeElement"/>
  <xsd:attribute ref="nameOfAttributeDefinedElsewhere"/>
</xsd:complexType>
```

attributeGroup

Use the `attributeGroup` element to define or reference a group of attributes. This is useful when multiple data types in the schema will use the same set of attributes. The syntax for defining an attribute group is as follows:

```
<xsd:attributeGroup name="groupname">
...
</xsd:attributeGroup>
```

Inside the `attributeGroup` element you place one or more attribute elements that define the attributes in the group. To reference the attribute group, use the following syntax:

```
<xsd:complexType name="YetAnotherType">
  <xsd:attributeGroup ref="nameOfAttributeGroup"/>
  <!- other type elements here ->
</xsd:complexType>
```

Anonymous Definitions

In most of the examples presented so far, data types have been assigned names (by means of the `name` attribute) and then each type has been associated with an element using the assigned name. You can also use what is termed *anonymous* definition, in which a data type is not assigned a name but rather is defined directly within the element it applies to. Here is an example of a nonanonymous definition that defines a complex type called "fullname" and the defines an element of that type:

```
<xsd:complexType name="fullname">
  <xsd:element name="firstname" type="xsd:string"/>
  <xsd:element name="lastname" type="xsd:string"/>
</xsd:complexType>
<xsd:element name="person" type="fullname"/>
```

To do the same thing anonymously, you simply enclose the complex type definition within the `element` element:

```
<xsd:element name="person">
  <xsd:complexType>
    <xsd:element name="firstname" type="xsd:string"/>
    <xsd:element name="lastname" type="xsd:string"/>
```

```
  </xsd:complexType>
</xsd:element>
```

The end result is the same for both forms. The anonymous definition is typically used in situations where the complex type will be used only once. By avoiding a separate definition, the overall complexity of the schema file is reduced.

The schema Element

At the heart of any XSD Schema is the `schema` element. This must be the root element in the schema file. Its attributes define the schema's namespaces. The `xmlns` attribute specifies the namespace for XSD Schemas, which is "http://www.w3.org/2001/XMLSchema." A namespace prefix must be included if defined—this is conventionally "xsd:", which has been used in the code examples in this chapter. You can use another prefix if you want, or you can omit the prefix, in which case the schema element names can be used as unqualified references (for example, `complexType` rather than `xsd:complexType`). You can define additional namespace/prefix combinations if needed—for example, if you will be referencing some custom data types.

The `targetNamespace` attribute specifies the schema's target namespace; in other words, the namespace that will be used to associate elements in an XML file with this schema.

Here is an example of a `schema` element:

```
<xsd:schema xmlns:xsd=" http://www.w3.org/2001/XMLSchema"
        targetNamespace="http://myURI/mySchema">
...
</xsd:schema>
```

Within the `schema` element you place the elements that define your schema. Specifically, the `schema` element can have the following elements as immediate children: `attribute`, `attributeGroup`, `element`, `group`, `simpleType`, and `complexType`.

Connecting a Schema to an XML File

The connection between an XML file and its XSD Schema (or Schemas) is not contained within the XML file itself, at least not directly. This is different from XDR Schemas, as covered in the previous chapter, where the name of the schema file was encoded directly in the XML file. With an XSD Schema, the connection is made by means of a namespace and in software. Here are the steps involved:

1. In the XML file, define a namespace prefix and use that prefix with the file's root element. Here's an example:

```
<?xml version="1.0" encoding="UTF-8"?>
<x:rootelementname xmlns:x="urn:whatever">
...
</x:rootelementname>
```

2. In your program (that uses the MSXML Parser), load the XSD schema file and associate it with the same namespace.
3. When your program loads the XML file, the namespace link will cause the parser to validate the XML file against the schema.

You'll see an example of this in the second demonstration program in Chapter 15. You can use this technique to apply different schemas to different parts of the document by using two or more namespaces and different prefixes to identify the elements to be validated against each schema.

An XSD Schema Demonstration

This section illustrates an actual use of an XSD Schema. The XML data file Recordings2.xml, shown in Listing 5.1, is based on the XML data file that was used for the demonstration of XDR Schemas in Chapter 4. The data is the same, and the only difference is the use of a namespace prefix instead of a schema file reference. The schema for this file, RecordingSchema.xsd, is shown in Listing 5.2. The XML file is constrained as follows:

- The root element is called "recordings."
- The <recordings> element can contain any number of child <recording> elements. Each <recording> element will correspond to one entry in the file—that is, to one item in the collection.
- Each <recording> element must contain one <title> element and one <performers> element. <title> is a string element. <performers> can contain one or more <performer> elements. <performer> is a string element.
- Each <recording> element can contain zero or one <comments> element, which is a string element.

- The <recording> element must contain an attribute named "media," which is an enumerated attribute with possible values "CD," "LP," and "tape."
- The <recording> element must also contain an attribute named "quality," which is a type `integer` attribute with permitted values between 0 and 10.

Listing 5.1 Recordings2.xml Is Based on the Data Model Defined by the XSD Schema in Listing 5.2

```
<?xml version="1.0" encoding="UTF-8"?>
<x:recordings xmlns:x="urn:recordings">
  <recording media="CD" quality="8">
    <title>
      Pandit Ravi Shankar
    </title>
    <performers>
      <performer>Ravi Shankar</performer>
      <performer>Kumar Bose</performer>
      <performer>Vidya Bataju</performer>
      <performer>Jeevan Govinda</performer>
    </performers>
  </recording>
  <recording media="LP" quality="6">
    <title>
      The Little Bach Book
    </title>
    <performers>
      <performer>Glenn Gould</performer>
    </performers>
    <comments>
      There is a scratch at the beginning of side 2.
    </comments>
  </recording>
  <recording media="CD" quality="9">
    <title>
      Bach: English Suites
    </title>
    <performers>
      <performer>Murray Perahia</performer>
    </performers>
    <comments>
       An exceptionally good performance.
```

```
    </comments>
  </recording>
</x:recordings>
```

Listing 5.2 RecordingSchema.xsd Is an XSD Schema for the XML File Recordings1.xml

```
<xsd:schema xmlns:xsd="http://www.w3.org/2001/XMLSchema">

<xsd:element name="recordings" type="recordinglist"/>

<!--This defines the type for the "media" attribute.-->
  <xsd:simpleType name="attrmedia">
    <xsd:restriction base="xsd:string">
      <xsd:enumeration value="CD"/>
      <xsd:enumeration value="LP"/>
      <xsd:enumeration value="tape"/>
    </xsd:restriction>
  </xsd:simpleType>

<!--This defines the type for the "quality" attribute.-->
  <xsd:simpleType name="attrquality">
    <xsd:restriction base="xsd:integer">
      <xsd:minInclusive value="0"/>
      <xsd:maxInclusive value="10"/>
    </xsd:restriction>
  </xsd:simpleType>

<!--This defines the complex type for the "performers" element.-->
<xsd:complexType name="performerlist">
  <xsd:sequence>
    <xsd:element name="performer" type="xsd:string" minOccurs="1"
maxOccurs="unbounded"/>
  </xsd:sequence>
</xsd:complexType>

<!--Defines the complex type for the "recording" element.-->
<xsd:complexType name="onerecording">
  <xsd:sequence>
    <xsd:element name="title" type="xsd:string"/>
    <xsd:element name="performers" type="performerlist"/>
    <xsd:element name="comments" type="xsd:string" minOccurs="0"/>
  </xsd:sequence>
```

```
  <xsd:attribute name="media" type="attrmedia" use="required"/>
  <xsd:attribute name="quality" type="attrquality" use="required"/>
</xsd:complexType>

<!--Defines the root element for the XML file.-->
<xsd:complexType name="recordinglist">
  <xsd:sequence>
    <xsd:element name="recording" type="onerecording" minOccurs="0"
maxOccurs="unbounded"/>
  </xsd:sequence>
</xsd:complexType>

</xsd:schema>
```

Summary

The XSD Schema vocabulary is the most powerful and flexible method for defining an XML data model. It offers significant advances over the original DTD method of defining a data model. These advantages include support for namespaces, an open-ended content model, more defined data types, and the use of XML syntax. Even so, the use of DTDs is still perfectly satisfactory for some applications. Being a W3C Recommendation, XSD Schema is preferred over the Microsoft-specific schema vocabulary, XDR Schema, which was covered in the previous chapter.

CHAPTER 6

Formatting XML Documents with Cascading Style Sheets

While XML provides a powerful means for storing structured data, it provides no information about how the data is to be displayed. This in fact is one of XML's advantages: The structure of the data is totally independent of the data presentation. When it is necessary to format the data in an XML file for presentation, the formatting details are placed in a *style sheet*. There are two approaches to style sheets: Cascading Style Sheets, which is covered in this chapter, and Extensible Stylesheet Language, which is covered in the next two chapters.

Style Sheet Fundamentals

One of the fundamental premises of XML is that data *storage* and data *presentation* are kept totally independent of each other. The logical structure of an XML document should place no restrictions on how its data can be presented. Likewise, the details of how data will be presented should place no limitations on how it can be structured. This is accomplished by keeping the presentation information physically separate from the XML data; the presentation information resides in its own file. The general term "style sheet" is used for XML presentation instructions.

While style sheets have been used for many years with Standard Generalized Markup Language (SGML), the specific style sheet technology called Cascading Style Sheets (CSS) was originally developed to control the display of HTML documents (Web pages). The CSS technology turns out to be well suited for XML documents also, and the first implementation of CSS, known as CSS1 (or CSS Level 1), became a W3C Recommendation in 1996. A more powerful and flexible version, CSS2, became a W3C Recommendation in 1998.

The existence of W3C Recommendations is not in itself enough to make a technology useful. Software support, particularly in browsers, is necessary if a style sheet Recommendation is to be really useful. As of this writing, Internet Explorer 5.5 provides good but not complete support for the CSS1 Recommendation, and it offers very limited support for the CSS2 Recommendation. Internet Explorer 6.0, which may be out by the time you read this, promises complete CSS1 support and "improved" CSS2 support.

A newer style sheet technology is Extensible Stylesheet Language, or XSL. The XSL technology is currently a W3C draft Recommendation, and its only browser support is Internet Explorer. While XSL does offer more advanced capabilities than CSS, it would be wrong to think of the two technologies as being in competition, with XSL fated to replace CSS at some time in the future. Rather, the two technologies serve different, albeit overlapping, needs and in fact are sometimes used together to good advantage.

The remainder of this chapter covers the CSS1 specification, which is the most widely used and has the widest support (most important for this book, in Internet Explorer). The final section of the chapter presents comparisons between CSS and XSL and some guidelines for deciding when to use one or the other. XSL is covered in the next two chapters.

CSS Basics

The syntax of CSS allows style constructs, such as fonts, colors, and positioning, to be associated with specific elements in an XML document. The style rules can be embedded directly in the XML document, but it is generally preferred to keep them in a separate file (which, like an XML file, is plain text). Each rule within CSS has the following general format:

```
selector { formatting }
```

`Selector` specifies a part of the XML file, and *`formatting`* specifies the style rules that will be used. In the simplest case, *`selector`* is the name of an XML element. Here is an example of a CSS rule:

```
companyname {
    font-family: Times, serif;
    font-size: 14pt;
```

```
    display: block;
}
```

This rule specifies that the XML element named "companyname" is to be displayed in the Times font, size 14 points, in the block style. If the Times font is not available, the software will select a serif font. The following sections explain CSS1 selectors and style rules in more detail. If a formatting specification includes more than one style rule, the rules must be separated by semicolons.

Be aware that the CSS1 Recommendation is very complicated and includes various aspects that are aimed primarily at HTML documents. The following treatment is by no means complete, and it is intended to explain just those CSS1 capabilities that will most often be needed by XML developers. For the complete CSS1 specification, please refer to `http://www.w3.org/TR/REC-CSS1.html`.

Why "Cascading"?

The term "cascading" is the result of two factors. One is the way style sheets interact. A document can have more than one style sheet associated with it. For example, one style sheet may be provided by the document author, and a second style sheet may be provided by the reader. There will also be a default set of style rules supplied by the display program. Style rules cascade in the following order: Author style rules override reader style rules and reader style rules override default style rules.

The other factor is the operation of inheritance. *If a certain aspect of formatting is not specified for a child element, it will (in most cases) inherit the formatting of its parent (enclosing) element. For example, a child element that has no font style rule will display in the font specified for its parent. The formatting "cascades" down the chain from parent to child.*

CSS Selectors

A CSS selector specifies which part or parts of an XML document will be affected by a set of formatting rules. A selector must be the first thing on a line of text in the CSS file. As was shown previously, the simplest type of selector is an XML element name. You can also select an element based on the value of a special attribute named `class`:

```
elementname.attributevalue { formatting }
```

Attributevalue is the value of the `class` attribute. Here's an example:

```
companyname.supplier {
    font-family: Times, serif;
    font-size: 14pt;
    display: block;
}
```

This rule specifies that the indicated formatting will be used for all "companyname" elements that have the `class` attribute set to the value "supplier." Consider this XML code:

```
<companyname>Acme Manufacturing</companyname>
<companyname class="supplier">ABC Lumber</companyname>
<companyname class="customer">Wilson Design Services</companyname>
```

Of these three XML elements, only the second one would have the previous CSS rule applied to it, and it will be displayed in 14-point Times font.

Another type of selector relies on an attribute value without specifying an element name. The syntax is as follows:

```
#value { formatting }
```

Value is the value of a special attribute named `id`. The formatting will be used for an element, regardless of its name, that has the *id* attribute set to *value*. Recall that an `id` attribute must have a value that is unique within the XML document. Here's an example of a CSS rule using this type of selector:

```
#emphasis {
    font-family: Times, serif;
    font-size: 14pt;
    display: block;
}
```

Of the following XML elements, this formatting would be applied only to the first one:

```
<lastname id="emphasis">Smith</lastname>
<firstname>Wilma</firstname>
<address id="small">123 Main Street</address>
<city id="large">anytown</city>
```

If you want the same formatting to apply to several elements in the XML file, you can specify this in a single rule by including all of the element names separated by commas. This rule specifies that the elements "firstname," "lastname," and "address" will all be formatted as indicated:

```
firstname, lastname, address {
    font-family: Times, serif;
    font-size: 14pt;
    display: block;
}
```

It is also possible to define more than one rule for an element. If the rules do not conflict, they will all be applied:

```
firstname {
    font-family: Times, serif
}
firstname {
    font-size: 14pt;
}
```

If the rules do conflict, the last one will take precedence. In this case, the element "firstname" will be displayed in 20-point font:

```
firstname {
    font-size: 14pt;
}
firstname {
    font-size: 20pt;
}
```

To ensure that a given rule will take precedence over all others, even those that come after it, add the `important` clause to the rule:

```
firstname {
    font-size: 14pt ! important;
}
```

```
firstname {
    font-size: 20pt;
}
```

In this case, the "firstname" element will be displayed in 14-point font because the `important` clause causes the formatter to ignore the second rule.

The `important` clause can also affect style sheet cascading. The default is for author style rules to override reader style rules, but if a reader style rule is marked with the `important` clause, it will not be overridden.

To create a selector that matches specific elements that are descendants of other specific elements, use both element names with a space between them. The following selector matches all "name" elements that are descendants of "person" elements:

```
person name {font-size: large}
```

To create a selector that matches specific elements that are immediate children of other specific elements, use both element names with the greater-than sign (>) between them. The following selector matches all "name" elements that are children of "person" elements:

```
person > name {font-size: large}
```

Finally, you can define a universal selector that will match all elements in the document. It will be applied only to those elements that do not have a more specific formatting rule that conflicts with the universal selector rule. A universal selector is created using an asterisk (*):

```
* {font-size: large}
```

CSS Style Rules

CSS1 formatting adheres to a simple box-oriented formatting model. Every formatted element will result in one or more rectangular boxes. Each box has a core content area surrounded by optional padding, border, and margin areas. This model is illustrated in Figure 6.1, and the elements are related as follows.

- The content area is where the data is displayed. The data may be text or an image. If the data is text, the display is controlled by the various `font` and `text` properties. If the data is an image, its size is controlled by the `height` and `width` properties. The `height` and `width` properties can be used with text elements also.
- The padding area provides some space between the element and its border. The size of this area is controlled by the `padding` properties.

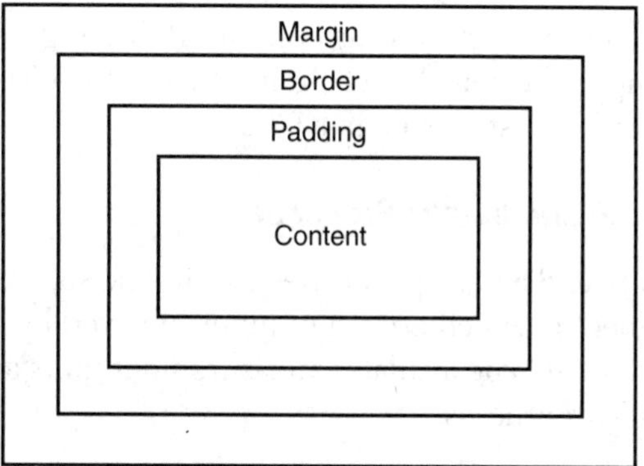

Figure 6.1: The CSS1 formatting model

The background of the padding area is the same as the background of the content area, as controlled by the `background` property.

- The border is an optional box drawn around the element. Its appearance is controlled by the `border` properties.
- The margin provides space around the element outside the border. In effect, the margin provides the spacing between the element and other elements that are being displayed. The margin size is controlled by the `margin` properties. The margin is transparent.

In the final output, the arrangement of the formatting boxes is determined primarily by the relationship between the elements in the XML document. The box for a parent element will contain the boxes for its child elements. These boxes are not visible in many cases and are best thought of as an aid to positioning.

The display Property

The `display` property controls how an element is displayed and whether it is displayed at all. There are four permitted settings for this property:

- `block`: The element is displayed in a box.
- `inline`: The element is displayed on the same line as adjacent content in an inline box.
- `list-item`: The element is displayed in a box preceded by a list item mark (a bullet).
- `none`: The element is not displayed.

The inline `display` property setting is used for elements that should not be separated from surrounding content. Italicizing a single word in a sentence is an example of when you would use this setting. The `display` property should be set for every style rule in a CSS.

The width and height Properties

The `width` and `height` properties specify the size of an element's display box. The values are specified as a number followed by a suffix indicating the unit of measurement. The available measurement units are as follows, with the suffix given in parentheses:

Centimeters (cm)
Ems (em)
Ens (en)
Inches (in)
Millimeters (mm)
Picas (pi)
Pixels (px)
Points (pt)

> **Measurement Units**
>
> *Certain of the measurement units may not be familiar to all readers. Picas and points are equal to 1/6 and 1/72 of an inch, respectively. Ems and ens are equal to the width of the letters "M" and "N," respectively. By using ems or ens as your measurement units, sizes can be made relative to the size of the font in use.*

You can mix measurement units within a style sheet, but it is good practice to settle on a single unit of measurement for certain types of elements and stick to it throughout. For example, you might use pixels for specifying the size of image elements and points for text elements.

The border Properties

The appearance of an element's border is controlled by the `border` properties. Note the use of the plural, because there is more than one border-related property. If all four borders (top, bottom, left, and right) are identical, you can set their appearance at the same time using the `border` property. If they are not the same, you must set them individually using the `border-top`, `border-bottom`, `border-left`, and `border-right` properties. You can specify three aspects of a border's appearance.

- Its width, or thickness, can be specified as "thin," "medium," or "thick" or as a numerical value followed by a measurement unit (the same units as described for the `width` and `height` properties).
- Its style can be specified using one of the terms described in Table 6.1. The default style is "none."
- Its color can be specified as a descriptive keyword (aqua, black, blue, fuchsia, gray, green, lime, maroon, navy, olive, purple, red, silver, teal, white, or yellow) or as a red-green-blue value expressed in the format rgb(*r*, *g*, *b*) where *r*, *g*, and *b* are numerical values from 0 to 255 that specify the relative levels of red, green, and blue in the final color.

Table 6.1 Style Settings for the `border` Properties

Border Style Setting	Description
`dashed`	A dashed line.
`dotted`	A dotted line.
`double`	A double line.
`groove`	A 3D groove using colors based on the `<color>` value.
`inset`	A 3D inset using colors based on the `<color>` value.
`none`	No border is drawn.
`outset`	A 3D outset using colors based on the `<color>` value.
`ridge`	A 3D ridge using colors based on the `<color>` value.
`solid`	A solid line.

The following border property setting results in a dotted blue border with all four sides 2 pixels thick:

```
border: 2px dotted blue;
```

The next border property setting results in a thick double yellow border:

```
border: thick double rgb(255, 255, 0);
```

The next border property setting results in a thin solid black border above and below the element, with no border on either side:

```
border-top: thin solid black;
border-bottom: thin solid black;
```

This border property setting results in elements "H1" and "H2" both having thick double borders on all four sides. For element "H1," the border is black on all four sides. For element "H2," the border is red on the bottom and black on the other three sides.

```
H1 H2 {
    border: thick double black;
}

H2 {
    border-bottom: red;
}
```

The margin and padding Properties

The margin and padding properties set the width of an element's margin and padding, respectively. The two properties work in the same way with the same syntax. This section explains the margin property. The same information also applies to the padding property.

You can set all four margins to the same width as follows:

```
margin: value
```

You can set different values with the following syntax:

```
margin: value1 value2 value3 value4
```

The four width values are applied to the top, right, bottom, and left margins, respectively. If one or two values are omitted, that margin takes its width from the opposite margin. Thus, the following style rule results in the top and bottom margins having `value1` and the left and right margins having `value2`:

```
margin: value1 value2
```

You can also use the `margin-top`, `margin-bottom`, `margin-left`, and `margin-right` properties to set the widths of the individual margins.

The width value for a margin can be specified in the following ways:

- As a numerical value followed by a measurement unit: The available measurement units were explained earlier in this chapter in the section on the `width` and `height` properties.
- As a numerical value followed by the percent sign (%): The margin width will be the specified percentage of the width set for the element's closest block-level ancestor.

The following CSS entry specifies that the "H1" element will be displayed with a 2-pixel margin, 0.5 em padding at the top and bottom, and 0.75 em padding at the left and right:

```
H1 {
    margin: 2px;
    padding: 0.5em 0.75em;
}
```

This entry specifies that the "H2" element will have 75 percent of the padding of its block-level ancestor at the left, top, and right, and 150 percent of the padding of its block-level ancestor at the bottom:

```
H2 {
    padding: 75%;
    padding-bottom: 150%;
}
```

The font Properties

The `font` properties specify the appearance of the font used to display text in an element. There are four such properties that are commonly used:

- `font-family`: You can give a specific family name, such as Times or Helvetica, and optionally a generic family name. The permitted generic family names are serif, sans-serif, cursive, fantasy, and monospace. The generic font family name is used to select a font if the system does not support the specific font family that was listed. You can actually specify multiple font families, and the first one that is available will be used. If the specific family name includes a space, the name must be enclosed in quotes.

- `font-size`: The size, or height, of the font, is specified in one of the measurement units described earlier in this chapter in the section on the `width` and `height` properties. Font sizes are usually given in points.
- `font-style`: This property specifies the style of the font as normal, italic, or oblique.
- `font-weight`: This property specifies the weight of the font as normal, bold, bolder, or lighter. This property can also be specified as one of the values 100, 200, 300, 400, 500, 600, 700, 800, or 900. The values 400 and 700 correspond to "normal" and "bold," respectively.

The following is an example of setting the "H1" element's font properties:

```
H1 {
font-family: "Times Roman", serif;
font-size: 20pt;
font weight: 600;
font-style: italic;
}
```

The text Properties

The `text` properties specify various aspects of how text is displayed. The following are the `text` properties that you will use most often.

- `text-decoration`: Specifies the text decoration. Possible values are underline, overline, line-through, and blink.
- `text-transform`: Specifies capitalization of text. Possible values are capitalize (first letter of words uppercase), uppercase, and lowercase.
- `text-align`: Specifies the alignment of text within its box. Settings are left, right, center, and justify. When the justify setting is used, the spacing between letters and/or words is adjusted to align both the left and right end of the lines with the margins.
- `text-indent`: Controls indentation of the first line of text. It can be specified as a length measurement using any of the units that were described earlier in this chapter in the section on the `width` and `height`

properties. It can also be specified as a percentage value, which is interpreted as a percentage of the parent element's width.

- `text-lineheight`: Specifies the vertical distance between lines of text (measured between the baselines). It can be specified as a number (1 means single spaced, 2 means double spaced, and so on), as a length measurement using any of the units described earlier in this chapter, or as a percentage of the element's font size.

The following example sets the "H1" element to display text underlined, centered, and with line spacing of 1.5 lines:

```
H1 {
text-decoration: underline;
text-align: center;
text-lineheight: 1.5;
}
```

The color and background-color Properties

These properties specify the color of an element's text and of its background. There are four ways to specify a color:

- As a descriptive keyword (aqua, black, blue, fuchsia, gray, green, lime, maroon, navy, olive, purple, red, silver, teal, white, or yellow)
- As a red-green-blue value expressed in the format rgb(*r*, *g*, *b*) where *r*, *g*, and *b* are numerical values from 0 to 255 that specify the relative levels of red, green, and blue in the final color
- As a red-green-blue value expressed in the format rgb(*r*%, *g*%, *b*%) where *r*, *g*, and *b* are numerical values from 0 to 100 that specify the relative levels of red, green, and blue in the final color
- As a hexadecimal value where the first two hex digits specify the red level, the second two digits specify the green level, and the third two digits specify the blue level

The following CSS rule specifies that the "H1" element will display as blue text on a light gray background.

```
H1 {
color: rgb(0, 0, 100);
background-color: rgb(75, 75, 75);
}
```

Creating and Referencing Style Sheets

A style sheet is a text document with no special elements. In other words, it contains nothing but the style rules. Traditionally, cascading style sheets are kept in files with the .css extension.

To reference a style sheet from within an XML document, use a processing instruction with the `xml-stylesheet` target. The syntax is as follows:

```
<?xml-stylesheet type="text/css" href="cssname"?>
```

Cssname is the name (including the path, if required) of the CSS file. This processing instruction should be placed in the XML file prolog, before any data. For example:

```
<xml version="1.0?>
<!DOCTYPE addresses SYSTEM "addresslist.dtd">
<?xml-stylesheet type="css/text" href="address.css"?>
<addresslist>
...
```

A CSS Demonstration

To complete this chapter, I will create two style sheets for the same XML data to show how greatly different display results can be obtained using CSS. The sample XML data file called MyCDRecordings.xml is shown in Listing 6.1. This XML file contains information about a collection of compact disc (CD) recordings. The data for each recording includes the title, the performer, the composer, the label and release number, and information about each track on the CD. Each <recording> element has a "class" attribute that provides a numerical rating of the recording on a scale of 1 to 10. You'll see soon why this attribute was given the name "class" rather than something more meaningful. The file contains data for only two recordings.

Listing 6.2 presents CDFormat.css, a simple style sheet for this data. This style sheet does not do anything fancy—it simply uses fonts and indentation to format the data in a clear manner. The "class" attribute is not used in any way. The result of formatting the data with this style sheet is shown in Figure 6.2.

Listing 6.1 MyCDRecordings.xml Contains Data about a Compact Disc Collection

```
<?xml version="1.0" encoding="UTF-8"?>
<?xml-stylesheet type="text/css" href="CDFormat.css"?>
<my_recordings>
<recording class="10">
  <title>Bach English Suites</title>
  <artist>Murray Perahia</artist>
  <composer>J. S. Bach</composer>
  <label>Sony Classical</label>
  <number>SK60277</number>
  <selection>
    <tracknumber>1</tracknumber>
    <tracktitle>English Suite No. 2 in A Minor</tracktitle>
  </selection>
  <selection>
    <tracknumber>2</tracknumber>
    <tracktitle>English Suite No. 4 in F Major</tracktitle>
  </selection>
  <selection>
    <tracknumber>3</tracknumber>
    <tracktitle>English Suite No. 3 in E Minor</tracktitle>
  </selection>
</recording>
<recording class="8">
  <title>Kind of Blue</title>
  <artist>Miles Davis</artist>
  <composer>Various</composer>
  <label>Columbia</label>
  <number>CK64935</number>
  <selection>
    <tracknumber>1</tracknumber>
    <tracktitle>So What</tracktitle>
  </selection>
  <selection>
    <tracknumber>2</tracknumber>
    <tracktitle>Freddie Freeloader</tracktitle>
  </selection>
  <selection>
    <tracknumber>3</tracknumber>
    <tracktitle>Blue in Green</tracktitle>
  </selection>
```

```
  <selection>
    <tracknumber>4</tracknumber>
    <tracktitle>All Blues</tracktitle>
  </selection>
  <selection>
    <tracknumber>5</tracknumber>
    <tracktitle>Flamenco Sketches</tracktitle>
  </selection>
  <selection>
    <tracknumber>6</tracknumber>
    <tracktitle>Flamenco Sketches (alternate take)</tracktitle>
  </selection>
</recording>
</my_recordings>
```

Listing 6.2 CDFormat.css Provides a Simple Style Sheet for the XML File in Listing 6.1

```
recording {
    display: block;
    margin-top: 24px;
    text-align: left;
    background-color: white;
}

title {
    display: block;
    color: black;
    font-family: Arial, sans-serif;
    font-size: 24pt;
    font-weight: bold;
}

artist, composer {
    display: block;
    color: black;
    font-family: Arial, sans-serif;
    font-size: 16pt;
}

label {
    display: inline;
```

```
    color: black;
    font-family: Arial, sans-serif;
    font-size: 12pt;
}

number {
    display: inline;
    color: black;
    font-family: Arial, sans-serif;
    font-size: 12pt;
}

selection {
    display: block;
    margin-left: 30px;
    color: black;
    font-family: Times, serif;
    font-size: 12pt;
}

tracknumber, tracktitle {
    display: inline;
}
```

The preceding example is a relatively simple demonstration of the power of style sheets. While it is perfectly adequate for some uses, you may want to use more elaborate formatting for certain situations. The CSS Recommendation provides plenty of flexibility, some of which is demonstrated by the style sheet in Listing 6.3. Specifically, this style sheet is designed to

- Display each recording in a box with a colored background and a border
- Use a different font color for the titles of recordings where the "class" attribute is equal to 10 (in other words, those recordings with the highest rating)
- List the track titles rather than use track numbers

This format might be more appropriate for printing than for screen display. In any case, it demonstrates some of the power of the CSS Recommendation. The output of the data using this style sheet is shown in Figure 6.3. It may not show up in the figure, but the data is displayed against a light blue background, and the title of the first recording is red.

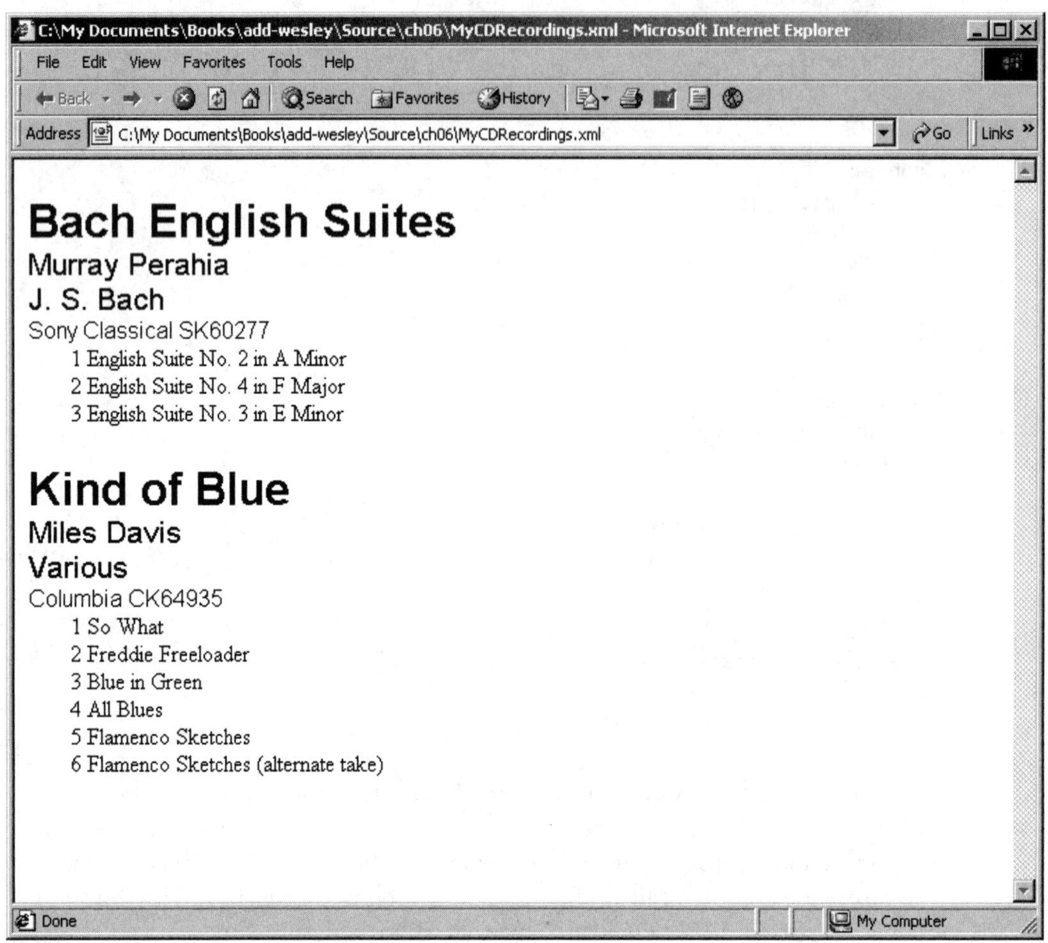

Figure 6.2 The data as formatted with the style sheet in Listing 6.2

One point about this style sheet deserves mention. The goal was to display the title of those recordings that have a perfect 10 rating in a different font color. This rating was encoded as the "class" attribute of the "recording" element. You saw earlier in this chapter how the formatting of elements with a specific value for the "class" attribute could be specified as follows (this is why the attribute name "class" was used):

```
elementname.attributevalue { formatting }
```

However, the "class" attribute is not associated with the element "title," which is the element whose formatting should be changed. Rather, it is associated with the parent element "recording." To achieve the desired result, the style sheet makes use of the cascading nature of the CSS Recommendation. Here's how it works:

1. The first style rule in the CSS file specifies the formatting for the "recording" element, including setting the foreground color to black. Because this element is the ancestor of all other elements, black becomes the default foreground color for all other elements as well.
2. The second style rule specifies formatting for "recording" elements that have the "class" attribute set to 10. The only rule here is setting the foreground color to red. Again, because "recording" is the top ancestor element, this setting will cascade down to all child elements.
3. The third style rule specifies formatting for "title," which is the element whose display color should be red or black depending on the value of the "recording" element's "class" attribute. These rules do not specify a foreground color, which means that the "title" element will display with whatever foreground color cascades down from its parent element, which in this case is "recording." As we have seen, either red or black will cascade down.
4. The style rules for all other child elements specifically set the foreground color to black. This means that they will display in black regardless of the color that cascades down from the "recording" element.

Listing 6.3 CDFormatFancy.css Provides a Sophisticated Style Sheet for the Data in Listing 6.1

```
recording {
    display: block;
    margin-top: 30px;
    text-align: center;
    color: black;
    border: 4px double black;
    background-color: rgb(150,150,250);
}

recording.10 {
    color: red;
}
```

```
title {
    display: block;
    font-family: Times, serif;
    font-size: 24pt;
    font-weight: bold;
}

artist, composer {
    display: block;
    color: black;
    font-family: Arial, sans-serif;
    font-size: 16pt;
}

label, number {
    display: inline;
    color: black;
    font-family: Arial, sans-serif;
    font-size: 12pt;
}

selection {
    display: block;
    color: black;
    font-family: Times, serif;
    font-size: 12pt;
}

tracktitle {
    display: block;
}

tracknumber {
    display: none;
}
```

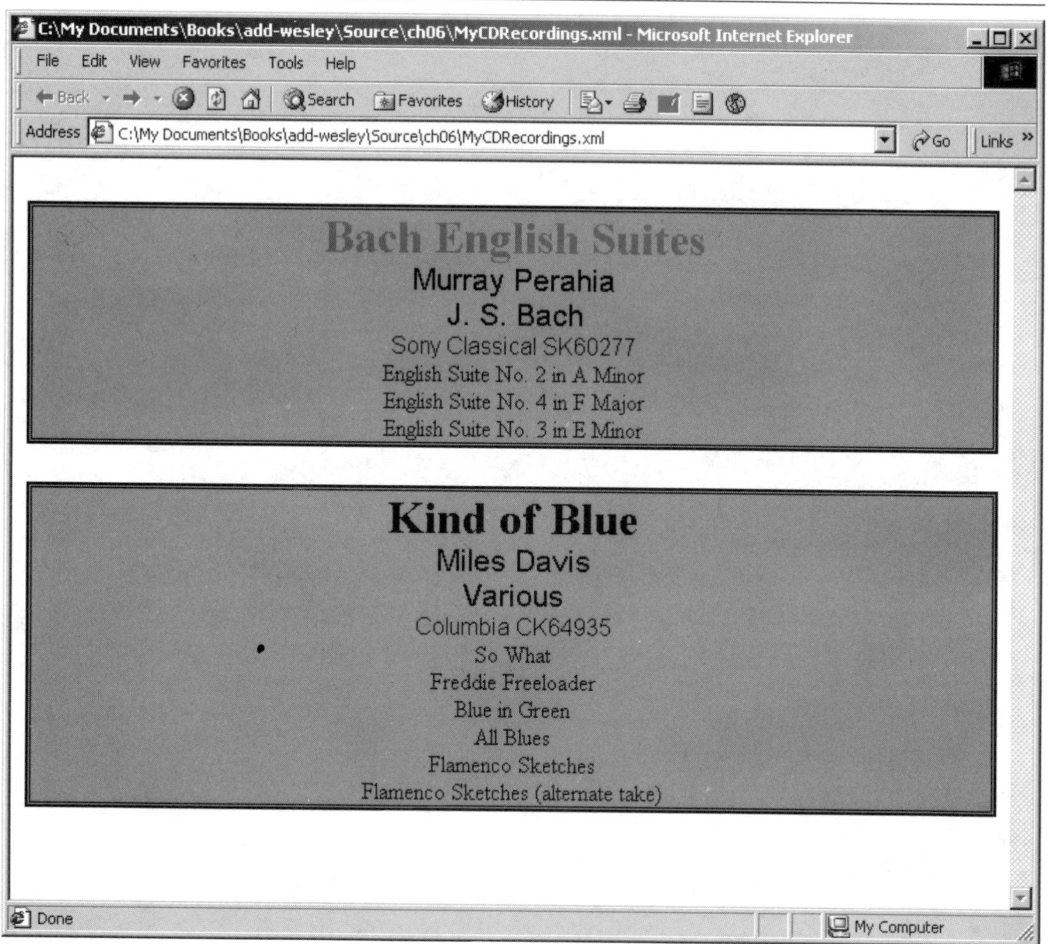

Figure 6.3 The data as formatted with the style sheet in Listing 6.3

Summary

The XML standard provides structure for data, but it intentionally has nothing to say about how the data is to be displayed. Cascading Style Sheets (CSS) was the first technology adapted to define display parameters for XML data. CSS was first developed to specify display for HTML documents, but it turns out to be well suited for XML data as well. The display specifications in a style sheet are separate from the XML data, which means that the same data can be displayed in different ways by applying different style sheets. Likewise, the same style sheet can be applied to multiple XML files, which provides great flexibility.

CHAPTER 7

Extensible Stylesheet Language and XSLT

The original technique for formatting XML data was Cascading Style Sheets (CSS), which the previous chapter covered. As with most early technologies, CSS has significant shortcomings that became more and more problematic as developers became more demanding. The response was to develop a new technology for formatting XML data called Extensible Stylesheet Language (XSL). In this chapter and the next, you will learn about the various parts of XSL and how the new technology compares with CSS. These two chapters cannot offer complete coverage of the topic. XSL is a large and complex specification, and entire books have been devoted to it. You will, however, learn the most essential information—more than enough to enable you to start working with XSL.

This chapter starts with an overview of XSL and its two components: XSL for Transformations (XSLT) and Formatting Objects (FO). The remainder of this chapter is devoted to XSLT, and FO is covered in the next chapter.

XSL Fundamentals

To understand XSL it is helpful to first look at one of the major limitations of CSS. When XML data is formatted using CSS, the appearance of the output can be controlled but the structure of the output cannot be changed. In other words, the parent/child/sibling relationships among the elements in the XML document cannot be changed and will be present in the formatted output. CSS does not provide the means to perform such tasks as rearranging data to be displayed in tables, calculating sums from numerical data, or combining elements from different parts of a document.

These factors made it clear that the new formatting technology had to be able to do more than just format the output. In addition, it needed the capability to transform XML documents, modifying the logical structure of the document by selecting, regrouping, and reordering elements as required by the specific application. Therefore, XSL was developed with two parts:

- XSL Transformations (XSLT) for transforming XML documents
- XSL Formatting Objects (FO) for formatting XML documents

These two components of XSL are independent of each other. The original idea seems to have been that you would use XSLT to transform an XML document so it would contain FO commands, and then display the result. It was soon realized that document transformations were a powerful and useful tool on their own, even when formatting for presentation was not the goal. Cross-application data transfer, for example, often required logical transformation of XML data that could be better accomplished with XSLT than with the proprietary technologies used previously.

Confusing Terminology

The terms XSL, XSLT, and FO are sometimes used in an inconsistent manner, and it can be confusing to the uninitiated. Officially, XSLT and FO are the two components of XSL. However, XSLT is sometimes treated as a separate entity, and XSL is used as a synonym for FO. This situation is due partly to the fact that XSLT is more often used by itself than as a preparation for FO. The confusion is not helped by the W3C documentation, which clearly states that XSLT and FO are components of XSL, but then presents XSLT as a Recommendation while XSL has only reached the status of Candidate Recommendation.

Both XSLT and FO are implemented as XML vocabularies. Thus, XSL style sheets are XML documents, with all the advantages that implies. To use XSL, you first create an XSL style sheet that contains the XSLT constructs to perform the desired transformations on your XML document. If the goal is to display the data using FO, the transformations will result in output that includes the FO commands to produce the desired formatting. The transformed XML is then processed by an FO-compliant rendering agent, such as a browser, to produce the final output. For other goals, such as creating an HTML file, there will be no FO commands in the output.

XSL and CSS

The relationship between XSL and CSS is not either/or. In fact, the two technologies are often used together for the following two purposes:

- When XSLT is used to transform an XML document to HTML for display in a browser, with the browser display controlled by CSS
- When XSLT is used to transform an XML document into an XML document with a different structure, and the resulting XML document is displayed using CSS

The combination of XSLT and CSS is popular for several reasons. One reason is that CSS, while not as powerful as FO, is a more mature technology with much wider software support. Another reason is that many developers already know CSS, whereas FO is a new and complex standard. Finally, CSS can be used to format HTML documents, while FO cannot.

XPath

One of the requirements for XSLT was a way to select parts of a document for transformation. The XSLT syntax for performing such selection was very similar to the XPointer language that was being developed for linking one document to another. The two were combined, and the result is called XPath (for XML Path language). XPath version 1 is a W3C Recommendation. The XPath specification is available at `http://www.w3.org/TR/xpath`.

You can think of XPath as a sublanguage inside an XSL style sheet. XPath expressions can perform many tasks. In addition to their main task of identifying parts of a document to process, XPath expressions can perform numerical calculations and string manipulation. For example, here is an instruction that outputs the sum of all "amount" elements in the "sale" elements in the document:

```
<xsl:value-of select="sum(//sale/@amount)"/>
```

Software Support

The Microsoft XML Parser version 4.0 supports the W3C Recommendations for XSLT and XPath. Support for other elements of XSL, specifically FO, are not yet available. It is important to note that Microsoft's support for the W3C XSLT Recommendation has been an evolutionary process. Earlier versions (before version 3.0) of the MSXML Parser, as are installed with Internet

Explorer version 5.*x*, provided only partial support, and also included some proprietary Microsoft extensions. Thus, XSL style sheets written to conform to the W3C Recommendation may not work on systems that do not have the latest versions of the MSXML Parser and Internet Explorer installed. Likewise, style sheets written for the earlier Microsoft XSLT implementation may not work on systems running MSXML version 4.0 and Internet Explorer version 5.5 (these are the latest versions as of this writing).

The situation is further complicated by the installation routine for MSXML version 3.0 (which was current until recently), which provides options for installing either in replace mode, which replaces any older version of MSXML with the new one, or in side-by-side mode, which retains the older version alongside the new one to provide compatibility for style sheets written to the old Microsoft specification. MSXML version 4.0 always installs in side-by-side mode, but what it is installed "next to" depends, of course, on what parser or parsers are already on your system.

If this is not enough confusion, there is also the question of the new Visual Studio .NET development tools, which are installed on many systems as beta software at the time of this writing and may be available as a commercial release by the time you read this. A new version of Internet Explorer, version 6.0, is part of that installation, and the details of its support of XML/XSL/XSLT are sketchy at present.

You can determine which parser versions are installed on your system by looking in your \Windows\System folder. The parsers exist as DLL files. The oldest parser you are likely to encounter is version 2.0, which is contained in MSXML.DLL. Later versions are in files named MSXMLXX.DLL, where "XX" is the version. For example, MSXML version 4.0 is in MSXML4.DLL.

Running Transforms

An XSL style sheet can be applied in several ways. If you load an XML file into Internet Explorer version 5.0 or later, and the XML file references a well-formed XSL style sheet, it may render properly in the browser. This, of course, applies to style sheets that transform XML into HTML, which is currently the most common use for XSLT. I use the phrase "may render" because the myriad of parser versions and Internet Explorer installations has resulted in a situation where XSL transforms do not always work as they should in Internet Explorer. This problem may well be resolved by the time you read this, but for now all you can do is try it. If Internet Explorer will not perform transforms for you, you can use the MSXSL utility, which I describe shortly.

You can also use the MSXML Parser in your programs to perform transforms. In a Visual Basic program, or using some other language, you can invoke MSXML to load an XML file, apply an XSL style sheet to it, and write the results of the transform to a new file. Techniques for using MSXML in your programs are covered later in the book in the chapters on individual programming languages.

The final way to apply transforms is to use the Microsoft MSXSL.EXE command-line utility. You can download this free program from the Downloads section of `http://msdn.microsoft.com/xml`. This small utility invokes MSXML (which must be installed separately) to apply an XSL style sheet to an XML document. The command line is as follows:

```
msxsl xml-file xsl-file -o output-file
```

`Xml-file` is the name of the XML file to transform, and *`xsl-file`* is the name of the XSL style sheet file. Note that even if the XML file specifies the name of its style sheet in the `<?xsl-stylesheet>` processing instruction (which you'll learn about soon), you must specify the name of the style sheet on the MSXSL command line. *`Output-file`* is the name of the file where the output of the transformation is to be placed. If you omit this argument, the output is displayed on the screen. If your Internet Explorer installation is not performing transforms properly, you can use MSXSL.EXE to create the transformed HTML file and then view that in the browser.

There is one quirk of the MSXSL utility to be aware of. Its default seems to be to write the output file to disk in UTF-16 encoding. This type of encoding causes problems with some programs that will use the transformed file—in particular, some of the formatting object rendering programs that are covered in the next chapter. To force the MSXSL utility to create output in UTF-8 format, use the `xsl:output` element to specify that the output be in UTF-8 encoding and in XML format. The syntax is as follows:

```
<xsl:output method="xml" encoding="utf-8"/>
```

This element is placed in the XSL style sheet immediately after the opening `xsl:stylesheet` element. You'll see an example of this in the demonstration style sheet presented at the end of Chapter 8.

XSLT and the Tree Model

Back in Chapter 2 you learned how an XML document can be represented by a parse tree, with the document itself as the root node and other components of the document, such as elements and attributes, represented by nodes in a branching pattern that follows the document's logical structure. It is important to understand that it is this node tree, and not the original document, that XSLT works with.

At one level, this distinction does not make any difference. You are still working with the document content, whether it is represented as the original document or as a parse tree. However, the terminology is different, and because XSLT works with the parse tree you will see parse tree terms such as "node set" and "branch" used rather than XML syntax terms such as "element" and "attribute." Much of XSLT involves selecting parts of the document to operate on, but what is really happening is selection of parts of the parse tree. Once you have worked with XSLT for a while, it will become second nature to think of an XML document in terms of its parse tree. For an example that may help clarify this concept, please refer to Listing 2.3 and Figure 2.1 in Chapter 2.

Style Sheet Structure

An XSL style sheet is an XML document, so the first tag will be the `<?xml>` processing instruction that is used in all XML documents. Next comes the `xsl:stylesheet` element, which serves as the outermost, or root, element of all XSL style sheets. This element specifies the XSL namespace as well as the version number. Here is the skeleton of an XSL style sheet:

```
<?xml version="1.0"?>
<xsl:stylesheet
    xmlns:xsl="http://www.w3.org/1999/XSL/Transform"
    version="1.0">
...
</xsl:stylesheet>
```

The `xsl:transform` element is a synonym for `xsl:stylesheet`.

> ***Style Sheet Namespaces***
>
> *The namespace for the W3C XSLT Recommendation is "http://www.w3.org/1999/XSL/Transform." You may come across the namespace "http://www.w3.org/TR/WD-xsl." This namespace belongs to the Working Draft of the XSLT specification, and the namespace changed when it became a Recommendation. It was this Working Draft that was supported by Internet Explorer version 5.0. Because MSXML now supports the W3C XSLT Recommendation, you should never need to use this alternate namespace unless you are working on a legacy project.*

Linking an XML Document to Its Style Sheet

To indicate the XSL style sheet that is to be used for an XML document, use the `xml-stylesheet` processing instruction. The syntax is as follows:

```
<?xml-stylesheet type="text/xsl" href="xsl-name"?>
```

`Xsl-name` is the URI of an external XSL file. The `xml-stylesheet` instruction is executed automatically only when the XML file is being displayed in a browser. With other XML applications, style sheets may be irrelevant and the instruction will be ignored, or the user will be able to select a style sheet manually.

A Style Sheet Example

Before you look at the details of XSLT syntax, it is useful to see a real, if simple, style sheet. This will make it easier to see how the parts fit together. Listing 7.1 shows a simple XML file that contains information about a collection of books: title, author, and publisher. Listing 7.2 shows an XSL style sheet that will transform the XML file into HTML for display in a browser. The lines in Listing 7.2 are numbered for reference and are explained in the text that follows the listings.

Listing 7.1 XML File That Will Be Transformed for Display by the XSL File in Listing 7.2

```
<?xml version="1.0"?>
<?xml-stylesheet type="text/xsl" href="list0702.xsl"?>
```

```
<books>
<book>
  <title>The Cambridge Biographical Encyclopedia</title>
  <author>David Crystal</author>
  <publisher>Cambridge University Press</publisher>
</book>
<book>
  <title>Travels with Charley</title>
  <author>John Steinbeck</author>
  <publisher>Putnam</publisher>
</book>
<book>
  <title>Crime and Punishment</title>
  <author>Fyodor Dostoyevsky</author>
  <publisher>Oxford</publisher>
</book>
</books>
```

Listing 7.2 XSL File That Will Transform the XML File in Listing 7.1 into HTML

```
<?xml version="1.0"?>
<xsl:stylesheet xmlns:xsl="http://www.w3.org/1999/XSL/Transform"
  version="1.0" >

<xsl:template match="/">
  <html><body>
  <h2>My Books</h2>
  <table border="2">
  <xsl:apply-templates select="/books/book"/>
  </table>
  </body></html>
</xsl:template>

<xsl:template match="book">
  <tr>
  <xsl:apply-templates/>
  </tr>
</xsl:template>

<xsl:template match="title | author | publisher">
  <td>
```

```
19.    <xsl:value-of select='.'/>
20.    </td>
21. </xsl:template>

22. </xsl:stylesheet>
```

Line 1: This is the standard XML processing tag.
Lines 2–3: This is the `xsl:stylesheet` opening tag. It is actually a single tag split over two lines because of its length.
Line 4: This is the start tag of an XSLT template that specifies processing actions to be taken for parts of the XML document. The match pattern in this case is "/" to specify the root node of the parse tree. This means that the actions specified in the template will be carried out once for the document.
Lines 5–7: These lines are HTML text to be written as-is to the transformed output.
Line 8: The `apply-templates` tag tells the processor to process other templates and insert the results in the output. In this case, the `select` pattern specifies that templates for "book" elements that are children of the "books" element are to be processed.
Lines 9–10: These lines are more HTML to be written to the output.
Line 11: This is the closing tag for the XSLT template.
Line 12: This is the opening tag for another template—this one to be applied to "book" elements.
Line 13: This is HTML to be written to the output.
Line 14: This is another `apply-templates` tag. Because there is no `select` value specified, templates for all child elements will be processed. In this case, it means that all children of the "book" element will be processed.
Line 15: This is HTML to be written to the output.
Line 16: This is the close tag for the template.
Line 17: This is yet another template. It will be applied to elements named "title," author," or "publisher."
Line 18: This is HTML to be written to the output.
Line 19: This `value-of` instruction writes the value of an XML element to the output. Setting the `select` attribute to "." specifies that the string value of the element is to be written.
Line 20: This is HTML to be written to the output.
Line 21: This is the close tag for the template.
Line 22: This is the end tag for the style sheet.

Depending on your Internet Explorer installation, you may be able to perform the transform and view the results simply by loading the XML file into the browser. If this does not work (as explained earlier in this chapter), you can apply this style sheet by using the MSXSL utility. The specific command will be as follows:

```
msxsl list0701.xml list0702.xsl -o list0703.html
```

The HTML output that is created by this style sheet is shown in Listing 7.3. If you examine the style sheet, and you also examine the output, you will be able to see how the XSLT processing instructions are applied to the XML document to result in the given output. Figure 7.1 shows the appearance of the output when viewed in Internet Explorer. You'll learn more about these and other XSLT commands in the remainder of the chapter.

Listing 7.3 HTML Output Created by the Style Sheet in Listing 7.2

```
<html><body>
<h2>My Books</h2>
<table border="2">
<tr>
<td>The Cambridge Biographical Encyclopedia</td>
<td>David Crystal</td>
<td>Cambridge University Press</td>
</tr>
<tr>
<td>Travels with Charley</td>
<td>John Steinbeck</td>
<td>Putnam</td>
</tr>
<tr>
<td>Crime and Punishment</td>
<td>Fyodor Dostoyevsky</td>
<td>Oxford</td>
</tr>
</table>
</body></html>
```

XSLT Templates

A *template* is an XSLT construct that defines output to be generated based upon certain criteria. The template criteria specify a part of the XML document—or more precisely, parts of the parse tree—to be processed. The

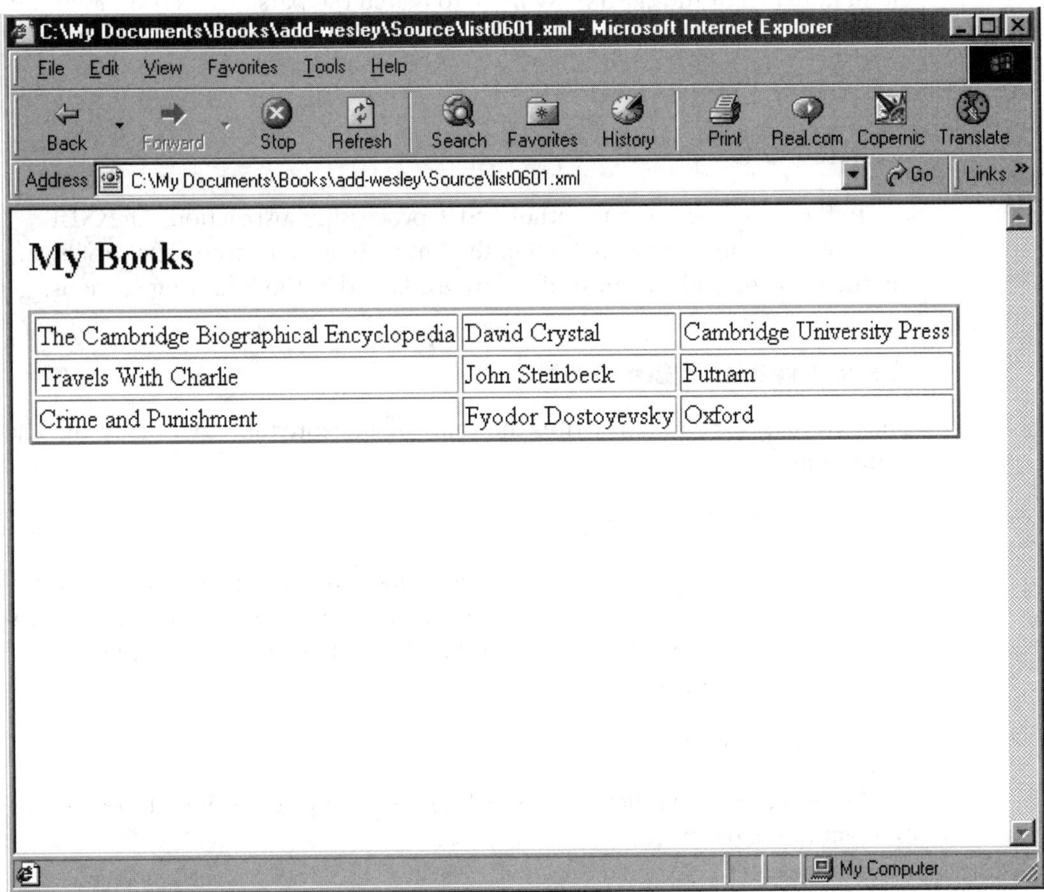

Figure 7.1: The output of the style sheet displayed in Internet Explorer

contents of the template, or the *template body,* define what output is to be generated when the template is executed. The `xsl:template` element has the following syntax:

```
<xsl:template match="pattern">
...
</xsl:template>
```

`Pattern` is the criterion for matching elements in the XML document—in other words, *`pattern`* matches a branch of the parse tree. You'll learn the details of patterns later in this chapter. At its simplest, a pattern is simply an

element name, or the slash (/) symbol, to match the parse tree's root node. For example, the following template will match all XML elements named "total":

```
<xsl:template match="total">
...
</xsl:template>
```

In the template body are other XSLT processing instructions, or XSLT elements, that are carried out when the template is processed. The processing instructions you will use most often are explained in the following sections.

The xsl:value-of Element

The `xsl:value-of` element writes the value of an expression to the output. The syntax is as follows:

```
<xsl:value-of select="expression"/>
```

`Expression` is the expression to be evaluated and output. This can be any XPath expression, as covered later in the chapter. A common use of `xsl:value-of` is to output the text data from an XML element, which is accomplished by using "." as the select expression:

```
<xsl:value-of select="."/>
```

For example, the following XSLT fragment writes the value of the "name" element to the output:

```
<xsl:template match="name">
  <xsl:value-of select="."/>
</xsl:template>
```

Literal Text

Literal text within a template body is output as is. Literal text is any text that is not part of an XSL tag. Here's an example:

```
<xsl:template match="name">
  <center><xsl:value-of select="."/></center>
</xsl:template>
```

This template outputs the text "<center>" followed by the value of the "name" element and finally the text "</center>." The text output in this manner must, of course, be legal XML.

You can also output literal text using the `xsl:text` instruction, which is described next.

The xsl:text Element

The `xsl:text` element outputs literal text. The syntax is as follows:

```
<xsl:text disable-output-escaping="value">
text
</xsl:text>
```

The `disable-output-escaping` argument is optional. If the argument is set to "yes," characters with special meaning to XML, such as < and >, are output as is. If the argument is set to "no," characters with special meaning to XML are output as the corresponding entity references (< and > in this case). The default is "no."

White space within an `xsl:text` element is output unchanged. This differs from white space by itself that is not in an `xsl:text` element, which is not output unless an enclosing element has the `xml:space` attribute set to "preserve." For example, if you want the output to consist of a person's first name followed by a space and then the person's last name, you write the following:

```
<xsl:value-of select="firstname"/>
<xsl:text> </xsl:text>
<xsl:value-of select="lastname"/>
```

The xsl:if Element

The `xsl:if` instruction encloses a set of instructions (template body) that will be processed only if a specified condition is True. The syntax is as follows:

```
<xsl:if test="criterion">
...
</xsl:if>
```

`Criterion` is an expression that is evaluated as being either True or False. The instructions contained in the `xsl:if` instruction are executed only if the test expression is True. For example, this instruction is processed only if the "category" attribute of the element being processed is equal to "drama":

```
<xsl:if test="@category='drama'">
...
</xsl:if>
```

Expressions are covered in detail in the section on XPath later in this chapter.

The xsl:choose Element

The xsl:choose element is used to define a choice among a number of alternatives. The syntax is as follows:

```
<xsl:choose>
  <xsl:when test="expression1">template-body1</xsl:when>
  <xsl:when test="expression2">template-body2</xsl:when>
  ...
  <xsl:otherwise>template-body</xsl:otherwise>
</xsl:choose>
```

The <xsl:choose> element can contain as many <xsl:when> elements as desired. There can be only one <xsl:otherwise> element, but it is optional. Here's how it works:

- The test expressions associated with the <xsl:when> elements are evaluated in order. When an expression evaluates as True, the associated template body is instantiated.
- Subsequent <xsl:when> elements are ignored even if their test expression is also True.
- If no test expression evaluates as True, the template body in the optional <xsl:otherwise> element is instantiated.
- If no test expression evaluates as True, and there is no <xsl:otherwise> element, then no template body is instantiated.

The following code fragment outputs the text "Large," "Medium," or "Small" based on the value of the "height" attribute:

```
<xsl:choose>
  <xsl:when test="@height < 10">Small</xsl:when>
  <xsl:when test="@height > 20">Large</xsl:when>
  <xsl:otherwise>Medium</xsl:otherwise>
</xsl:choose>
```

The xsl:for-each Element

The `xsl:for-each` element sets up a loop that is executed repeatedly for each node in a set of nodes. The syntax is as follows:

```
<xsl:for-each select="expression">
...
</xsl:for-each>
```

`Expression` is any XPath expression returning a node set. The instructions within the `xsl:for-each` element are executed once for each node in the set. Inside an `xsl:for-each` loop, the function `position()` returns the number of the node currently being processed (the first node is position 1), and the `last()` function returns the number of the last node in the node set. You'll learn more about XSL functions later in this chapter. These two functions let you do things such as determine when the first node is being processed (`position() = 1`) or when the last node is being processed (`position() = last()`).

The `xsl:for-each` instruction processes the nodes in the same order they exist in the document, unless an `xsl:sort` instruction is used to change the sort order.

The following XSLT instructions iterate over every "city" element that is a child of a "state" element. The values of the "name" and "budget" elements and of the "population" attribute are output. The cities are sorted alphabetically by name. The output is HTML that will display the data in a table.

```
<xsl:for-each select="state/city">
  <xsl:sort select="name"/>
  <tr>
    <td><xsl:value-of select="name"/></td>
    <td><xsl:value-of select="budget"/></td>
    <td><xsl:value-of select="@population"/></td>
  </tr>
</xsl:for-each>
```

The same results as `xsl:for-each` can also be obtained with the `xsl:apply-templates` instruction.

The xsl:apply-templates Element

The `xsl:apply-templates` instruction processes a set of nodes. Its actions are essentially identical to the `xsl:for-each` instruction. The syntax is as follows:

```
<xsl:apply-templates select="expression"/>
```

`Expression` is any XPath expression returning a node set. If *`expression`* is omitted, the default node set consisting of all the children of the current node is used. When this instruction is encountered, the XSLT processor locates and processes all templates that are defined (in `xsl:template` instructions) for the nodes in the specified node set. The `xsl:apply-templates` instruction processes the nodes in the same order they exist in the document, unless an `xsl:sort` instruction is used to change the sort order. When one or more `xsl:sort` instructions are used, the format is as follows:

```
<xsl:apply-templates select="expression">
  <!--xsl:sort instructions go here-->
</xsl:apply-templates>
```

Here is an example that is slightly modified from Listing 7.2. Its operation is explained in the text that follows the code.

```
1. <xsl:template match="/">
2.   <xsl:apply-templates select="/books/book">
3.     <xsl:sort select="title"/>
4.   </xsl:apply-templates>
5. </xsl:template>

6   <xsl:template match="book">
7.    <xsl:apply-templates/>
8.  </xsl:template>

9.  <xsl:template match="title | author | publisher">
10.   <xsl:value-of select='.'/>
11. </xsl:template>
```

Lines 2–4 are an `xsl:apply-templates` instruction that will be applied to "book" elements that are children of the "books" element. The `xsl:sort` instruction on line 3 specifies that the "book" elements will be processed in order according to the "title" element.

Lines 6–8 define a template for "book" elements. This is the template that will be executed one time for each "book" element as a result of the `xsl:apply-templates` instruction on lines 2–4. This template contains another `xsl:apply-templates` instruction that has no `select` attribute and therefore will iterate through all the child elements of the "book" element.

Lines 9–11 define a template for the "title," "author," and "publisher" elements (these are the children of the "book" element). The `xsl:apply-templates` instruction on line 7 will cause this template to be executed as follows:

- For the “title” element in the first “book” element.
- For the “author” element in the first “book” element.
- For the “publisher” element in the first “book” element.
- For the “title” element in the second “book” element.
- . . .
- For the “publisher” element in the last “book” element.

Using xsl:for-each versus xsl:apply-templates

In most XSLT programming, the `xsl:for-each` *and* `xsl:apply-templates` *instructions can be used interchangeably. In certain more complex situations you may want to choose one or the other (although they can certainly be mixed in the same XSL file). The* `xsl:for-each` *instruction requires that you specify a node set, which in turn requires that you have knowledge of the XML document's logical structure. In contrast,* `xsl:apply-templates` *can work with the default node set, which is defined simply as all child nodes of the current node. You can use this default node set without having detailed knowledge of the logical structure of the XML document.*

The xsl:sort Element

The `xsl:sort` element is used to specify the order in which nodes are processed by an `xsl:apply-templates` or `xsl:for-each` element. The `xsl:sort` element can appear only within these two elements. The syntax is as follows:

```
<xsl:sort select="expression"/>
```

Expression defines the sort key. The `select` attribute is optional. If it is omitted, the sort is done based on the string value of the node data. The three other optional attributes for the `xsl:sort` element are described in Table 7.1.

If there is more than one `xsl:sort` element with an `xsl:apply-templates` or `xsl:for-each` element, the data is sorted according to the first `xsl:sort` expression, then by the second, and so on. The following are some examples of using the `xsl:sort` element to process the “item” children of the current node, sorting them alphabetically by the “supplier” attribute:

Table 7.1 Optional Attributes for the `xsl:sort` Element

Attribute	Description
`case-order`	Set to "upper-first" or "lower-first" to specify whether uppercase or lowercase letters are collated first. The default is language dependent.
`data-type`	Set to "text" or "number" to specify whether the data is to be collated alphabetically or numerically. The default is "text."
`order`	Set to "ascending" or to "descending" to specify the sort order. The default is "ascending."

```
<xsl:apply-templates select="item">
  <xsl:sort select="@supplier"/>
</xsl:apply-templates>
```

The following would do the same as the preceding example, except when two or more items have the same supplier they would be sorted numerically by the "price" attribute:

```
<xsl:apply-templates select="item">
  <xsl:sort select="@supplier"/>
  <xsl:sort select="@price" data-type="number"/>
</xsl:apply-templates>
```

The following sorts the nodes in reverse document order:

```
<xsl:sort select="position()" data-type="number" order="descending"/>
```

XPath Patterns

A *pattern* specifies a node set. Patterns are used in the `match` attribute of `xsl:template` elements to specify which nodes the template applies to. In effect, a pattern specifies rules, or criteria, that a node must meet to be

Table 7.2 Patterns That Match by Element Name and Position

Example	Matches
`book` or `//book`	Any element named "book"
`/book`	Elements named "book" that are children of the root node
`holdings/book`	Elements named "book" that are children of the element named "holdings"
`/holdings/book`	Elements named "book" that are children of the element named "holdings," which is in turn a child of the root element
`holdings//book`	Elements named "book" that have the "holdings" element as an ancestor
`holdings/*/book`	Elements named "book" that have a "holdings" grandparent (parent of its parent)
`holdings[book]`	Elements named "holdings" that have a child named "book"

included in the node set. The criteria can include the name of a node (an element or attribute name), the position of a node relative to other nodes, or the data stored in an element or an attribute.

To match an element by name, use the name. To match any name, use an asterisk (*). To specify an element by its name and also by its position relative to other elements, use the slash (/) or double slash (//) characters. Table 7.2 shows some examples.

A part of a pattern in square brackets is called a *predicate* and it modifies the preceding part of the pattern. In general, the use of a predicate follows this syntax:

```
a[b]
```

This means "select nodes that meet criterion 'a' but only when 'b' is true."

To match based on attribute names, use the `attribute::` syntax or the at sign (@). Note that there is a distinction between matching an element node that has a certain attribute and matching the attribute node itself. Table 7.3 shows some examples.

Table 7.3 Patterns That Match by Attribute Name

Example	Matches
`attribute::title`	Attributes named "title"
`@title`	Attributes named "title" (synonym for `attribute::title`)
`*[@title]`	Any element node with an attribute named "title"
`holdings/*[@title]`	Any child element of the "holdings" element that has an attribute named "title"

Table 7.4 Patterns That Match by Attribute and Element Values

Example	Matches
`book[@title="War and Peace"]`	"Book" elements that have the "title" attribute with the value "War and Peace."
`book[title="War and Peace"]`	"Book" elements that have the "title" child element with the value "War and Peace."
`id["75443"]`	A node with a type `ID` attribute equal to "75443." An attribute is type `ID` if it is defined as this type in the document schema. The name of the attribute is irrelevant.

You can also create patterns that define node sets based on the data—that is, the text in elements (text nodes) and the value of attributes. Table 7.4 shows some examples of this type of pattern.

XPath Expressions

An *expression* is an XPath construct that can be evaluated as a string, a number, a node set, or a Boolean (True/False value). Expressions have two general uses in an XSL style sheet:

- To select data from the source document for processing
- To manipulate data and perform calculations for output to the result document

The first of these uses for expressions was covered earlier in this chapter in the section on patterns—a specific type of expression that evaluates to a node tree. In this section, you will learn about using XPath expressions for data manipulations and calculations.

> ***Expressions and Patterns***
>
> *You will sometimes see the terms "pattern" and "expression" used as if they mean the same thing, but they do not. A pattern is one kind of expression. Thus, all patterns are expressions but not all expressions are patterns. A pattern always specifies a node set, while an expression can evaluate to specify a node set or various other things, such as a string or a number.*

Variables

A *variable* is used as a storage location for information while an XSL style sheet is executing. Unlike variables in other programming languages, an XSL variable cannot be changed. In other words, it is assigned an initial value and that value cannot be changed—it acts like a symbolic constant in programming languages such as Visual Basic and Java. Thus, the name "variable" is not accurate, but that's the term used in the W3C Recommendation so we are stuck with it.

To define a variable, use the `xsl:variable` element. There are two equivalent forms of syntax. The first defines the variable value as an attribute:

```
<xsl:variable name="name" select="value"/>
```

The second syntax form defines the variable value between start and end tags:

```
<xsl:variable name="name">
value
</xsl:variable>
```

`Name` is the name of the variable, and `value` is the value assigned to it. The value can be a string (text), a number, a True/False value, a result tree, or a node set. Here are some examples:

```
<xsl:variable name="city" value="'Chicago'"/>
<xsl:variable name="interest" value="0.05"/>
<xsl:variable name="nodeset1" value="/addresses/person"/>
<xsl:variable name="ToPrinter" value="true()"/>
```

Two of these examples merit further explanation. In the first one, note that the text value being assigned to the variable is enclosed in double *and* single quotes. This is required to indicate that the value is text and not a node set. Consider the following:

```
<xsl:variable name="city" value="Chicago"/>
```

In the preceding example, " "Chicago" would be interpreted as an element name and not a string because it is not enclosed in single and double quotes. You can reverse the order of the double and single quotes: '"Chicago"'. If you use the start/end tag syntax, the quotes are not necessary:

```
<xsl:variable name="city">
Chicago
</xsl:variable>
```

The fourth example assigns the Boolean value True to the variable. Because XSL does not have constants to represent the values True and False, you must use the functions `true()` and `false()` for this purpose. You'll learn more about functions later in this chapter.

To reference a variable within the XSL style sheet, use the variable name preceded by the dollar sign ($). For example, assuming that the variable "nodeset1" has been assigned a node set value, the following code creates a template that will be applied to that node set:

```
<xsl:template match="$nodeset1">
...
</xsl:template>
```

The following code establishes an `if` element that executes only if the value of the variable "total" is less than 1,000:

```
<xsl:if test="$total < 1000">
```

```
...
</xsl:if>
```

If you reference a variable that has not been assigned a value, an error occurs.

Variables and Namespaces

Variable names are often simple names, such as “company” or “sales-total.” A variable name can also be qualified by a namespace prefix, such as “red:company” or “blue:sales-total.” Names with different prefixes are considered to be the same if the prefixes refer to the namespace. For example, the variable names “red:company” and “blue:company” are considered to be the same only if the prefixed “red” and “blue” refer to the same namespace. A variable name without a prefix does not use the default namespace, but rather has a null namespace.

Variable Scope

The *scope* of a variable refers to the parts of the style sheet where the variable may be referenced. A variable’s scope is determined by the location where it is declared. Variables declared at the top level of the style sheet—that is, outside of any template body—are global and can be referenced anywhere in the style sheet. Variables declared within a template body are local and can be referenced only within that template body. The following XSL code fragment illustrates variable scope:

```
<?xml version="1.0"?>
<xsl:stylesheet xmlns:xsl="http://www.w3.org/1999/XSL/Transform"
   version="1.0" >
<xsl:variable name="company" value="Acme"/>

<xsl:template match="/">
<xsl:variable name="division" value="Sales"/>
<!-- Variables $company and $division but not $title
 are is scope here. -->
</xsl:template>

<xsl:template match="book">
<xsl:variable name="title" value="Manager"/>
<!-- Variables $company and $title but not $division
 are in scope here. -->
</xsl:template>
```

Examples of Using Variables

Perhaps the most common use for variables is to avoid repeating a common expression that is used in multiple locations throughout the style sheet. This can make the style sheet more readable, and it also makes it easier to change the value of the expression, as it needs to be done in only one location. Suppose your style sheet will need to select node trees consisting of people in your address book that are family members, as indicated by the "type" attribute. You could create a variable to hold the expression, as shown here:

```
<xsl:variable name="family"
   select="/addresses/person[@type='family']"/>
```

Then you would use the variable wherever you needed to refer to this node tree:

```
<xsl:template select="$family">
...
<xsl:template>
```

Variables can also be used to expand the value of an attribute. Suppose there is an optional attribute named "amount." When the amount is greater than zero, the attribute is included, but when the amount is zero, the attribute is omitted. You need the value of "amount" for calculations, but when the attribute is omitted, the value is not available. You can deal with this situation using the following code:

```
<xsl:variable name="amount">
  <xsl:choose>
    <xsl:when test="@amount">
      <xsl:value-of select="@amount"/>
    </xsl:when>
    <xsl:otherwise>
      0
    </xsl:otherwise>
  </xsl:choose>
</xsl:variable>
```

This code results in the variable "$amount" having the value of the "amount" attribute when it is present or zero when it is not present. You can use the variable in your calculations to obtain the desired results.

> ***Variables and Parameters***
>
> *XSL has an element called a* parameter *that is defined with the* `<xsl:parameter>` *tag. Parameters work exactly like variables except that the value assigned to them is considered a default value. Some XSL processors permit the user to pass parameter values to the style sheet, replacing the default values.*

Operators

An *operator* performs an action on information in the style sheet. XSL operators fall into three categories. The mathematical operators perform the common mathematical operations of addition, subtraction, division, multiplication, and modulus. The comparison operators compare two expressions and return True if the comparison is True and False if it is not. The logical operators manipulate logical (True/False) expressions. The XSL operators are explained

Table 7.5 The XSL Mathematical, Comparison, and Logical Operators

Operator	Operation	Example
`+`	Addition	"$total + 10" adds 10 to the value of the variable $total.
`-`	Subtraction	"$X - $Y" subtracts the value of $Y from the value of $X.
`*`	Multiplication	"$X * $Y" multiplies $X by $Y.
`div`	Division	"5 div 2" returns 2.5.
`mod`	Modulus	Remainder after division. "10 mod 4" returns 2.
`=`	Equal to	"5 = 4" returns False.
`!=`	Not equal to	"5 != 4" returns True.
`>`	Greater than	"5 > 4" returns True.

(continued)

Table 7.5 (*cont.*)

Operator	Operation	Example
>=	Greater than or equal to	"5 >= 6" returns False.
<	Less than	"5 < 6" returns True.
<=	Less than or equal to	"5 <= 4" returns False.
and	And	"Exp1 and Exp2" returns True if Exp1 and Exp2 are both True; otherwise, it returns False.
or	Or	"Exp1 or Exp2" returns True if either Exp1 or Exp2 is True or if both are True; otherwise, it returns False.
!	Not	"!Exp" returns True if Exp is False and False if Exp is True.

in Table 7.5. Note that because the characters < and > have special meaning in XML, they are normally represented by < and > respectively. In the table, however, they are printed as themselves for the sake of clarity.

> ***Parentheses in Expressions***
>
> *You can use parentheses in an expression to control the order in which operations are performed. Anything within parentheses is evaluated first. For example, suppose you want to add the variables $X and $Y and multiple the sum by 5. If you write "$X + $Y * 5" you will not get the desired result because $Y will be multiplied by 5 first, and then the result will be added to $X. To force the addition to be performed first, use parentheses like this: "($X + $Y) * 5".*

The following code snippets give some examples of using the XSL operators. This expression returns True only if $X is less than $Y and $Y is greater than 10:

```
($X &lt; $Y) and ($Y &gt; 10)
```

This expression returns True if $X is an even number:

```
($X mod 2) = 0
```

This code returns True if $X or $Y, but not both of them, is greater than 10:

```
(($X &gt; 10) or ($Y &gt; 10)) and !(($X + $Y) &gt; 20)
```

Functions

A *function* is a built-in XSL component that returns a value. Because functions return values, they can be considered expressions. Functions are sometimes used by themselves, and sometimes they are used as a component of a more complex expression. Some functions take *arguments,* which are used to pass data to the function. Here's an example: The function `contains()` is used to determine if one string is contained within another. If you want to determine if the attribute named "type" contains the string "person," you call the function as follows:

```
contains(@type, "person")
```

The function will return True if the "type" attribute value is "personal," "business person," and so on.

XSL functions fall into several categories. It is beyond the scope of this book to provide information on all the available functions. You can find information on the full function set at `http://www.w3.org/TR/xpath`. For the purposes of this chapter, presentation will be limited to the most commonly needed functions, as shown in Table 7.6. Some functions require addition explanation or examples, which are provided following the table.

The boolean() Function

The `boolean()` function converts its single argument to a True/False value according to the rules described in Table 7.7.

The `boolean()` function is useful for a variety of tasks, such as determining whether a string is zero length or a node set is empty.

Table 7.6 Commonly Needed Functions

Category	Function	Description
String manipulation	`concat(s1, s2, ...)`	Takes two or more arguments. The return value is the arguments converted to strings and joined end to end.
	`contains(s1, s2)`	Returns True if string *s1* contains string *s2*. Returns False otherwise.
	`starts-with (s1, s2)`	Returns True if string *s1* starts with string *s2*. Returns False otherwise.
	`string-length(s1)`	Returns the length, in characters, of string *s1*. If the argument is omitted, returns the length of the string value of the context node.
	`substring(s1, start, length)`	Returns a substring from *s1* starting at position *start* and *length* characters long.
Aggregation	`count(ns)`	Returns the number of nodes in the node set *ns*. See the text following the table for details.
	`sum(ns)`	Sums numerical values over the node set *ns*. See the text following the table for details.
Boolean	`false()`	Returns the Boolean value False.
	`true()`	Returns the Boolean value True.
	`not(b)`	Returns the logical not of the Boolean expression *b*. Returns True if *b* is False and vice versa.
Current context	`last()`	Returns the current context size (the number of nodes it contains). See the text following the table for details.

(continued)

Table 7.6 *(cont.)*

Category	Function	Description
	`position()`	Returns the value of the current context position. See the text following the table for details.
Arithmetic	`ceiling(n)`	Returns the smallest integer that is greater than or equal to the value *n*.
	`floor(n)`	Returns the largest integer that is less than or equal to the value *n*.
	`round(n)`	Returns the integer that is closest to the value *n*, Fractional values of .5 and below are rounded down, and values above .5 are rounded up.
Data conversion	`boolean(a)`	Converts its argument *a* to a True or False value. See the text following the table for details.
	`format-number(v, f)`	Converts the value *v* to a string using the formatting instructions specified by *f*. See the text following the table for details.
	`number(a)`	Converts its argument *a* to a number. See the text following the table for details.
	`string(a)`	Converts its argument *a* to a string. See the text following the table for details.

The format-number() Function

The `format-number()` function is used to format numerical values for output. The syntax is as follows:

```
format-number(value, format)
```

Table 7.7 Return Value Rules of the `boolean()` Function

Argument Type	Returns True If	Returns False If
Boolean	The argument is True.	The argument is False.
Node set	The node set is not empty.	The node set is empty.
Number	The argument evaluates to a nonzero value.	The argument evaluates to zero.
Result tree fragment	The fragment contains nonempty text nodes.	The fragment only contains empty text nodes.
String	The argument evaluates to a string with length greater than zero.	The argument evaluates to a zero-length string.

`Value` is an expression evaluating to a numerical value. *`Format`* is a string that defines the format to use. The rules for creating format strings are quite complex, having been designed to handle every possible eventuality. You can find complete information on the W3C Web site at `http://www.w3.org/TR/xslt`. I present only basic information here.

The format string is made up of certain characters representing digits and symbols. For example, the format string "$#.00" will display a number with a leading dollar sign and two decimal places. Table 7.8 explains these formatting characters. Some examples are presented following the table.

Table 7.8 Characters Used in Format Strings

Character	Meaning
`0` (zero)	A digit will always be displayed at this position.
#	A digit will be displayed unless it is a redundant leading or trailing zero.
$	Displays a leading dollar sign.

(continued)

Table 7.8 *(cont.)*

Character	Meaning
. (decimal point)	Specifies the position of the decimal point.
, (comma)	Specifies the location of digit separators.
-	Specifies the minus sign.
%	The number is multiplied by 100 and displayed as a percentage.
' (apostrophe)	Displays special characters as themselves. For example, '#' displays #.

The following are some examples of using the `format-number()` function, with the function given followed by the return value:

```
format-number(12.34, "#.#")
12.3

format-number(12.34, "#.00")
12.34

format-number(-12.34, "#.00")
-12.34

format-number(12.34, "000.000")
012.340

format-number(0.66, "##%")
66%

format-number(666000000, "$,###")
$666,000,000
```

You will see more examples of using the `format-number()` function in Listing 7.5.

The count() and sum() Functions

The `count()` and `sum()` functions are used when processing a node set. The `count()` function returns the number of nodes in the set. The syntax is as follows:

```
count(ns)
```

Ns is an expression evaluating to a node set. The value returned is the number of nodes that are members of the set. This value does not include nodes that are descendants of member nodes but that are not members in their own right.

`Count()` can be used in calculations such as averages, as will be demonstrated when the `sum()` function is described. It also has some specialized uses. One such use is to determine whether the current node is a member of a specific node set. This is done using the union operator | (explained in the sidebar) and the . (period) symbol, which evaluates as the current node. If the union of a node set and the current node contains the same number of nodes as the node set alone, the current node is part of the node set. This would be coded as follows, using an `xsl:if` element to demonstrate (assuming that "$ns1" is a variable referring the node set of interest):

```
<xsl:if test="count(ns1 | .) = count(ns1)">
...
</xsl:if>
```

The elements within the `xsl:if` element will be executed only if the current node is a member of the node set referenced by $ns1.

> ***The Union Operator***
>
> *The union operator | combines two sets into a single set. If* ns1 *and* ns2 *are node sets, the expression* (ns1 | ns2) *evaluates as a node set that contains the nodes in* ns1 *and the nodes in* ns2*. If a node was part of both* ns1 *and* ns2*, it will be present only once in the result node set.*

The `sum()` function calculates the total of a set of numeric values over a node set. The node set can refer to a text element or an attribute. The syntax is as follows:

```
sum(ns)
```

Ns is an expression evaluating to a node set. For example, this expression returns the sum of all "amount" elements that are children of the "sale" element:

```
sum(sale/amount)
```

The following expression returns the sum of all "weight" attributes of the "item" element, which is a child of the "inventory" element:

```
sum(inventory/item/@weight)
```

This expression sums the values of those "item" elements that have the "weight" attribute greater than 10:

```
sum(item[@weight &gt; 10])
```

While the `sum()` function can be very useful, it has some limitations. First, all of the values to be totaled must be explicitly present as nodes (elements or attributes) in the source document. You cannot perform any preprocessing of the data. Second, if any value is not a number or is absent, the `sum()` function returns the special value `NaN`, representing "Not a Number."

The code in Listing 7.4 and Listing 7.5 demonstrates using the `sum()` and `count()` functions. This code also demonstrates using the `format-number()` function, which is covered previously in this chapter in the section "The format-number Function." Listing 7.4 presents an XML file containing data from a sales database, with information stored both as elements and as attributes. Listing 7.5 shows a style sheet for processing this XML file. The HTML output that results from processing these files with MSXSL.EXE is shown in Listing 7.6. This HTML, displayed in Internet Explorer in Figure 7.2, shows the raw data in a table and then displays summary data that was obtained using the `sum()` and `count()` functions.

Listing 7.4: XML File Containing Sales Data

```
<?xml version="1.0"?>
<?xml-stylesheet type="text/xsl" href="list0705.xsl"?>
<inventory>
<item numbersold="26">
  <name>Hammer</name>
  <sales>543.25</sales>
</item>
<item numbersold="12">
```

```
  <name>Wrench</name>
  <sales>901.15</sales>
</item>
<item numbersold="31">
  <name>Screwdriver</name>
  <sales>255.00</sales>
</item>
<item numbersold="6">
  <name>Chisel</name>
  <sales>99.95</sales>
</item>
</inventory>
```

Listing 7.5 Style Sheet for Displaying the XML Data in Listing 7.4

```
<?xml version="1.0"?>
<xsl:stylesheet xmlns:xsl="http://www.w3.org/1999/XSL/Transform"
version="1.0">

<xsl:variable name="items" select="/inventory/item"/>

<xsl:template match="/">

  <!-- Get the sum of all "sales" elements -->
  <xsl:variable name="totalsales"
    select="sum(/inventory/item/sales)"/>
  <!-- Get the sum of all "numbersold" attributes -->
  <xsl:variable name="numitemssold"
    select="sum(/inventory/item/@numbersold)"/>
  <!-- Get the average sale per item by dividing the total sales
  by the count of "item" elements -->
  <xsl:variable name="averagesale"
    select="$totalsales div count(/inventory/item)"/>

  <html><body>
  <h1>Sales Figures</h1>
  <table cellpadding="6" border="2">
  <tr>
  <td><b>Item</b></td>
  <td><b>Sales</b></td>
  <td><b>Number sold</b></td>
  </tr>
```

```
  <xsl:for-each select="$items">
    <tr>
    <td><xsl:value-of select="name"/></td>
    <td><xsl:value-of select="format-number(sales, '$#.00')"/></td>
    <td><xsl:value-of select="@numbersold"/></td>
    </tr>
  </xsl:for-each>

  </table>
  <p>Total sales =
  <xsl:value-of select="format-number($totalsales, '$#.00')"/>
  </p>
  <p>Number items sold =
  <xsl:value-of select="$numitemssold"/>
  </p>
  <p>Average sales =
  <xsl:value-of select="format-number($averagesale, '$#.00')"/>
  per item.</p>
  </body></html>
</xsl:template>

</xsl:stylesheet>
```

Listing 7.6 The HTML Produced When the XML File in Listing 7.4 Is Transformed by the XSLT in Listing 7.5

```
<html><body>
<h1>Sales Figures</h1>
<table cellpadding="6" border="2">
<tr>
<td><b>Item</b></td>
<td><b>Sales</b></td>
<td><b>Number sold</b></td>
</tr>
<tr>
<td>Hammer</td>
<td>$543.25</td>
<td>26</td>
</tr>
<tr>
<td>Wrench</td>
<td>$901.15</td>
```

```
<td>12</td>
</tr>
<tr>
<td>Screwdriver</td>
<td>$255.00</td>
<td>31</td>
</tr>
<tr>
<td>Chisel</td>
<td>$99.95</td>
<td>6</td>
</tr>
</table>
<p>Total sales =
  $1799.35</p>
<p>Number items sold =
  75</p>
<p>Average sales =
  $449.84
  per item.</p>
</body></html>
```

The last() and position() Functions

The `last()` and `position()` functions are used to obtain information about the current context. They take no argument and return information as follows:

- `last()` returns a numerical value specifying how many nodes are in the current context.
- `position()` returns a numerical value giving the position within the current context or, expressed another way, the position of the context node within the current context. The value returned can range from 1 to `last()`.

These functions are used when processing a node set—for example, using the `xsl:for-each` element. There are many things that you can do with one or both of these functions. One possibility is to label the output with item numbers. For example, you could output a list a books like this:

```
1: War and Peace
2: The Covenant
3: Middlemarch
```

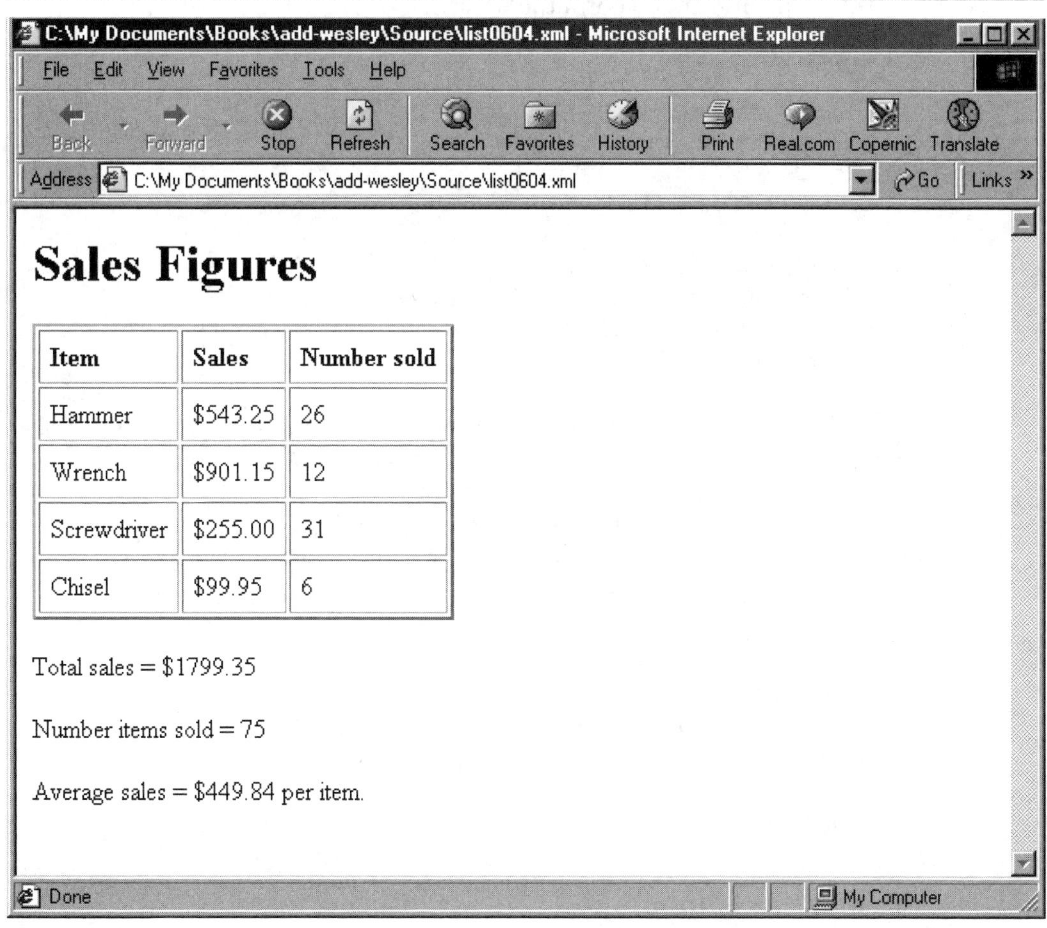

Figure 7.2 The XML data from Listing 7.4 displayed using the style sheet in Listing 7.5

This is the code required, assuming the book title is stored in the "title" element:

```
<xsl:template match="book">
  <xsl:value-of select="position()"/>: <xsl:value-of select="title"/>
</xsl:template>
```

You could also create output like this:

```
Book 1 of 20: War and Peace
Book 2 of 20: The Covenant
Book 3 of 20: Middlemarch
```

Here's the code for this output:

```
<xsl:template match="book">
  Book <xsl:value-of select="position()"/> of
  <xsl:value-of select="last()"/>: <xsl:value-of select="title"/>
</xsl:template>
```

When using `last()` in a repeating loop, as in this example, you can store the value of `last()` in a variable and then output the value of the variable. By calling `last()` only once you improve performance.

Another use for these functions is to determine when processing has reached the last node in the context. For example, you might want to display a list of books and put a horizontal line after the last one. Here's how:

```
<xsl:template match="book">
  <xsl:value-of select="title"/>
  <xsl:if test="position() = last()">
    <hr/>
  </xsl:if>
</xsl:template>
```

The number() Function

The `number()` function converts its argument to a number and returns the result. Table 7.9 explains the conversion rules.

Here are some examples:

```
number(5.5) returns 5.5
number("5.5") returns 5.5
number("abc") returns NaN
number(false()) returns 0
```

In most situations, conversion of other data types to numbers is performed automatically, so there are few instances when this function is needed.

Table 7.9 Conversion Rules for the `number()` Function

Argument	Type Conversion
Boolean	Returns 1 for True, 0 for False.
Node set	The node set is converted to a string using the rules for the `string()` function (covered in the next section). The result is converted to a number following the rule for string arguments.
Numeric	The value is not changed.
Result tree fragment	The result tree is converted to a string using the rules for the `string()` function (covered in the next section). The result is converted to a number following the rule for string arguments.
String	Leading and trailing white space is removed. If the remaining string is recognized as a number, the corresponding value is returned. If the string cannot be recognized as a number, the special value "NaN" is returned.

The string() Function

The `string()` function returns its argument converted to a string. The argument is optional. Table 7.10 explains the conversion rules.

Conversion of data to string form is usually performed automatically, so there are few occasions when the `string()` function is needed. One time it is needed is when you want to perform a string comparison instead of a node set comparison. For example, the following code tests if any "name" child of the current node has the value "Alice Walker":

```
<xsl:if test="name='Alice Walker'">
```

If you want to test if the first "name" child has the value "Alice Walker," you would write:

```
<xsl:if test="string(name)='Alice Walker'">
```

Note, however, that the same result could be obtained as follows:

```
<xsl:if test="name[1]='Alice Walker'">
```

Table 7.10 Conversion Rules for the `string()` Function

Argument	Conversion
Boolean	Returns either "false" or "true."
Node set	The string value of the node that is first in document order. If the node set is empty, an empty string is returned.
Numeric	Integers are returned with no decimal point. Floating point values are returned with at least one digit on each side of the decimal point. Zero is returned as "0." Special return values are "NaN," "Infinity," and "–Infinity."
Omitted	The default argument is a node set containing the context node.
Result tree fragment	The values of all descendant text nodes concatenated in order.
String	The string is unchanged.

Summary

Extensible Stylesheet Language (XSL) is an extremely powerful tool. It has two parts: XSLT for performing transforms and FO for providing output formatting. XSLT enables you to define a set of constructs, or rules, that take an XML file as input and transform it in just about any way you desire. The output might be a new XML file with a different structure, a file containing FO commands for data rendering, or an HTML file for display in a browser. In fact, the use of XSLT to transform XML to HTML is currently its most common use. A good understanding of XSLT will open up many new possibilities for the XML developer.

CHAPTER 8

Formatting Objects

Formatting Objects, or FO, is one of the two components of Extensible Stylesheet Language (XSL). The other component, XSL for Transformations (XSLT), was covered in the previous chapter. This chapter covers the fundamentals of FO. Before getting started, I should mention that as of this writing Microsoft provides no support for FO. What, then, is this chapter doing in a book on Microsoft technologies? The rationale is that FO is such a powerful and promising specification that Microsoft support will almost surely come—perhaps even by the time you read this. There is no guarantee of this, of course.

FO Basics

FO is an XML vocabulary that is used to describe the formatting and display of data that is contained in an XML document. It is one of two XML formatting techniques, the other being Cascading Style Sheets (CSS, covered in Chapter 6). FO is a work in progress. As of this writing, it is a W3C Candidate Recommendation as part of XSL version 1.0, and that is what the material in this chapter is based on. There are, however, some known issues with the current specification, and there will likely be some minor changes before FO achieves Recommendation status.

The situation is somewhat confused by W3C's lack of clarity in defining the relationships among FO, XSLT, and XSL. Technically, both FO and XSLT are subsumed under the XSL umbrella, but XSLT version 1.0 has achieved W3C Recommendation status (as of November 16, 1999) while XSL (and its FO component) remains a Candidate Recommendation.

FO is an XML vocabulary, meaning that FO "instructions" are written as XML elements using XML syntax. You will, however, almost never write FO directly, but rather you will create an XSL style sheet containing XSLT instructions to transform the original XML document into an XML document that contains the data to be displayed and the FO instructions that specify how it is to be displayed. You learned how to use XSLT in the previous chapter, but there the emphasis was on transforming XML to HTML for display in a browser. In this chapter, examples are presented as FO-XML documents so you can see the FO elements required to obtain a particular result. You'll see an example of using XSLT to transform XML to XML-FO at the end of this chapter.

A DTD for FO Documents

Because FO is an XML vocabulary, it is possible to define a schema that can be used to validate FO-XML documents. Any such schema is unavoidably provisional due to the fact that FO is not a fixed standard. It can still be useful, however, if applied with suitable precautions. You can find a schema for FO-XML (in the form of a DTD) at `http://www.renderx.com/Tests/validator/fo2000.dtd.html`.

The next step is to feed the transformed document into an FO-compliant rendering agent for display or other output—and there's the rub. There are currently no browsers, and very few programs of any kind, that support FO. Microsoft has no FO support in any of its offerings, although such support is almost certain to appear in the future. This means that a third step is required. The document must be transformed a third time, into a format such as Portable Document Format (PDF) or TeX, for which rendering agents are available. As of this writing, the following are some sources for third-party products that work with FO:

- Apache Project (FOP): `http://xml.apache.org/fop/`
- RenderX (XEP): `http://www.renderx.com/`
- Antenna House (Antenna House XSL Formatter): `http://www.antennahouse.com/`
- Oxford University Computing Services (Passive TeX): `http://users.ox.ac.uk/~rahtz/passivetex/`
- Unicorn Enterprises (XML Toolkit): `http://www.unicorn-enterprises.com/#products_ufo`

You can turn to one of these sources or wait for Microsoft to start supporting FO. I have found FOP and XEP both to be quite useful. They use FO to output a PDF file that can be viewed either locally or on the Web using free tools supplied by Adobe (`http://www.adobe.com/`). FOP is an open source program, and you can download and use it for free. Note, however, that some familiarity with Java is required to get it installed and running. XEP is a commercial product, but a time-limited evaluation version is available free of charge.

FO may seem like a bit of an orphan at the current time, with no browser support and limited support of any kind. This situation is sure to change. For complex formatting and nonvisual situations, FO offers (or will offer) so much more than CSS. Its widespread adoption in the near future is a very good bet. In any case, please bear in mind that FO is an evolving standard, and it is also quite complex. This chapter provides an introduction to FO as currently defined by W3C.

The FO Model

The FO formatting model is based on rectangular areas. An area may contain text, an image, empty space, and/or other areas. Your FO-XML file defines these areas, and when the FO renderer processes the FO-XML file it interprets the formatting objects in the file to determine where the various areas are to be placed on the page. Each formatting object (that is, each FO element) usually creates a single area, but in some situations, such as when a paragraph must be split between two pages, multiple areas may be generated by a single formatting object.

An FO area has a content area that contains the area's content: text, image, and so on. The content area is surrounded by padding that represents space between the content and an optional border. Finally, the border is surrounded by additional space, or the *margin*. This arrangement is illustrated in Figure 8.1.

FO has two types of areas. A *block* area represents a rectangular area on a page that holds content such as a paragraph or an entry in a bulleted list. In addition to content, a block area can contain other block areas and inline areas. An *inline* area represents part of a line, such as a single word or a footnote reference. An inline area can contain text as well as other inline areas. To get a feel for these two types of areas, consider the paragraph you are reading. The paragraph as a whole would represent a block area, while each of the italicized words in the paragraph would represent an inline area contained within the block area.

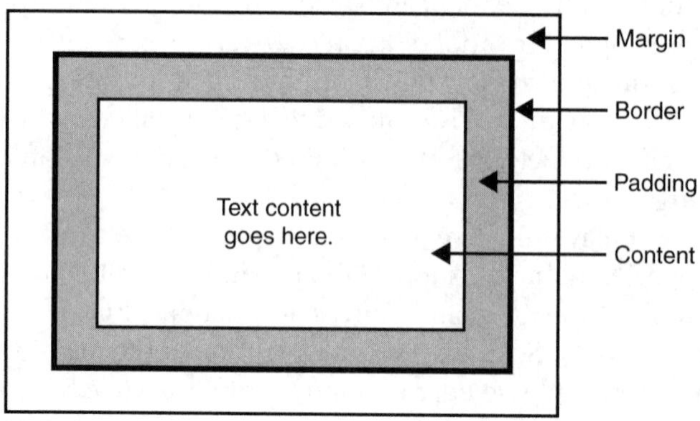

Figure 8.1 The content/padding/border/margin structure of an FO area

FO Document Structure

Because FO documents are XML documents, they follow all the rules of XML syntax. The elements in the document are FO elements in the FO namespace. These elements contain the document data and instruct the FO rendering agent as to how the data is to be formatted. FO files are sometimes given the .fob or .fo extension, but you are just as likely to see the .xml extension.

The root element of all FO documents is the `fo:root` element. This element encloses all other FO elements and also defines the FO namespace. Here's an example:

```
<?xml version="1.0?">
<fo:root xmlns:fo="http://www.w3.org/1999/XSL/Format">
...
</fo:root>
```

All FO elements, therefore, use the `fo:` prefix. Within the root element, two elements are required.

- The `fo:layout-master-set` element contains other elements that describe the overall page layout, with specifications such as page size, orientation (landscape or portrait), and margin sizes.
- The `fo:page-sequence` element contains actual data as well as the instructions for how that data is to be placed on the pages.

Defining Master Pages

The current FO implementation supports only one kind of master page: `fo:simple-page-master`. A *master page* represents a rectangular page with a specified height and width and margin sizes. When you define a master page, you also assign it a name, as the `master-name` attribute, that is used to reference the page. An FO-XML document can define more than one master page. At this point, you are defining a page but not putting any content on it. Here is an example of an FO element defining a master page with the name "opening":

```
<fo:simple-page-master margin-right="1in" margin-left="1in"
                       margin-top="0.5in" margin-bottom="0.5in"
                       page-width="8.5in" page-height="11in"
                       master-name="opening">
...
</fo:simple-page-master>
```

If you do not specify the margin and page size attributes in the `fo:simple-page-master` element, the FO renderer will apply reasonable defaults based on the output media in use.

Inside the margins, a page is divided into five regions. These regions, and their relationships to the page margins, are illustrated in Figure 8.2. These

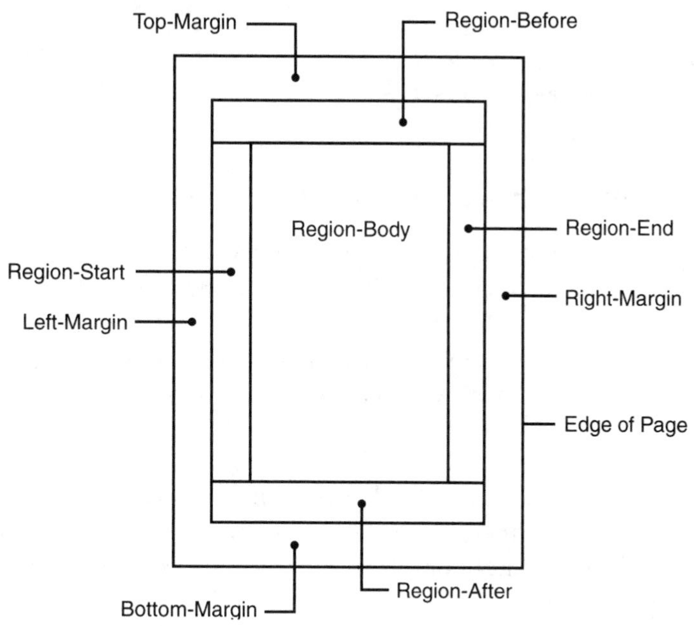

Figure 8.2: The regions and margins of an FO master page

regions are represented by the elements `fo:region-start`, `fo:region-end`, `fo:region-before`, `fo:region-after`, and `fo:region-body`.

Within the `fo:simple-page-master` element, you place other FO elements that specify the size of the regions and the data to be placed in each region. By default, all the regions except for the body region have zero size, and the body region occupies all the space within the margins. To give a region (other than the body region) a nonzero size, set its `extent` attribute. You must also set the body region's margins (which are separate from the page margins) to account for the size of any other regions. If you do not, content displayed in the body region will overlap content displayed in the other regions. The following example defines a page where the start, end, before, and after regions are each 0.5 inch, and the body region's margins have been set to 0.75 inch to make room for the other regions:

```
<fo:simple-page-master margin-right="1in" margin-left="1in"
                       margin-top="0.5in" margin-bottom="0.5in"
                       page-width="8.5in" page-height="11in"
                       master-name="opening">
   <fo:region-body margin-right="0.75in" margin-left="0.75in"
                   margin-top="0.75in" margin-bottom="0.75in"/>
   <fo:region-start extent="0.5in"/>
   <fo:region-end extent="0.5in"/>
   <fo:region-before extent="0.5in"/>
   <fo:region-after extent="0.5in"/>
</fo:simple-page-master>
```

Putting Content on a Page

Once you have defined one or more pages, you use the `fo:page-sequence` element to actually place content on pages. The general syntax is as follows:

```
<fo:page-sequence master-name="name">
<!-- content is placed here -->
</fo:page-sequence>
```

Name is the name of the page defined with an `fo:simple-page-master` element, as described earlier in the chapter. This specifies that the output created by the content of this `fo:page-sequence` element will use the indicated page specifications.

Within the `fo:page-sequence` element, you place content using one or both of the following elements:

- The `fo:flow` element contains content that is to be flowed from page to page without repeating.
- The `fo:static-content` element contains content that will be repeated on every page.

If an `fo:page-sequence` element contains both of these child elements, the `fo:static-content` element(s) must be placed before the `fo:flow` element(s).

The fo:flow Element

The `fo:flow` element holds content that will be flowed onto the pages. This means that the content will fill up one page and then flow to the next page as needed—given content is never repeated on more than one page. The text you are reading in this book, for example, would have been placed on the page using an `fo:flow` element. To specify which page region the content is to be placed in, use the `fo:flow` element's `flowname` attribute. The possible values for this attribute are as follows, corresponding to the five page regions that were explained earlier in this chapter:

- `xsl-region-body`
- `xsl-region-before`
- `xsl-region-after`
- `xsl-region-start`
- `xsl-region-end`

There cannot be more than one flow into the same region within a given page sequence. This means that within an `fo:page-sequence` element there can be at most five `fo:flow` children—one for each region. In most situations, however, there will be only a single `fo:flow` element placing content in the body region.

Each `fo:flow` element contains child elements that hold the actual content. These child elements include `fo:block`, `fo:block-container`, `fo:table-and-caption`, `fo:table`, and `fo:list-block` elements. These are explained later in this chapter. For now, Listing 8.1 presents a complete FO-XML file and shows how to use the `fo:flow` element to place a block of text on a page in the body region. The text in this example, a paragraph from this chapter, is not long enough to flow to another page, but it would flow if it were longer.

Listing 8.1 Using the `fo:flow` Element to Place Text on a Page

```
<?xml version="1.0"?>
<fo:root xmlns:fo="http://www.w3.org/1999/XSL/Format">
```

```
<fo:layout-master-set>
    <fo:simple-page-master margin-right="1in" margin-left="1in"
                        margin-top="0.5in" margin-bottom="0.5in"
                        page-width="8.5in" page-height="11in"
                        master-name="standard">
      <fo:region-body/>
    </fo:simple-page-master>
</fo:layout-master-set>

<fo:page-sequence master-name="standard">
    <fo:flow flow-name="xsl-region-body">
      <fo:block>
The fo:flow element holds content that will be flowed onto the pages.
This means that the content will fill up one page then flow to the next
page, as needed - given content is never repeated on more than one page.
The text you are reading in this book, for example, would be placed on
the page using an fo:flow element. To specify which page region the con-
tent is to be placed in, use the fo:flow element's flowname attribute.
The possible values for this attribute are as follows, corresponding to
the five page regions that were explained earlier in this chapter:
      </fo:block>
    </fo:flow>
</fo:page-sequence>

</fo:root>
```

The fo:static-content Element

The `fo:static-content` element holds content that will appear on every page, such as a header or a footer. Like the `fo:flow` element, the `fo:static-content` element has the `flowname` attribute that specifies which of the five page regions the static content is to be placed in, and it also can contain the same child elements, such as `fo:block`. Listing 8.2 is a modification of the FO-XML file from Listing 8.1 to display a header on every page. Figure 8.3 shows the PDF file generated from this FO-XML file. To generate this PDF file, follow the instructions for FOP or whatever FO to PDF converter you are using.

Listing 8.2: Using the `fo:static-content` Element to Place a Header on Every Page

```
<?xml version="1.0"?>
<fo:root xmlns:fo="http://www.w3.org/1999/XSL/Format">
```

```
<fo:layout-master-set>
    <fo:simple-page-master margin-right="1in" margin-left="1in"
                           margin-top="0.5in" margin-bottom="0.5in"
                           page-width="8.5in" page-height="11in"
                           master-name="standard">
  <fo:region-before extent="0.5in"/>
  <fo:region-body margin-top="0.5in"/>
    </fo:simple-page-master>
</fo:layout-master-set>

<fo:page-sequence master-name="standard">
    <fo:static-content flow-name="xsl-region-before">
      <fo:block>
XML the Microsoft Way
      </fo:block>
    </fo:static-content>
    <fo:flow flow-name="xsl-region-body">
      <fo:block>
The fo:flow element holds content that will be flowed onto the pages.
This means that the content will fill up one page then flow to the next
page, as needed - given content is never repeated on more than one page.
The text you are reading in this book, for example, would be placed on
the page using an fo:flow element. To specify which page region the con-
tent is to be placed in, use the fo:flow element's flowname attribute.
The possible values for this attribute are as follows, corresponding to
the five page regions that were explained earlier in this chapter:
      </fo:block>
    </fo:flow>
</fo:page-sequence>

</fo:root>
```

Content Elements

Content elements are those FO elements that directly hold the document content. The type of content element determines certain aspects of how the content is formatted. Other aspects of formatting, such as font appearance and size, are controlled by element attributes that are covered later in the chapter.

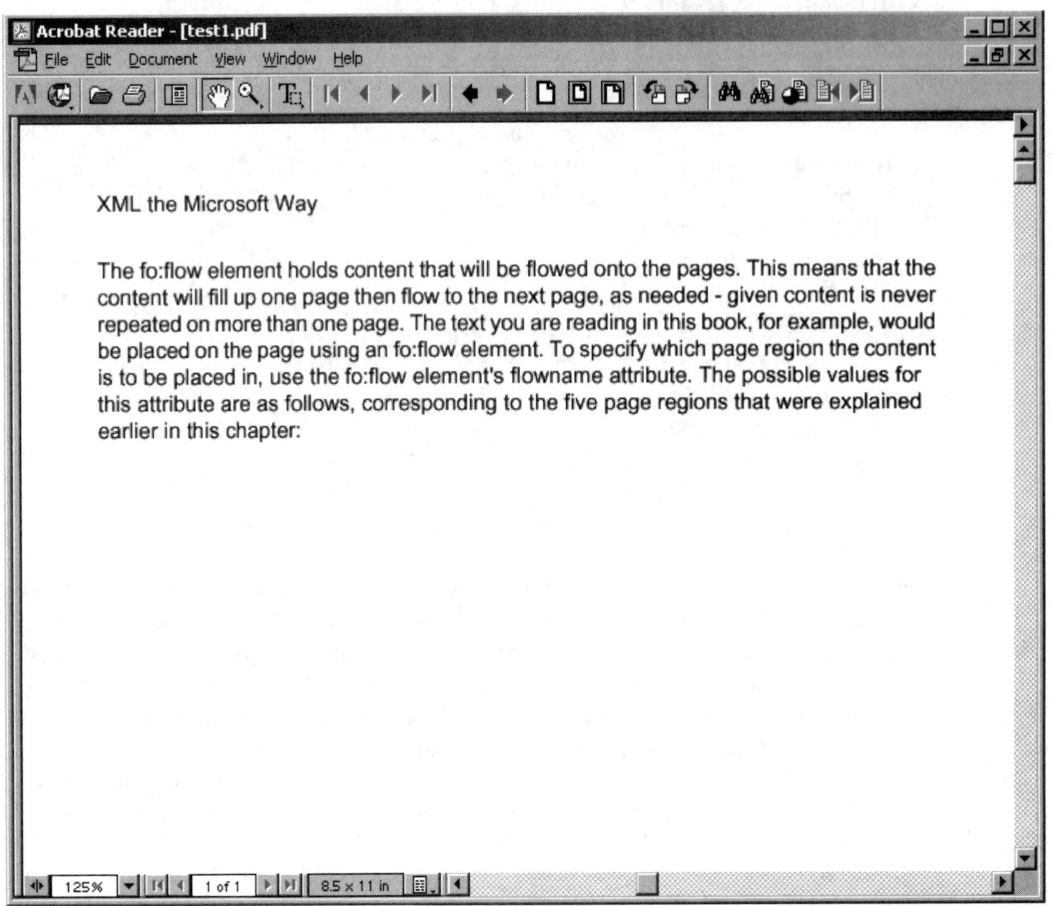

Figure 8.3 The output of the FO-XML file in Listing 8.2

The fo:block Element

The `fo:block` element represents a rectangular region of output. If the element contains only text (that is, only content), you can think of it as representing a paragraph in the output. However, the `fo:block` element is a lot more flexible than that. In addition to content, an `fo:block` element can contain other `fo:block` elements, inline areas, images, and so on. If one block area contains other block areas as child elements, the arrangement, or *stacking*, of the blocks is normally handled automatically by the renderer.

The fo:inline Element

The `fo:inline` element is used to apply formatting to sections of text. This element has no direct effect on the layout of the page. The `fo:inline` element can contain other inline elements, a technique that is useful for combining font attributes. For example, the FO elements shown in Listing 8.3 use nested `fo:inline` elements to create an inline section that is displayed in italics with a subsection that is displayed in italics with a larger font. The output of this FO code (assuming it was embedded in a complete FO file) is shown in Figure 8.4.

Listing 8.3 FO Fragment That Uses the `fo:inline` Element

```
<fo:flow flow-name="xsl-region-body">
<fo:block>
Normal Normal Normal Normal Normal
<fo:inline font-style="italic">
Italics Italics Italics Italics
<fo:inline font-size="larger">
Larger italics
</fo:inline>
Italics Italics Italics
</fo:inline>
Normal Normal Normal Normal Normal Normal Normal
</fo:block>
</fo:flow>
```

The fo:footnote Element

The `fo:footnote` element is used to create a footnote. You place this element in the text where the footnote reference (for example, an asterisk) will appear. The `fo:footnote` element contains the symbol or other marker that will denote the footnote, and it also contains an `fo:footnote-body` child element that contains the actual footnote text. The body of the footnote is placed at the bottom of the page in the after region. The following is FO code that will create a simple footnote using an asterisk as a reference:

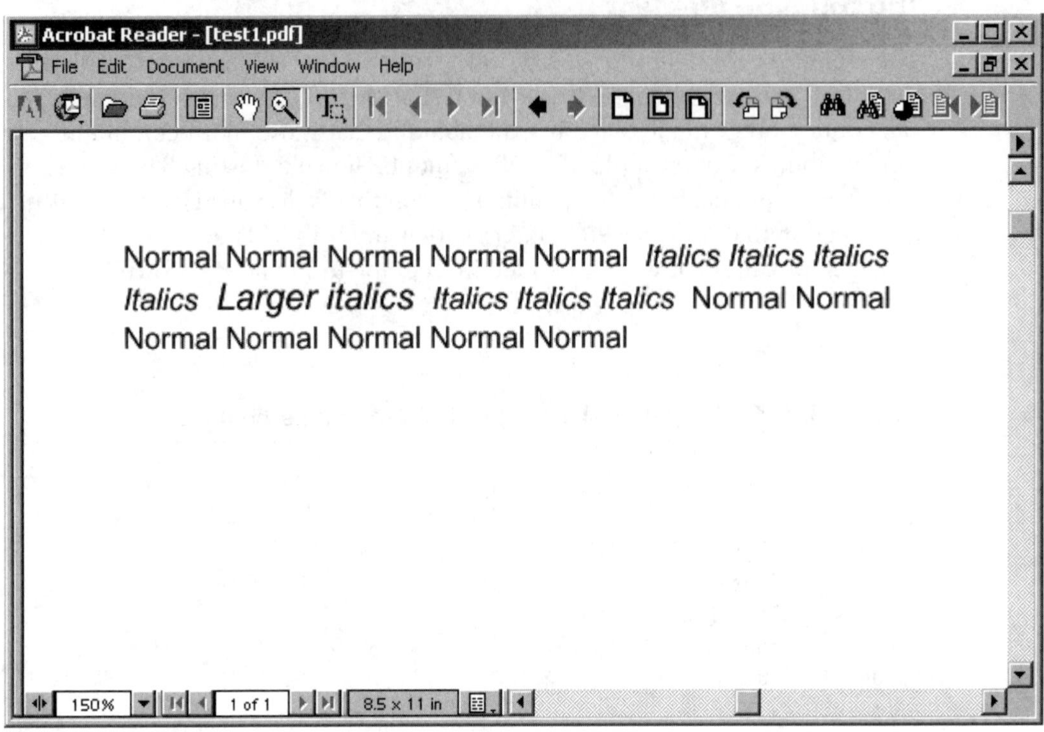

Figure 8.4 The output produced by the FO code fragment in Listing 8.3

```
<fo:footnote>
*
<fo:footnote-body>
* This topic is discussed in detail in the next chapter.
</fo:footnote-body>
</fo:footnote>
```

You can use `fo:inline` elements within an `fo:footnote` element to control the formatting of the footnote elements. The following example expands on the previous one, using `fo:inline` child elements to display the asterisks as superscripts and the footnote body in a smaller font:

```
<fo:footnote>
<fo:inline vertical-align="super">
*
</fo:inline>
<fo:footnote-body>
```

```
<fo:inline font-size="smaller">
<fo:inline vertical-align="super">
*
</fo:inline>
This topic is discussed in detail in the next chapter.
</fo:inline>
</fo:footnote-body>
</fo:footnote>
```

The fo:external-graphic Element

The `fo:external-graphic` element is used to insert a graphic into a document. This is an inline element with the following syntax:

```
<fo:external-graphic src="fileURL"/>
```

FileURL is the relative or absolute URL of the graphic. Here is an example:

```
<fo:external-graphic src="http://www.somewhere.com/images/logo.gif"/>
```

Be aware that the graphic formats you can use will depend on the support of the specific rendering engine you are using. JPEG and GIF images are the most commonly supported formats.

While the `fo:external-graphic` element is itself an inline element, you can force it to be treated as a block element by wrapping it in an `fo:block` element:

```
<fo:block>
<fo:external-graphic src="http://www.somewhere.com/images/logo.gif"/>
</fo:block>
```

To specify the size of the graphic, use the `height` and `width` attributes. You can use various units of measure for these attributes, as detailed later in this chapter in the section "FO Attributes." For example, the following will display the image 2 inches tall and 3 inches wide:

```
<fo:external-graphic src="http://www.somewhere.com/images/logo.gif"
    height="2in" width="3in"/>
```

If you set these properties to "auto," the image will be displayed at its native size. Most renderers default to "auto" and will display an image at its native size if the `height` and `width` properties are omitted.

The fo:list-block Element

The `fo:list-block` element is used to create bulleted, numbered, and other types of lists. The `fo:list-block` element contains the entire list. Each item in the list is represented by the following two child elements:

- An `fo:list-item-label` element that contains the bullet or number of the item
- An `fo:list-item-body` element that contains the list item itself (as block-level elements)

Alternatively, each `fo:list-item-label` / `fo:list-item-body` pair can be enclosed within an `fo:list-item` element, but this has no effect on the output and is generally omitted for renderers that do not require this element. The FO code in Listing 8.4 shows an FO-XML file that creates a bulleted list. The output is shown in Figure 8.5.

Listing 8.4 Portion of an FO-XML File to Create a Bulleted List

```
<fo:page-sequence master-name="standard">
<fo:flow flow-name="xsl-region-body">
<fo:block>
Please bring the following items to your interview:
</fo:block>
<fo:list-block>
<fo:list-item-label><fo:block>*</fo:block></fo:list-item-label>
<fo:list-item-body>
<fo:block>A current resume.</fo:block>
</fo:list-item-body>
<fo:list-item-label><fo:block>*</fo:block></fo:list-item-label>
<fo:list-item-body>
<fo:block>Your college diploma.</fo:block>
</fo:list-item-body>
<fo:list-item-label><fo:block>*</fo:block></fo:list-item-label>
<fo:list-item-body>
<fo:block>A recent photograph.</fo:block>
</fo:list-item-body>
</fo:list-block>
</fo:flow>
</fo:page-sequence>
```

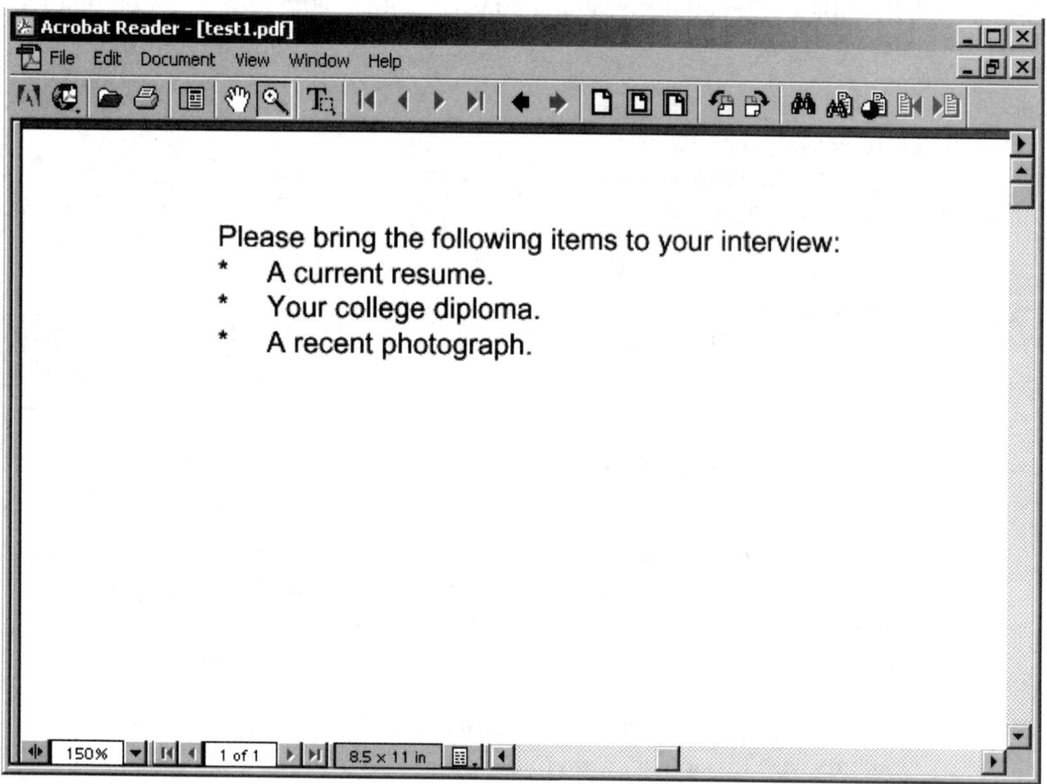

Figure 8.5 The bulleted list created by the code in Listing 8.4

The fo:table-and-caption and fo:table Elements

To create a table with a caption, use the `fo:table-and-caption` element. This element contains two children: an `fo:table-caption` element that contains the table caption and an `fo:table` element that contains the body of the table. If your table does not require a caption, use the `fo:table` element instead of `fo:table-and-caption` and omit the `fo:table-caption` child.

The fo:table-caption Element

The `fo:table-caption` element contains block-level elements that specify the table's caption. The default location for the caption is before the table, but you can change this by setting the `fo:table-and-caption` element's `caption-side` attribute to one of the following values: before, after, start, end, top, bottom, left, or right. The following shows how to create a table with a caption that follows the table:

```
<fo:table-and-caption caption-side="bottom">
  <fo:table-caption>
    <fo:block font-weight="bold" font-size="14pt">
    This is the caption text.
    </fo:block>
  </fo:table-caption>
  <fo:table>
    <!-- place table contents here -->
  </fo:table>
</fo:table-and-caption>
```

The fo:table-body Element

The `fo:table-body` element contains various child elements that define the actual content of the table. In many ways, the logic of laying out a table in FO is the same as with Cascading Style Sheets (see Chapter 6), although the terminology is different. In the simplest case, an `fo:table-body` element will contain one `fo:table-row` element for each row in the table, and each `fo:table-row` element will contain one `fo:table-cell` element for each cell, or column, in the row. Finally, the `fo:table-cell` elements contain block-level elements with the actual table content.

This basic FO table structure is illustrated in Listing 8.5, which shows the `fo:table` element required to create the simple table shown in Figure 8.6. You can see that this is a barebones table with no caption or borders.

Listing 8.5: An `fo:table` Element to Create a Simple Table

```
<fo:table>
  <fo:table-body>
  <fo:table-row>
    <fo:table-cell>
      <fo:block>Cell 1</fo:block>
    </fo:table-cell>
    <fo:table-cell>
      <fo:block>Cell 2</fo:block>
    </fo:table-cell>
  </fo:table-row>
<fo:table-row>
    <fo:table-cell>
      <fo:block>Cell 3</fo:block>
```

```
      </fo:table-cell>
      <fo:table-cell>
        <fo:block>Cell 4</fo:block>
      </fo:table-cell>
    </fo:table-row>
<fo:table-row>
      <fo:table-cell>
        <fo:block>Cell 5</fo:block>
      </fo:table-cell>
      <fo:table-cell>
        <fo:block>Cell 6</fo:block>
      </fo:table-cell>
    </fo:table-row>
</fo:table-body>
</fo:table>
```

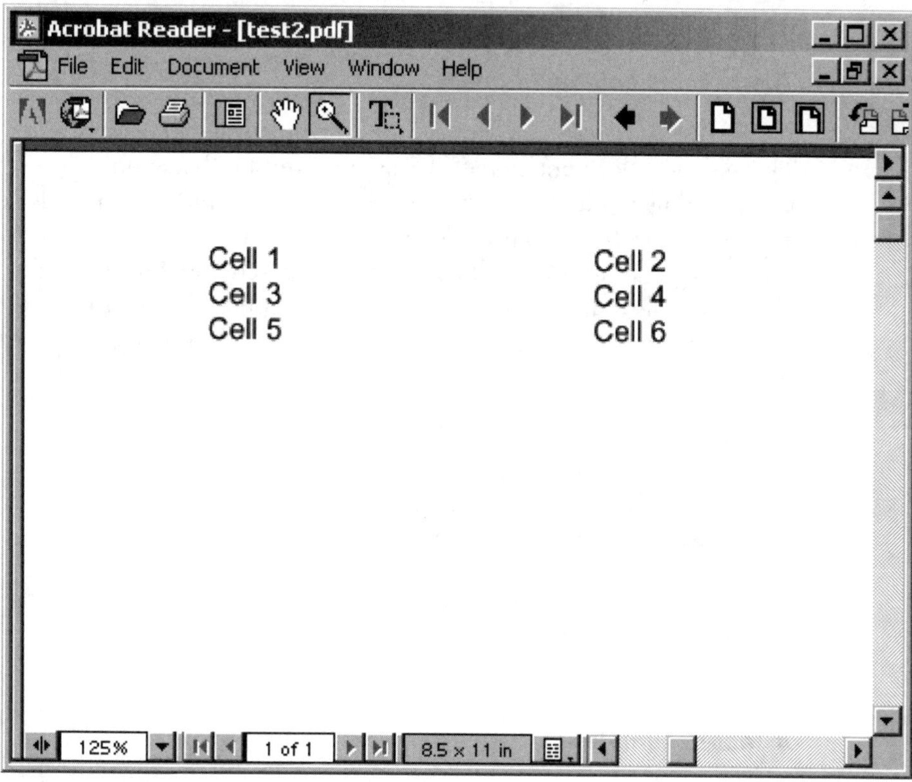

Figure 8.6 The table created by the `fo:table` element in Listing 8.5

The fo:table-header and fo:table-footer Elements

The `fo:table-header` and `fo:table-footer` elements are used to create a header and footer for the table, respectively. A header and footer can be thought of as the first and last rows of the table, which may need special formatting in some situations. They are both optional elements. These elements contain `fo:table-cell` elements that in turn contain the actual text content of the header or footer. The `fo:table-cell` elements can be on their own, or if the header or footer needs more than one row, they can be contained within `fo:table-row` elements. The following example will contain a one-row, two-column header:

```
<fo:table-header>
  <fo:table-cell>
    <fo:block>Header content 1</fo:block>
  </fo:table-cell>
  <fo:table-cell>
    <fo:block>Header content 2</fo:block>
  </fo:table-cell>
</fo:table-header>
```

The fo:table-column Element

The `fo:table-column` element is used to define the characteristics of a column. This element does not actually create a column—that is done when content is inserted using the `fo:table-cell` element—but rather it specifies certain aspects of how the column will appear, such as its width and background. By using an `fo:table-column` element, you can avoid applying attributes individually to all cells in that column. Here is an example of using the `fo:table-column` element to specify that the columns in a three-column table have widths of 0.5, 2, and 3 inches:

```
<fo:table>
   <fo:table-column column-width="0.5in"/>
   <fo:table-column column-width="2in"/>
   <fo:table-column column-width="3in"/>
   <fo:table-body>
    <!-- row and cell elements go here -->
   </fo:table-body>
</fo:table>
```

A Table Example

To pull together what you have learned about creating tables with FO, this section presents a complete example of an FO-XML file that will create a table with a caption, a header, different width rows, and different border styles. This example uses some of the FO attributes that will be covered in the next section, but for the most part their meanings should be clear. Listing 8.6 presents the complete FO-XML file, and Figure 8.7 shows the output.

Listing 8.6 FO-XML File to Create a Table with a Caption

```
<?xml version="1.0"?>
<fo:root xmlns:fo="http://www.w3.org/1999/XSL/Format">

<fo:layout-master-set>
    <fo:simple-page-master margin-right="2in" margin-left="2in"
                           margin-top="0.5in" margin-bottom="0.5in"
                           page-width="8.5in" page-height="11in"
                           master-name="standard">
 <fo:region-body />
    </fo:simple-page-master>
</fo:layout-master-set>

<fo:page-sequence master-name="standard">
<fo:flow flow-name="xsl-region-body">

<fo:table-and-caption>
<fo:table-caption>
  <fo:block>Table 1: Company Officers as of January 1, 2001</fo:block>
</fo:table-caption>
<fo:table margin-top="0.25in" padding="4px">
  <fo:table-column column-width="2in"/>
  <fo:table-column column-width="3in"/>
  <fo:table-header border-width="2px" border-style="solid">
    <fo:table-cell padding="px">
      <fo:block font-weight="bold">Name</fo:block>
    </fo:table-cell>
    <fo:table-cell padding="4px">
      <fo:block font-weight="bold">Title</fo:block>
    </fo:table-cell>
  </fo:table-header>
    <fo:table-body>
    <fo:table-row>
      <fo:table-cell padding="4px" border-width="1px" border-
style="solid">
        <fo:block>Alice Hernandez</fo:block>
      </fo:table-cell>
```

```
      <fo:table-cell padding="4px" border-width="1px" border-
style="solid">
        <fo:block>Chief Executive Officer</fo:block>
      </fo:table-cell>
    </fo:table-row>
    <fo:table-row>
      <fo:table-cell padding="4px" border-width="1px" border-
style="solid">
        <fo:block>Winston Livingstone</fo:block>
      </fo:table-cell>
      <fo:table-cell padding="4px" border-width="1px" border-
style="solid">
        <fo:block>Chief Operating Officer</fo:block>
      </fo:table-cell>
    </fo:table-row>
    <fo:table-row>
      <fo:table-cell padding="4px" border-width="1px" border-
style="solid">
        <fo:block>Akiko Yamaguchi</fo:block>
      </fo:table-cell>
      <fo:table-cell padding="4px" border-width="1px" border-
style="solid">
        <fo:block>Chief Financial Officer</fo:block>
      </fo:table-cell>
    </fo:table-row>
  </fo:table-body>
</fo:table>
</fo:table-and-caption>

</fo:flow>
</fo:page-sequence>

</fo:root>
```

FO Attributes

Many of the details of formatting with FO are controlled by attributes assigned to the various FO elements. Sometimes called FO properties, these attributes control things such as font appearance and size, background color, border style and width, and margins. FO supports over 200 different attributes, and most of them can be applied to more than one kind of FO element. You have seen some examples in the FO demonstration listings that were

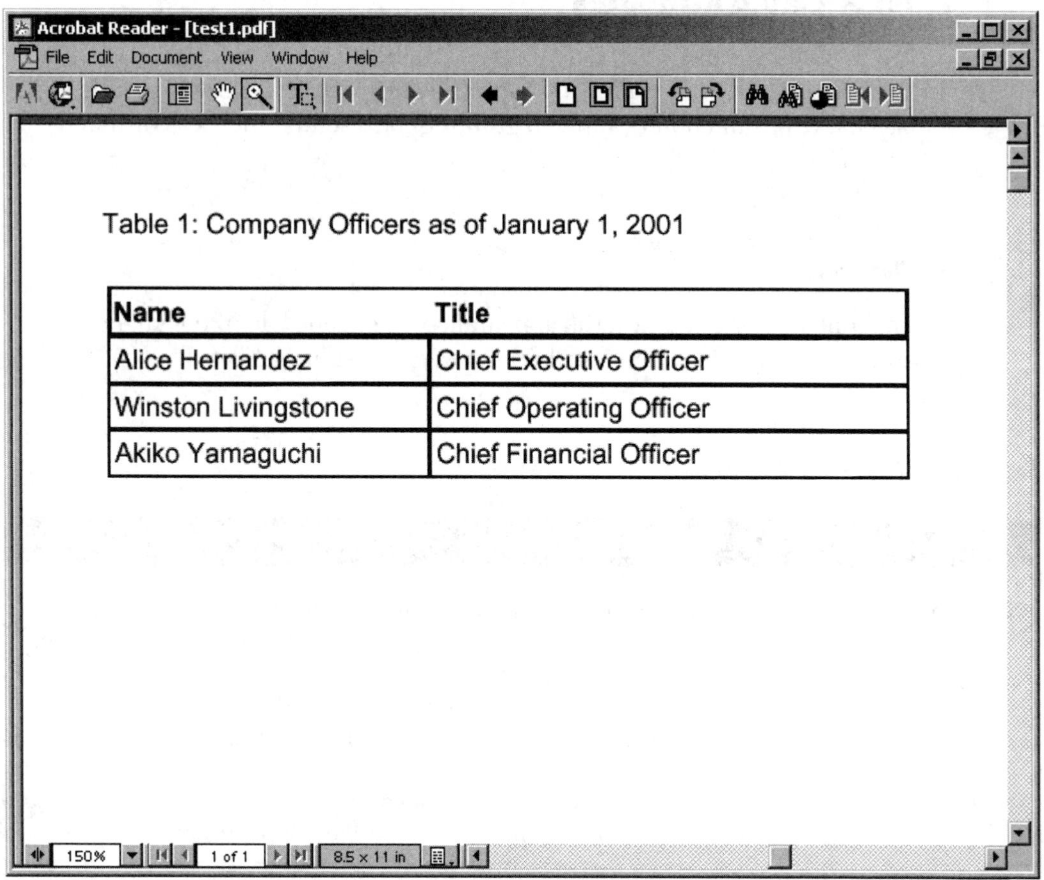

Table 1: Company Officers as of January 1, 2001

Name	Title
Alice Hernandez	Chief Executive Officer
Winston Livingstone	Chief Operating Officer
Akiko Yamaguchi	Chief Financial Officer

Figure 8.7 The table created by the FO-XSL file in Listing 8.6

presented earlier in the chapter. In this section, I provide details on the FO attributes that are most commonly needed.

As with CSS properties, FO attributes exhibit what I call the "trickle-down effect." This means that, in many cases, attributes set for an element will be inherited by the element's descendants unless the same attributes are explicitly set for them. Inheritance can simplify some FO coding tasks because you can set certain attributes once and have them affect multiple parts of the output. The rules of inheritance are tricky, however, and FO rendering engines implement them in different ways, so you'll need to do some experimenting to see exactly where inheritance does and doesn't work.

Text-Related Attributes

Any formatting object that contains text can be assigned various text-related attributes. These are divided into several categories. Some apply to individual characters and others apply to groups of characters, such as words and sentences.

The Font Attributes

The font attributes control the appearance, size, and style of the characters used to display text. These attributes are described in Table 8.1.

Table 8.1 The Font Attributes

Attribute	Description
`font-family`	The name of the preferred font family (typeface). You can list two or more family names in order of preference separated by commas. For example "Helvetica, Arial, sans" specifies that the Helvetica font is the first choice, the Arial font is the second choice, and any sans-serif font is the third choice.
`font-size`	The vertical size of the font consisting of a number followed by a unit. For example, "12pt" specifies 12-point size.
`font-stretch`	The width of the font specified as one of the following values: keyword `condensed expanded`, `extra-condensed`, `extra-expanded`, `narrower`, `normal`, `semi-condensed`, `semi-expanded`, `ultra-condensed`, `ultra-expanded`, or `wider`.
`font-style`	The style of the font specified as one of the following values: `italic`, `normal`, `oblique`, `reverse-normal`, or `reverse-oblique`.
`font-variant`	Either `normal` or `small-caps`
`font-weight`	The thickness of the strokes making up the font specified as one of the following values: `100`, `200`, `300`, `400`, `500`, `600`, `700`, `800`, `900`, `bold`, `bolder`, `lighter`, or `normal`.

The color Attribute

The `color` attribute specifies the color of text in a block or inline area. You can specify color as a hexadecimal RGB value or as one of the following keywords: `aqua`, `black`, `blue`, `fuchsia`, `gray`, `green`, `lime`, `maroon`, `navy`, `olive`, `purple`, `red`, `silver`, `teal`, `white`, or `yellow`. In this example, the word "dangerous" is displayed in red while the remainder of the sentence is in blue:

```
<fo:block color="#0000FF">
It is <fo:inline color="#FF0000">dangerous</fo:inline> to
play with guns!</fo:block>
```

The line-height Attribute

The `line-height` attribute controls the vertical spacing between lines of text. The default is for lines to be spaced according to the size of the font in use. To effectively double-space text, set the `line-height` attribute to twice the font size, as in this example:

```
<fo:block font-size="12pt" line-height="24pt">
<!-- text goes here -->
</fo:block>
```

The Text Alignment Attributes

There are two text alignment attributes: `text-align` and `text-align-last`. The `text-align` attribute specifies how all lines of text in a block, except the last one, are aligned within their area. The `text-align-last` attribute controls the alignment of the last line of text. If the `text-align-last` attribute is omitted, the last line is aligned like the other lines. Possible settings for these attributes are as follows:

- `start`: Left-aligned in languages written left to right
- `center`: Centered
- `end`: Right-aligned in languages written left to right
- `justify`: Expanded with extra space as necessary to fill the entire line (same as full justification in most word processors)
- `left`: Left-aligned regardless of the writing direction
- `right`: Right-aligned regardless of the writing direction
- `inside`: Align with the inside edge of facing pages: the right edge on the left page and the left edge on the right page

- `outside`: Align with the outside edge of facing pages: the left edge on the left page and the right edge on the right page

The Indent Attributes

The indent properties control how lines are indented from the edge of the box that the text is displayed in. Indentation is specified in length units, with negative values specifying an outdent (a hanging indent). Indents are specified relative to the start and end edges, which depend on the direction that the language being used is written. For English, the left edge is the start edge. The four indent attributes are as follows:

- `start-indent`: Indents all lines from the start edge
- `end-indent`: Indents all lines from the end edge
- `text-indent`: Indents the first line of text from the start edge
- `last-line-end-indent`: Indents the last line of text from the end edge

Note that the first line's indentation will be the sum of the `text-indent` and `start-indent` settings. This example indents all lines 1 inch from the left edge, with the first line outdented by 0.6 inch:

```
<fo:block text-indent="-0.6in" start-indent="1.0in">
<!-- text goes here -->
</fo:block>
```

Block Attributes

Certain attributes apply specifically to block areas, as opposed to their contents. They have to do with spacing between and within blocks, and with borders. When using these attributes, you may want to refer to the content/padding/border/margin structure of an FO area, as described earlier in this chapter.

The Background Attributes

The background attributes control the appearance of an area's background. They are identical in many ways to the background properties used in CSS. The FO background attributes are described in Table 8.2.

The following example defines a block area with a background image that will be placed at the upper-left corner of the box and be repeated as needed to fill the box:

Table 8.2 The Background Attributes

Attribute	Description
`background-attachment`	Set to `scroll` to permit the background to scroll within the enclosing area or to `fixed` to have the background fixed within its enclosing area.
`background-color`	Sets the background color as a hexadecimal RGB value, a color keyword, or the keyword `transparent`.
`background-image`	Specifies the URI of an image to be used as the background or the keyword `none`.
`background-position`	Specifies the position of a background image. Set to `left`, `right`, `bottom`, `middle`, `top`, or to a pair of length values specifying the vertical and horizontal distance between the top-left corner of the image and the top-left corner of the padding area.
`background-repeat`	Specifies how an image is to be repeated if it is smaller than its box. Set to `repeat`, `no-repeat`, `repeat-x`, or `repeat-y`.

```
<fo:block background-image="\images\chalk.gif"
          background-position="0,0"
          background-repeat="repeat"
Block content goes here.
</fo:block>
```

The Size Attributes

The size attributes control the size of a box's content area. The total size of a box includes its size plus its padding, margins, and border. The size attributes are as follows:

- `height`
- `width`
- `max-height`
- `max-width`

- min-height
- min-width

These attributes can be set to any value consisting of a number followed by a unit abbreviation. You can also set the height and width attributes to “auto,” which is the default value and results in the box being sized according to its content. In no circumstances will a box be made larger or smaller than the sizes specified by the max-xxx and min-xxx attributes. The following example displays the text in a box with a content area with height of 1 centimeter and width determined automatically, but no less than 2 centimeters:

```
<fo:block height="1cm" min-width="2cm">
This is the text to display.
</fo.block>
```

The Margin Properties

The margin properties control the size of a box’s margin, the area between its border and surrounding boxes. There are two ways to set a box’s margins. The first is provided for compatibility with CSS and provides the following five attributes:

- margin-top
- margin-bottom
- margin-left
- margin-right
- margin

Use the first four attributes to set individual margins or the margin attribute to set all four margins to the same value. Each of these attributes can be set to a specific length value or to a percentage. The percentage settings are calculated using the box’s containing block, except for the margin-top and margin-bottom attributes in page context, where the page box height is used.

The second way to set margins is better suited to the FO model and should be used where possible. The four relevant attributes are as follows:

- space-before (top margin)
- space-after (bottom margin)
- start-indent (left margin)
- end-indent (right margin)

The last two attributes were mentioned earlier in this chapter in the section "The Indent Attributes." Taken together, these four attributes can be used to effectively control the margin of a box area. Each of these attributes can be set to a single length value. They can also be set using the following syntax:

```
"min;max;ideal;discard;force"
```

- `min` is a length value specifying the smallest size that can be used.
- `max` is a length value specifying the largest size that can be used.
- `ideal` is a length value specifying the ideal size to use.
- `discard` is an optional keyword specifying that any extra space will be discarded.
- `force` is an optional keyword specifying that this space specifier overrides any conflicting space specifiers.

Here is an example of using these attributes to specify that a block of text will have a minimum of 0.1 inch, a maximum of 0.5 inch, and ideally 0.25 inch of space on all four sides:

```
<fo:block space-before="0.1in;0.5in;0.25in"
          space-after="0.1in;0.5in;0.25in"
          start-indent="0.1in;0.5in;0.25in"
          end-indent="0.1in;0.5in;0.25in">
This is the text that will be displayed.
</fo:block>
```

The Border Attributes

The border attributes specify the type of border that will be displayed around a block area. There are two sets of parallel attributes: one set for compatibility with CSS syntax and another set more in tune with FO syntax. You can use either, as you choose. The border-related attributes take the following general form:

```
border-XXX-YYY
```

XXX specifies the border being set and can be one of the following:

- `before` or `top`: The upper border
- `after` or `bottom`: The lower border
- `start` or `left`: The left border
- `end` or `right`: The right border

Table 8.3 Style Settings for the Border Attributes

Border Style Setting	Description
`dashed`	A dashed line.
`dotted`	A dotted line.
`double`	A double line.
`groove`	A 3D groove using colors based on the `color` attribute.
`inset`	A 3D inset using colors based on the `color` attribute.
`none`	No border is drawn. This is the default.
`outset`	A 3D outset using colors based on the `color` attribute.
`ridge`	A 3D ridge using colors based on the `color` attribute.
`solid`	A solid line.

YYY specifies the aspect of the border being set and can be one of the following:

- `color`: The color of the border specified as a color keyword or as a hexadecimal RGB value
- `style`: The style of the border using one of the keywords in Table 8.3
- `width`: The width of the border using a length value

You can also use the shorthand border attributes, which have the form `border-`*YYY*, to set all four sections of an area's border at once. This example creates an area with a 4-pixel-wide dotted blue border on all sides:

```
<fo:block border-style="dotted"
          border-color="blue"
          border-width="4px">
This is the text displayed in the area.
</fo:block>
```

An XSLT-FO Demonstration

All the examples in this chapter were presented in FO-XML code. You will, however, almost never write FO-XML code directly. Rather, you will create an XSL style sheet that contains the XSLT commands to transform the original XML document into an FO-XML document. Then, the resulting FO-XML document can be processed by a rendering agent to produce the final output. Knowing how XSLT works, and knowing the FO elements and attributes that are needed to produce the desired result, you can design your XSL style sheet accordingly.

It is, however, always helpful to see a working example of a technique, and that's what I present in this section. Listing 8.7 shows a simple XML file that contains some inventory data. The objective is to create an XSL style sheet that will transform Listing 8.7 into an FO-XML document to display the data as a table with a heading and a caption. The XSL style sheet is shown in Listing 8.8.

The resulting FO-XML file is shown in Listing 8.9. Note that the actual output of the MSXSL processor will not be formatted nicely like in this listing, but that should not matter as FO-XML files are usually not read or edited by humans. Finally, the output generated by the FO-XML file, after being converted to a PDF file, is shown in Figure 8.8.

Listing 8.7 XML Data File to be Transformed by the XSL Style Sheet in Listing 8.8

```
<?xml version="1.0"?>
<?xml-stylesheet type="text/xsl" href="list0808.xsl"?>
<inventory>
  <item>
    <name>Greek Olives</name>
    <stockno>GK1332</stockno>
    <weight>15oz</weight>
    <cost>2.25</cost>
  </item>
  <item>
    <name>Tomato paste</name>
    <stockno>ZN332</stockno>
    <weight>32oz</weight>
    <cost>1.95</cost>
  </item>
  <item>
    <name>Olive oil</name>
    <stockno>FQ098</stockno>
```

```
    <weight>8oz</weight>
    <cost>4.00</cost>
  </item>
  <item>
    <name>Anchovies</name>
    <stockno>DF9987</stockno>
    <weight>4oz</weight>
    <cost>1.17</cost>
  </item>
  <item>
    <name>Wine vinegar</name>
    <stockno>UJ877</stockno>
    <weight>16oz</weight>
    <cost>3.54</cost>
  </item>
</inventory>
```

Listing 8.8 XSL Style Sheet to Transform Listing 8.7 into an FO-XML Document

```
<?xml version="1.0"?>
<xsl:stylesheet xmlns:xsl="http://www.w3.org/1999/XSL/Transform"
     version="1.0"
     xmlns:fo="http://www.w3.org/1999/XSL/Format">
<xsl:output method="xml" encoding="utf-8"/>
<xsl:template match="/">
<fo:root>
  <fo:layout-master-set>
    <fo:simple-page-master margin-right="1in" margin-left="1in"
                           margin-top="0.5in" margin-bottom="0.5in"
                           page-width="8.5in" page-height="11in"
                           master-name="only">
      <fo:region-body/>
    </fo:simple-page-master>
  </fo:layout-master-set>

  <fo:page-sequence master-name="only">
    <fo:flow flow-name="xsl-region-body">
    <fo:table-and-caption>
      <fo:table-caption>
        <fo:block>New Product Listing</fo:block>
      </fo:table-caption>
      <fo:table margin-top="0.25in" >
      <fo:table-header border-bottom-width="2px"
```

```
                    border-bottom-style="solid">
        <fo:table-cell><fo:block>Item</fo:block></fo:table-cell>
        <fo:table-cell><fo:block>Item #</fo:block></fo:table-cell>
        <fo:table-cell><fo:block>Size</fo:block></fo:table-cell>
        <fo:table-cell><fo:block>Cost</fo:block></fo:table-cell>
      </fo:table-header>
      <fo:table-body>

      <xsl:apply-templates/>

      </fo:table-body>
      </fo:table>
      </fo:table-and-caption>
    </fo:flow>
  </fo:page-sequence>
</fo:root>

</xsl:template>

<xsl:template match="item">
  <fo:table-row>
    <fo:table-cell>
      <fo:block><xsl:value-of select="name"/></fo:block>
    </fo:table-cell>
    <fo:table-cell>
      <fo:block><xsl:value-of select="stockno"/></fo:block>
    </fo:table-cell>
    <fo:table-cell>
      <fo:block><xsl:value-of select="weight"/></fo:block>
    </fo:table-cell>
    <fo:table-cell>
      <fo:block><xsl:value-of select="cost"/></fo:block>
    </fo:table-cell>
  </fo:table-row>

</xsl:template>

</xsl:stylesheet>
```

Listing 8.9 FO-XML File Generated by Applying the XSL Style Sheet in Listing 8.8 to the XML File in Listing 8.7

```
<?xml version="1.0" encoding="utf-8"?>
<fo:root xmlns:fo="http://www.w3.org/1999/XSL/Format">
```

```
<fo:layout-master-set>
<fo:simple-page-master margin-right="1in" margin-left="1in" margin-
top="0.5in" margin-bottom="0.5in" page-width="8.5in" page-height="11in"
master-name="only">
<fo:region-body />
</fo:simple-page-master>
</fo:layout-master-set>
<fo:page-sequence master-name="only">
<fo:flow flow-name="xsl-region-body">
<fo:table-and-caption>
<fo:table-caption>
<fo:block>New Product Listing</fo:block>
</fo:table-caption>
<fo:table margin-top="0.25in">
<fo:table-header border-bottom-width="2px" border-bottom-style="solid">
  <fo:table-cell><fo:block>Item</fo:block></fo:table-cell>
  <fo:table-cell><fo:block>Item #</fo:block></fo:table-cell>
  <fo:table-cell><fo:block>Size</fo:block></fo:table-cell>
  <fo:table-cell><fo:block>Cost</fo:block></fo:table-cell>
</fo:table-header>
<fo:table-body>
  <fo:table-row>
    <fo:table-cell><fo:block>Greek Olives</fo:block></fo:table-cell>
    <fo:table-cell><fo:block>GK1332</fo:block></fo:table-cell>
    <fo:table-cell><fo:block>15oz</fo:block></fo:table-cell>
    <fo:table-cell><fo:block>2.25</fo:block></fo:table-cell>
  </fo:table-row>
  <fo:table-row>
    <fo:table-cell><fo:block>Tomato paste</fo:block></fo:table-cell>
    <fo:table-cell><fo:block>ZN332</fo:block></fo:table-cell>
    <fo:table-cell><fo:block>32oz</fo:block></fo:table-cell>
    <fo:table-cell><fo:block>1.95</fo:block></fo:table-cell><
  /fo:table-row>
  <fo:table-row>
    <fo:table-cell><fo:block>Olive oil</fo:block></fo:table-cell>
    <fo:table-cell><fo:block>FQ098</fo:block></fo:table-cell>
    <fo:table-cell><fo:block>8oz</fo:block></fo:table-cell>
    <fo:table-cell><fo:block>4.00</fo:block></fo:table-cell>
  </fo:table-row>
  <fo:table-row>
    <fo:table-cell><fo:block>Anchovies</fo:block></fo:table-cell>
    <fo:table-cell><fo:block>DF9987</fo:block></fo:table-cell>
    <fo:table-cell><fo:block>4oz</fo:block></fo:table-cell>
    <fo:table-cell><fo:block>1.17</fo:block></fo:table-cell>
```

```
      </fo:table-row>
      <fo:table-row>
        <fo:table-cell><fo:block>Wine vinegar</fo:block></fo:table-cell>
        <fo:table-cell><fo:block>UJ877</fo:block></fo:table-cell>
        <fo:table-cell><fo:block>16oz</fo:block></fo:table-cell>
        <fo:table-cell><fo:block>3.54</fo:block></fo:table-cell>
      </fo:table-row>
    </fo:table-body>
    </fo:table>
    </fo:table-and-caption>
    </fo:flow>
    </fo:page-sequence>
    </fo:root>
```

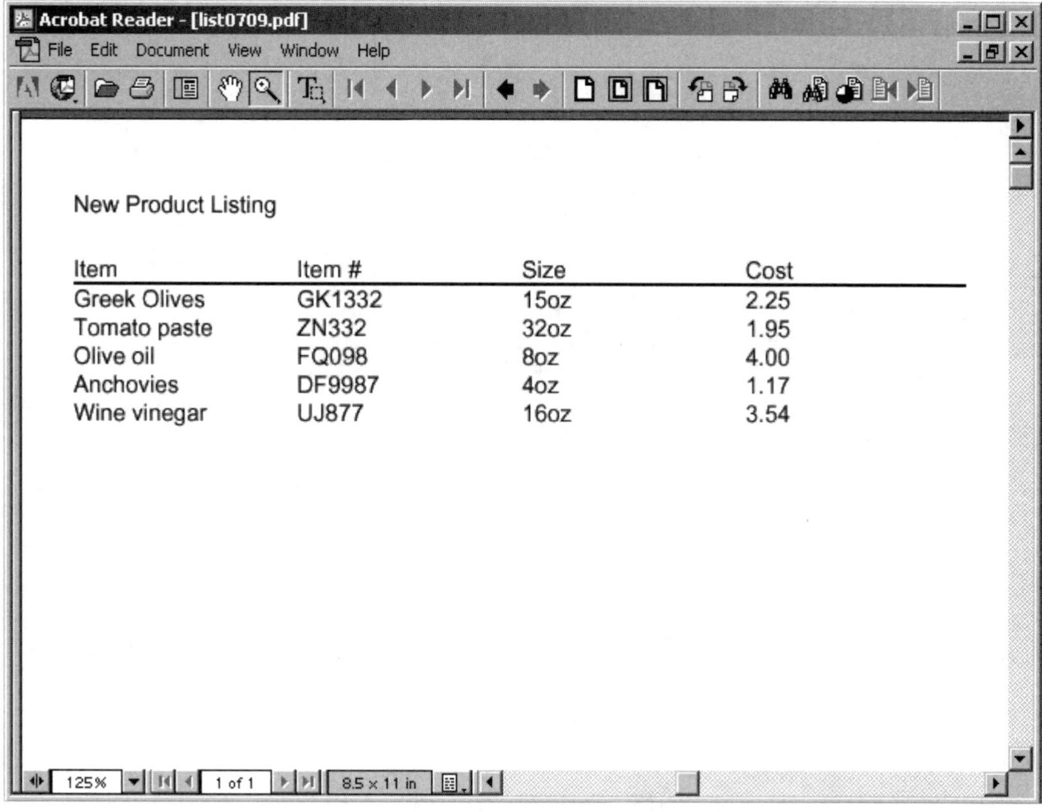

Figure 8.8 The output of the FO-XML file generated by the example code

Summary

Formatting Objects (FO) is a very promising technology with limited but growing support. As of this writing, it is supported by various software vendors but not by Microsoft. It offers significant advantages over Cascading Style Sheets (CSS) for complex formatting, and it also has the potential to handle situations where nonvisual output is required. Even so, CSS remains a valuable tool and is in fact preferred in many situations over FO because of its relative simplicity and much wider support. Over the next few years, however, FO will almost surely increase in importance.

CHAPTER 9

XLink and XPointer

XLink and XPointer are related standards in that they both act as a sort of "look here" signpost. As a result, I cover them in the same chapter. However, the two standards differ in *what* they point at. At the risk of oversimplifying to some extent, XLink is designed to create links between entire documents, or resources. In contrast, XPointer is used to link to specific locations within a document. Their uses are related but distinct. As of this writing, XLink is a W3C Recommendation and XPointer is a Candidate Recommendation.

XLink

XML Linking Language, or XLink, uses XML syntax to define links between resources, with a resource being essentially any accessible file, whether an XML file or a file in some other format. In this way, XLink is similar to the hyperlinks that are used in HTML documents, but XLink is a lot more powerful, with the capability to define bidirectional and even more complex links. For example, XLink has the capability to perform various tasks such as creating a table of contents or an index for a document, or defining one or more paths a student can take through an online course.

While XLink is currently a W3C Recommendation, in terms of implementation it is a new, emerging technology. It has a great deal of promise, but at the time of this writing support is limited. For example, browser support for XLink is limited to treating XLinks as simple, one-directional links that work the same way as HTML hyperlinks. Your custom applications can support more XLink features, and improved support in browsers is on the way.

XLink provides two general types of links. A *simple* link defines a one-way link to a resource and provides essentially the same functionality as a regular HTML link. An *extended* link describes a set of one- or two-directional links between a set of two or more resources, and as such it provides significantly enhanced functionality over HTML links.

Simple Links

A simple link defines a one-way link between a starting resource and an ending resource. The starting resource is always an XML element that is defined as a link by means of XLink syntax. The ending resource is identified by a URI. The URI can, but does not have to be, a URL. A simple XLink link is directly analogous to the standard HTML link that most people are familiar with.

Any XML document that uses XLink must define the XLink namespace. The namespace is "http://www.w3.org/1999/xlink," and the namespace prefix associated with it is traditionally "xlink." Although another prefix can be used, it would serve, I think, only to confuse people. The namespace must be defined at or above the highest (that is, closest to the root) element in the document that uses XLink, and it is often done in the root element. For example, in an XML document whose root element is "books," you could define the namespace like this:

```
<books xmlns:xlink=" http://www.w3.org/1999/xlink">
...
</books>
```

Once the namespace is defined, the minimum steps required to create a simple link are to add the following two attributes to the element:

- `xlink:type` specifies the type of the link. For a simple link, the type is "simple."
- `xlink:href` specifies the target URI of the link.

The following example creates a link to the indicated URL:

```
<AnyElement xlink:type="simple"
            xlink:href="http://www.somewhere.com/info.txt">
...
</AnyElement>
```

> ***XLink and Document Schemas***
>
> *If a document is going to be validated against a schema, the schema must take XLink attributes into account. In the preceding example, the schema for the* `AnyElement` *element must specify that the element can (or must, depending on your needs) have the* `xlink:type` *and* `xlink:href` *attributes.*

You can use XLink to create links from document elements that also hold other elements and data. The following is an example of a "book" element that contains information on a book as well as a link to an image of the author:

```
<book xlink:type="simple"
      xlink:href="http://www.somewhere.com/images/tolstoy.jpg">
  <title>War and Peace</title>
  <author>Leo Tolstoy</author>
  <category>fiction</category>
</book>
```

You can also create elements that have no children or content, but serve only as a link. Here's an example:

```
<mylink xlink:type="simple"
        xlink:href="http://www.somewhere.com/summary.htm"/>
```

A link can have a title and a description specified by the `xlink:title` and `xlink:role` attributes, respectively. The `xlink:title` attribute is typically used for a short text note that might, for example, be displayed as a tool tip for the link. The `xlink:role` attribute is a URI that provides information about the resource being pointed to by the link. The information pointed to by the `xlink:role` attribute is generally not meant to be read by the user, but rather it can be used by the software that is processing the link. Here is an example of assigning a title and a role to a link:

```
<book xlink:type="simple"
      xlink:href="http://www.somewhere.com/images/tolstoy.jpg">
      xlink:title="Picture of Tolstoy"
      xlink:role="http://www.tolstoy.org"
  <title>War and Peace</title>
  <author>Leo Tolstoy</author>
  <category>fiction</category>
</book>
```

It is important to note that use of the `title` and `role` attributes is entirely up to the processing application. The URI pointed to by the `role` attribute may indicate a file that will be read, or it may just serve as a form of unique identification (similar to a namespace).

A simple link can also contain attributes that define the behavior of the link. The `xlink:show` attribute defines what happens when the link is activated, and the `xlink:actuate` attribute specifies when the link should be activated.

Table 9.1 Settings for the `show` Attribute

Value	Description
`embed`	The linked resource will be displayed embedded in the current document.
`new`	The linked resource will be displayed in a new window.
`other`	The link behavior is defined elsewhere.
`replace`	The linked resource will replace the current document.
`none`	There are no constraints on link behavior.

Table 9.2 Settings for the `actuate` Attribute

Value	Description
`onLoad`	The link is activated when the document is loaded.
`onRequest`	The link is activated when some event occurs—for example, when the user clicks the link.
`other`	The link activation behavior is defined elsewhere.
`none`	There are no constraints on link activation.

Settings for the `show` and `actuate` attributes are described in Table 9.1 and Table 9.2.

Extended Links

An extended link describes a collection of resources and the paths among them. An individual resource in the collection can be linked to any or all of the other resources, to none of them, and even back to itself. In effect, an extended link defines relationships between resources. The link says nothing about what is actually done with these relationships—that is up to the processing software. At present, software support of extended links is essentially nonexistent, so the types of uses that will be devised for extended links remains to be seen.

To create an extended link, use the `xlink:type` attribute with the value "extended." The following example defines the "bookreview" element as an extended link:

```
<bookreview xlink:type="extended">
...
</bookreview>
```

An extended link can have `xlink:title` and `xlink:role` attributes that serve the same purposes as they do in a simple link. Other link details are provided by elements that are placed within the link element. These elements are as follows:

- `locator`: Identifies a remote resource
- `resource`: Defines a local resource
- `arc`: Defines traversal information between two resources
- `title`: Defines a title for the link

The locator Element

The `locator` element identifies an individual remote resource that is part of the extended link. A `locator` element has five attributes associated with it.

- `xlink:type`: Required. Must be set to "locator."
- `xlink:href`: Required. The URL of the remote resource.
- `xlink:role`: Optional. A URI that provides information about the resource being pointed to by the link.
- `xlink:title`: Optional. The title of the link.
- `xlink:label`: Optional. A name identifying the resource. A label must be provided if the link is to be referenced in an `arc` element.

The `xlink:role` and `xlink:title` attributes play the same role here as they do with a simple link. Here is an example of an extended link:

```
<booklink xlink:type="extended" xlink:title="Some book reviews">
  <review xlink:type="locator"
          xlink:title="War and Peace"
          xlink:role="http://www.mysite.com/tolstoy"
          xlink:href="http://www.mysite.com/war_and_peace.htm"/>
```

```
  <review xlink:type="locator"
          xlink:title="Swann's Way"
          xlink:role="http://www.mysite.com/proust"
          xlink:href="http://www.mysite.com/swanns_way.htm"/>
  <review xlink:type="locator"
          xlink:title="Absalom, Absalom!"
          xlink:role="http://www.mysite.com/faulkner"
          xlink:href="http://www.mysite.com/absalom_absalom.htm"/>
</booklink>
```

What would happen if an XLink application processed the document containing this extended link? That would be totally up to the application, but one possibility would be that it would display a list of the books in a pop-up menu. The user would select a book to view the review, and based on the `xlink:role` attribute, additional information about the book's author could be presented as well. The processing software could also provide links between the resources—for example, while a user views the review of *War and Peace,* links to the other two reviews might be displayed. This is potentially very powerful stuff, and it goes well beyond what can be done with HTML.

The resource Element

The `resource` element defines a local resource. The information provided by a local resource is contained in the element itself and is not external to the XML file. A `resource` element must have the `xlink:type` attribute set to "resource." It can also have optional `xlink:title`, `xlink:role`, and `xlink:label` attributes that serve the same purposes as described previously for the `locator` element. In almost all cases, a `resource` element will contain child elements that hold the actual information.

The following example builds on the example presented previously for the `locator` element. It adds `resource` elements that provide information about each book's author and original language.

```
<booklink xlink:type="extended" xlink:title="Some book reviews">
  <bookinfo xlink:type="resource"
    <title>War and Peace</title>
    <author>Leo Tolstoy</author>
    <language>Russian</language>
  </bookinfo>
  <bookinfo xlink:type="resource"
    <title>Swann's Way</title>
    <author>Marcel Proust</author>
    <language>French</language>
```

```
  </bookinfo>
  <bookinfo xlink:type="resource"
    <title>Absalom, Absalom!</title>
    <author>William Faulkner</author>
    <language>English</language>
  </bookinfo>
  <review xlink:type="locator"
          xlink:title="War and Peace"
          xlink:role="http://www.mysite.com/tolstoy"
          xlink:href="http://www.mysite.com/war_and_peace.htm"/>
  <review xlink:type="locator"
          xlink:title="Swann's Way"
          xlink:role="http://www.mysite.com/proust"
          xlink:href="http://www.mysite.com/swanns_way.htm"/>
  <review xlink:type="locator"
          xlink:title="Absalom Absalom!"
          xlink:role="http://www.mysite.com/faulkner"
          xlink:href="http://www.mysite.com/absalom_absalom.htm"/>
</booklink>
```

Again, the use that the processing application makes of the information in the `resource` elements is completely open.

The arc Element

The `arc` element specifies traversal information among an extended link's participating resources. In order to use a resource in an `arc` element, the `resource` or `locator` element must be assigned a name using the `xlink:label` attribute. The `arc` element has the following attributes:

- `xlink:type`: Required. Must be set to "arc."
- `xlink:title`: Optional. The title of the `arc`.
- `xlink:arcrole`: Optional. A URI that provides information about the link (similar to the `xlink:role` attribute for other elements).
- `xlink:show`: Optional. Specifies what happens when the link is activated.
- `xlink:actuate`: Optional. Specifies when the link is activated.
- `xlink:from`: Optional. Identifies the "from" resource by its `xlink:label` attribute. If omitted, all resources in the extended link are treated as sources.

- `xlink:to`: Optional. Identifies the "to" resource by its `xlink:label` attribute. If omitted, all resources in the extended link are treated as targets.

The following is an example that expands on the earlier example of book review resources. Each `locator` element is given an `xlink:label` attribute to identify it. Then, `arc` elements are added to define the following traversals:

- From *War and Peace* to *Swann's Way*
- From *Swann's Way* to *Absalom, Absalom!*
- From *Absalom, Absalom!* to *War and Peace*

Note that in this example the `arc` elements are actually named "arc," but this is not required.

```
<booklink xlink:type="extended" xlink:title="Some book reviews">
  <review xlink:type="locator"
          xlink:title="War and Peace"
          xlink:role="http://www.mysite.com/tolstoy"
          xlink:href="http://www.mysite.com/war_and_peace.htm"
          xlink:label="A"/>
  <review xlink:type="locator"
          xlink:title="Swann's Way"
          xlink:role="http://www.mysite.com/proust"
          xlink:href="http://www.mysite.com/swanns_way.htm"
          xlink:label="B"/>
  <review xlink:type="locator"
          xlink:title="Absalom, Absalom!"
          xlink:role="http://www.mysite.com/faulkner"
          xlink:href="http://www.mysite.com/absalom_absalom.htm"
          xlink:label="C"/>
  <arc xlink:type="arc" xlink:from="A" xlink:to="B"
       xlink:actuate="onRequest" xlink:title="Next review"/>
  <arc xlink:type="arc" xlink:from="B" xlink:to="C"
       xlink:actuate="onRequest"" xlink:title="Next review"/>
  <arc xlink:type="arc" xlink:from="C" xlink:to="A"
       xlink:actuate="onRequest" xlink:title="Next review"/>
</booklink>
```

The processing application can use the `arc` information in whatever way is needed. For example, Next and Previous buttons could be provided to move forward and backward between book reviews using the defined traversals. This example presents a very simple set of traversals, and more complex ones are possible, including bidirectional traversals (from A to B and from B to A) and multibranched traversals (from A to B, C, and D).

The title Element

The `title` element can appear as a child of `extended`, `locator`, `resource`, or `arc` elements, and it can contain its own child elements. Using the `title` element provides more flexibility than using the `xlink:title` attribute. For example, different data can be provided for different languages:

```
<name xlink:type="title" xml:lang="en">Peter</name>
<name xlink:type="title" xml:lang="fr">Pierre</name>
<name xlink:type="title" xml:lang="sp">Pedro</name>
```

How the information in `title` elements is used is completely up to the processing application.

XPointer

XPointer is a syntax for identifying specific locations within XML documents. In some ways, XPointer provides the same capabilities as the `#name` reference in HTML `<a>` anchor tags, permitting a user to navigate directly to a specific location in the document. The HTML syntax, however, has a significant limitation in that every location that you want to jump to must be identified with an `<a>` tag. XPointer permits you to reference any part of an XML document without the need for special tags. Typically, XPointer is used in conjunction with XLink: The document, or resource, is identified with XLink and a specific part of the document is identified with XPointer. Sometimes an XPointer expression, or more concisely just an XPointer, is called a *fragment identifier.*

All XPointers have the following syntax:

```
xpointer(expression)
```

`Expression` identifies the part of the document being pointed to. The `xpointer` keyword identifies the scheme and currently is the only scheme available. In the future, the scheme may be used to identify a particular version of XPointer or another language for locating parts of documents.

Be aware than an XPointer does not always refer to a single, unique location in a document. An XPointer can identify zero, one, or more than one location. A "location" reference by an XPointer is usually a document element, but it can also be a range of elements, a point, a section of text, or an attribute node.

XPointers in Links

An XPointer references a location in a document, but which document? To specify an XPointer in an external document, reference the document using XLink syntax, and then follow the XLink with the number sign (#) and the XPointer. Here's an example:

```
http://www.mysite.com/data.xml#xpointer(expression)
```

You can also use XPointers on their own to reference locations within the current document. You still need to precede the XPointer with the number sign (#).

Using XPath Expressions with XPointer

XPointer is an extension of the XPath language covered in Chapter 7, and in fact, the syntax is quite similar. You can create a valid XPointer by constructing an XPath expression and enclosing it in the parentheses of `xpointer()`. Following are some examples of using XPath expressions to create XPointers. You can refer to Chapter 7 if you need more information on the syntax of XPath expressions.

- `xpointer(/booklist/book[1])`: Points to the first "book" element that is a child of the root "booklist" element
- `xpointer(book[title="War and Peace"])`: Points to the "book" element that has a child "title" element containing the text "War and Peace"
- `xpointer(*[@title])`: Points to any element that has an attribute named "title"
- `xpointer(id["heading"])`: Points to an element with a type `ID` attribute with the value "heading"

In many situations, XPath syntax is all you will need to create an XPointer. Sometimes, however, you will need to use the XPointer extensions, those elements of XPointer syntax that are not part of XPath. These extensions are described in the following sections.

Bare Names

A *bare name* XPointer is a convenient way to identify an element by means of a type `ID` attribute. Recall that an `ID` attribute is an attribute that is declared to have type `ID` in the XML document's schema. An element can have at most one type `ID` attribute, and the attribute does not need to be named "ID." Bare name XPointers cannot be used with documents that do not have schemas, because a schema is required to create type `ID` attributes.

A bare name is not enclosed in `xpointer()` but is placed by itself following the number sign (#). The following link points to an element with a type `ID` attribute that has the value "fiction":

```
http://www.mysite.com/books.xml#fiction
```

Child Sequences

You use a *child sequence* to reference a child element in terms of its relationship with its ancestor elements. When using this technique, the names or data of the elements are irrelevant. You can use child sequences to locate an element with respect to the document or root element with this syntax:

```
#/1/3/2
```

The preceding example references the second child of the third child of the root element. In this syntax, `/1` refers to the root element. You can also combine a child sequence with a bare name as shown here:

```
#fiction/2/1
```

This XPointer references the first child of the second child of the element that has a type `ID` attribute with the value "fiction."

Points

A *point* is used to refer to a specific location that is not a node in an XML document. This is in contrast to XPath expressions, bare names, and child sequences, which are limited to referencing individual nodes or sets of nodes. A point can refer to locations such as the first word of the third paragraph or the year portion of a date. A point can reference just about anything in an XML document, including the content of comments and processing instructions. A point cannot, however, be inside an entity reference, although it can be inside the entity's replacement text.

A point is identified first by its container node. Remember that an XML node can be an element, an attribute, a namespace, a text node, or a comment. Within that node, points exist as follows:

- If the node contains children, a point exists immediately before and after each of the child nodes, as well as after the node's opening tag and before the node's closing tag.
- If the node does not contain children, a point exists before and after each character in the node's string value.

This is demonstrated by the following XML element:

```
<book category="fiction">
    <title>War and Peace</title>
    <author>Leo Tolstoy</author>
</book>
```

The "book" node has children, so the points it contains are defined by its opening and closing tags as well as its child nodes. The location and number of the "book" node's points are indicated by the numbers in curly braces (note that point numbering starts at 0):

```
<book category="fiction">{0}
   {1}<title>War and Peace</title>{2}
   {3}<author>Leo Tolstoy</author>{4}
{5}</book>
```

The text node child of the "title" element contains 13 points numbered 0 through 12. The first is before the "W" and the last is before the final "e."

To create an XPointer that references a point, use the `point` node test in an XPath expression. The general syntax is as follows:

```
expression/point[position()=n]
```

`Expression` is an XPath expression that identifies the node containing the point, and *`n`* is the index of the desired point. Here is an XPointer that references the point before the first character in the first "book" element's "category" attribute value:

```
xpointer(//book[position()=1]/@category/point[position()=0]
```

There are two functions provided by the XPointer specification that simplify the task of referencing the point immediately before or immediately after an element or text node: `start-point()` and `end-point()`. Each function takes as its argument an XPath expression identifying the element or text node. For example, this XPointer references the point immediately before the second "book" element:

```
xpointer(start-point(//book[position()=2]))
```

When working with points, an error occurs if a `point` node test points to a location before the start or after the end of the referenced node. The processing application can respond to or ignore such errors as desired.

Ranges

A *range* represents the parsed character data between two points. It can contain any part of an XML document, from a few characters to the entire root node. A range need not contain entire nodes. XPointer provides four functions for creating ranges.

The range() Function

The `range()` function takes an XPath expression as its argument and returns a range for each node that is selected by the XPath expression. For example, for a node that is an element, this function returns a range that includes the element's start tag, end tag, and everything in between. Here is an XPointer using the `range()` function:

```
xpointer(range(//book))
```

If there is only one "book" element, this XPointer selects the entire element, including its start and end tags. If there are multiple "book" elements, it returns one range for each such element. If there are no "book" elements, it returns no range.

Here is another `range()` example:

```
xpointer(range(//book[position()=1]/*))
```

This returns one range for each child of the first "book" element.

The range-inside() Function

The `range-inside()` function works exactly the same as the `range()` function except when applied to element nodes. In that case, `range-inside()` returns the content of the element without the start and end tags, while `range()` returns the entire element including the start and end tags.

The range-to() Function

The `range-to()` function returns a range including everything from a specified start location up to and including a specified end location. The syntax is as follows:

```
xpointer(start-expression/range-to(end-expression))
```

`Start-expression` and *`end-expression`* are XPath expressions identifying the start node and end node, respectively. The following example references everything starting with the "book" element and ending with the next "author" element:

```
xpointer(//book/range-to(year))
```

The string-range() Function

The `string-range()` function differs from the other range-related functions in that it operates only on the text of a document, minus all markup. In other words, tags are ignored. The syntax is as follows:

```
xpointer(string-range(expression, text))
```

`Expression` is an XPath expression identifying the nodes to process. *`Text`* is the text to locate. For example, this XPointer references a range for every occurrence of the text "Tolstoy" in all "author" elements:

```
xpointer(string-range(//author, "Tolstoy"))
```

You can include two optional arguments to offset the range with respect to the found text. The syntax is as follows:

```
xpointer(string-range(expression, text, offset, length))
```

The returned range will begin *`offset`* characters from the found text and will include *`length`* characters.

Summary

XLink and XPointer are distinct but related vocabularies that are used to identify and link to resources. XLink provides links between resources, supporting simple one-directional links as well as more sophisticated multidirectional links. XPointer identifies specific locations within a resource and has the significant advantage of not requiring any special tag to serve as a link target. While software support for XLink and XPointer is limited at present, this situation is sure to change.

CHAPTER 10

Using the Document Object Model

The Document Object Model (DOM) is one of the most important tools that you have for working with XML documents. If you write programs that access and manipulate the data in XML documents, you'll probably use DOM. (The other tool for programmatically working with XML documents, the Simple API for XML, or SAX, is covered in Chapter 11.) DOM is part of the MSXML Parser and can be used from programming languages such as Visual Basic and Java, and also from scripts. This chapter covers DOM itself. In later chapters you will see examples of using DOM from various languages.

DOM Overview and Background

The purpose of DOM is to provide programmatic access to the content and structure of an XML document. This includes reading data from the document as well as modifying data and changing the structure by, for example, adding new elements. Many of the most important applications for XML documents require this kind of access. But why is a special DOM needed? After all, an XML document is just plain text, and a programmer should be able to write code that reads and writes the file directly. True enough, but the programming involved is quite complex and prone to errors. The idea behind DOM is to encapsulate all that functionality in an object that programmers can use. Regardless of which programming language you are using, you can call DOM to perform the needed tasks. Likewise, regardless of which XML parser you are using, as long as it supports DOM, you can use the same calls to access and manipulate an XML document. You'll also hear DOM described as an API because it provides an interface that applications programs can call to work with XML documents.

Here is a simple example to illustrate the use of DOM. The following code fragment, written in Visual Basic, uses the DOM interface in the MSXML Parser to read data from an XML document. The line numbers are referred to following the listing.

```
1. Dim xmlDoc As New MSXML2.DOMDocument
2. Dim ElementName As String
3. Dim ElementValue As String
4. xmlDoc.Load("c:\my documents\data.xml")
5. ElementName = xmlDoc.documentElement.firstChild.baseName
6. ElementValue = xmlDoc.documentElement.firstChild.text
```

In brief, this code does the following:

Line 1 creates an instance of the `DOMDocument` object.
Lines 2 and 3 create variables to store the information read from the XML document.
Line 4 loads the specified XML document into the parser. After this line of code executes, the XML document is accessible using the variable "xml-Doc."
Line 5 reads the name of the document's first child element.
Line 6 reads the text data of the document's first child element.

In this chapter, all code examples will be given in Visual Basic. Even if your preferred programming language is something else, you should be able to follow the code examples. Using DOM with other languages will be covered in later chapters.

This chapter does not provide exhaustive coverage of DOM. Such an undertaking would be a book in itself. Rather, I concentrate on the fundamental components of DOM—those that you will need most often in your programming. You can find complete information on DOM in the MSXML online Help that is installed as part of the MSXML development package.

DOM and the Tree Model

One way to describe an XML document is using a tree model. You saw some mention of the tree model earlier in the book, but it is worth restating because it is an important part of understanding DOM. In the tree model, everything in the document—elements, attributes, processing instructions, comments, and so on—is a *node.* There is a root node that represents the document itself, and all other nodes branch off from it, either directly or indirectly. Traditionally,

XML trees are visualized with the root at the top. The following terminology is used:

- *Parent:* The node one step above a given node. All nodes except the root node have a parent.
- *Child:* A node one step below a given node. A node can have zero, one, or more children.
- *Descendant:* Any node below a given node on the same branch.
- *Ancestor:* Any node above a given node on the same branch.
- *Sibling:* A node with the same parent as a given node.
- *Leaf:* A node with no children.

Consider the node tree in Figure 10.1. The relationships in this tree include the following:

- Node A is the parent of nodes B, C, and D. Likewise, node C is the parent of node E. This could also be expressed by saying that nodes B, C, and D are children of node A, and that node E is a child of node C.
- Nodes B, C, and D are siblings. Nodes G and H are also siblings. However, nodes E and F are not siblings. While they are at the same level in the tree, they have different parents.
- Nodes E, G, and H are descendants of node C.
- Nodes D and A are ancestors of node F.
- Nodes B, F, G, and H are leaves.

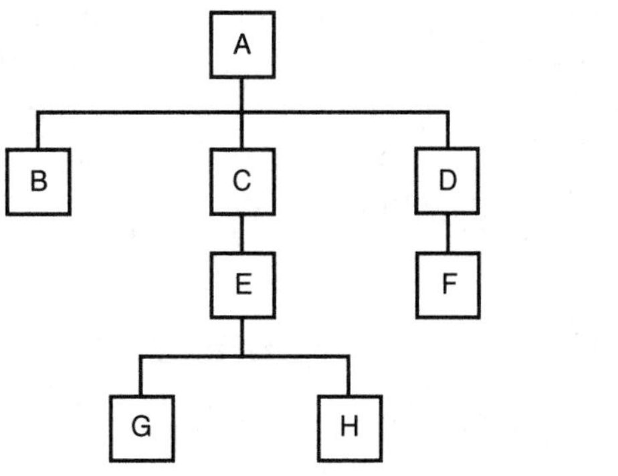

Figure 10.1: A node tree that demonstrates relationships between nodes

Part of the tree model is the concept of "walking the tree." Starting anywhere on the document tree (often at the root), you can traverse the nodes and branches to reach any desired location in the tree. This concept is evident in many of the aspects of DOM that you will learn in this chapter. For example, in the code fragment given earlier in this chapter, you see the keyword `firstChild`, which refers to the first child element of a given element. In essence, using this term "walks" from a starting node to its first child node.

DOM, Microsoft, and W3C

There are several levels of DOM, due in part to the fact that the standard has been evolving over time. The earliest DOM was designed to work with HTML documents, and it is sometimes referred to as DOM level 0. DOM level 1 was designed for XML, and it incorporates the tree model described previously, as well as DOM level 0 for HTML. DOM level 2 expands on level 1 by adding an events model, support for namespaces, and a model for style sheets. DOM level 3 will add a variety of advanced features to level 2, including XPath support and access to keyboard input.

As regards W3C, the DOM situation is complex because of the various DOM levels and also the fact that levels 2 and 3 have been divided into subsections. You can find the details on the W3C Web site, but in a nutshell here is where things stand as of this writing: DOM levels 1 and 2 are W3C Recommendations, while level 3 is a Working Draft.

How does this relate to Microsoft technologies? The DOM that is implemented in MSXML version 4.0 is an extension of the W3C level 1 Recommendation. In other words, Microsoft has added things—mostly properties and methods—to the W3C Recommendation. If you know the W3C DOM, the Microsoft implementation will seem familiar to you, but it will have available additional features for you to use. As always, this is a mixed blessing. The Microsoft DOM is more powerful than the W3C DOM, but it is nonstandard. Some or all of the Microsoft extensions may be incorporated into a future W3C DOM Recommendation, but there is no guarantee this will happen.

Overview of Working with DOM

Before I get into the details of DOM, I'll provide you with an overview of the process in very simple form:

1. Create an instance of the `DOMDocument` object. This object is at the top of the DOM hierarchy.

2. Load the XML document into the `DOMDocument` object. An XML file can be loaded from a disk file or, when writing Active Server Pages (ASP) scripts, from a `Request` object.
3. Use the objects, properties, and methods of DOM to obtain information about the document's content and structure and to modify the content and structure as needed.
4. If the document was modified, save it to disk or to a `Response` object.

This sounds simple enough, but as they say, "The devil is in the details." The remainder of this chapter provides information on how to use DOM to work with XML documents. The coverage is not exhaustive, but it focuses on those areas that are most likely to be needed by a programmer. Examples are presented in Visual Basic. Later chapters cover using DOM with Visual Basic in more detail (Chapter 15) and using DOM with C++ (Chapter 16) and with C# (Chapter 13).

The DOMDocument Object

You will use the `DOMDocument` object in everything you do with DOM. It is referred to by its version-independent ID `MSXML2.DOMDocument`, which automatically refers to the latest version of the MSXML Parser that is installed on your system. Note that even in MSXML version 4.0, the object library name is MSXML2 to retain code compatibility with previous versions of MSXML. One of the first things your code will do is create one or more instances of the `DOMDocument` object, using the syntax of the language you are using for your project. In the remainder of this chapter, assume that "xmlDoc" is a reference to an instance of this object.

Table 10.1 presents a summary of the `DOMDocument` methods and properties that are covered in this chapter. (Note that in the table, method names are followed by parentheses.) Details are explained in the sections that follow.

Loading and Saving XML Documents

Before you can do anything with an XML document, it must be loaded into the parser. It will then be available through the `DOMDocument` object. To load an XML file, use the `load()` method. The syntax is as follows:

```
xmlDoc.load(source)
```

Table 10.1 Properties and Methods of the `DOMDocument` Object

Property/Method	Use	See Section
`abort()`	Aborts an asynchronous download	Loading and Saving XML Documents
`async`	Controls whether or not asynchronous download is permitted	Loading and Saving XML Documents
`load()`	Loads an XML file for processingDocuments	Loading and Saving XML
`loadXML()`	Loads an XML string for processing	Loading and Saving XML Documents
`parseError`	Contains information about the latest parsing error	Dealing with Errors
`preserveWhiteSpace`	Specifies if all white space is to be preserved	Setting Parse Options
`readyState`	Contains information about the state of document processing	Loading and Saving XML Documents
`resolveExternals`	Specifies if external definitions are to be resolved	Setting Parse Options
`save()`	Saves an XML document	Loading and Saving XML Documents
`validateOnParse`	Specifies whether the document is to be validated against its DTD or its Schema	Setting Parse Options

`Source` is either the name (and, if needed, the path) to the XML file or a reference to a Microsoft Internet Information Services (IIS) `Request` object. The method returns True if the load was successful and False if it failed (for

example, if the file was not found). Note that loading a document automatically parses it. Parse errors are not reflected in the method's return value, but rather in the `parseError` property, which is explained in the "Dealing with Errors" section later in this chapter.

The loading of a document is usually performed asynchronously, which means that the `load()` method returns control to your program before the loading and parsing is complete. To force synchronous loads, set the `async` property to False. You can determine the state of asynchronous loading by examining the `readyState` property. During an asynchronous load, the `readyState` property will have one of the following four values:

- 1: Loading is in progress but no data is available yet.
- 2: Loading is complete but the object model is not available yet.
- 3: Parsing is partially complete. The object model is available only on the data that has been parsed.
- 4: Parsing is complete (although not necessarily successful).

Your program can use the `onreadystatechange` event to detect when this property changes. This event is explained in the "DOMDocument Events" section later in this chapter. To abort the loading of an XML document before it is complete, call the `abort()` method.

To load an XML document or fragment that exists as a string in a program variable, use the `loadXML()` method. The syntax is as follows:

```
xmlDoc.loadXML(s)
```

s is a string containing the XML. The result is the same as if the XML had been in a file and loaded with the `load()` method.

To save XML from a `DOMDocument` object, use the `save()` method. The syntax is as follows:

```
xmlDoc.save(S)
```

S can be a filename or a `Response` reference. *S* can also be a reference to another `DOMDocument` object, in which case the XML is loaded into the second `DOMDocument` object and parsed just as if it has been loaded from a file. Here's an example:

```
Dim xmlDoc1 As New DOMDocument
Dim xmlDoc2 As New DOMDocument
xmlDoc1.load("sample.xml")
xmlDoc1.save(xmlDoc2)
```

After this code executes, both xmlDoc1 and xmlDoc2 contain the same XML.

Dealing with Errors

The return value of the `load()` and `loadXML()` methods indicates if the XML was loaded successfully but tells you nothing about the details of any parsing errors that may have occurred. For this purpose, you use the `DOMDocument` object's `parseError` property. This property returns a reference to a `DOMParseError` object, and this object's properties provide information about the most recent parse error as described in Table 10.2. All of these properties are read-only.

> ***The `load()` Return Value and Parsing Errors***
>
> *According to the Microsoft documentation, the `load()` method is supposed to return True if the XML file loaded successfully, regardless of parsing errors. In reality, it will return False if there is a parsing error, even if the file loaded successfully. To deal with this, when `load()` returns False you can test the `parseError.errorCode` property to determine if the error was a load error or a parse error.*

Table 10.2 Properties of the `DOMParseError` Object

Property	Description
`ErrorCode`	Returns a number identifying the error or 0 if there has been no error
`filepos`	Returns the absolute file position of the error (the number of characters from the start of the file)
`line`	Returns the number of the line where the error occurred
`linepos`	Returns the position of the character on the line where the error occurred
`reason`	Returns a brief description of the error
`srcText`	Returns the full text of the line where the error occurred
`url`	Returns the URL of the XML document containing the error

The `DOMParseError` object's properties provide you with significant flexibility in dealing with parse errors. Listing 10.1 shows an example. This Visual Basic code will load an XML file and test to see if a parse error occurred. If so, the line containing the error is displayed along with a pointer to the error location and the error description. Figure 10.2 shows the error message displayed by this code. If you want to try out this code, you can use it with any XML file that contains an error, such as an element's end tag not matching the start tag.

Listing 10.1 Visual Basic Code to Process and Display a Parsing Error

```
xmlDoc.Load ("c:\my documents\xml\test1.xml")

If xmlDoc.parseError.errorCode <> 0 Then
    s = "Error on line " & xmlDoc.parseError.Line & vbCrLf
    s = s & xmlDoc.parseError.srcText & vbCrLf
    s = s & Space(xmlDoc.parseError.linepos)
    s = s & " - " & xmlDoc.parseError.reason
    MsgBox s
Else
    MsgBox "XML file parsed successfully."
End If
```

Setting Parse Options

The MSXML Parser has several parse options that you can set programmatically before an XML document is loaded. One of these options, the `async` property, was discussed earlier in the "The DOMDocument Object" section. These options, which are accessed as properties of the `DOMDocument` object, are all True/False values.

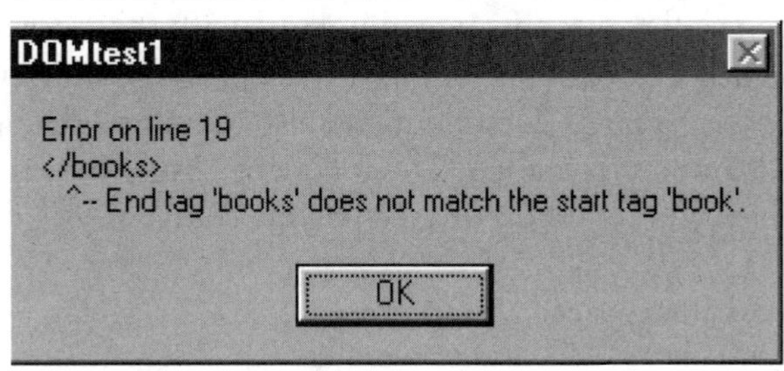

Figure 10.2: The error message displayed by the code in Listing 10.1

- `validateOnParse`: If True (the default), the document is validated against its DTD or Schema (if any). If False, validation is not performed and the document is checked only for well-formedness.
- `resolveExternals`: If True (the default), external definitions are resolved during parsing. This allows default attributes and data types to be defined on elements from the schema and use of the DTD as a file-inclusion mechanism.
- `preserveWhiteSpace`: If False (the default), white space is preserved as specified by `xml:space` attributes in the document. If True, all white space is preserved—the equivalent of having an `xml:space="preserve"` attribute in every element in the document.

DOMDocument Events

The DOM object model exposed by the MSXML Parser supports two events, which are Microsoft extensions to DOM. You can use these events to detect when loading XML data asynchronously to determine when data is available for processing. Using these events, your program can start processing data before the load process is complete. The events are as follows:

- The `ondataavailable` event fires whenever new data becomes available. This is applicable when data is being loaded asynchronously.
- The `onreadystatechange` event fires when the `readyState` property changes.

To use these events, you must declare the instance of the `DOMDocument` object using the `WithEvents` keyword, as shown here:

```
Dim WithEvents xmlDoc As DOMDocument
Set xmlDoc = New DOMDocument
```

You can use these events in conjunction with the `readyState` property (explained earlier in the chapter) to display progress messages to the user when processing a large document and also to initiate data processing before the entire document is loaded. The following Visual Basic event procedure illustrates how you might do this, displaying status messages in a text box:

```
Private Sub xmlDoc_onreadystatechange()

  Select Case xmlDox.readyState
    Case 1
      txtStatus.Text = "The document is loading."
```

```
    Case 2
      txtStatus.Text = "The document has loaded."
    Case 3
      txtStatus.Text = "The document is being parsed."
    Case 4
      txtStatus.Text = "Document processing is complete."
  End Select

End Sub
```

Accessing the Tree

Once you have loaded an XML document into the `DOMDocument` object, you are ready to access the XML tree created by the parser. In most situations, you will do this by means of the `documentElement` property, which returns a reference to the root element of the XML tree (or `Null` if no root exists, which would happen if no document had been loaded). The reference returned by this property is to an `IXMLDOMElement` object. This object is used throughout the tree to represent all element nodes, and as such it is a very important part of DOM and will be covered in detail later in this chapter. For now it is sufficient to know that the `IXMLDOMElement` object has properties and methods that enable you to "walk the tree." For example:

- The `firstChild` property references the element's first child element.
- The `lastChild` property references the element's last child element.
- The `childNodes` property returns a list of all the element's child nodes.

Thus, once you have a reference to the root element obtained from the `DOMDocument` object's `documentElement` property, you can access any part of the XML document tree by using these and other properties. You'll learn how later in the chapter.

The DOM Object Model

A surprisingly small number of objects is at the heart of DOM. Because DOM represents the document as a tree, most of these object types represent a type of node in the tree. Those objects that you will work with most frequently are summarized in Table 10.3. They are explained in detail in the sections that follow.

Table 10.3 Frequently Used Object Types in DOM

Object	Represents
IXMLDOMAttribute	An attribute.
IXMLDOMCDATAsection	A CDATA section (text not interpreted as XML).
IXMLDOMComment	An XML comment.
IXMLDOMElement	An XML element.
IXMLDOMNode	A generic node. Use this object type when you are not sure what type of node your code will be working with. A type IXMLDOMNode can refer to an element node, a text node, and so on.
IXMLDOMNodeList	A list of nodes.
IXMLDOMText	The text content of an entity or attribute.

Navigating the Document Tree

Given that you have a reference to any document element—including its root element as obtained from the DOMDocument object's documentElement property—you can obtain references to other elements using the properties described in this section. All but one of these properties returns a reference to an IXMLDOMElement object or the value Null if no such element exists. The exception is the childNodes property, which returns an IXMLDOMNodeList object. The following section explains how to use this object.

- firstChild: The first child element (in document order).
- lastChild: The last child element (in document order).
- childNodes: A list of all the child elements. The list will have length 0 if there are no children.
- nextSibling: The next sibling element (as determined by the parent node's child list).
- previousSibling: The previous sibling element (as determined by the parent node's child list).
- parentNode: The parent node.

Table 10.4 Using the Tree Navigation Properties

Task	Property to Use
Reference the second child of element N	`N.firstChild.nextSibling`
Reference the first sibling of element N	`N.parentNode.first.Child`
Determine if element N has any children	If `N.firstChild` is not `Null`
Reference the last child element of node N's grandparent element	`N.parentNode.parentNode.lastChild`

Using these properties, it is possible to start anywhere in the document tree and move to any element in the tree, as well as perform other tasks related to the document tree. Table 10.4 presents some examples.

If you will be performing several manipulations on an element, you may find it more convenient to create a separate reference to the element rather than using the sometimes cumbersome syntax shown in Table 10.4. The following code fragment illustrates how to do so in Visual Basic, and techniques are similar in other languages. The result is that the variable "el" references the last child of the first child of the document's root element, and you can now use "el" wherever you need to refer to that element.

```
Dim xmlDoc As New DOMDocument
Dim el As IXMLDOMElement

xmlDoc.Load ("test1.xml")
Set el = xmlDoc.documentElement.firstChild.lastChild
```

Element Nodes and Text Nodes

One aspect of DOM that some people find confusing is the relationships among an element node (represented by the `IXMLDOMElement` object), an attribute node (represented by the `IXMLDOMAttribute` object), and a text node (represented by the `IXMLDOMText` object).

- Any XML element is represented by an element node.
- If the element has child elements, each child is also represented by an element node.

- If the element contains text, it is represented by a text node.
- If the element has attributes, each attribute is represented by an attribute node.
- The text data of each attribute is represented by a text node.

Consider the following XML fragment:

```
<person type="friend">
Akiko Yamaguchi
<phone>555-1212</phone>
<fax>555-3434</fax>
</person>
```

The “person” element is represented by an element node. It has four children:

- One attribute node representing the “type” attribute
- One text node representing the data “Akiko Yamaguchi”
- Two element nodes representing the “phone” and “fax” elements

The “type” attribute node has a single child: a text node representing the data “friend.”

The text node has no children.

Each of the two child element nodes has a single text node child representing the element’s data.

This tree fragment is represented schematically in Figure 10.3. The reason that these relationships are confusing at times is because you can usually

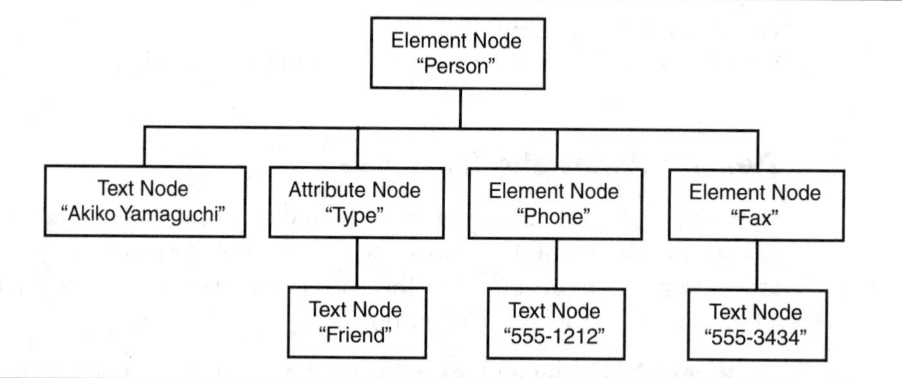

Figure 10.3 The tree diagram of the XML fragment presented in the text

access the data in a text node without explicitly navigating to the text node. For example, to retrieve the data "Akiko Yamaguchi" in the example, you need only navigate to the element node for the "person" element. Be aware, however, that there is often a text node in the branch even if you do not reference it explicitly.

Using a Node List

Using a node list, as returned by the `IXMLDOMElement` object's `childNodes` property, can be a very powerful technique for working with the DOM tree. The node list is returned as a reference to an `IXMLDOMNodeList` object. This object has one property and three methods for accessing the individual elements in the list.

- The `length` property returns the number of elements in the list.
- The `item(n)` method returns the `n`th element in the list. Elements are numbered starting at 0, so `n` can range from 0 to `length - 1`.
- The `nextNode()` method returns the next element in the list. The first time it is called, this method returns the first element, the second time it is called it returns the second element, and so on. It returns `Null` if there are no elements in the list or if the current element is the last element.
- The `reset()` method reinitializes the list so that the `nextNode()` method again will return the first element in the list.

The advantage of using a node list is that it simplifies the task of iterating through all of an element's child elements. There are two ways to do this: Either call the `item()` method in a loop, passing values of `n` starting at 0 and ending at `length-1`, or call the `nextItem()` method repeatedly until it returns `Null`. The following code fragment shows how to iterate through all the child elements of the document's root element using the first of these techniques:

```
Dim xmlDoc As New DOMDocument
Dim nl As IXMLDOMNodeList
Dim i As Integer

xmlDoc.Load ("test1.xml")

Set nl = xmlDoc.documentElement.childNodes
For i = 0 To nl.length - 1
' Process child nodes here.
Next i
```

Reading Element and Attribute Data

Once you have navigated to the desired element in the document tree, you can access its information—that is, the element's text and its attributes. You can also access information from the element's descendants.

Reading Element Data

Aside from any attributes, an XML element, or node, can contain data in two forms: as text and as part of a child element. For example, consider this XML fragment:

```
<item>
Hammer
<partno>X-2123</partno>
<cost>9.95</cost>
</item>
```

"Hammer" is text contained within the "item" element, which is represented by a text node (an `IXMLDOMText` object), while "X-2123" and "9.95" are text contained within child elements (represented by `IXMLDOMElement` objects). Once you have a reference to an element, you can read either its text data or all of its data (that is, its text data plus the data of its descendants). You can also access the element's name and the raw XML of the element. The properties of the `IXMLDOMElement` and `IXMLDOMText` objects that provide access to data are described in Table 10.5.

Getting an element's text data is not quite as simple as it might appear on the surface. It was explained earlier in this chapter (in the "Element Nodes and Text Nodes" section) how the text content of an XML element (for example, "Hammer" in the preceding example) is represented by a text node or, more specifically, an `IXMLDOMText` object. Each block of text within an element is represented by a separate `IXMLDOMText` object. Consider this example (which admittedly is badly written XML but is perfectly legal):

```
<parent>
Some text data
More text data
<child>Child's text data</child>
Yet more text data
</parent>
```

Table 10.5 Properties of the `IXMLDOMElement` and `IXMLDOMText` Objects for Reading Element Data

Property	Description
`nodeType`	A numerical value specifying the type of node. Element nodes return the value `NODE_ELEMENT` (value = 1) and text nodes return the value `NODE_TEXT` (value = 3).
`nodeTypeText`	A string describing the node type—"element" or "text" for element and text nodes.
`nodeValue`	For text nodes, the contained text including white space. For element nodes, the value `Null`.
`tagName`	The name of the element.
`Text`	For element nodes, a string containing the element's own text data plus the text data of all of its descendants. For text nodes, the node text with white space normalized.
`xml`	Returns the element's XML. For element nodes, this consists of the opening and closing tags and everything between them. For text nodes it is the same as the `nodeValue` property.

The "parent" node has three child nodes:

- An `IXMLDOMText` node containing the data "Some text data<lf>More text data" where "<lf>" represents a line feed
- An `IXMLDOMElement` node named "child"
- A second `IXMLDOMText` node containing the data "Yet more text data"

The result of this arrangement is that in order to read an element's text data, you must examine each of its child elements to see whether it is a text node or an element node. Then, for each text node, use the `Text` property (or `nodeValue` property, if you want the white space preserved) to obtain the text. The Visual Basic code in Listing 10.2 presents a function to perform this task. Passed an element node, the function returns a string containing all of the node's text data. If it contains no text data, an empty string is returned. This function ignores data in any child nodes.

Listing 10.2: Visual Basic Function to Return All Text Data from an Element Node

```
Public Function GetTextDataFromNode(node As IXMLDOMElement) As String

' Passed an element node, returns a string containing all the
' text data contained in the element (not in its child elements).
' Data from multiple text nodes is separated by a CRLF.

Dim i As Integer
Dim buf As String

For i = 0 To node.childNodes.length - 1
    If node.childNodes.Item(i).nodeType = NODE_TEXT Then
        buf = buf & node.childNodes.Item(i).Text & vbCrLf
    End If
Next i

GetTextDataFromNode = buf

End Function
```

The procedure for obtaining data from child nodes follows a similar logic. Your code will need to loop through all the child elements looking for type `NODE_ELEMENT` elements and extracting their data as needed. Listing 10.4 shows an example of Visual Basic code to perform this task using the XML file in Listing 10.3. After this code has run, the variable "buf" contains the information from the XML file formatted for display as shown here:

```
title: The Cambridge Biographical Encyclopedia
author: David Crystal
publisher: Cambridge University Press

title: Travels with Charley
author: John Steinbeck
publisher: Putnam

title: Crime and Punishment
author: Fyodor Dostoyevsky
publisher: Oxford
```

Two points about this code merit additional comment. Note the technique used to obtain a reference to the root XML element. The children of the

DOMDocument object will include the root XML element, but they will also include other elements such as processing instructions and comments. To obtain a reference to the root XML element, it is necessary to loop through the children of the DOMDocument looking for the correct node.

The second point has to do with the complexity of the code. In this example, the logical structure of the XML file was known ahead of time, so the code could be written specifically for that structure and therefore is relatively simple. In situations where you do not know the XML structure ahead of time, the code is unavoidably more complex.

Listing 10.3 Books.xml Is Used by the Code in Listing 10.4

```
<?xml version="1.0"?>
<books>
<book type="reference" year="1994">
  <title>The Cambridge Biographical Encyclopedia</title>
  <author>David Crystal</author>
  <publisher>Cambridge University Press</publisher>
</book>
<book type="fiction" year="1936">
  <title>Travels with Charley</title>
  <author>John Steinbeck</author>
  <publisher>Putnam</publisher>
</book>
<book type="fiction" year="1902">
  <title>Crime and Punishment</title>
  <author>Fyodor Dostoyevsky</author>
  <publisher>Oxford</publisher>
</book>
</books>
```

Listing 10.4 Visual Basic Code to Extract Element Names and Data from the XML File in Listing 10.3

```
Dim xmlDoc As New DOMDocument
Dim anyNode As IXMLDOMNode
Dim el1 As IXMLDOMElement
Dim el2 As IXMLDOMElement
Dim el3 As IXMLDOMElement
Dim buf As String
Dim s as String
```

```
xmlDoc.Load ("c:\my documents\xml\books.xml")

' Locate the document root element named "books".
Set el1 = Nothing
For Each anyNode In xmlDoc.childNodes
    If anyNode.nodeName = "books" Then
        Set el1 = anyNode
        Exit For
    End If
Next anyNode

' If el1 is nothing then the "books" node was not found.
If el1 Is Nothing Then
    MsgBox "Root 'books' element not found."
    Unload Me
End If

' Having found the root "books" element, loop through
' its children, gathering data into buf.
For Each el2 In el1.childNodes
    For Each el3 In el2.childNodes
        buf = buf & el3.tagName & ": " & el3.Text & vbCrLf
    Next el3
    buf = buf & vbCrLf
Next el2
```

Reading Attribute Data

To access an element's attributes, use the `IXMLDOMElement` object's `attributes` property. This property returns a reference to an `IXMLDOMNamedNodeMap` object, which is a collection that permits access to individual attributes by name or by index position. Each individual attribute is represented by an `IXMLDOMAttribute` object. The properties and methods of an `IXMLDOMNamedNodeMap` object that are used most often are described in Table 10.6. (Note that in the table, parentheses follow a method's name.)

The `IXMLDOMAttribute` object has properties that provide access to the attribute name and data. They are as follows:

- `baseName` returns the attribute's name.
- `Text` returns the attribute's value.

Reading the attribute data from an element is demonstrated by the Visual Basic code in Listing 10.5. This example makes use of the XML file presented

Table 10.6 Frequently Needed Properties and Methods of the IXMLDOMNamedNodeMap Object

Property/Method	Description
getNamedItem(*name*)	Returns an IXMLDOMAttribute object for the attribute with the specified name or Null if the specified attribute does not exist
item(*n*)	Returns an IXMLDOMAttribute object for the *n*th attribute, with *n* ranging from 0 to length-1, or Null if the *n*th attribute does not exist
length	Returns the number of attributes

earlier in Listing 10.3. The code goes through all of the "book" elements, extracting the names and values of the attributes and concatenating the data in the variable "buf." After running the code, this variable will contain the following:

```
type: reference
year: 1994

type: fiction
year: 1936

type: fiction
year: 1902
```

Listing 10.5 Visual Basic Code to Display the Names and Values of the Attributes of the First-Level Child Node of the Books.xml File in Listing 10.3

```
Dim xmlDoc As New DOMDocument
Dim anyNode As IXMLDOMNode
Dim nnm As IXMLDOMNamedNodeMap
Dim at As IXMLDOMAttribute
Dim i As Integer
Dim buf As String
Dim s As String
```

```
xmlDoc.Load ("c:\my documents\xml\test2.xml")

' Locate the document root element named "books".
Set el1 = Nothing
For Each anyNode In xmlDoc.childNodes
    If anyNode.nodeName = "books" Then
        Set el1 = anyNode
        Exit For
    End If
Next anyNode

' If el1 is nothing then the "books" node was not found.
If el1 Is Nothing Then
    MsgBox "Root 'books' element not found."
    Unload Me
End If

' Now get the attributes for each child and place in buf.
buf = ""
' Loop through all of the child nodes.
For Each el2 In el1.childNodes
    ' Get the attributes for this child node.
    Set nnm = el2.Attributes
    ' Loop for each attribute of this child node.
    For i = 0 To nnm.length - 1
        ' Add the attribute name and value to the buffer.
        buf = buf & nnm.Item(i).baseName & ": " & nnm.Item(i).Text
        buf = buf & vbCrLf
    Next i
    buf = buf & vbCrLf
Next el2
```

Getting Other Document Information

An XML document contains information in addition to element text and attributes. Using DOM, you can access any information in the document that is required by your application. This section summarizes the techniques you can use to obtain these other kinds of data.

Processing Instructions

An XML processing instruction is represented by a type `XMLDOMProcessingInstruction` node, and it will typically be a child of the `DOMDocument` object. The node type for this node is NODE_PROCESSING_INSTRUCTION, with a value of 7. Use the nodeValue property to obtain the instruction text. For example, here is the most common XML processing instruction element:

```
<?xml version="1.0"?>
```

The nodeValue property of the corresponding node returns this text:

```
version="1.0"
```

Comments

An XML comment is represented by a type IXMLDOMComment node and can be located anywhere in the document (except within a CDATA section). The node type for this node is NODE_COMMENT with the value 8. Use the nodeValue property to retrieve the comment text.

Document Type

The document type information refers to the DOCTYPE tag in an XML document. These tags can contain the name of the root element as well as information about the document's DTD or Schema. The DOCTYPE element is represented by the IXMLDOMDocumentType node. The node type for this node is NODE_DOCUMENT_TYPE with the value 10. Use the nodeValue property to retrieve the node's text.

CDATA Sections

A CDATA section is used to enclose text that is to be ignored by the XML parser. A CDATA section can appear within an XML element and is represented by a type IXMLDOMCDATASection node. This node has type NODE_CDATA_SECTION with a value of 4. The nodeValue property returns the text contained within a CDATA section.

Modifying Document Data and Structure

DOM gives you the ability not only to read data from an XML document, but also to modify the document. You can make the one of the following types of modifications.

- You can modify the document data without changing its structure by changing the data associated with existing elements and attributes.

- You can modify the document structure by adding, deleting, or rearranging elements and attributes.

These modifications are covered in turn in the sections that follow.

Modifying Document Data

Modifying document data without changing its structure is fairly straightforward. You need to locate the node you want to change using the techniques that were covered in the first part of this chapter, and then set the property that corresponds to the data you want to change. You also must save the XML if you want the change to be persistent. The following Visual Basic example changes the "year" attribute of the first child of the root element to "1992." It is assumed that "rootNode" is a reference to the document's root XML element.

```
rootNode.firstChild.Attributes.getNamedItem("year").Text = "1992"
```

The principle is the same when changing other data, whether it is text in an element, the content of a `CDATA` section, a processing instruction, or a comment. An XML document is saved using the `DOMDocument` object's `Save` method, as detailed earlier in this chapter.

Modifying Document Structure

DOM provides you with the ability to modify the structure of an XML document. These modifications consist of adding and deleting nodes (elements) as well as adding and deleting attributes.

Adding and Deleting Nodes

The process of adding a new node to the document consists of two steps:

1. Create the new node (an element, processing instruction, attribute, and so on). At this point, the node exists in your program but has not yet been inserted in the document tree.
2. Insert the new node at the desired location in the document.

To create a new node, you use the methods exposed by the `DOMDocument` object, as Table 10.7 details. Each of these methods creates a node of the specified type and returns a reference to it. The reference for any type of node can be stored in a variable of type `IXMLDomNode`, or you can use a variable of the

Table 10.7 Methods of the `DOMDocument` Object for Creating New Nodes

Method	Description
`CreateAttribute(`*`name`*`)`	Creates an attribute node with the specified name
`createCDATASection(`*`data)`*	Creates a `CDATA` section containing the specified data
`createComment(`*`comment`*`)`	Creates a comment node containing the specified comment
`createElement(`*`name`*`)`	Creates an element node with the specified name
`createProcessingInstruction(`*`target, data`*`)`	Creates a processing instruction with the specified target and data
`createTextNode(`*`text`*`)`	Creates a text node containing the specified text

type specific for the node being created (`IXMLDOMElement` for an element node, for example), although this offers no advantage.

The one shortcoming of these methods is that they do not permit the creation of nodes with namespace prefixes. If you need to create nodes with namespace prefixes, you must use the `createNode` method. The syntax is as follows (assuming that "xmlDoc" is a reference to a type `DOMDocument` object):

```
xmlDoc.createNode(type, name, namespace)
```

The method returns a reference to the new node. ***`Type`*** is a constant specifying the type of node to create, as described in Table 10.8. ***`Name`*** in the name of the node and is interpreted according to the type of node. ***`Namespace`*** is an optional argument specifying the namespace URI. If this argument is omitted, the node is created in the document's default namespace.

There is one more way to create a new node for insertion into the document: Clone an existing node. To clone a node, use the `cloneNode` method, which is available for all node types. The syntax is as follows:

```
nodeToClone.cloneNode(deep)
```

Table 10.8 Details of the `createNode` Method

Node Type Constant	Interpretation of the *name* Argument
`NODE_ATTRIBUTE`	The name of the attribute

`NODE_CDATA_SECTION`
`NODE_COMMENT`
`NODE_TEXT`
	Ignored—pass an empty string

`NODE_ELEMENT`	The name of the element
`NODE_PROCESSING_INSTRUCTION`	The target of the instruction (the name following the <?)

`NodeToClone` is a reference to the node you are cloning. `Deep` is a Boolean value. Set `deep` to True to clone the node and all of its children, or set it to False to clone only the node and its attributes. The method returns a reference to the newly cloned node.

When you create a new node using one of these techniques, it is an orphan and has no position in the document tree. The next step is to insert the new node at the desired location. To insert a new node, you must first obtain a reference to an existing node that will be the parent of the new node. In some situations you also need a reference to an existing node that will be a sibling of the new node. Then, you call one of the methods listed in Table 10.9.

Table 10.9 Methods for Inserting Nodes into the Document Tree

Method	Description
`parent``.insertBefore(`*`new`*`, `*`ref`*`)`	Inserts node *`new`* as a child of *`parent`*, as the left sibling of (that is, just before) existing child node *`ref`*. If *`ref`* is `Null` the new node is inserted as the last child of *`parent`*. Returns a reference to the newly inserted node.
`parent``.replaceChild(`*`new`*`, `*`ref`*`)`	Replaces existing child node *`ref`* with node *`new`*. Returns a reference to the replaced node.
`parent``.appendChild(`*`new`*`)`	Appends node *`new`* as the last child node of *`parent`*. Returns a reference to the new node.

When inserting nodes into a document using these methods, you need to be aware that certain types of changes are not permitted because they would not conform to the permitted structure of an XML document. For example, a `CDATA` node cannot be the child of a document node. Trying to make such changes will cause an error.

To delete a node, use the `removeChild()` method. The syntax is as follows:

```
parentremoveChild(child)
```

`Parent` is the parent node, and *`child`* is the node to be removed. The method returns a reference to the returned node.

Adding and Deleting Attributes

While attributes are nodes, the procedure for adding and deleting them is different because attributes are accessed via an `IXMLNamedNodeMap` object, as explained earlier in this chapter in the "Reading Attribute Data" section. This means that you must use this object's methods to add or delete attributes. To add an attribute, first create the new attribute node (type `IXMLDOMAttribute`) using the `createAttribute()` method that was described earlier in this chapter. Set the attribute's `baseName` and `Text` attributes to set its name and value, respectively. Then, use the named node map's `setNamedItem()` method to add the attribute. The syntax is as follows:

```
nodemap.setNamedItem(node)
```

`Nodemap` is a reference to the named node map you are adding the attribute to (obtained from the `element` node's `attributes` property). *`Node`* is a reference to the new attribute node. If an attribute of the same name already exists, it is replaced with the new one. Otherwise, a new attribute is added.

To delete an attribute, use the `removeNamedItem()` method. The syntax is as follows:

```
nodemap.removeNamedItem(name)
```

`Nodemap` is a reference to the named node map you are removing the attribute from, and *`name`* is the name of the attribute to be removed. The method returns a reference to the removed attribute or `Null` if the named node map did not contain an attribute of the specified name.

A Demonstration

In this section, I present a short Visual Basic demonstration program that shows you how to perform many of the document modifications that have been covered in this chapter. The original XML file is shown in Listing 10.6. The modifications to be made are as follows:

- Add a comment to the document.
- Add another "book" element, including its children, as the last child of the "books" element.
- Put the data for a new book into the new "book" element.
- For all "book" elements, delete the "year" attribute and replace it with a "date" attribute that contains the same data.

The code to perform these tasks is presented in Listing 10.7. The comments in the code explain what is going on, and even if Visual Basic is not your preferred language you should be able to follow them. The resulting XML file is shown in Listing 10.8.

Listing 10.6 Books2.xml Is the Original XML File

```
<?xml version="1.0"?>
<books>
  <book year="1994">
    <title>The Cambridge Biographical Encyclopedia</title>
    <author>David Crystal</author>
    <publisher>Cambridge University Press</publisher>
  </book>
</books>
```

Listing 10.7 Visual Basic Code to Perform the Required Modifications on Books2.xml

```
Dim xmlDoc As New DOMDocument
Dim anyNode As IXMLDOMNode
Dim newAtt As IXMLDOMAttribute
Dim at As IXMLDOMAttribute
Dim rootElement As IXMLDOMElement
Dim clonedElement As IXMLDOMElement
Dim s As String
Dim buf As String

' Load the source document.
xmlDoc.Load ("c:\my documents\xml\books2.xml")

' Check for parse errors.
```

```
If xmlDoc.parseError.errorCode <> 0 Then
    s = "Error on line " & xmlDoc.parseError.Line & vbCrLf
    s = s & xmlDoc.parseError.srcText & vbCrLf
    s = s & Space(xmlDoc.parseError.linepos)
    s = s & "^- " & xmlDoc.parseError.reason
    MsgBox s
    Unload Me
End If

' Locate the document root element named "books".
Set rootElement = Nothing
For Each anyNode In xmlDoc.childNodes
    If anyNode.nodeName = "books" Then
        Set rootElement = anyNode
        Exit For
    End If
Next anyNode

' If rootElement is nothing then the "books" node was not found.
If rootElement Is Nothing Then
    MsgBox "Root 'books' element not found."
    Unload Me
End If

' Add a comment to the document, inserting it before
' the root XML element.
Set anyNode = xmlDoc.createComment("Document modified by P. Aitken")
xmlDoc.insertBefore anyNode, rootElement

' Make a clone, including children, of the first
' child element of the root element.
Set clonedElement = rootElement.firstChild.cloneNode(True)

' Put the new data in the cloned element's child elements.
clonedElement.childNodes.Item(0).Text = "Bartlett's Familiar Quotations"
clonedElement.childNodes.Item(1).Text = "John Bartlett"
clonedElement.childNodes.Item(2).Text = "Little, Brown"

' Put new data in the cloned element's "year" attribute.
clonedElement.Attributes.getNamedItem("year").Text = "1992"

' Insert the cloned element as the last child of the
' root element.
```

```
rootElement.appendChild clonedElement

' Change all "year" attributes to "date",
' keeping the same data.
For Each anyNode In rootElement.childNodes
    ‘ Get the value of the "year" attribute.
    buf = anyNode.Attributes.getNamedItem("year").Text
    ‘ Create a new attribute node named "date".
    Set newAtt = xmlDoc.createAttribute("date")
    ' Set the new attribute’s value.
    newAtt.Text = buf
    ' Add the new attribute to the element.
    anyNode.Attributes.setNamedItem newAtt
    ' Remove the "year" attribute.
    anyNode.Attributes.removeNamedItem "year"
Next anyNode

' Save the modified document
xmlDoc.save "c:\my documents\xml\books_mod.xml"
```

Listing 10.8 Books_mod.xml Is the Modified XML File Created by the Code in Listing 10.7

```
<?xml version="1.0"?>
<!--Document modified by P. Aitken-->
<books>
  <book date="1994">
    <title>The Cambridge Biographical Encyclopedia</title>
    <author>David Crystal</author>
    <publisher>Cambridge University Press</publisher>
  </book>
  <book date="1992">
    <title>Bartlett's Familiar Quotations</title>
    <author>John Bartlett</author>
    <publisher>Little, Brown</publisher>
  </book>
</books>
```

DOM and XSLT

DOM provides the capability of applying XSLT transformations to XML documents. If an XML document contains a reference to an XSL style sheet, and you load the document into DOM, the style sheet is not automatically applied. In other words, the DOM tree node will contain the original XML and not the transformed XML. In order to apply XSLT transforms, you use the `transformNode()` method. The syntax is as follows:

```
nodeToTransform.transformNode(nodeContainingXSLT)
```

NodeToTransform is the node that contains the XML to be transformed (as a node tree). *NodeContainingXSLT* is a node that contains the XSLT transformation style sheet. The method returns a string containing the results of the transformation. The concept of a node is very broad in DOM and includes the `DOMDocument` object. Thus, you can use this method to transform an entire XML file by applying the transformation instructions in an XSL file. For example, the following Visual Basic code applies the transforms in summary.xsl to the XML in salesdata.xml and stores the result in the variable "buf":

```
Dim xmlDoc As New DOMDocument
Dim xslDoc As New DOMDocument
Dim buf as String

xmlDoc.Load ("c:\my documents\xml\salesdata.xml")
xslDoc.Load ("c:\my documents\xml\summary.xsl")
buf = xmlDoc.transformNode(xslDoc)
```

Summary

The Document Object Model (DOM) is an extremely powerful tool for working with the content of XML files. DOM maintains an entire XML document as a branching, treelike structure of nodes. Each component of the XML file—elements, processing instructions, comments, attributes, and so on—is represented by a node. The branch pattern, starting with the root node that corresponds to the document's root element, represents the relationships between the nodes. Using DOM you can access any data in the document as well as modify the document's data and structure.

CHAPTER 11

The Simple API for XML Interface

The Simple API for XML, or SAX, is an application programming interface that provides tools for manipulating the contents of an XML document. In this respect, SAX is like DOM, the Document Object Model, which was covered in the previous chapter. SAX, however, takes a very different approach and is suitable for different XML processing tasks than DOM. SAX is supported by the MSXML Parser. This chapter shows you how to use SAX, and it also explains factors to consider when you are deciding whether to use SAX or DOM.

SAX Overview and Background

SAX development began in 1997 as a collaborative effort between several individuals who were members of the XML-DEV mailing list. SAX did not involve W3C or any corporations—it was the brainchild of a group of XML developers who were frustrated with the poor quality and lack of standardization of currently available XML parsers. The first version of SAX was released in 1998. Written in Java and designed for use with Java, it was public domain "freeware" that anyone could use without payment.

SAX rapidly became a popular tool for XML developers. Even though DOM, with its W3C support, was being developed during this period, SAX remained popular partly because it was better at certain tasks than DOM. Developers wanted the flexibility to choose between DOM or SAX—or a combination of both—depending on their specific XML development needs. Microsoft has incorporated support for the latest version of SAX into its MSXML Parser. While SAX was originally developed as an API to be used with Java, Microsoft has packaged SAX to be usable from Visual Basic and C++ as well.

Where does SAX fit into the world of standards and recommendations? It doesn't, really, because SAX is better thought of as a set of guidelines and not a strict standard. Microsoft's SAX implementation follows these guidelines, but it is meaningless to ask whether Microsoft follows "the SAX standard" because there is no such thing. At the present time, there is no effort by W3C to develop a SAX recommendation.

Event-Driven Interface

SAX provides an *event-driven interface* to an XML document. This means that, as SAX reads an XML document, it generates events as it finds specific items in the XML file. Your application can respond to these events, or ignore them, as required. For example, look at this small XML file:

```
<?xml version="1.0"?>
<books>
  <book>
    <author>Herman Melville</author>
    <title>Moby Dick</title>
  </book>
</books>
```

When a SAX processor reads this file, it will generate the following events:

```
StartDocument()
StartElement("books")
StartElement("book")
StartElement("author")
Characters("Herman Melville")
EndElement("author")
StartElement("title")
Characters("Moby Dick")
EndElement("title")
EndElement("book")
EndElement("books")
EndDocument()
```

How your application responds to these events is totally up to you, the programmer. At one extreme, an application could respond to every event and build a representation of the entire XML document in memory. At the other extreme, an application could respond only to events that signal the start of a "title" element, looking for a specific book title.

In contrast, DOM makes essentially no use of events. DOM reads the entire XML document and constructs a node tree. This node tree is stored in memory where an application can access it using the DOM API calls.

SAX versus DOM

The completely different processing models of SAX and DOM result in each API having a distinct set of advantages and disadvantages. For a given programming task, there is rarely any difficulty in deciding which is better.

DOM reads the entire document and constructs the corresponding node tree. This means that DOM places significant demands on the CPU and on memory resources, particularly with large documents, as there is a great deal of information that must be processed and stored in memory. DOM tends to be slower, too. In other words, when DOM processes a large document, there may be a significant delay between the start of processing and the time that the node tree becomes available to your application. On the plus side, DOM provides random access to the document because all content is present in memory at one time. DOM also provides significantly greater power when it comes to modifying the document.

SAX reads the XML document from beginning to end and generates events based on the document content. The document is never stored in memory, either as raw text or as a node tree. Demands on the CPU and memory resources are not nearly as demanding as DOM, and the processing is faster. However, because the entire document is never available as a whole, random access to content is not possible. You application needs to "know" ahead of time what it is looking for and respond to the corresponding events. Furthermore, SAX is weak when it comes to modifying an XML document. Changes to document data are possible, but changes to document structure are not.

Based on these descriptions of the differences between DOM and SAX, it is usually fairly easy to determine which one best suits your needs. Here are some guidelines:

Use SAX when

- Memory and processing resources are a consideration, particularly for large documents.
- You are looking for specific pieces of information in the document. For example, in a library catalog, use SAX when you need to locate all works by a specific author.
- You do not need to modify the document structure.

Use DOM when

- You need random access to all of the document's content.
- You need to modify the document structure.
- You need complex XPath filtering.
- You need to perform XSLT transformations.

The SAX Interface

SAX is made available to your programs by means of a set of classes, or interfaces, that are part of the MSXML installation. In your Visual Basic or Visual C++ program, you will implement those SAX interfaces that your program will use. Each of these interfaces has methods that correspond to events that can occur during the processing of an XML document. In your program, you will implement (write code for) those methods that correspond to events that you need to detect.

Here's a specific example. The Content Handler interface receives notification (events) corresponding to logical parts of the XML document. One of its methods is `characters()`, which is called whenever the SAX processor encounters character data in the document, with the character data passed as an argument. If your application needs to read character data from the document, you will implement the `characters()` method with code to perform the needed actions with the data. If you do not need to read the character data, do not implement the `characters()` method and character data will be ignored.

It is important to note that SAX methods are unlike typical methods in that, with only a few exceptions, you do not call them from your program. Rather, they are called by the SAX processor as needed. Technically, this is known as a *call back.* Visual Basic programmers should think of the SAX methods as event handlers.

Visual Basic versus Visual C++

SAX was originally written to be used in Java programs, but the Microsoft implementation packages SAX to be used from Visual Basic and Visual C++. Most of the information regarding SAX is the same regardless of the language you are using. There are some minor differences, however, such as the names of the interfaces. In this section I use the Visual Basic interface names and present examples using Visual Basic syntax. Later in the chapter I explain the differences that are involved for Visual C++ programmers.

The Content Handler Interface

The `Content Handler` interface is the primary interface that is implemented when using SAX. The Visual Basic class name for this interface is `IVBSAXContentHandler`. This interface receives notification as the processor encounters different items within the document content: elements, processing instructions, and so on.

The startDocument() and endDocument() Methods

The `startDocument()` and `endDocument()` methods are called at the start and the end of document processing. They are always the first and the last methods called by the processor. The `endDocument()` method is also called when the processor encounters an unrecoverable error and terminates processing. Neither of these methods takes any arguments.

The startElement() and endElement() Methods

The `startElement()` method is called when the SAX reader encounters the opening tag of an XML element. The syntax is as follows:

```
startElement(strNamespaceURI, strLocalName, strQName, oAttributes)
```

The method arguments are as follows:

- *`strNamespaceURI`* is the namespace URI of the element, or a blank string if the default namespace is in use.
- *`strLocalName`* is the name of the element.
- *`strQName`* is the element name with its namespace prefix. If there is no namespace prefix, `strQName` returns the same value as `strLocalName`.
- *`oAttributes`* is an `IVBSAXAttributes` object containing the element's attributes. This interface is explained later in the chapter.

The `endElement()` method is called when the SAX reader encounters the element's closing tag. The syntax is as follows:

```
endElement(strNamespaceURI, strLocalName, strQName)
```

The arguments for this method are the same as described previously for the `startElement()` method.

The characters() Method

The `characters()` method is called whenever the SAX reader encounters character data. The syntax is as follows:

```
characters(data)
```

`Data` is a string containing the characters that were read. You need to be aware that the `character()` method is called for all characters, including white space. For example, look at this fragment of XML:

```
<item>
  <name>Hammer</name>
  <partnumber>H1234</partnumber>
</item>
```

When SAX is processing this XML, the `characters()` method will be called for

- The newline character after the `<item>` tag
- The two spaces before the `<name>` tag
- The text "Hammer"
- The newline character after the `</name>` tag
- The two spaces before the `<partnumber>` tag
- The text "H1234"
- The newline character after the `</partnumber>` tag

This means that you must examine the data passed to the `characters()` method to determine whether it is "real" data or white space.

The processingInstruction() Method

The `processingInstruction()` method is called whenever the SAX reader encounters an XML processing instruction. The syntax is as follows:

```
processingInstruction(strTarget, strData)
```

`StrTarget` is the target of the instruction, and *`strData`* is the instruction itself. For example, here is a processing instruction:

```
<?xml-stylesheet href="report.css" type="text/css" title="Report" ?>.
```

When it encounters this instruction, the SAX reader will call the `processingInstruction()` method and pass "xml-stylesheet" as the target, and the remainder of the instruction as the data. Note that the standard XML processing instruction `<?xml version="1.0"?>` is not reported by the `processingInstruction()` method.

Implementing IVBSAXContentHandler in Visual Basic

The following is a brief description of how to implement the `IVBSAXContentHandler` interface in Visual Basic version 6.0. Chapter 15 presents a complete Visual Basic SAX program.

1. Add a reference to MSXML to the project by opening the References dialog box and placing a check mark next to Microsoft XML v4.0.
2. Add a new Class module to the project. Change the class's `Name` property to something descriptive, such as "SAXContentHandler."
3. In the Class module code window, enter the line of code `Implements IVBSAXContentHandler`.
4. In the drop-down list at the top left of the code window, be sure that `IVBXSAXContentHandler` is selected.
5. In the drop-down list at the top right of the code window, select the property or method you want to implement, and then add the desired code to the method.
6. Repeat step 5 for additional methods.

Note that you must include every method in the class even if you will not be using it, or the class will not compile. For example, you must include an empty `endDocument()` method in the class even if your application will not use this method.

The Error Handler Interface

The `Error Handler` interface provides the mechanism for handling parsing errors. The Visual Basic name for this interface is `IVBSAXErrorHandler`. This interface has one currently implemented method: `fatalError()`. The syntax is as follows:

```
fatalError(Locator, strErrorMessage, nErrorCode)
```

`Locator` is a type `IVBSAXLocator` object that can be used to determine the location of the error. This is explained later in this chapter. *`StrErrorMessage`* is

a string containing a description of the error. `NErrorCode` is a numerical value specifying the error code.

The `IVBSAXLocator` object provides information about the location in the XML document where the error occurred. This object has two properties, `columnNumber` and `lineNumber`, that identify the location (with column 1 being the first character position on a line). Specifically, the location identified is immediately after the cause of the error. You can use this information, along with the other information passed to the `fatalError()` method, to display an informative error message to the user. Listing 11.1 shows Visual Basic code to display such a message, with the output shown in Figure 11.1.

Listing 11.1 Visual Basic Implementation of the `fatalError()` Method for Reporting a SAX Parsing Error to the User

```
Private Sub IVBSAXErrorHandler_fatalError(ByVal oLocator As _
 MSXML2.IVBSAXLocator, strErrorMessage As String, _
 ByVal nErrorCode As Long)

Dim msg As String

msg = "The parser encountered an error: " & vbCrLf
msg = msg & "  Error code: " & nErrorCode & vbCrLf
msg = msg & "  Description: " & strErrorMessage
msg = msg & "  Location: just before line "
msg = msg & oLocator.lineNumber & " column " & oLocator.columnNumber

MsgBox msg

End Sub
```

Figure 11.1 An error message displayed by the `fatalError()` method in Listing 11.1

When the SAX reader encounters an error, the application's own error mechanism is triggered after the `fatalError()` method is called. However, the error information is not passed to the application. For example, if a SAX reader error occurs in a Visual Basic program, an error will be triggered but the `Err` object will not contain information about the error. The usual approach to handling SAX reader errors is to disable or suspend the application's own error handing (for example, with Visual Basic's `On Error Resume Next` statement) and perform all error handling by means of the `fatalError()` method.

The Microsoft SAX documentation mentions two other methods of the Error Handler interface: `error()` for reporting nonfatal parser errors and `ignorableWarning()` for reporting parser warnings. These methods both take the same arguments as the `fatalError()` method. However, they are not functional in the current SAX reader implementation because all errors are reported as fatal errors. You can expect this situation to change in the future.

Implementing IVBSAXErrorHandler in Visual Basic

The following is a brief description of how to implement the `IVBSAXErrorHandler` interface in Visual Basic version 6.0. Chapter 15 presents a complete Visual Basic SAX program.

1. If you have not already done so, add a reference to MSXML to the project by opening the References dialog box and placing a check mark next to Microsoft XML v4.0.
2. Add a new Class module to the project. Change the class's `Name` property to something descriptive, such as "SAXErrorHandler."
3. In the Class module code window, enter the line of code `Implements IVBSAXErrorHandler`.
4. In the drop-down list at the top left of the code window, be sure that `IVBXSAXErrorHandler` is selected.
5. In the drop-down list at the top right of the code window, select the `fatalError` method, and then add the desired code to the method.
6. Repeat step 5 for the `error()` and `ignorableWarning()` methods. These methods will remain empty, but they must be present for the class to compile.

The SAXXMLReader Interface

The `SAXXMLReader` interface is implemented to manage the parsing and processing of an XML document. You can think of this interface as being at the

Table 11.1 Properties and Methods of the `SAXXMLReader` Interface

Property or Method	Description
`contentHandler`	Sets the content handler interface to be used by the reader.
`errorHandler`	Sets the error handler interface to be used by the reader.
`parseURL(`*`source`*`)`	Instructs the reader to load and parse the specified XML document. *`Source`* is a URL identifying a local or remote file.

"top" of the hierarchy when you implement SAX in an application. The Visual Basic class name is `SAXXMLReader40` for the version-dependent class (tied to MSXML version 4.0) or `SAXXMLReader` for the version-independent class (to use the most current version of MSXML that is available on the system). The interface has methods and properties that are used to control the processing of the XML, as shown in Table 11.1. The methods of the `SAXXMLReader` interface are traditional methods that you call from your program and not methods that are called in response to events. (Note that in Table 11.1, methods are shown with parentheses following the name.)

These are the steps required to use the `SAXXMLReader` interface:

1. Create an instance of the `SAXXMLReader` interface.
2. Set its `contentHandler` property to the implementation of the `IVBSAXContentHandler` interface that you have created.
3. Set its `errorHandler` property to the implementation of the `IVBSAXErrorHandler` interface that you have created.
4. Call the `parseURL()` method, passing it the URL of the XML file to be processed.

Listing 11.2 presents a fragment of Visual Basic code that illustrates these steps. It is assumed that your project includes content handler and error handler classes named "SAXContentHandler" and "SAXErrorHandler," respectively.

Listing 11.2 Minimum Visual Basic Code to Use the SAX Reader to Process a Document

```
Dim reader As New SAXXMLReader
Dim contentHandler As New SAXContentHandler
Dim errorHandler As New SAXErrorHandler

Set reader.contentHandler = contentHandler
Set reader.errorHandler = errorHandler

On Error Resume Next
reader.parseURL "c:\my documents\xml\books.xml"
```

You'll see a complete Visual Basic SAX program in Chapter 15.

The Attributes Interface

The `Attributes` interface provides access to attributes within an XML document. The Visual Basic class name is `IVBSAXAttributes`. You obtain a reference to this interface from the `startElement()` method of the `IVBSAXContentHandler` interface. Thus, whenever the SAX reader encounters the start of an XML element, it calls the `startElement()` method and passes, as one of the method arguments, an `IVBSAXAttributes` object. You then use the object's methods and its one property to access the element's attributes. These methods and property are described in Table 11.2.

Here's an example of accessing attributes in an XML file. The following Visual Basic code, placed in the content handler's `startElement()` method, will read all the attributes of every element in the XML file. The attribute's name and value are assigned to variables for further processing (not included here).

```
If oAttributes.length > 0 Then
    For i = 0 To oAttributes.length - 1
        name = oAttributes.getLocalName(i)
        value = oAttributes.getValue(i)
    Next i
End If
```

Here's another example. This code will obtain the "price" attribute of every element named "saledata" and add the value to the variable "total," resulting in this variable containing the sum of all "price" attribute values over the entire XML file.

Table 11.2 Methods and the One Property of the `IVBSAXAttributes` Interface

Method or Property	Description
`getIndexFromName(`*`URI`*`, `*`Name`*`)`	Returns the 0-based index of the specified attribute. `Name` is the attribute name, and *`URI`* is the namespace URI or, if the attribute has no namespace URI, an empty string.
`getLocalName(`*`index`*`)`	Returns the name of the specified attribute, where *`index`* can range from 0 to `length-1`.
`getValue(`*`index`*`)`	Returns the value of the specified attribute, where *`index`* can range from 0 to `length-1`.
`getValueFromName(`*`URI`*`, `*`Name`*`)`	Returns the value of the specified attribute. *`Name`* is the attribute name, and *`URI`* is the namespace URI or, if the attribute has no namespace URI, an empty string.
`length`*	Returns the number of attributes.

* This is the object's one property.

```
If strLocalName = "saledata" Then
    total = total + oAttributes.getValueFromName("", "price")
End If
```

The Lexical Handler Interface

The `Lexical Handler` interface is an optional extension to SAX that permits an application to receive information about comments, the document type definition, `CDATA` sections, and entities within an XML document. The Visual Basic class name is `IVBSAXLexicalHandler`. You do not have to implement this interface in your SAX application unless you need its capabilities. The interface has several methods that are called when the SAX reader encounters the corresponding type of document content.

The comment() Method

The `comment()` method is called when the SAX reader encounters a comment, whether the comment is inside or outside the document element. The syntax is as follows:

```
comment(data)
```

Data is a string containing the comment text.

The startCDATA() and endCDATA() Methods

The `startCDATA()` and `endCDATA()` methods are called when the SAX reader encounters the beginning and end of a `CDATA` section. These methods take no arguments and do not provide access to the content of the `CDATA` section. To read the `CDATA` text you use the `characters()` method of the `IVBSAXContentHandler` interface, as described earlier in this chapter. The `startCDATA()` and `endCDATA()` methods are provided only to provide notification of the start and end of a `CDATA` section.

The startDTD() and endDTD() Methods

The `startDTD()` and `endDTD()` methods are called when the SAX reader encounters the start and end of a document type declaration. The syntax for the `startDTD()` method is as follows:

```
startDTD(Name, PublicID, SystemID)
```

Name is the name of the document's root element. *PublicID* is the declared public identifier for the external DTD subset, or `Null` if none is declared. *SystemID* is the declared system identifier for the external DTD subset, or `Null` if none is declared. Here's an example. Suppose the XML file being processed contains the following document type declaration:

```
<!DOCTYPE books SYSTEM "books.dtd">
```

The information passed to the `startDTD()` method will be

- *Name:* "books"
- *PublicID:* Null
- *SystemID:* "books.dtd"

Implementing IVBSAXLexicalHandler in Visual Basic

The following is a brief description of how to implement the `IVBSAXLexicalHandler` interface in Visual Basic version 6.0. Chapter 15 presents a working Visual Basic SAX program.

1. If you have not already done so, add a reference to MSXML to the project by opening the References dialog box and placing a check mark next to Microsoft XML v4.0.
2. Add a new Class module to the project. Change the class's `Name` property to something descriptive, such as "SAXLexicalHandler."
3. In the Class module code window, enter the line of code `Implements IVBSAXLexicalHandler`.
4. In the drop-down list at the top left of the code window, be sure that `IVBXSAXLexicalHandler` is selected.
5. In the drop-down list at the top right of the code window, select the method to implement, and then add the desired code to the method.
6. Repeat step 5 for the remaining interface methods. Your class must contain all methods, even if some of them are empty.

To connect the `Lexical Handler` class that you just created to the SAX reader, the procedure is different than the one you learned earlier for the `Content Handler` and `Error Handler` classes. You must use the `putProperty()` method, which has the following syntax:

```
putProperty property, value
```

`Property` is the property identifier, and *`value`* is the value of the property. For the SAX reader, property identifiers are URIs (like namespaces). The idea is the same: to ensure that each property has a unique identifier. For example, the property identifier to assign a `Lexical Handler` is "http://xml.org/sax/properties/lexical-handler." Thus, the steps are as follows:

1. Define a `Lexical Handler` class as described previously.
2. Create an instance of the class in your code.
3. Use the `putProperty()` method to assign the handler instance to the SAX reader using the "http://xml.org/sax/properties/lexical-handler" property identifier.

The following code demonstrates the preceding steps. It assumes that the instance of the `IVBSAXLexicalHandler` class that you created is named "XMLLexicalHandler."

```
Dim reader As New SAXXMLReader
Dim lexicalHandler As New XMLLexicalHandler
```

```
reader.putProperty "http://xml.org/sax/properties/lexical-handler", _
   lexicalHandler
```

SAX and Visual C++

The Microsoft SAX implementation can be used from Visual C++ equally as well as from Visual Basic. The MSXML Parser installation includes a good C++ SAX demo. For now I present a brief overview of the differences between the VC++ wrapper and the Visual Basic wrapper.

- SAX interfaces start with the "I" prefix rather than "IVB." Thus, the Content Handler interface is `IVBSAXContentHandler` in Visual Basic and `ISAXContentHandler` in VC++.
- Errors are reported as `IerrorInfo` parameters rather than as strings.
- Strings are represented as `wchar_t*/int` rather than as `BSTR`.
- Type `long` return values in Visual Basic are `HRESULT` in VC++.

The procedures for using SAX in VC++ are the same as for Visual Basic, although of course the implementation details differ.

Summary

The Simple API for XML (SAX) provides an event-driven interface to the contents of an XML document. It reads the document from start to finish and as it encounters the various items in the file (elements, processing instructions, attributes, and so on) it triggers an event to signal the parent application that the item is available. Your application can make use of each item—or not—as its requirements dictate. Compared with DOM, SAX operates much faster and places significantly lower demands on your processor and memory. SAX is less flexible than DOM, however, as it permits forward-only reading of an XML document (in contrast to DOM's random access) and does not permit changes to a document's structure. In many situations, SAX is the preferred method of accessing the contents of an XML document.

CHAPTER 12

The Simplified Object Access Protocol

The Simplified Object Access Protocol, commonly known as SOAP, is a technique that uses XML to transport information over the Internet. More specifically, SOAP provides a way to invoke object methods, and to retrieve the results of those methods, using a standard and widely adopted technology. SOAP is intimately tied in with the idea of Web services, which permit programs to access other programs remotely regardless of their location and without human interaction. This chapter provides an introduction to Web services and SOAP.

Web Services

The Web originated as a way to deliver content over the Internet. A browser requested a page, the server sent the page, and the browser displayed it. This sounds simple enough, but it was revolutionary at the time, and many interesting and useful things have been done using this basic model. As the Internet evolved, however, people wanted to do more. Rather than delivering only content in the form of Web pages, the Internet was envisioned as a tool to deliver services, and the simple request/response model was not up to the task. The idea of Web services was born, but a method of implementing it was needed.

What exactly are Web services, and how do they differ from the original Web-as-content-provider model? In a nutshell, Web services perform tasks. For example, suppose an online retailer wants to outsource their credit card processing. The processing could be offered as a Web service by the credit card company, and the merchant's ordering system would use this service to verify charges as part of the ordering process, with information being exchanged via the Internet.

What information would be exchanged in such a transaction? The merchant would send to the credit card company something similar to the following:

```
Transaction number: 12345678
Transaction type: charge
Card number: 1234123412341234
Expiration: 12/2002
Amount: 59.95
```

The computers at the credit card company would receive this information and perform the transaction. Assuming the charge went though successfully, the following information might be returned to the merchant:

```
Transaction number: 12345678
Result: Successful
```

The merchant could then confirm the order and initiate shipping procedures. On the other hand, if the charge did not go through, the reply message might be something like this:

```
Transaction number: 12345678
Result: Failed
Reason: Over limit
```

On receiving this reply, the merchant could prompt the customer for another payment method. This is a simple example, and Web services can get a lot more complex. A client may request multiple services, or a Web service provider may itself request services as part of providing its service. Whether simple or complex, it is clear that the service requester and the service provider must agree on the format, or protocol, by which the service request and any required responses are to be made. Technically, this type of communication is called a *remote procedure call (RPC).*

In the early days of Web services, there were no established standards. Each Web service provider developed their own proprietary protocols. This led to a variety of problems and inefficiencies. A merchant that wanted to switch to a different credit card processor, for example, had to modify their software to use the new service provider's RPC protocols. Clearly, some standards were needed.

Two technologies were developed to provide the kind of intercomputer communication that was required to create and deploy Web services (although these technologies do a lot more than RPCs). The Common Object Request Broker Architecture (CORBA) was developed by the Object Management Group, and the Distributed Component Object Model (DCOM) was developed by Microsoft. Without going into any details, suffice it to say that both of these standards achieved widespread adoption but, from the standpoint of the

Web services developer, they suffered from several shortcomings, including the following:

- They are better suited for server-server communication than for client-server communication.
- They have serious problems working through firewalls.
- They are difficult to set up and administer.
- They cannot talk to each other.

This situation was the impetus for the development of SOAP.

> ***UDDI***
>
> *Universal Description, Discovery, and Integration (UDDI) is a business registry where providers of Web services publish information about the services that they expose. UDDI uses XML, SOAP, and HTTP. Thus, software can make use of this registry to locate relevant Web services and then, by means of their WSDL and WSML files (explained later in the chapter), obtain the details necessary to use the services. Microsoft has created a UDDI Software Development Kit that simplifies that task of programmatically accessing the UDDI business registry. You can locate this SDK and related information by going to* `http://msdn.microsoft.com/` *and searching for "uddi."*

SOAP Basics

In the early stages of developing a new RPC protocol, it was realized that the success of any new protocol would depend on it being both simple and flexible. It should require no new technologies and should be platform-agnostic, meaning that it can be easily implemented on essentially any combination of operating system and software. The answer was found in two existing technologies: XML to structure the data and HTTP (HyperText Transfer Protocol) to transport the data across the Internet. (SOAP can also use the SMTP protocol, but that is beyond the scope of the present discussion.)

What exactly is HTTP? It is the protocol that is used to transport hypertext files—that is, Web pages—over the Internet. Anytime you view a Web page, HTTP is being used to send your request to the Web server and transmit the Web page back to your computer. HTTP is one of the oldest technologies on the Web, and certainly the most widely used, which means that it has essentially universal software and platform support. While originally designed for Web pages, HTTP can send any text data over the Internet—and XML files are text data. To give you an idea of the simplicity of HTTP, here is a legal HTTP request message:

```
POST /token HTTP/1.1
Host: www.someserver.com
Content-Type: text/plain
Content-Length: 27

This is the message content
```

The first line of the request has three components:

- `POST` identifies the message as an HTTP POST request (the other commonly used type of HTTP request, GET, is used for retrieving Web pages).
- `/token` is an identifier (known technically as the Request-URI) that identifies the target of the request.
- `HTTP/1.1` specifies the HTTP version that is being used.

The second line identifies the host that the request is being sent to. This can be a URL, as in this example, or an IP address.

The third line identifies the type of the message content—plain text in this case. You specify "text/xml" if the request contains XML.

The fourth line gives the length, in characters, of the message content. This is followed by a blank line and the message content.

In a nutshell, then, SOAP is a standard for passing requests and responses between computers, using XML to structure the information and HTTP to transport the information. SOAP does not care in the least about the operating system, programming language, or object model in use on either end of the transaction. As of this writing, SOAP version 1.1 has been submitted to W3C as a Note (`http://www.w3.org/TR/2000/NOTE-SOAP-20000508/`). A Note is a proposal to form a Working Group, and it is used as the basis for discussion without implying any endorsement by W3C.

> **SOAP and HTTP**
>
> *Strictly speaking, SOAP is not tied to the HTTP protocol. Other protocols for transmitting text data between computers can be used as well. Because SOAP started with HTTP, and HTTP is by far the most common transport protocol currently in use, the discussion in this chapter will focus on HTTP.*

SOAP and Microsoft

Microsoft actively supports SOAP, and in fact played a key role in its development. For development tools that are current as of this writing (the Visual Studio version 6.0 languages), Microsoft provides the SOAP Toolkit. This toolkit gives developers a set of classes for creating both SOAP clients and servers. You can download the toolkit from `http://msdn.microsoft.com/xml/general/soapland2.asp`. For Microsoft's new development tools (the .NET Framework and Visual Studio .NET), SOAP support is built in.

SOAP Requests

A SOAP request, or call, is transported in an HTTP POST message. The only modification to the standard HTTP POST format is the addition of a fifth header field named `SOAPAction`. This field contains a URI that indicates the intent of the SOAP request. There are no restrictions on the format or content of the URI. The information provided in this field can be used by the server to appropriately filter SOAP requests. If this field is set to an empty string ("") it means that the intent of the request is indicated by the HTTP-Request URI (the second part of the first line of the HTTP headers). If there is no value for `SOAPAction`, it means that there is no indication of a message's intent. Here is an example of the HTTP header fields for a SOAP request:

```
POST /PriceQuote HTTP/1.1
Host: www.pricequoteserver.com
Content-Type: text/xml
Content-Length: nnnn
SOAPAction: "http://www.whatever.com/this#that"
```

Remember that the content of the `SOAPAction` field and of the HTTP-Request URI (in this example, "/PriceQuote") are specific to the service being requested. The HTTP server that handles the `POST` message will be programmed to use this information to determine what to do in response to the message.

The content of the SOAP message, separated from the HTTP headers by a blank line, consists of a mandatory `Envelope` element that in turn contains an optional `Header` element and a mandatory `Body` element.

The Envelope Element

The `Envelope` element is the mandatory top-level element of the SOAP message. It contains the definition of the `Envelope` namespace "http://schemas.

xmlsoap.org/soap/envelope/" and may also contain additional implementation-specific attributes. Here is an example of an Envelope element:

```
<SOAP-ENV:Envelope
  xmlns:SOAP-ENV="http://schemas.xmlsoap.org/soap/envelope/">
...
</SOAP-ENV:Envelope>
```

Using "SOAP-ENV" for the namespace prefix is not required, but it is common practice. You will see that SOAP syntax typically uses namespace qualification for all elements and attributes. Technically, the use of namespaces is not required—a SOAP application is permitted to treat a SOAP message that does not define the Envelope namespace as if the namespace were correctly defined ("http://schemas.xmlsoap.org/soap/envelope/"). However, if a SOAP message defines an incorrect namespace, a SOAP application is required to reject the message.

The Header Element

The Header element is optional, and if present it must be the first child of the Envelope element. This element is used to extend the SOAP message in areas such as authentication and message processing. Immediate child elements of the Header element must be namespace-qualified. The elements that will be included as children of the Header element will be application-specific, but there are two attributes that are part of the SOAP specification: actor and mustUnderstand.

The actor attribute is related to the fact that a SOAP message may pass through one or more SOAP intermediaries before reaching its final destination. The Header can be used to include information that is intended for a specific intermediary. In this situation, you use the actor attribute to identify, by means of a URI, the intermediary that a Header child element is intended for. If an element does not specify the actor attribute, it is assumed to be intended for the final message destination. Here is an example:

```
<SOAP-ENV:Header>
   <t:ProcessCode xmlns:t="some-URI" SOAP-ENV:actor="URI">
     11
   </t:ProcessCode>
</SOAP-ENV:Header>
```

The information in the ProcessCode element is intended for the SOAP intermediary identified by *URI*. An intermediary will remove any elements intended specifically for it.

The `mustUnderstand` attribute is used to indicate to the final recipient of an element that proper processing of the element content is mandatory (`mustUnderstand="1"`) or optional. If this attribute is set to "1" the recipient must process the element data (as indicated by the element name) or must fail. If this attribute is set to "0" or is omitted, processing of the element is optional.

The Body Element

The `Body` element is a required part of a SOAP message. It must be either the first child within the `Envelope` element or the first element following the `Header` element. The `Body` element itself must be namespace-qualified, and its immediate child elements may be namespace-qualified. The content of the `Body` element is always intended for the final recipient of the SOAP message. The SOAP specification defines only one child element that can appear in the `Body` element: the `Fault` element (which is covered later in the chapter). Other child elements within the `Body` element are application-specific. The following is an example of a simple but complete SOAP message (without the HTTP headers):

```
<SOAP-ENV:Envelope
  xmlns:SOAP-ENV="http://schemas.xmlsoap.org/soap/envelope/">
   <SOAP-ENV:Body>
       <x:GetPrice xmlns:x="http://www.mysite.com">
           <item>Left handed widget</item>
       </x:GetPrice>
   </SOAP-ENV:Body>
</SOAP-ENV:Envelope>
```

The encodingStyle Attribute

Any SOAP element can use the `encodingStyle` attribute to specify the serialization rules that are used by that element and its children—in other words, the way data is encoded within the message. If this attribute is not set, no particular encoding style is assumed. When used, the `encodingStyle` attribute value is set to a URI that identifies the serialization rules to be used. The SOAP specification includes a set of serialization rules identified by the URI "http://schemas.xmlsoap.org/soap/encoding/."

Using the M-POST Message

While SOAP requests are usually sent using the HTTP verb POST, they can also be sent using the M-POST verb (if the server is set up to accept such messages). The M- prefix is part of HTTP extensions, marking a message as having mandatory headers that must be processed and understood. You can find details on the HTTP mandatory extensions at `http://www.w3.org/Protocols/HTTP/ietf-http-ext/`.

Web Services Description Language and Web Services Meta Language

Web Services Description Language (WSDL) and Web Services Meta Language (WSML) are integral parts of SOAP. These languages, which follow XML syntax, are used to create files that reside on the server and provide information about the services that the server offers.

As its name suggests, a WSDL file provides information about the services that are provided and the specific operations that are supported by each service. For example, a WSDL file could identify a service called "CreditCard-Processing" and within that service it could further identify the specific operations of "ChargePurchase," "ChargeCashAdvance," and "Charge-Refund." The WSDL file will also contain information about the specific format that a client must use in order to use the service. In order to call a Web service, a client will retrieve a copy of the WSDL file and use the information it contains to format the SOAP request.

A WSML file provides additional information about service requests and is specific to Microsoft's SOAP implementation. A WSML file maps specific service requests to specific software objects and methods on the server.

Creating WSDL and WSML files from scratch can be a tedious process. Fortunately, Microsoft's SOAP Toolkit (covered in the next section) provides a tool, the WSDL/WSML Generator, to automate the process.

The Microsoft SOAP Toolkit

Many aspects of Web services and SOAP programming are greatly simplified by the Microsoft SOAP Toolkit. This toolkit is available for free download from the Microsoft Web site (`http://msdn.microsoft.com/soap`). As of this writing, the toolkit is in its first beta release, so the information presented here is subject to change.

The SOAP Toolkit provides a set of objects that you can use on both the server side and the client side of SOAP to simplify development. These objects come in two groups. The *high-level* SOAP API provides the simpler programming model and is applicable to most SOAP programming situations. The *low-level* SOAP API is more complex to program but provides a greater level of control that is necessary for some situations. The current discussion is limited to the high-level API.

The client-side components in the current SOAP Toolkit run on Windows 98, Windows ME, Windows NT (Service Pack 6), and Windows 2000 (Service Pack 1). The server-side objects run on Windows 2000 and Windows NT (Service Pack 6).

Server-Side Programming

The programming required on the server side consists of the following.

- Create a class that provides the services. You can use any programming tool that can create a COM object, such as a Microsoft Visual Basic ActiveX DLL. The name of the DLL file is the service name, and the names of the public methods (functions) in the class are the operations exposed by the service. The class must be registered on the server. Note that if you use Visual Basic to create the Web service DLL, it must be compiled with the "Retained in memory" and "Unattended execution" options enabled.
- Use the WSDL/WSML Generator to create the WSDL/WMDL files for the service. Note that the class must have an associated type library in order to use the WSDL/WSML Generator.
- Use Internet Information Server (IIS, the Microsoft Web server software) to create a virtual root and assign it the same name as the DLL file.
- Create an Active Server Pages (ASP) file that includes script code to receive the request from the client and invoke the service (you'll see how to do this soon). The ASP script uses the `SoapServer` object (provided by the SOAP Toolkit) to perform these tasks.
- Place the ASP file, the WSDL file, and the WSML file in the folder associated with the IIS virtual root.

The `SoapServer` object automates almost all of the tasks involved in receiving and responding to a SOAP request. It has only two members. The `Init()`

method initializes the `SoapServer` object using the information in the WSDL and WSML files. The syntax is as follows:

```
SoapServer.Init wsdl, wsml
```

The two arguments are the names and paths to the WSDL and WSML files, respectively.

The second method of the `SoapServer` object is `SoapInvoke()`. This method processes the SOAP request and returns the response to the client. The syntax is as follows:

```
SoapServer.SoapInvoke Request, Response
```

The arguments refer to two objects that are provided by ASP. The `Request` object contains the request sent by the client, which in this case will be a SOAP request. The `Response` object sends the output of the Web service back to the client. Before calling the `SoapInvoke()` method, the ASP script should set the `Response` object's `ContentType` property to "text/xml" because that is the format of SOAP requests.

The following VBScript fragment shows how an ASP script would receive and respond to a Web services request. You should note that the role of the ASP script is solely to serve as an intermediary between the client requesting the service and the service itself. Unlike the usual usage of ASP pages, the output of the script is not HTML to display in the client browser. Rather, it is data generated by the service in response to the request that is sent to the client, which then accesses the data via the client-side SOAP API.

```
<%@ LANGUAGE=VBScript %>
<% Response.ContentType="text/xml"
set SoapServer = CreateObject("MSSOAP.SoapServer")
wsdl = Server.MapPath("MyWebService.wsdl")
wsml = Server.MapPath("MyWebService.wsml")
SoapServer.Init wsdl, wsml
SoapServer.SoapInvoke Request, Response
%>
```

Client-Side Programming

Client-side programming with the SOAP Toolkit is based on the `SoapClient` object. This object has a single method, `mssoapinit()`, that connects it to the SOAP server. The syntax is as follows:

```
mssoapinit wsdlfile, servicename, portname
```

`Wsdlfile` is a required argument that specifies the URL of the WSDL file for the service being accessed. `Servicename` is an optional argument specifying the name of the service. If this argument is omitted, is a blank string, or is `Null`, the first service listed in the WSDL file is used. `Portname` specifies the port type of the service that will be requested. If it is omitted, the first port in the specified service is used.

> ***Services and Port Names***
>
> *A given Web server can expose multiple services that are defined in the same WSDL file. Each individual service can have one or more ports, and within each port the service's operations are defined. The operations correspond to the methods of the service that the client calls. By permitting multiple ports, a Web service can expose two different operations that have the same name, as long as they are defined under different port type elements in the WSDL files. In most situations, however, each service will have only a single port associated with it.*

The following Visual Basic code demonstrates how to use the `mssoapinit()` method to connect to a Web service:

```
Dim soapclient As New MSSOAPLib.soapclient
soapclient.soapinit "http://www.myserver.com/mywebservice.wsdl", "", ""
```

The method for creating an instance of the `soapclient` object will depend on the language you are using. For example, in VBScript you use the `CreateObject()` method. Note that the identifier for this object differs depending on the situation. As shown previously, the identifier is `MSSOAPLib.soapclient`, whereas in script you must use `MSSOAP.soapclient`. These inconsistencies are likely due to the fact that the SOAP Toolkit is a beta product. By the time you read this, the naming should be consistent.

The WSDL/WSML Generator

The Microsoft SOAP Toolkit provides a utility program that can generate WSDL and WSML files from your Web service class. This is a terrific help, as the process of creating these files manually is difficult and time-consuming. The program is named WSDLGEN.EXE, and it is installed in the Binaries subfolder under the main SOAP Toolkit installation folder (c:\program

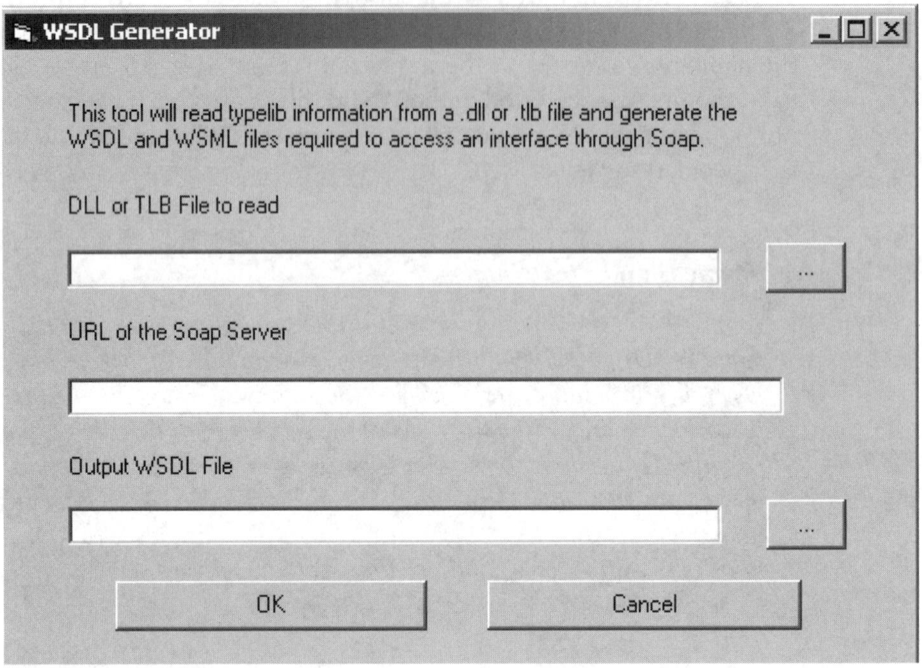

Figure 12.1 The WSDLGEN utility

files\MSSoapSDK by default). When you run the program, it displays the dialog box shown in Figure 12.1. The information required is as follows:

- The name (including the path) of the DLL containing the Web service class you created, or the name of the associate type library (TLB) file.
- The URL of the ASP file that contains the script to interface the client to the server. For example, "http://www.myserver.com/soap.asp."
- The name (including the path) of the WSDL file to generate.

The utility creates both WSDL and WSML files and places them in the specified folder.

A SOAP Toolkit Demonstration

SOAP may sound rather complicated, but with the utilities provided by Microsoft it can be surprisingly simple to get a Web service up and running. In this section, I walk you through the steps of creating, deploying, and testing a

Web service using the SOAP Toolkit. There are two approaches to this. You can create and "deploy" the service on any local development system that has IIS running. This is the approach I take in the demonstration. You then use the local URL that IIS is set up to use, which is typically `http://localhost/` or `http://127.0.0.1/`. The alternative is to deploy the service on a remote Web server where you have your Web page (again, IIS is required). This requires uploading the service DLL to the Web server, and it also requires you to "execute" permission for that folder on your Web site. If you administer the site yourself, you know how to take care of these details. Otherwise, your site administrator should be able to help.

Creating the Service Class

A Web service can do just about anything you can imagine, but for the present purposes I am going to keep things simple. The goal is to demonstrate the use of the SOAP Toolkit rather than to create a service that is really useful. The service that I create provides three operations:

- Return the current time on the server.
- Reverse the order of characters in a string.
- Add two numbers.

You can create a Web service using any programming language that supports the creation of COM objects. This example uses Microsoft Visual Basic version 6.0. Here are the steps to follow:

1. Open Visual Basic and start a new ActiveX DLL project. Assign a project name; for the demonstration, I use "MyWebService."
2. Add the code from Listing 12.1 to the class.
3. Select Properties from the project menu and turn on the "Unattended execution" and "Retained in memory" options.
4. Select Make MyWebService.dll from the File menu.

After you complete these steps, the file MyWebService.dll will be present in the folder you selected. If you are developing locally, it can stay there, as long as it is registered (which is done automatically). If you are deploying remotely, you need to upload this file to the server. At this point the service is complete.

Listing 12.1 The Code for the Web Service Class

```
' WebService1. Class to provide Web services to
' demonstrate the MS SOAP Toolkit.
```

```
Public Function Sum(ByVal n1 As Double, ByVal n2 As Double) As Double

' Returns the sum of two numbers.
Sum = n1 + n2

End Function

Public Function ServerTime() As String

' Return the current time.
ServerTime = Time

End Function


Public Function ReverseString(ByVal s As String) As String

' Reverses the order of characters in a string.

Dim i As Integer
Dim buf As String

' Check for empty string.
If s = "" Then
    ReverseString = ""
    Exit Function
End If

buf = ""

For i = Len(s) To 1 Step -1
  buf = buf & Mid(s, i, 1)
Next i

ReverseString = buf

End Function
```

Creating the ASP File

You can use any text editor to create an ASP file. The ASP file contains the code shown in Listing 12.2. After you create the ASP file, save it as MyWebService.asp to the virtual root in your Web site (local or remote).

Listing 12.2 MyWebService.asp Provides the Interface between the SOAP Client and the Web Service

```
<%@ language=vbscript%>
<% response.contenttype="text/xml"
set soapserver = createobject("MSSOAP.SoapServer")
wsdl = Server.MapPath("MyWebService.wsdl")
wsml = Server.MapPath("MyWebService.wsml")
SoapServer.Init wsdl, wsml
SoapServer.SoapInvoke request, response
%>
```

Creating the WSDL and WSML Files

The next step is to run the WSDLGEN utility and create the WSDL and WSML files for your project. For this project, the three pieces of information needed by the utility are as follows:

- The name and path of the MyWebService.dll file you created. Even if you are deploying remotely, you can use your local copy of the DLL file for this purpose.
- The URL of the ASP file you just created. For local deployment this might be "http://localhost/MyWebService.asp."
- The name to use for the WSDL file, MyWebService.wsdl. If you are deploying locally, include the path to the folder corresponding to the IIS virtual root. If you are deploying remotely, you can create the WSDL and WSML files anywhere on your local disk and then upload them to your remote Web folder.

Creating the Client Program

You can create a SOAP client using any development method that can use COM objects. I will show you a Visual Basic client and then a VBScript client.

To create the Visual Basic client, start Visual Basic and create a new Standard EXE project. Then follow these steps:

1. Select References from the Project menu to display the References dialog box. Put a check mark next to "Microsoft SOAP Type Library." (Note that this identification may change with the final release version of the SOAP Toolkit.)
2. On the project's form, add a Text Box control and set its `Multiline` property to True. Size the Text Box so that it is at least several lines tall.

3. Add two Command Buttons, one with the caption "Access Service" and the other with the caption "Quit."
4. Add the code from Listing 12.3 to the form. Note that this code contains event procedures for the two Command Buttons that you placed on the form. If necessary, change the URL of the WSDL file to point to your local or remote server.

After saving your files, you can run the project. When it displays the dialog box, click the Access Service button. The client will send the SOAP request to the server and display the returned data in the Text Box, as shown in Figure 12.2.

Listing 12.3 Code in the Visual Basic SOAP Client Program

```
Private Sub cmdAccessService_Click()


Dim soapclient As New MSSOAPLib.soapclient
Dim buf As String


' Initialize the SOAP client.
soapclient.mssoapinit "http://127.0.0.1/MyWebService.wsdl", "", ""


buf = "The time at the server is " & soapclient.ServerTime() & vbCrLf
buf = buf & "'Hello' backwards is " & soapclient.ReverseString("Hello")
& vbCrLf
buf = buf & "The sum of 1 and 2 is " & soapclient.Sum(1, 2)
Text1.Text = buf

Set soapclient = Nothing

End Sub

Private Sub cmdQuit_Click()

Unload Me

End Sub
```

Creating a SOAP client in VBScript is even simpler than in Visual Basic. You can run the script using the Windows Script Host. These are the steps to follow:

1. Use a text editor to create a file named "MyWebService.vbs" containing the script code in Listing 12.4. As before, change the URL or your WSDL file as needed.

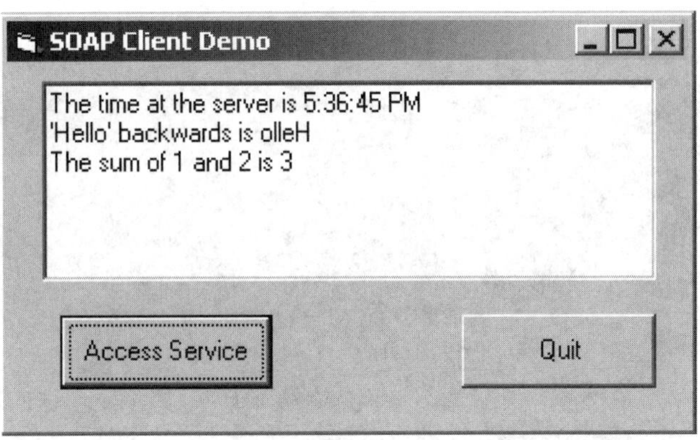

Figure 12.2 The Visual Basic SOAP client displaying data obtained from the Web service

2. Open a Command Prompt window and navigate to the folder where you saved MyWebService.vbs.
3. Type "cscript mywebservice.vbs" at the command prompt and press Enter.

When the script runs, it will access the Web service and display the returned data in the Command Prompt window, as shown in Figure 12.3.

Listing 12.4: A SOAP Client Written in VBScript

```
set soapclient = CreateObject("MSSOAP.SoapClient")
soapclient.mssoapinit "http://127.0.0.1/MyWebService.wsdl", "", ""
wscript.echo soapclient.ReverseString("Hello")
wscript.echo soapclient.ServerTime()
wscript.echo soapclient.Sum(1, 2)
```

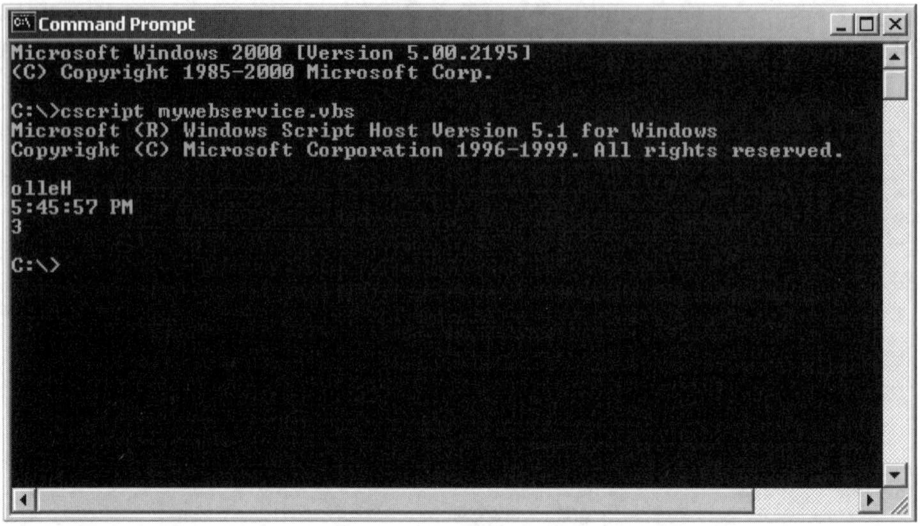

```
Command Prompt
Microsoft Windows 2000 [Version 5.00.2195]
(C) Copyright 1985-2000 Microsoft Corp.

C:\>cscript mywebservice.vbs
Microsoft (R) Windows Script Host Version 5.1 for Windows
Copyright (C) Microsoft Corporation 1996-1999. All rights reserved.

olleH
5:45:57 PM
3

C:\>
```

Figure 12.3 Running the VBScript SOAP client

Summary

The Simplified Object Access Protocol (SOAP) defines a way for existing Internet protocols to be used to transmit information required for interactive Web services. SOAP messages use XML to structure their contents; hence the interest to XML developers. Microsoft's SOAP Toolkit provides a set of classes for creating both SOAP clients and servers, and greatly simplifies the task of the SOAP programmer.

CHAPTER 13

XML and the .NET Framework

The .NET (pronounced "dot net") Framework is the foundation of Microsoft's next generation of development tools. Given the increasing importance of XML in all areas of programming and data processing, the inclusion of powerful, integrated XML support in .NET is not surprising. This chapter provides a brief overview of .NET and then details the XML tools that are provided by the Framework and the Visual Studio .NET development environment. Code samples in this chapter are written in the C# language. This is a new language introduced with Visual Studio .NET.

.NET Overview

Microsoft's .NET initiative has its origins in the increasing importance of the Web in almost all areas of application development. Previous development tools, exemplified by Visual Studio version 6.0, were designed for the needs of a decade ago, when the ruling paradigm was applications that were standalone or were distributed over a local area network (LAN). As the need for Web-related capabilities grew, ad hoc solutions were crafted as enhancements to existing tools. Because the Web capabilities were not built into the development tools from the beginning, however, there were inevitable problems with deployment, maintenance, and efficiency.

Things are different with .NET. The .NET Framework provides a comprehensive set of classes that are designed for just about any programming task you can imagine. From the very beginning, the Framework was designed to integrate Web-related programming functionality. The Framework can be used by any of Microsoft's three programming languages: Visual Basic, C++, and C# (pronounced "C sharp"). The new releases of Visual Basic and C++ will be familiar to anyone who has used earlier versions, although there are numerous changes to accommodate the .NET architecture. C# is new language that is similar to Java in many respects, although there are significant differences between the two. Some observers consider C# to be a Java replacement made necessary because legal problems have forced Microsoft to stop supporting Java (or Visual J++, as Microsoft's version of Java was called).

For the XML developer, .NET was designed to support XML from the ground up. There are no add-ons required, such as the MSXML Parser or the SOAP Toolkit. Everything you need is provided by the Framework. Please remember that as of this writing, the .NET Framework is a beta product. It is believed that the XML support is fairly stable, but it is possible that there will be some changes before the final product is released (which may happen by the time you read this).

The System.XML Assembly

XML support in .NET is provided by the classes in the System.XML namespace, or assembly. An assembly is a collection of related classes. In the case of System.XML, the classes are related by having to do with XML processing. The primary classes are as follows:

- `XmlTextReader`: Provides forward-only, fast, noncached access to XML data
- `XmlValidatingReader`: Used in conjunction with the `XmlTextReader` class to provide the capability for DTD, XDR, and XSD schema validation
- `XmlDocument`: Implements both level 1 and level 2 of the W3C Document Object Model specification (`http://www.w3.org/TR/DOM-Level-1/` and `http://www.w3.org/TR/DOM-Level-2/`)
- `XmlTextWriter`: Permits generation of XML documents that conform to the W3C XML 1.0 specification
- `XmlNavigator`: Supports evaluation of XPath expressions

Note that the Simple API for XML (SAX) is not supported in .NET. Similar functionality is provided by the `XmlTextReader` class, although there are significant differences, which are detailed later in the chapter.

The XmlTextReader Class

The `XmlTextReader` class is designed for fast, resource nonintensive access to the contents of an XML file. Unlike the `XmlDocument` class, the `XMLTextReader` class does not create a node tree of the entire document in memory. Rather, it processes the XML as a forward-only stream. The entire XML document is never available at the same time (as is the case with the `XmlDocument` class)—your code can extract individual items from the XML file as they stream by.

In some ways the `XmlTextReader` class is similar to the SAX model covered in Chapter 11, and in fact, the .NET programmer would tend to use the `XmlTextReader` class for the same types of processing that SAX would be used for. There is a major difference between the two models, however. SAX uses a *push* model in which the XML processor uses events to inform the host program that node data is available, and the program can use the data or not as its needs dictate. The data is pushed from the XML processor to the host, and it can be accepted or ignored. As an analogy, think of a Chinese dim sum restaurant where the available food is brought around on carts and you select what you want.

In contrast, the `XmlTextReader` class uses a *pull* model. The host program requests that the XML processor read a node, and then requests data from that node as needed. The host program pulls the data from the processor as it is needed. Pull processing is analogous to a traditional restaurant where you request items from a menu. A pull model has numerous advantages over a push model for XML processing. Perhaps most important is that a push model can easily be built on top of a pull model, while the reverse is not true.

The `XmlTextReader` class operates by stepping through the nodes of an XML document, one at a time, under the control of the host program. At any given time, there is a current node. For the current node, the host program can determine the type of the node, its attributes (if any), its data, and so on. Once the needed information about the current node has been obtained, the program will step to the next node. In this manner the entire XML file can be processed.

The `XmlTextReader` class has a large number of public properties and methods. The ones you will need most often are explained in Table 13.1 and Table 13.2.

Table 13.1 Commonly Needed Properties of the `XmlTextReader` Class

Property	Description
`AttributeCount`	Returns the number of attributes of the current node
`Depth`	Returns the depth (nesting level) of the current node
`EOF`	Returns True if the XML reader is at the end of the file

(*continued*)

Table 13.1 *(cont.)*

Property	Description
`HasAttributes`	Returns True if the current node has attributes
`HasValue`	Returns True if the current node can have a value
`IsEmptyElement`	Returns True if the current node is an empty element (for example, <ElementName/>)
`Item`	Returns the value of an attribute
`LocalName`	Returns the name of the current node without any namespace prefix
`Name`	Returns the name of the current node with any namespace prefix
`NodeType`	Returns the type of the current node as an `XmlNodeType` (see Table 13.3)
`Value`	Returns the value of the current node

Table 13.2 Commonly Needed Methods of the `XmlTextReader` Class

Method	Description
`Close()`	Closes the XML file and reinitializes the reader.
`GetAttribute(att)`	Gets the value of an attribute. *`Att`* is a number specifying the position of the attribute, with the first attribute being 0, or a string specifying the name of the attribute.
`IsStartElement()`	Returns True if the current node is a start element or an empty element.
`MoveToAttribute(att)`	Moves to a specific attribute. *`Att`* is a number specifying the position of the attribute, with the first attribute being 0, or a string specifying the name of the attribute.

Table 13.2 *(cont.)*

Method	Description
`MoveToElement()`	Moves to the element that contains the current attribute.
`MoveToFirstAttribute()`	Moves to the first attribute.
`MoveToNextAttribute()`	Moves to the next attribute.
`Read()`	Reads the next node from the XML file. Returns True on success or False if there are no more nodes to read.

Table 13.3 `XmlNodeType` Values Returned by the `NodeType` Property

Value	Meaning
`Attribute`	An attribute
`CDATA`	A `CDATA` section
`Comment`	A comment
`Document`	The document node (root element)
`DocumentType`	A `DOCTYPE` element
`Element`	An element (opening tag)
`EndElement`	The end of an element (closing tag)
`EntityReference`	An entity reference
`ProcessingInstruction`	An XML processing instruction
`Text`	The text content of an element
`XmlDeclaration`	The XML declaration element

The basic steps required to use the `XmlTextReader` class are as follows:

1. Create an instance of the class, passing the name of the XML file to process as an argument to the class constructor.
2. Create a loop that executes the `Read()` method repeatedly until it returns False, which means that the end of the file has been reached.
3. In the loop, determine the type of the current node.
4. Based on the node type, either ignore the node or retrieve node data as needed.

Listing 13.1 presents an example of using the `XmlTextReader` class. It is an ASP Web page, with the script components written using the C# language. The script opens an XML file and processes it using the `XmlTextReader` class. The root element in the file, its child element, and their attributes and data are formatted as HTML and written to the output for display in the browser.

The script defines a class called `DisplayXmlFile` that does all of the work. This class contains one public method, `ReadDoc()`, that is passed the name of the XML file to be processed and returns the HTML to be displayed in the document. It also contains two private methods: `ProcessXml()`, which performs the actual processing of the XML file, and `Spaces()`, which is a utility function to provide indentation to format the output.

The script also contains a procedure named `Page_Load()`. This is an event procedure that is called automatically when the browser first loads the page. Code in this procedure creates an instance of the `DisplayXml` class, and then calls its `ReadDoc()` method, passing the name of the XML file to be processed. The HTML returned by this method is displayed by assigning it to the `InnerHTML` property of a `<div>` element in the page.

Figure 13.1 shows the output when this script is used to process Listing1506.xml, an XML file that is presented in Chapter 15. Though not visible in the figure, the data (attribute and element values) are displayed in blue while the remainder of the document is in black.

Listing 13.1 Using the `XmlTextReader` Class to Read Data from an XML File

```
<%@ Import Namespace="System.Xml" %>

<script language="C#" runat=server>

  public class DisplayXmlFile
  // This is the class that reads and processes the XML file.
```

```
{
  StringBuilder result = new StringBuilder();

  public string ReadDoc(String XmlFileName) {
    XmlTextReader xmlReader = null;
  try  {
      // Create an instance of the XMLTextReader.
     xmlReader = new XmlTextReader(XmlFileName);
     // Process the XML file.
     ProcessXml(xmlReader);
     }
  catch (Exception e){
     result.Append("The following error occurred: " +
          e.ToString());
     }
      finally
     {
     if (xmlReader != null)
     xmlReader.Close();
     }
      return result.ToString();
  }

private void ProcessXml(XmlTextReader xmlReader) {
  // This method reads the XML file and generates the output HTML.
  while (xmlReader.Read()) {
   // Process a start of element node.
   if (xmlReader.NodeType == XmlNodeType.Element) {
     result.Append(spaces(xmlReader.Depth*3));
     result.Append("&lt;" + xmlReader.Name);
     if (xmlReader.AttributeCount > 0) {
       while (xmlReader.MoveToNextAttribute()) {
         result.Append(" " + xmlReader.LocalName +
           "=<font color=#0000ff>" + xmlReader.Value +
           "</font> ");
       }
     }
       result.Append("&gt;<br>");
   // Process an end of element node.
   } else if (xmlReader.NodeType == XmlNodeType.EndElement) {
       result.Append(spaces(xmlReader.Depth*3));
       result.Append("&lt;/" + xmlReader.Name + "&gt;<br>");
   // Process a text node.
   } else if (xmlReader.NodeType == XmlNodeType.Text) {
```

```
          if (xmlReader.Value.Length != 0) {
            result.Append(spaces(xmlReader.Depth*3));
            result.Append("<font color=#0000ff>" + xmlReader.Value +
              "<br></font>");
      }
    }
  }
 }

private string spaces(int n) {

// Returns the specified number of non-breaking
// spaces ( ).

    string s = "";
    for (int i=0; i < n; i++) {
     s += " ";
    }
    return s;
  }
} //End DisplayXmlFile Class

private void Page_Load(Object sender, EventArgs e){

   // Create a class instance.
   DisplayXmlFile DisplayXmlFileDemo = new DisplayXmlFile();

   // Add the HTML generated by the class to the HTML document.
   show.InnerHtml =
DisplayXmlFileDemo.ReadDoc(Server.MapPath("list1506.xml"));
}

</script>
<html>
<head>
</head>
<body>
  <font size="4">Using the XmlTextReader Class</font><p>
  <div id="show" runat="server"/>
</body>
</html>
```

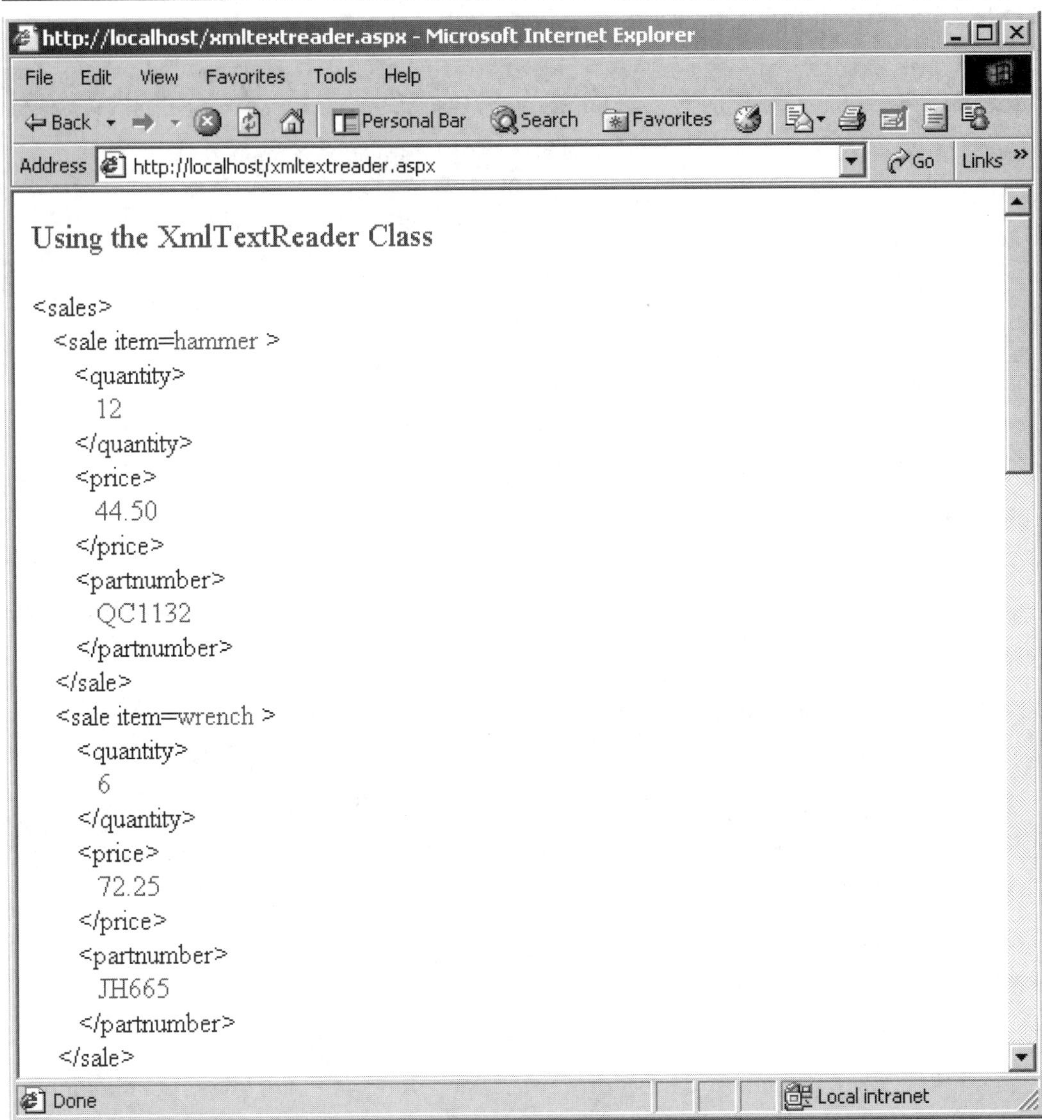

Figure 13.1 An XML file displayed in Internet Explorer by the script in Listing 13.1

The XmlValidatingReader Class

The `XmlValidatingReader` class is used to validate an XML file against a DTD or a schema (either XDR or XSD). This class is used in conjunction with the `XmlTextReader` class and provides the same access to the document contents.

Table 13.4 `ValidationType` Constants for the `ValidationType` Property

Constant	Description
`Auto`	Validates using information contained in the XML document (a DTD defined in a `DOCTYPE` element, a "schemalocation" attribute, or an inline schema). If no validation information is found, it acts as a nonvalidating parser.
`DTD`	Validate against a DTD.
`None`	Does not validate.
`Schema`	Validate against an XSD Schema.
`XDR`	Validate against an XDR Schema.

The properties and methods of these two classes are essentially identical. The differences between them lie in two properties of the `XmlValidatingReader` class that are related to validation.

The `ValidationType` property specifies the type of validation to be performed. The possible settings for this property are the `ValidationType` constants described in Table 13.4.

The `ValidationEventHandler` property is used to inform the XML reader of the event procedure you have created to handle validation errors. This event procedure takes the following form:

```
public void ValidationCallBack(object sender, ValidationEventArgs args)
// Code to handle error goes here.
}
```

The name of the procedure can be anything you like. When a validation error occurs, the procedure is called by the XML reader with information about the error contained in the `args` argument. Use `args.ErrorCode` and `args.Message` to obtain a numerical code and text description of the error, respectively. You can also use the `LineNumber` and `LinePosition` properties of the `XMLTextReader` class to get information about the location of the error in the XML file.

To inform the `XmlValidatingReader` object of your event handler, use the following syntax (assuming that "vrdr" is an instance of the class):

```
vrdr.ValidationEventHandler +=
        new ValidationEventHandler( NameOfEventHandler );
```

Note that you do not have to specify a handler for validation errors. If you do not, the reader will throw an exception when a validation error occurs. The advantage of using a validation error handler is that multiple validation errors can be detected and reported during a single pass over the XML file.

The general procedure for using the `XmlValidatingReader` class to validate an XML document is as follows. This assumes that the XML file contains the DTD/schema to be used for validation, either inline or as a reference.

1. Create an instance of the `XmlTextReader` class and load the XML file into it.
2. Create an instance of the `XmlValidatingReader` class and pass it a reference to the `XmlTextReader` class created in step 1.
3. Create an event handler procedure to handle validation errors. Code in this procedure can display messages to the user, set flags, or perform other actions as required by the program.
4. Set the `XmlValidatingReader` object's `ValidationType` and `ValidationEventHandler` properties.
5. Call the `XmlValidatingReader` object's `Read()` method repeatedly until the end of the XML file is reached.

The program in Listing 13.2 shows an example of how to do these tasks. This is a console, or command-line, application written in C# (a console application runs in a "DOS box"). Passed the name of an XML file as a command-line argument, the program validates the file against the DTD or schema information contained or referenced in the file. If the validation is successful, a message to that effect is displayed. If there is a validation error, or an exception is thrown, the relevant information is displayed to the user.

Listing 13.2 C# Program to Demonstrate the `XmlValidatingReader` Class

```
using System;
using System.IO;
using System.Xml;
using System.Xml.Schema;

public class ValidateXML
  {
```

```
    private XmlTextReader rdr = null;
    private XmlValidatingReader vrdr = null;
    private Boolean succeeded = true;

    public ValidateXML(string filename)
    // This method performs the validation.
      {
        try
        {
          //Create an XmlTextReader.
          rdr = new XmlTextReader( filename );
          // Create an XmlValidatingReader.
          vrdr = new XmlValidatingReader( rdr );
          // Set validation type to DTD.
          vrdr.ValidationType=ValidationType.DTD;
          // Set the validation callback method.
          vrdr.ValidationEventHandler +=
             new ValidationEventHandler( ValidationCallBack );
          // Read the XML document.
          while (vrdr.Read()) {}
          // Display success or failure message.
          if (succeeded)
             Console.WriteLine("Validation succeeded.");
          else
             Console.WriteLine("Validation failed.");
        }
        catch (Exception e)
        {
          Console.WriteLine( "Xml Exception: " + e.ToString() );
        }
        finally
        {
          if ( rdr != null )
            rdr.Close();
          if ( vrdr != null )
            vrdr.Close();
          }
      }

  public static void Main(string[] args)
    {
    // Execution starts here.
    // The class reference.
      ValidateXML validate;
    // Ensure that 1 command line argument (the XML file name) was passed.
```

```
    if (args.Length != 1)
      Console.WriteLine("Usage: validate xmlfilename");
    else
      validate = new ValidateXML(args[0]);
  }

public void ValidationCallBack( object sender, ValidationEventArgs args
)
  {
  // This callback method is called when a validation error occurs.
    succeeded = false;
    // Display error information to the user.
    Console.Write( "\r\n\tValidation error: " + args.Message );
    if ( rdr.LineNumber > 0 )
      Console.WriteLine( "Line: " + rdr.LineNumber + " Position: " +
        rdr.LinePosition );
  }
}
```

The XmlTextWriter Class

The `XmlTextWriter` class provides the ability to write properly formed XML to a file or other stream. The XML created conforms to the W3C XML specification version 1.0, and also to the Namespaces in XML specification. Using this class is straightforward:

1. Create an instance of the class, passing the name of the file to be used for output and the type of encoding to use. Pass a null reference for the encoding argument to use UTF-8 encoding.
2. Set object properties as needed to control the formatting of the output.
3. Call object methods to write elements and attributes to the file.
4. Close the file.

The properties and methods of the `XmlTextWriter` class that you will use most often are described in Table 13.5 and Table 13.6.

The program in Listing 13.3 demonstrates how to use the `XmlTextWriter` class. This is a C# console application that creates a new XML file named XmlOutput.xml. Some data is written to the file, and then it is closed. Finally, the file is read back using the `XmlTextReader` class and then written to the console. Reading the file with `XmlTextReader` is often a good idea to verify that the file is well-formed. The results of running the program are shown in Figure 13.2.

Table 13.5 Commonly Needed Properties of the `XmlTextWriter` Class

Property	Description
`Formatting`	Specifies the formatting of the output. Possible settings are `Formatting.Indented` to indent child elements with respect to their parents. Set to `Formatting.None` for no indentation (the default).
`Indentation`	Specifies how many characters to indent by for each level in the element hierarchy when `Formatting` is set to indented. The default is 2.
`IndentChar`	Specifies the character to use for indenting when `Formatting` is set to indented. The default is the space character. Must be a valid white space character.
`Namespaces`	Set to True to enable namespace support, and set to False for no namespace support. The default is True.
`QuoteChar`	Specifies the character to use for quoting attribute values. Must be either the double quote (") or the single quote ($). The default is the double quote.

Table 13.6 Commonly Needed Methods of the `XmlTextWriter` Class

Method	Description
`Close()`	Closes the output stream or file.
`Flush()`	Flushes the writer buffer to the output file or stream.

`WriteAttributeString(`*`localName, value`*`)`
 	
`WriteAttributeString(`*`localName, ns, value`*`)`
 	
`WriteAttributeString(`*`prefix, localName, ns, value`*`)`
	Writes an attribute with the specified local name and value. Use the other forms of the method to include as namespace URI and a prefix.

`WriteCData(`*`text`*`)`	Writes a CDATA section containing *`text`*.
`WriteComment(`*`text`*`)`	Writes an XML comment containing *`text`*.

(continued)

Table 13.6 *(cont.)*

Method	Description
`WriteDocType(`*`name`*`, `*`pubid`*`, `*`sysid`*`, `*`subset`*`)`	Writes a `DOCTYPE` element. *`Name`* is a required argument specifying the name of the `DOCTYPE`. The other arguments are optional and are for writing `PUBLIC` "*`pubid`*," `SYSTEM` "*`sysid`*," and [*`subset`*] to the `DOCTYPE` element.
`WriteElementString(`*`localName`*`, `*`value`*`)` `WriteElementString(`*`localName`*`, `*`ns`*`, `*`value`*`)`	Writes an element with the specified local name and value. Use the second form of the method to include a namespace URI.
`WriteEndAttribute()`	Completes an attribute started with `WriteStartAttribute()`.
`WriteEndDocument()`	Closes any open elements or attributes.
`WriteEndElement()`	Writes the closing tag for an element started with `WriteStartElement()`. If the element is empty it will be closed with a short end tag: <element />.
`WriteFullEndElement()`	Writes the closing tag for an element started with `WriteStartElement()`. If the element is empty it will be closed with a separate end tag: <element></element>.
`WriteProcessingInstruction(`*`name`*`, `*`text`*`)`	Writes a processing instruction with the specified name and text.
`WriteRaw(`*`text`*`)`	Writes raw text to the output.
`WriteStartAttribute(`*`localName`*`, `*`ns`*`)` `WriteStartAttribute(`*`prefix`*`, `*`localName`*`, `*`ns`*`)`	Writes the start of an attribute with the specified local name and namespace URI. Use the second form of the method to add a prefix to the local name.
`WriteStartDocument()` `WriteStartDocument(`*`standalone`*`)`	Writes the XML declaration with the version "1.0." Use the second form of the method to include "standalone=yes" or "standalone=no" in the declaration.

(continued)

Table 13.6 *(cont.)*

Method	Description

`WriteStartElement(localName)`
`WriteStartElement (localName, ns)`
`WriteStartElement (prefix, localName, ns)`
	Writes a start element with the specified local name. Use the other forms of the method to include a namespace URI and a prefix in the element.

`WriteWhitespace(string)`	Writes white space to the output. If *`string`* contains non–white space characters, an exception occurs.

Listing 13.3 Console Application Demonstrating the `XmlTextWriter` Class

```
using System;
using System.IO;
using System.Xml;

class XmlWriter
{
    private const string m_FileName = "XmlOutput.xml";

    static void Main()
    {
        XmlTextWriter w = null;
        XmlTextReader rdr = null;

        try
        {
        w = new XmlTextWriter(m_FileName, null);
        w.Formatting = Formatting.Indented;
        w.Indentation = 4;

        //Start the document.
        w.WriteStartDocument();

        //Write the root element.
        w.WriteStartElement( "contacts" );
```

```
// Start a "person" element.
w.WriteStartElement( "person" );

//Write a "category" attribute.
w.WriteAttributeString("category", "personal");

//Write a "name" element.
w.WriteElementString("name", "John Adams");

//Write a "phone" element.
w.WriteElementString("phone", "555-555-1212");

//Write an "email" element.
    w.WriteElementString("email", "john.adams@nowhere.net");

//Close the "person" element.
w.WriteEndElement();

//Write another "person" element.
    w.WriteStartElement( "person" );
    w.WriteAttributeString("category", "business");
    w.WriteElementString("name", "Mandy Pearson");
    w.WriteElementString("phone", "555-444-3232");
    w.WriteElementString("email", "mandyp@overthere.org");
    w.WriteEndElement();

// Close the root element.
w.WriteEndElement();

//Flush and close.
w.Flush();
w.Close();

//Read the file back in and display it.
rdr = new XmlTextReader( m_FileName );
XmlDocument xmlDoc = new XmlDocument();
// Preserve white space for readability
xmlDoc.PreserveWhitespace = true;
xmlDoc.Load( rdr );
// Write the content to the console
Console.Write( xmlDoc.InnerXml );
}
catch (Exception e)
{
```

```
                Console.WriteLine( "Exception: ", e.ToString() );
                }
                finally
                {
                Console.WriteLine();
                Console.WriteLine( "Processing completed." );
                if ( rdr != null )
                   rdr.Close();
                if ( w != null )
                   w.Close();
                }
            }
        }
```

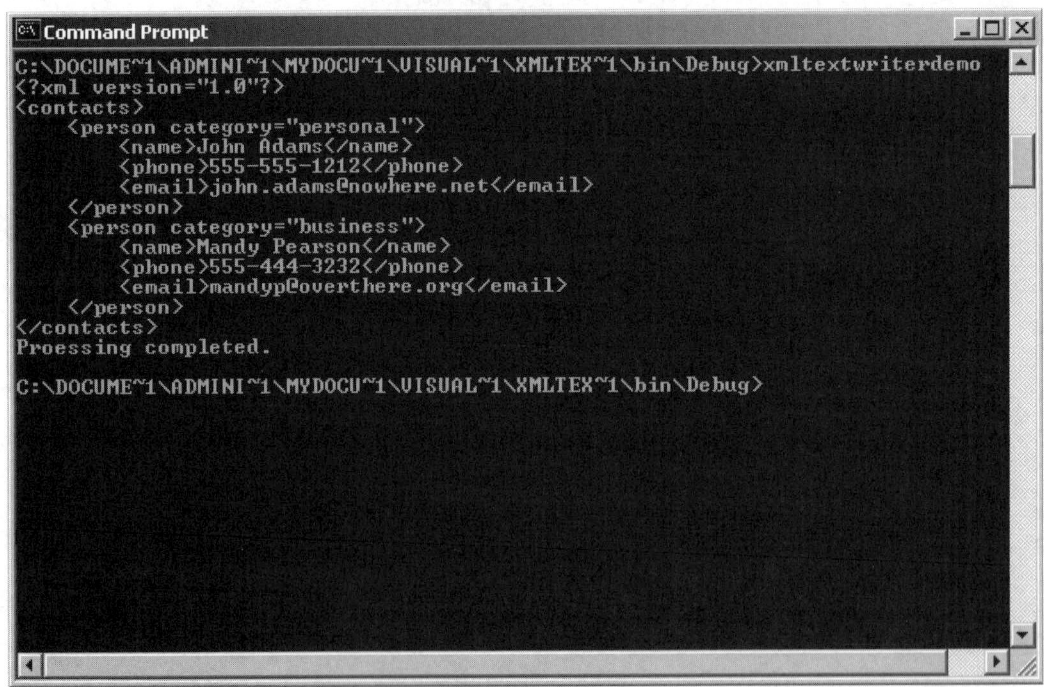

Figure 13.2 Running the C# console application in Listing 13.3

The XmlDocument Class

The `XmlDocument` class provides support for the Document Object Model (DOM) levels 1 and 2, as defined by W3C. This class represents the entire XML document as an in-memory node tree, and it permits both navigation and editing of the document. The DOM implemented by the `XmlDocument` class is essentially identical to the DOM implemented by the MSXML Parser, as was covered in detail in Chapter 10. The properties and methods are the same, and rather than duplicating that information here I suggest that you turn to that chapter.

When do you use the `XmlDocument` class in preference to the `XmlTextReader` class? The criteria are similar to those for deciding between using the MSXML DOM and the Simple API for XML.

Use `XmlTextReader` when

- Memory and processing resources are a consideration, particularly for large documents.
- You are looking for specific pieces of information in the document. For example, in a library catalog, use `XmlTextReader` when you need to locate all works by a specific author.
- You do not need to modify the document structure.
- You want to only partially parse the document before handing it off to another application.

Use `XmlDocument` when

- You need random access to all of document's contents.
- You need to modify the document structure.
- You need complex XPath filtering.
- You need to perform XSLT transformations.

There are various ways to use the `XmlDocument` class. You can use it alone, applying the class methods and properties to "walk the tree" and make changes. You can also use the `XmlDocument` class in conjunction with the `XPath-Navigator` class, which provides more sophisticated navigational and editing capabilities as well as XPath support. The following sections look at both. The first section presents a C# demonstration of using the `XmlDocument` class to modify the contents of an XML file. The second section explains how to use the `XPathNavigator` class.

Using the XmlDocument Class to Modify an XML Document

The first demonstration of the `XmlDocument` class shows how to use it to modify the contents of an XML document. In this case the task is to add a new <person> element to the XML file shown in Listing 13.4 and save the modified file under the name OutputFile.xml. The program, shown in Listing 13.5, is a C# console application, and the code is fully commented so you can figure out how it works.

Listing 13.4 InputFile.xml Is the File to Be Modified

```
<?xml version="1.0"?>
<contacts>
    <person category="personal">
        <name>John Adams</name>
        <phone>555-555-1212</phone>
        <email>john.adams@nowhere.net</email>
    </person>
    <person category="business">
        <name>Mandy Pearson</name>
        <phone>555-444-3232</phone>
        <email>mandyp@overthere.org</email>
    </person>
    <person category="family">
        <name>Jack Sprat</name>
        <phone>000-111-2222</phone>
        <email>jack001@earth.net</email>
    </person>
</contacts>
```

Listing 13.5 C# Program to Modify the Contents of InputFile.xml

```
using System;
using System.IO;
using System.Xml;

class Class1
{
private const string m_InFileName = "InputFile.xml";
private const string m_OutFileName = "OutputFile.xml";

    static void Main()
    {
```

```
        bool ok = true;
        XmlDocument xmlDoc = new XmlDocument();

        try
        {`
          //Load the input file.
          xmlDoc.Load( m_InFileName );
          //Create a new "person" element.
          XmlElement elPerson = xmlDoc.CreateElement( "person" );
          //Add the "category" attribute.
          elPerson.SetAttribute( "category", "family" );
          //Create "name," "phone," and "email" elements.
          XmlElement elName = xmlDoc.CreateElement( "name",
             "Ann Winslow" );
          XmlElement elPhone = xmlDoc.CreateElement( "phone",
             "000-000-0000" );
          XmlElement elEmail = xmlDoc.CreateElement( "email",
             "anne123@there.net" );
          //Add them as children of the "person" element.
          elPerson.AppendChild( elName );
          elPerson.AppendChild( elPhone );
          elPerson.AppendChild( elEmail );
          //Get a reference to the document's root element.
          XmlElement elRoot = xmlDoc.DocumentElement;
          //Add the "person" element as a child of the root.
          elRoot.AppendChild( elPerson );
          //Save the document.
          xmlDoc.Save( m_OutFileName );
        }
        catch ( Exception e )
        {
          ok = false;
          Console.WriteLine( "Exception: " + e.Message );
        }
        finally
        {
          if (ok)
            Console.WriteLine( "Element added successfully." );
          else
            Console.WriteLine( "An error occurred." );
        }
      }
    }
```

Using XPathNavigator with XmlDocument

The XPathNavigator class is designed specifically to facilitate navigating through XML that is contained in an XmlDocument object. It provides a cursor model, meaning that the navigator almost always has a position within the document's node tree. Many of the actions you can take with the navigator are performed relative to the current position, such as "move to the next node." When an action is performed successfully, the cursor is left pointing at the location where the action occurred. When an action fails, the cursor remains at its original position. You can always use the MoveToRoot() method to move the cursor to the document's root node.

Much of the power of the XPathNavigator class comes from its support for XPath expressions. You can select all of the nodes that match an XPath expression, and then conveniently work with them. However, many of the uses of this class do not in fact involve XPath expressions and hence its name is a bit misleading. These are the steps required to work with the XPathNavigator class if you are not going to use XPath expressions:

1. Create an instance of the XmlDocument class.
2. Load the XML document into the XmlDocument object.
3. Call the XmlDocument object's CreateNavigator() method to create an instance of the XPathNavigator class and return a reference to it.
4. Use the XPathNavigator object's properties and methods to move around the document and access its content.

The following code fragment shows how the preceding steps would be done in C#:

```
XmlDocument xmlDoc = new XmlDocument;
xmlDoc.Load( "original.xml" );
XPathNavigator nav = xmlDoc.CreateNavigator();
// Work with navigator here.
```

If you want to use XPath expressions, you call the XPathNavigator object's Select() method, which returns a type XPathNodeIterator that contains the nodes matching the XPath expression. This is explained later in this chapter.

When the XPathNavigator is first created, it is by default positioned on the document's root node. Even so, many programmers call the MoveToRoot() method to ensure that they know where they are starting. Then a call to MoveToFirstChild() moves to the first element in the file, typically the <?xml version="1.0"?> node. At this point, a typical approach is to call MoveToNext()

repeatedly until you reach the document's root element (the <contacts> element in Listing 13.4). Then you can use the various methods to move around the document as needed. You'll see this in the first demonstration program later in this chapter.

Note that there is some potential confusion regarding the use of the term "root" because the root node as seen by `XPathNavigator` is not the same as the document's root element. The root node encompasses the entire XML document, and the root element is a child node of this root node.

The `XPathNavigator` class has a large number of properties and methods, and many of them are infrequently needed. Rather then presenting all of them here, I have limited coverage to those properties and methods that you most often need. (You can refer to the .NET online documentation for information on the others.) Table 13.7 lists these properties and methods of the `XPathNavigator` class. Following the tables, I present two sample programs that use the `XPathNavigator` class.

Demonstrating XPathNavigator

This first demonstration shows how to use the `XPathNavigator` class to "walk" the tree of an XML document. The demonstration makes use of the XML data

Table 13.7 Commonly Used Properties and Methods of the `XPathNavigator` Class

Property/Method	Description
`GetAttribute (`*`name, ns`*`)`	Returns the value of the attribute with the specified name and namespace URI. Returns null if a matching attribute is not found.
`HasAttributes`	Returns True if the current node has attributes. Returns False if the current node has no attributes or is not an element node.
`HasChildren`	Returns True if the current node has child nodes.
`IsEmptyElement`	Returns True if the current node is an empty element (such as <element/>).
`LocalName`	Gets the name of the current node without its namespace prefix.

(continued)

Table 13.7 (*cont.*)

Property/Method	Description
`Matches (XPathExpr)`	Returns True if the current node matches the specified XPath expression. The argument can be a string or a type `XPathExpression`.
`MoveTo()`	Moves to the first sibling of the current node. Returns True if there is a first sibling node or False if not or if the current node is an attribute node.
`MoveToAttribute (name, ns)`	Moves to the attribute with the matching local name and namespace URI. Returns True if a matching attribute is found or False if not.
`MoveToFirstChild()`	Moves to the first child of the current node. Returns True on success or False if there is no child node.
`MoveToID(id)`	Moves to the node that has a type `ID` attribute with the specified value. Returns True on success or False if there is no matching node.
`MoveToNext()`	Moves to the next sibling of the current node. Returns True on success or False if there are no more siblings or if the current node is an attribute node.
`MoveToNextAttribute()`	Moves to the next attribute node. Returns True on success or False if there are no more attribute nodes or if the current node is not an attribute node.
`MoveToParent()`	Moves to the current node's parent. Returns True on success or False if the current node has no parent (is the root node).
`MoveToPrevious()`	Moves to the previous sibling node. Returns True on success or False if there is no previous sibling or if the current node is an attribute node.
`MoveToRoot()`	Moves to the root node. This method is always successful and has no return value.
`Name`	Returns the name of the current node with namespace prefix (if any).

(continued)

Table 13.7 *(cont.)*

Property/Method	Description
`NodeType`	Returns an `XPathNodeType` value identifying the type of the current node. See Table 13.8 for possible values.
`Select(`*`match`*`)`	Selects a node set that matches the specified XPath expression and returns a type `XPathNodeIterator`. The argument can be a string or a type `XPathExpression`.
`Value`	Returns the text value of the current node—for example, the value of an attribute node or the text in an element node.

Table 13.8 Members of the `XPathNodeType` Enumeration Returned by the `XPathNavigator` Class's `NodeType` Property

Constant	Description
`All`	All node types
`Attribute`	Attribute node
`Comment`	Comment node
`Element`	Element node
`Namespace`	A namespace node (for example, `xmlns="xxx"`)
`ProcessingInstruction`	A processing instruction (not including the XML declaration)
`Root`	Root node
`SignificantWhitespace`	A node that contains white space and has `xml:space` set to "preserve"
`Text`	A text node (the text content of an element or attribute)
`Whitespace`	A node that contains only white space characters

file presented later in the book in Listing 18.5. This file contains a database of books and is structured as shown in this fragment:

```
<books>
<book category="reference">
  <title>The Cambridge Biographical Encyclopedia</title>
  <author>David Crystal</author>
  <publisher>Cambridge University Press</publisher>
</book>
...
</books>
```

The objective of the demonstration is to let the user select a category of books, and then display a list of all matching books. It is created as a Web application. The user selects the category on an HTML page, as shown in Listing 13.6. This page presents a list of categories from which the user selected. The request is sent to the ASP.NET application in Listing 13.7. The code in this page uses an `XPathNavigator` object to move through the XML file. Specifically, the code locates each <book> element and checks its "category" attribute. If the value of this attribute matches the category requested by the user, the program walks through the <book> element's children (the title, author, and publisher elements), extracts their data, and outputs it in the form of an HTML table. The results of a search are shown in Figure 13.3.

Listing 13.6 The HTML Page That Lets the User Select a Book Category

```
<html>
<head>
<title>Book search</title>
</head>
<body>
<h2>Find books by category.</h2>
<hr/>
<form method="GET" action="list1307.aspx">
<p>Select your category, then press Submit.</p>
<p>Category:
<select name="category" size="1">
  <option value="biography">Biography</option>
  <option value="fiction">Fiction</option>
```

```
  <option value="reference">Reference</option>
<select>
</p>
<p><input type="submit" value="Submit"/>
</p><hr/>
</form>
</body>
</html>
```

Listing 13.7 ASP.NET Script That Uses the `XPathNavigator` Class to Access XML Data

```
<%@ Import Namespace="System.Xml" %>
<%@ Import Namespace="System.Xml.XPath" %>
<script language="C#" runat="Server">
 void Page_Load(object sender, EventArgs e) {
   try {
      XmlDocument xmlDoc = new XmlDocument();
      xmlDoc.Load(Server.MapPath("list1805.xml"));
      XPathNavigator nav = xmlDoc.CreateNavigator();
      //Get the query string submitted by the client.
      NameValueCollection coll = Request.QueryString;
      string category = coll.Get( "category" );
      //Move to the document's root element.
      nav.MoveToRoot();
      //Move to the first child.
      nav.MoveToFirstChild();
      while (nav.LocalName != "books")
          nav.MoveToNext();
      //At this point we are positioned at the root element.
      //Move to the first child (the first <book> element).
      nav.MoveToFirstChild();
      //Start writing the HTML to the output.
      Response.Write( "<html><body>");
      Response.Write("<h2>Books in the '" + category +
          "' category:</h2><hr/>");
      //Write out the table headings.
      Response.Write(" <table cellpadding='4'>" );
      Response.Write( "<thead><tr>" );
      Response.Write( "<th>Title</th><th>Author</th>" );
      Response.Write( "<th>Publisher</th></tr></thead>" );
      Response.Write( "<tbody>" );
```

```
        bool more = true;
        while (more)
        {
          //Is this book in the selected category?
          if (nav.GetAttribute( "category", "") == category)
          {
          //Move to the first child (<title>) and write its data.
          nav.MoveToFirstChild();
          Response.Write( "<tr><td>" + nav.Value + "</td>");
          //Move to next (<author>).
          nav.MoveToNext();
          Response.Write( "<td>" + nav.Value + "</td>");
          //Move to next (<publisher>).
          nav.MoveToNext();
          Response.Write( "<td>" + nav.Value + "</td></tr>");
          //Move back to the parent <book> node.
          nav.MoveToParent();
          }
          //Move to the next <book> node, if any.
          more = nav.MoveToNext();
        }
        //Finish the table.
        Response.Write( "</tbody></table><hr/></body></html>");
        }
        catch(Exception ex) {
            Response.Write(ex.ToString());
        }
    }
  </script>
```

Using the Select() Method and the XPathNodeIterator Class

The `XPathNavigator` class has the `Select()` method, which permits you to select a node set that matches an XPath expression. The method returns an object of type `XPathNodeIterator` that contains the matching nodes. If there are no matching nodes, the `XPathNodeIterator` object's `Count` property will be 0; otherwise, this property returns the number of nodes. For example, this code assumes that the variable `selectExpr` contains the XPath expression that you want to use:

```
XmlDocument xmlDoc = new XmlDocument();
xmlDoc.Load( "InputFile.xml" );
```

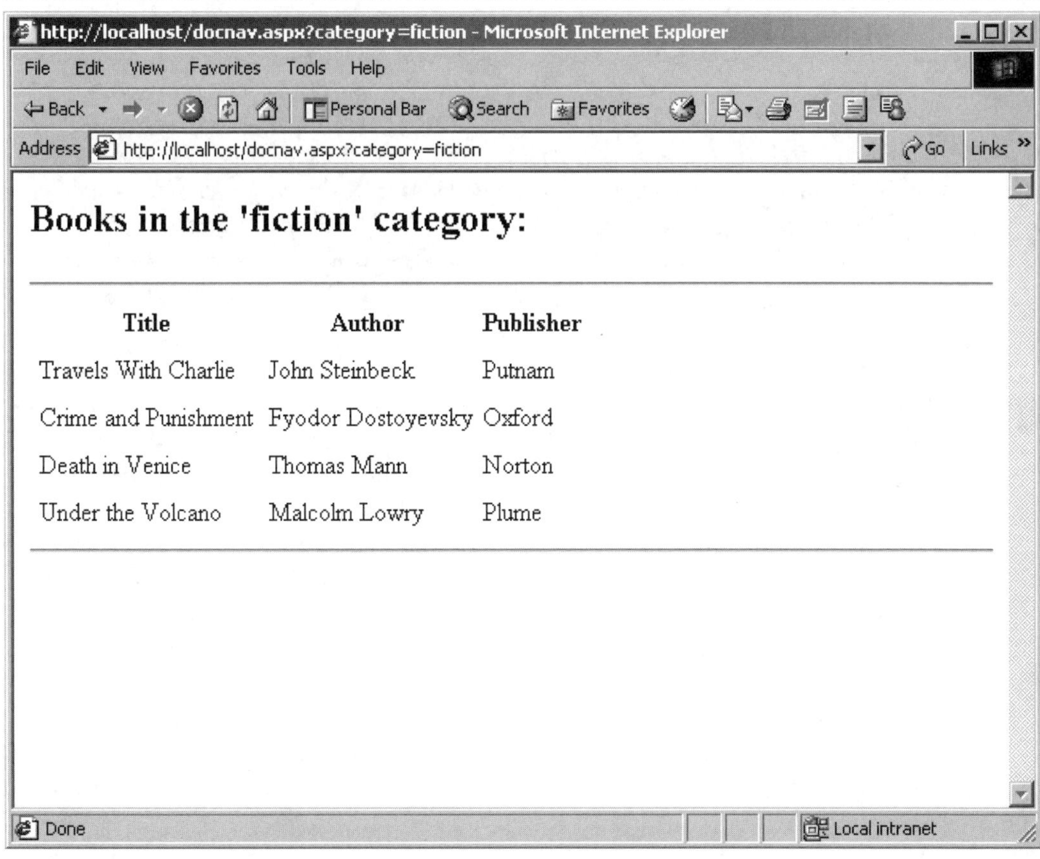

Figure 13.3 The results of a book query displayed by Listing 13.7

```
XPathNavigator nav = xmlDoc.CreateNavigator();
XPathNodeIterator xpi = nav.Select( selectExpr );
if ( xpi.Count != 0 )
{
  // At least one matching node was found.
}
else
{
  // No matching nodes were found.
}
```

When to Use XPathNodeIterator

There's not much that really requires the use of the `XPathNodeIterator` *class, but it does make certain tasks more efficient. You can always locate the node(s) that you want by using the* `XPathNavigator` *class's methods to move around the document tree and examine nodes as you go. However, the ability to quickly select a subset of nodes based on an XPath expression can make this sort of brute force technique unnecessary.*

Table 13.9 describes members of the `XPathNodeIterator` class. You will note that the `Current` property returns a reference to an `XPathNavigator` object that is positioned on the current node. However, you cannot use this `XPathNavigator` object to move away from the current node (unless you first clone it)—you can use it only to get information about the current node.

To demonstrate using the `Select()` method and the `XPathNodeIterator` class, I turn again to the XML file Inputfile.xml from Listing 13.4. The goal of this application is to list the names of all the people in the XML database. In other words, the application needs to go through the XML file, select all <name> nodes, and display their values. This could be done using the "brute force" method of going through all the nodes in the document, but the code is a lot simpler if you use the `Select()` method. This is a console application that opens the file and displays the names on the screen. Listing 13.8 presents the source code.

Table 13.9 Members of the `XPathNodeIterator` Class

Member	Description
`Count`	Returns the index of the last selected node or 0 if there are no nodes.
`Current`	Returns a type `XPathNavigator` positioned on the current node.
`CurrentPosition`	The 1-based index of the current node.
`MoveNext()`	Moves to the next selected node. Returns True on success or False if there are no more selected nodes.

Listing 13.8: Using `XPathNavigator` and `XPathNodeIterator` to Access XML Data

```
using System;
using System.IO;
using System.Xml;
using System.Xml.XPath;

namespace XPathNavDemo
{
  class SearchXML
  {
    static void Main(string[] args)
    {
      SearchXML ex = new SearchXML();
    }

    public SearchXML()
    {
      try
      {
        XmlDocument xmlDoc = new XmlDocument();
        xmlDoc.Load( "InputFile.xml" );
        XPathNavigator nav = xmlDoc.CreateNavigator();
        // Select all the <name> nodes.
        string select = "descendant::person/name";
        XPathNodeIterator xpi = nav.Select(select);
        if ( xpi.Count != 0 )
        {
          // At least one <name> node was found.
          // Move through them and display the values.
          Console.WriteLine("The following people are in this file:");
          while     (xpi.MoveNext())
            Console.WriteLine(xpi.Current.Value);
        }
        else
          Console.WriteLine("No <name> elements found.");
      }
      catch ( System.Exception ex )
      {
        Console.WriteLine("Exception: " + ex.Message );
      }
      finally
      {
```

```
                Console.ReadLine();
            }
        }
    }
}
```

Summary

The .NET Framework provides a rich and comprehensive set of classes that support almost every imaginable aspect of desktop and Internet-enabled computing. Coupled with the Visual Studio .NET programming environment, .NET represents Microsoft's response to the new challenges facing developers as the Internet assumes greater importance in all aspects of computing. .NET includes excellent support for XML development, with several classes for reading, writing, modifying, and navigating XML documents.

CHAPTER 14

Extensible Hypertext Markup Language and Web Pages

Extensible Hypertext Markup Language (XHTML) is an XML vocabulary that was designed to as the next step in the evolution of Hypertext Markup Language (HTML) as the standard language for building Web pages. XHTML keeps most of the original syntax of HTML while removing most of its disadvantages. This chapter explains the syntax of XHTML, provides information on how to convert existing HTML documents to XHTML, and describes the use of the most commonly needed XHTML tags.

Some HTML Background

From the very beginning, HTML has been the language of the Web. It started out as a remarkably simple markup language, providing a set of tags sufficient to format Web pages into paragraphs and headings, to apply some rudimentary formatting, and to display images. As the use of the Web increased, Web publishers became more demanding and sophisticated about what they wanted to do with their pages, and the limited vocabulary of HTML was very quickly considered inadequate. The solution? Add more tags to the HTML vocabulary to provide the needed functionality.

Of course, new tags are useless unless they are supported by the browsers that are in use. Back in the days when there was competition in the market for Windows platform browsers, when you could not be fairly sure that Internet Explorer was the target browser, this led to a very messy situation. Netscape would add support for some new tags to its browser, Microsoft would add support for some other tags to its browser, and so on. Even when various browsers supported the same tags, they might do so in different ways. Web page designers had to test their HTML code in all the popular browsers to make sure it displayed properly.

Another result of this unplanned growth of HTML was that browsers were specifically designed to be loose in enforcing HTML syntax. Users would be turned away by a browser that reported an error every time it encountered a new tag or a minor syntax error. In turn, Web page designers were sloppy in adhering to "proper" HTML syntax because the browsers did not require it. If the page displayed okay, that was enough.

This does not mean that no efforts were made to standardize HTML. The most recent standard, HTML 4.01 (a W3C Recommendation since 1999, available at `http://www.w3.org/TR/html4/`), was a significant step toward updating HTML to account for the way the language was being used in the real world. Even so, HTML still suffered from some shortcomings.

- It lacked the syntactic rigor that would permit completely unambiguous parsing and processing of a document.
- It retained some elements and attributes that are related to document presentation only and not to document structure. This violates the complete separation of structure and presentation that is a central aspect of other markup languages.

XML to the Rescue

XML has none of the shortcomings of HTML, so it might seem that replacing HTML with XML is an obvious solution to these problems. Remember, however, that XML is not itself a markup language but rather a metalanguage—in other words, XML is a specification that can be used to create markup languages. The solution, then, was to use the XML specification to create a new markup language that would retain the advantages of traditional HTML while removing its disadvantages. The result is XHTML, an XML vocabulary designed specifically for Web page design.

Is XHTML really that different from the latest HTML specification? No, it is not. If you are familiar with any HTML, and HTML 4.01 in particular, the elements of XHTML will look very familiar. Aside from the advantages of enforcement of syntax and separation of structure and content, XHTML offers several additional advantages over HTML:

- *Extensibility:* Because XHTML is an XML vocabulary, it is inherently extensible. New elements and attributes can be added without affecting existing language elements. As Web publishing needs change, XHTML can evolve along with them.

- *Standardization:* XHTML forces users to adhere to its standard, unlike HTML where standards existed but were often ignored by browsers and developers. With an enforced standard, the many problems caused by proprietary code will disappear, and the sloppy coding practices common among Web developers should vanish as well.
- *Improved linking:* XHTML provides more sophisticated options for linking as compared with HTML's basic hyperlink. You can, for example, create a single link that points to multiple resources.

Will XHTML replace HTML soon? I don't think this is very likely. HTML is widely used and deeply entrenched, and it is perfectly satisfactory for many applications. Thus, there is no reason for millions of Web pages to be upgraded to XHTML. A more likely scenario is that XHTML will be used for many new Web projects. XHTML is best viewed as a long-term replacement for HTML.

XHTML Schemas

Any XML vocabulary is defined by a schema, and XHTML is no exception. The schema for XHTML is defined by three different DTDs, meaning that there are actually three varieties of XHTML. They are as follows:

- *XHTML Strict:* This is the most restrictive XHTML. It is used for documents that require a clean structural markup with no presentation elements at all. An XHTML document that follows the strict schema requires a Cascading Style Sheet to specify how it is to be displayed.
- *XHTML Transitional:* This type of XHTML provides greater flexibility than the strict DTD, and it permits the inclusion of presentation markup elements that specify display characteristics independent of a style sheet. This is the most commonly used version of XHTML, and it can be considered the default.
- *XHTML Frameset:* You use this variant of XHTML when you need to create frames (multiple windows) in the browser.

The type of XHTML for a specific document is indicated by its `DOCTYPE` declaration, which is covered shortly. The remainder of this chapter deals with Transitional XHTML.

Structure of an XHTML Document

An XHTML document is an XML document, and if well-formed, it will follow the same rules that you learned for XML documents earlier in this book. There are, however, certain items that are specific to XHTML documents. The first required element is the `DOCTYPE` declaration, which must include information indicating which of the three XHTML DTDs the document is using. For the Strict XHTML DTD:

```
<!DOCTYPE html PUBLIC "-//W3C//DTD XHTML 1.0 Strict//EN""
    "http://www.w3.org/TR/xhtml1/DTD/xhtml1-strict.dtd">
```

For the Transitional XHTML DTD:

```
<!DOCTYPE html PUBLIC "-//W3C//DTD XHTML 1.0 Transitional//EN"
    "http://www.w3.org/TR/xhtml1/DTD/xhtml1-transitional.dtd">
```

For the Frameset XHTML DTD:

```
<!DOCTYPE html PUBLIC "-//W3C//DTD XHTML 1.0 Frameset//EN"
    "http://www.w3.org/TR/xhtml1/DTD/xhtml1-frameset.dtd">
```

The second required element is the root element, which must be named `html`. This element must declare the XHTML namespace:

```
<html xmlns="http://www.w3.org/1999/xhtml">
...
</html>
```

There are three additional required elements, all of which are taken from HTML and serve the same purpose as they do in regular HTML. All three are placed within the `<html>` element:

- A `<head>` element
- A `<title>` element as a child of the `<head>` element
- A `<body>` element as a sibling of the `<head>` element

With these basic requirements in mind, it is a simple matter to create a short XHTML document. Listing 14.1 shows a very simple XHTML document, and Figure 14.1 shows how that document appears when loaded into Internet Explorer.

Listing 14.1 A Simple XHTML Document

```
<?xml version="1.0"?>
<!DOCTYPE html PUBLIC "-//W3C//DTD XHTML 1.0 Transitional//EN"
    "http://www.w3.org/TR/xhtml1/DTD/xhtml1-transitional.dtd">
<html xmlns="http://www.w3.org/1999/xhtml">
  <head>
    <title>Your first XHTML document</title>
  </head>
  <body>
    <h1>Your first XHTML document.</h1>
    <hr/>
    <p>This is a very simple XHTML document!</p>
  </body>
</html>
```

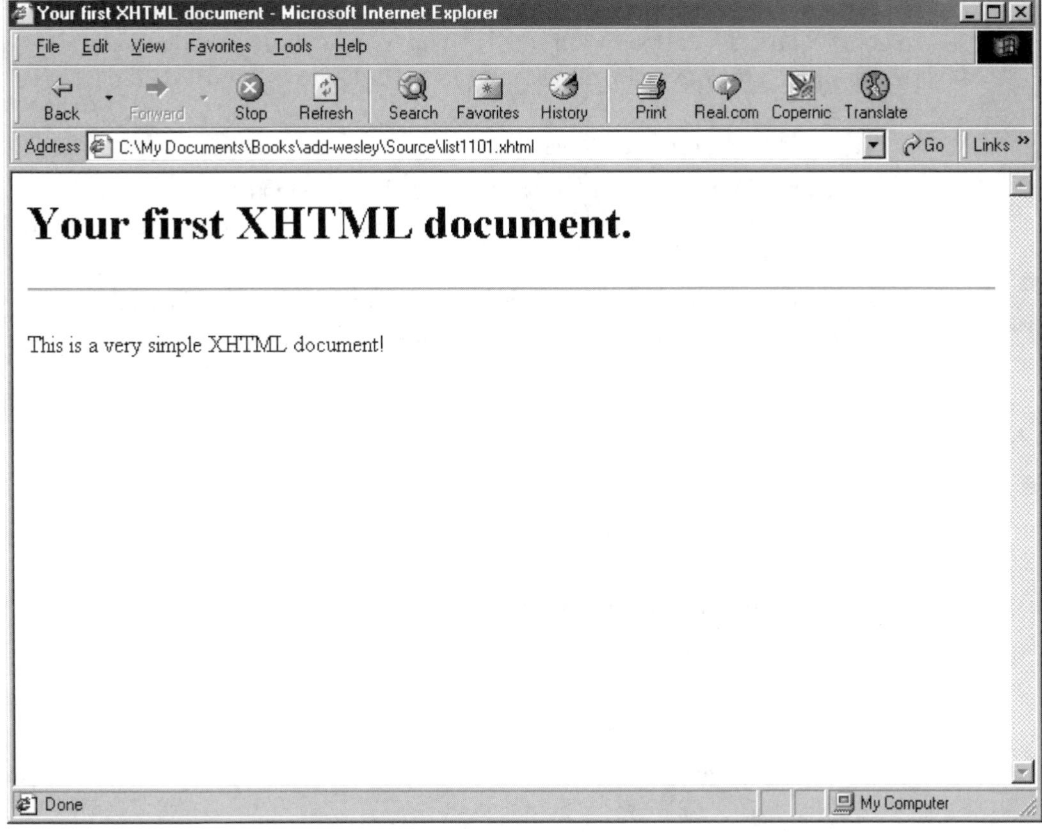

Figure 14.1 The XHTML document in Listing 14.1 displayed in a browser

XHTML documents can be given the XHTML extension, but use of the HTML or HTM extension is permitted also. As XML documents, they could also be given the XML extension, but if you try to view a document with the XML extension in Internet Explorer, it applies the default style sheet and displays the document content, rather than formatting the document for browser display.

If you are familiar with HTML, much of Listing 14.1 will be familiar to you. The document is broken into `<head>` and `<body>` elements. The `<head>` element contains a `<title>` element with the document's title, and the `<body>` element contains standard HTML elements for a heading, a horizontal line, and a paragraph.

Converting HTML to XHTML

Because XHTML is based on HTML 4.01, it is usually a fairly simple matter to convert an HTML document to XHTML. This section provides a step-by-step approach to converting an existing HTML document into XHTML.

1. Add the required `DOCTYPE` element, as described earlier in this chapter.
2. The HTML document should already have an `html` element as its root element. Add the XHTML namespace information to the opening `html` element.
3. Convert all element and attribute names to lowercase. This step is required because XML is case-sensitive. For example:

   ```
   <Title Category="Classical">
   ```

   must be changed to:

   ```
   <title category="Classical">
   ```

4. Make sure all attribute values are quoted. HTML permits attribute values to be unquoted, but XHTML does not. For example:

   ```
   <table border=4 cellpadding=2>
   ```

   must be changed to:

   ```
   <table border="4" cellpadding="2">
   ```

5. Change all instances of attribute minimalization. HTML permits some attributes to be specified as a value alone and not as a name=value pair. In this <select> tag, for example, the "multiple" value is a minimized attribute:

   ```
   <select name="colors" size="6" multiple>
   ```

   To comply with XHTML rules, this must be converted to a name=value pair, as follows:

   ```
   <select name="colors" size="6" multiple="multiple">
   ```

6. Terminate all stand-alone elements. HTML permits a variety of elements to exist without a closing tag. Included are <p>, <li>, <hr>, <br>, and <img>. XHTML does not permit this—any and all elements must be explicitly terminated. For elements that enclose content, you must add a closing tag at the end of the content, such as making sure every paragraph not only begins with <p>, but also that it ends with </p>. For elements that do not enclose content, you can add a slash at the end of the element. For example, change <img src="logo.gif"> to <img src="logo.gif"/>.
7. Ensure that all elements are properly nested. XHTML requires that every child element be totally enclosed in its parent, whereas HTML is forgiving in this respect. The following would be fine in HTML for marking text as bold and italic:

   ```
   <b><i>This is the text</b></i>
   ```

   For XHTML, it will have to be modified as follows so that the italic element closes before the bold element does:

   ```
   <b><i>This is the text</i></b>
   ```

8. Replace occurrences of the characters &, <, and > in character data or attribute values with & < and >.
9. Add hyphens to comments so they follow XML comment style. For example, <!Comment> becomes <!--Comment-->.
10. Enclose <script> and <style> code in CDATA sections. If your HTML includes VBScript, JavaScript, or CSS code, it must be enclosed in a CDATA section to prevent the processing software from trying to

interpret it as XML markup. In HTML, script code is normally handled like this, hiding it within a comment (so it does not display in the browser):

```
<script type="text/vbscript">
<!--
script code here
-->
</script>
```

XML processors, however, typically ignore comment text, which results in the script code not being executed. In XHTML, enclose your script code in `CDATA` sections rather than comments. For the preceding code to be acceptable in an XHTML document, it must be edited as follows:

```
<script type="text/vbscript">
<![CDATA[
script code here
]]>
</script>
```

> ***Automatic HTML to XHTML Conversion***
>
> *If you have large HTML files to convert to XHTML, you certainly will not want to convert them by hand. Several conversion utilities are available; my favorite is Tidy, which was written by Dave Raggett of W3C. It is a free utility that can save you many hours of work. Visit the Tidy Web site (`http://www.w3.org/People/Raggett/tidy/`) for information and downloads.*

HTML Tags to Avoid

The current XHTML standard does a good job of supporting essentially all HTML elements, but future versions will not. Certain HTML elements are being deprecated, which means that they are supported in the current XHTML (version 1.0) but will most likely be unsupported in future versions. These deprecated elements are as follows:

```
base
basefont
center
font
frame
frameset
iframe
isindex
menu
noframes
s
strike
u
```

You can see that these are, for the most part, presentation-related elements. The objective is to move XHTML away from having any presentation-related elements, and to use style sheets for all aspects of formatting and display. For ease of Web site maintenance and upgrade, you are advised to avoid or minimize the use of these elements in your XHTML documents.

XHTML Elements

If you are familiar with HTML, you can, by following the guidelines presented earlier in this chapter, apply your knowledge to the creation of XHTML documents. If you do not know HTML, the information in this section will help you get started working with XHTML. This is by no means a complete XHTML reference, but it is aimed at presenting the fundamentals of those XHTML elements and attributes that you commonly need when authoring Web pages. At the end of the chapter I present a complete XHTML document that demonstrates the use of many of the elements described here.

<head>

The `<head>` element is one of two children of an XHTML document's root `<html>` element (the other being the `<body>` element). The `<head>` element does not contain any document content, but rather it contains elements that provide information about the document and how it is to be formatted. The only required child of the `<head>` element is `<title>`.

<title>

The `<title>` element contains the document's title. The title is used for various purposes, such as displaying in a browser's title bar or in a history list. Document titles are also used by some search engines, such as Yahoo, when they categorize a Web site. You must include a `<title>` element in the document head, and you should always provide a concise, descriptive title for every page. For example:

```
<title>Books by William Faulkner</title>
```

<script>

The `<script>` element encloses script code or references script code in an external file. Within the `<script>` element, the code itself must be enclosed in a `CDATA` section. This element takes two attributes:

- `type`: Required. Identifies the MIME type of the script code—most often `text/vbscript` or `text/javascript`.
- `src`: Optional. Specifies the URL of the file containing the script code.

Here is an example of using the `<script>` tag to enclose script code in a document:

```
<script type="text/vbscript">
<![CDATA[
script code here
]]>
</script>
```

This example references script code located in an external file:

```
<script type="text/vbscript" src="http://www.mysite.com/calc.vbs">
</script>
```

You cannot use the `src` attribute and have script code inside the tag at the same time.

<style>

The `<style>` element contains formatting information for the document, typically in CSS format. There are two attributes for this element.

- `type`: Required. Specifies the MIME type of the style information. Use `text/css` to specify that you are using the CSS level 1 specification.
- `title`: Optional. Specifies a descriptive title for the `<style>` element.

Here is an example of a `<style>` element containing style specifications:

```
<style type="text/css">
  body {font: 12pt Ariel; color: blue;margin-left: 0.5in}
  h1 {font: 20pt Ariel; font-weight: bold}
  p {font: 10pt Times; line-height: 14pt}
</style>
```

<body>

The `<body>` element contains the document's content. It takes no attributes. Child elements within the body section of the document define the structure of the content and control certain aspects of its formatting. These child elements can be divided into several categories that are covered in this section.

- *Text-level elements* affect sections of text such as a word or phrase, and are used for formatting tasks such as making a single word bold or italic.
- *Block-level elements* apply to larger sections of text, such as paragraphs and headings.
- *List elements* are used for bulleted, numbered, and other types of lists.
- *Hyperlink elements* provide links between documents and parts of documents.
- *Image elements* display external images in the document.
- *Table elements* are used to create tables of information.

Other categories of XHTML elements that are beyond the scope of this book are as follows:

- *Form elements* are used to create interactive forms where the user can enter information and make choices.
- *Frame elements* are used to divide a browser window into multiple panes, each displaying different information.
- *Executable content elements* are used to embed objects, such as ActiveX controls and Java applets.

Table 14.1 Text-Level Elements That Describe Specific Formatting

Element	Description
`<big>`	Displays text in a larger font size
`<bold>`	Displays text in boldface
`<em>`	Marks emphasized text. Typically rendered in italics.
`<i>`	Displays text in italics
`<small>`	Displays text in a smaller font size
`<strong>`	Marks strongly emphasized text. Typically rendered in boldface.
`<sub>`	Displays text as a subscript
`<sup>`	Displays text as a superscript
`<tt>`	Displays text in a fixed width (monospace) font (typically Courier)

Text-Level Elements

The text-level elements control the formatting and appearance of sections of text. The format for these elements is as follows:

```
<element-name>Text to be affected</element-name>
```

The text-level elements can be nested to achieve the desired effect. There are two types of text-level elements. The first type, listed in Table 14.1, specifies that a particular formatting be applied, and the result is generally predictable across browsers. The second type of element, listed in Table 14.2, describes the meaning of a section of text—for example, marking it as an address or a citation. The exact rendering of such elements is less standardized than the first type and will be browser-dependent to some degree.

Table 14.2 Text-Level Elements That Describe the Meaning of Text

Element	Description
`<abbr>`	Marks text as an abbreviation. Applicable to browsers that are not vision-based. A speech-based browser could look up the abbreviation and pronounce the full word.
`<acronym>`	Marks text as an acronym. A speech-based browser could spell out the individual letters of the acronym rather than trying to pronounce it as a word.
`<address>`	Marks text as a postal or e-mail address. Typically rendered in italics.
`<cite>`	Marks text as a citation. Typically rendered in italics.
`<code>`	Marks text as computer code. Typically rendered in a monospace font such as Courier.
`<del>`	Marks text that has been deleted. Used in collaborative documents where one reviewer will need to see text that was deleted by the previous reviewer. Takes two optional attributes: `cite` is the URL of a document that explains why the revision was made, and `datetime` is a timestamp indicating when the deletion was made, in the format YYYYMMDDThh:mm:ss.
`<ins>`	Works as `<del>` but for inserted text.
`<q>`	Marks text as a direct quotation to be displayed inline. Takes two optional attributes: `cite` is the URL of the source document, and `lang` specifies the language of the citation.

Block-Level Elements

The block-level elements are used to format larger sections of a document and to divide it into logical sections such as headings and paragraphs. These elements are described in Table 14.3.

Table 14.3 Block-Level Elements

Element	Description
`<blockquote>`	Marks text as a block quote that is to be displayed indented from the regular body text. The optional `cite` attribute can be used to point to the URL of the source document.
`<h1>` through `<h6>`	Mark text as a heading. The `<h1>` element marks a top-level heading and the elements `<h2>` through `<h6>` mark lower level headings. Headings are typically displayed in boldface with some extra space above and below, with smaller fonts used for lower levels.
`<p>`	Marks text as a paragraph. In Transitional XHTML, you can use the `style` attribute to specify text alignment (for example, `style="align: right"`) but the use of a style sheet is preferred.
`<pre>`	Marks text as being already formatted. White space is not ignored and text is rendered in a fixed-width font. Often used for presenting tables of information.
`<span>`	Marks text as having a specific style applied. The `style` attribute contains name=value pairs providing the details of the style. For example: `style="font-weight: bold; color: red"`.

List Elements

List elements are a type of block-level formatting used to create various kinds of lists. There are three types of list available:

- A *definition* list consists of terms each followed by its definition.
- A *numbered* list consists of numbered items. It is sometimes called an *ordered* list.
- A *bulleted* list, such as this one. It is sometimes called an *unordered* list.

To create a definition list, use the following syntax:

```
<dl>
  <dt>Term 1</dt>
```

```
  <dd>Definition of term 1</dd>
  <dt>Term 2</dt>
  <dd>Definition of term 2</dd>
  <dt>Term 3</dt>
  <dd>Definition of term 3</dd>
</dl>
```

To create a numbered list, use the following syntax. The numbers are added automatically by the browser.

```
<ol>
  <li>First item</li>
  <li>Second item</li>
  <li>Third item</li>
</ol>
```

To create a bulleted list, use the following syntax. The bullets are added automatically by the browser.

```
<ul>
  <li>First item</li>
  <li>Second item</li>
  <li>Third item</li>
</ul>
```

You can use text-level elements within lists to control the formatting of list elements. For example, the following definition list will display all of its terms in boldface:

```
<dl>
  <dt><b>Term 1</b></dt>
  <dd>Definition of term 1</dd>
  <dt><b>Term 2</b></dt>
  <dd>Definition of term 2</dd>
  <dt><b>Term 3</b></dt>
  <dd>Definition of term 3</dd>
</dl>
```

Hyperlink Elements

Only a single hyperlink element is currently supported by XHTML. This is the anchor element, denoted by the `<a>` tag. This element can serve either as the destination of a link or as the source, depending on the attributes used. When used as a destination, or named anchor, the <a> element serves as a bookmark, providing a named location in the document to which the user can navigate. Use the following syntax to create a named anchor:

```
<a name="anchorname">
anchor text here
</a>
```

Anchorname is the name identifying the anchor. The text of the anchor is not displayed any differently, but is only marked internally as being a named anchor.

To set up a source hyperlink, you must include the `href` attribute in the <a> tag, which specifies the link target. To link to an external document, use the URL (absolute or relative) of the document, as in this example:

```
<a href="http://www.mysite.com/resume.htm">View my resume</a>
```

To link to a named anchor in the current document, use the number sign (#) followed by the name of the anchor:

```
<a href="#index">Go to the index</a>
```

To link to a named anchor in an external document, use the URL of the document followed by the number sign (#) and the name of the anchor:

```
<a href="http://www.onlinestore.com/buy.htm#order">Place an order</a>
```

A hyperlink can include various optional attributes, as described in Table 14.4.

The text in a source hyperlink is displayed differently than surrounding text, typically in a different color and underlined. Note that the content of a hyperlink can be an image as well as text.

Image Elements

The <img/> tag is used to place an image in a document. This is a stand-alone element, with all information provided by attributes. At its simplest, the <img/> element includes two attributes: `src`, which specifies the relative or absolute URL of the image file, and `alt`, which specifies a text description of the image. Here's an example:

```
<img src="images/logo.jpg" alt="company logo"/>
```

Table 14.4 Optional Attributes for Hyperlink Elements

Attribute	Description
`accesskey`	Denotes a key that, combined with the Alt key, can be used to activate the hyperlink. For example, `accesskey="D"` will enable users to press Alt-D to activate the link.
`tabindex`	Specifies the hyperlink's position in the document's tabbing order.
`target`	When the document uses frames, specifies the name of the frame into which the target document should be loaded.
`type`	Specifies the MIME type of the target resource.

When used in this simple form, the image is displayed at its native size, one screen pixel for each pixel in the image. The value of the `alt` attribute is displayed if the image file cannot be found, and it may be used by nonvisual browsers as well. Optional attributes of the `<img/>` element are as follows:

- `height`: The display height of the image, in pixels
- `width`: The display width of the image, in pixels
- `longdesc`: The URL of a resource that contains a detailed description of the image

By setting the `height` and `width` attributes, you can display an image at a size other than its native size. Even when you want the image displayed at its native size, setting these attributes to the native size can speed up display. When these attributes are specified, the browser can, when it encounters the `<img/>` element, set aside space for the image and continue rendering the remainder of the page while the image downloads. If these attributes are not specified, the browser must wait until the entire image is downloaded before it can set aside space for the image and continue displaying the rest of the page.

Image Maps

XHTML supports a feature called image maps, *whereby an image is divided into defined regions and each region serves as a hyperlink to a different target. Users can click different locations on the image to navigate to different URLs. Image maps are beyond the scope of this book, but you can find information about them in many HTML references.*

Table Elements

XHTML's table elements are used to organize parts of a document into tabular format. These elements can be used to create regular tables in row-and-column format, and they can also be used to create unusual page layouts. You can control the width of columns, height of rows, borders between cells, and various other aspects of table appearance. All tables are defined by the `<table>` element and its children. The `<table>` element takes several attributes:

- `border`: The width of the table border, in pixels.
- `cellpadding`: The amount of space between a cell's contents and its edge, in pixels.
- `cellspacing`: The amount of space between adjacent cells, in pixels.
- `frame`: Specifies which parts of the table's outer border are displayed. Table 14.5 describes settings for this attribute.

Table 14.5 Settings for the `<table>` Element's `frame` Attribute

Value	Border Display Location
`above`	At the top of the table
`below`	At the bottom of the table
`border`	All four sides of the table
`box`	Identical to `border`
`hsides`	On the left and right sides of the table
`lhs`	On the left side of the table

(continued)

Table 14.5 (*cont.*)

Value	Border Display Location
rhs	On the right side of the table
vsides	On the top and bottom of the table
void	No border displayed

- rules: Specifies how borders are displayed around individual cells. Table 14.6 describes settings for this attribute.
- summary: A brief text summary of the table.
- width: Specifies the width of the table in pixels or as a percentage of the browser's screen width.

Within the <table> element you place one or more of the following child elements to define the content of the table:

- <caption>: The table caption
- <col/>: Defines a table's columns
- <thead>: The table header
- <tfoot>: The table footer
- <tbody>: The table body
- <tr>: Placed within a <thead>, <tfoot>, or <tbody> element to define a table row

Table 14.6 Settings for the rules Attribute

Value	Border Display Location
all	Between all rows and columns
cols	Between all columns
groups	Between groups defined with the <thead>, <tbody>, and <tfoot> elements none No inner borders are displayed
rows	Between all rows

- `<th>`: Placed within a `<tr>` element to define a header cell whose contents will be displayed in boldface and centered horizontally
- `<td>`: Placed within a `<tr>` element to define a normal cell whose contents will be displayed left-aligned in a normal font

The <thead> and <tfoot> Elements

The `<thead>` and `<tfoot>` elements define a table header and footer, respectively. The header and footer are part of the table itself, but are defined as separate elements to enable different formatting to be applied. Both elements are optional. The following attributes can be set to control the appearance of the header or footer:

- `align`: Specifies the horizontal alignment of text. Permitted values are `left`, `right`, `center`, `justify`, and `char`. The `char` setting aligns text on a specific character.
- `char`: When `align` is set to `char`, specifies the alignment character. For example, to align monetary values on the decimal point, set `align="char"` and `char="."`.
- `charoff`: Specifies the offset distance from the alignment character.
- `valign`: Specifies the vertical alignment of text. Permitted values are `top`, `middle`, `bottom`, and `baseline`.

For each row in the header or footer, include one child `<tr>` element. For each column in the header or footer, include one `<td>` or `<th>` element in each `<tr>` element. The `<td>` or `<th>` element contains the text to be displayed.

The <col/> Element

The `<col/>` element is used to define characteristics of a column in the table. This element does not contain content or actually create a column, but only specifies things such as the column width and alignment. It is particularly useful for defining the width of columns that, if not specified, will default to being as small as permitted by the column's data. The `<col/>` element has the following attributes:

- `align`: Specifies the horizontal alignment of text in the column. Permitted values are `left`, `right`, `center`, `justify`, and `char`. The `char` setting aligns text on a specific character.
- `char`: When `align` is set to `char`, specifies the alignment character. For example, to align monetary values on the decimal point, set `align="char"` and `char="."`.

- charoff: Specifies the offset distance from the alignment character.
- span: Specifies how many columns this <col/> element applies to. The default is 1.
- valign: Specifies the vertical alignment of text. Permitted values are top, middle, bottom, and baseline.
- width: Specifies the width of the column in terms of pixels or as a percentage of the entire table width.

Place one <col/> element in your table definition for each column in the table. They apply to the table columns in order, from left to right. The exception to this rule is when you specify a span value of more than 1. For example, the following specifies that the left and middle columns of a three-column table will each be 40 percent as wide as the table, and that the right column will be 20 percent as wide:

```
<col width="40%"/>
<col width="40%"/>
<col width="20%"/>
```

The same result could be obtained as follows:

```
<col width="40%" span="2"/>
<col width="20%"/>
```

The <tbody> Element

The <tbody> element contains all the table rows that are not part of the header or footer. This element can have the same four attributes that were described for the <thead> and <tfoot> elements. For each row in the table body, the <tbody> element will contains one <tr> child element.

The <tr> Element

The <tr> element defines a row in the table body, header, or footer. This element can have the same four attributes that were described for the <thead> and <tfoot> elements. For each cell, or column, in the row, the <tr> element will contain one <th> or <td> child element.

The <td> and <th> Elements

The <td> and <th> elements are used to define individual cells in a table row, and to hold the cell contents. They operate the same way except that content in a `<th>` element is by default centered and in boldface, whereas content in a `<td>` element is left-aligned and in normal font. These elements are placed as children of a `<tr>` element, and normally each `<tr>` element will contain one `<td>` or `<th>` element for each column in the table. The exception is when the `colspan` attribute is used to specify that a cell span more than one column. These elements have the following attributes:

- `align`: Specifies the horizontal alignment of text in the cell. Permitted values are `left`, `right`, `center`, `justify`, and `char`. The `char` setting aligns text on a specific character.
- char: when `align` is set to `char`, specifies the alignment character. For example, to align monetary values on the decimal point, set `align="char"` and `char="."`.
- `charoff`: Specifies the offset distance from the alignment character.
- `colspan`: Specifies how many columns this cell spans. The default is 1.
- `rowspan`: Specifies how many rows this cell spans. The default is 1.
- `valign`: specifies the vertical alignment of text. Permitted values are `top`, `middle`, `bottom`, and `baseline`.

A Table Demonstration

The XHTML document in Listing 14.2 demonstrates some of the table-related elements that have been covered in this chapter. The resulting table is shown in Figure 14.2.

Listing 14.2 XHTML Document Demonstrating Some Table Elements

```
<?xml version="1.0"?>
<!DOCTYPE html PUBLIC "-//W3C//DTD XHTML 1.0 Transitional//EN"
    "http://www.w3.org/TR/xhtml1/DTD/xhtml1-transitional.dtd">
<html xmlns="http://www.w3.org/1999/xhtml">
  <head>
  <title>Demonstrating XHTML tables.</title>
  </head>
  <body>
  <table width="95%" frame="void" rules="all" cellpadding="4px">
  <col width="40%" span="2"/>
  <col width="20%"/>
  <caption align="left"><b><big>A sample XHTML Table</big></b>
```

```
    </caption>
    <thead>
      <tr>
        <th>Name</th>
        <th>Citizenship</th>
        <th>Age</th>
      </tr>
    </thead>
    <tbody>
      <tr>
        <td>Ann O'Malley</td>
        <td>Ireland</td>
        <td>31</td>
      </tr>
      <tr>
        <td>Winnie Baxter</td>
        <td colspan="2" align="center">Information not available</td>
      </tr>
      <tr>
        <td>Dmitri Konstantin</td>
        <td>Russia</td>
        <td>53</td>
      </tr>
      <tr>
        <td>Adrian Gomez</td>
        <td>Mexico</td>
        <td>44</td>
      </tr>
    </tbody>
    </table>
    </body>
  </html>
```

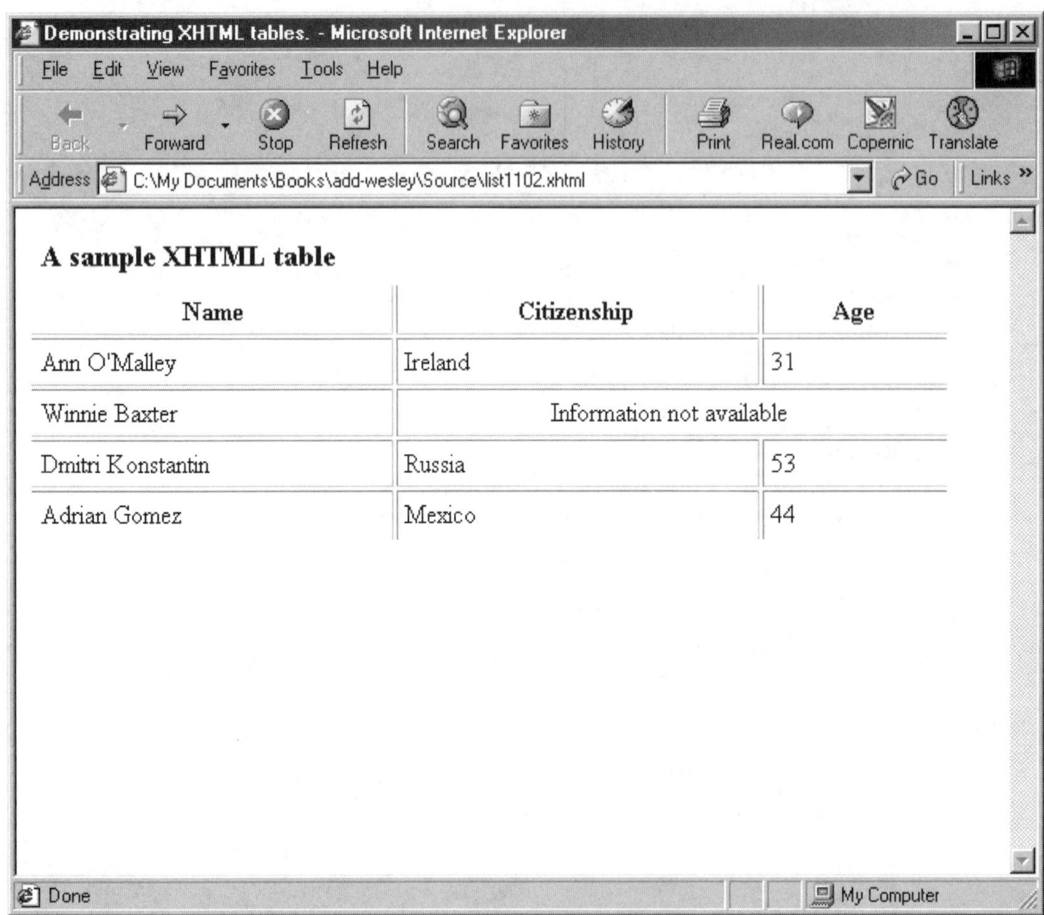

Figure 14.2 The table created by Listing 14.2

Miscellaneous Elements

There are two additional elements that did not fit into any of the other categories in this section:

- `<br/>`: Inserts a blank line in the document. Can be used to place blank space between paragraphs.
- `<hr/>`: Places a horizontal line in the document.

An XHTML Demonstration

I end this chapter with a demonstration XHTML file that pulls together many of the things you have learned in this chapter. The document, presented in Listing 14.3, includes the following:

- Use of an embedded style sheet to override the browser's default formatting
- Definition of and a link to a named anchor in the document
- A link to an external resource
- Numbered and bulleted lists
- Tables to arrange elements on the page
- An image

Note that the image that is displayed is linked from my personal home page. This image should remain available, but if you cannot access it, or if you do not have an Internet connection, you can change the XHTML to point at an image on your local drive. The document is shown displayed in Internet Explorer in Figure 14.3.

Listing 14.3 Demonstration XHTML File

```
<?xml version="1.0"?>
<!DOCTYPE html PUBLIC "-//W3C//DTD XHTML 1.0 Transitional//EN"
    "http://www.w3.org/TR/xhtml1/DTD/xhtml1-transitional.dtd">
<html xmlns="http://www.w3.org/1999/xhtml">
  <head>
    <title>An XHTML Demonstration.</title>
    <!-- This embedded style sheet specifies the font for the <h1>
      element and for the document body. These styles override the
      browser default styles. -->
    <style type="text/css">
      h1 {font: 20pt Times; font-weight: bold}
      body {font: 12pt Times; line-height: 14pt}
    </style>
  </head>
  <body>
  <!-- The following heading also serves as a named anchor.-->
  <a name="top"><h1>This is a level 1 heading.</h1></a>
  <!--This table is used to place a numbered list and
  a bulleted list next to each other.-->
```

```
<table frame="void" width="90%">
 <col width="50%" span="2"/>
 <tbody>
  <tr>
    <td>
    <ol>
      <li>First numbered item</li>
      <li>Second numbered item</li>
      <li>Third numbered item</li>
    </ol>
    </td>
    <td>
    <ul>
      <li>First bulleted item</li>
      <li>Second bulleted item</li>
      <li>Third bulleted Item</li>
    </ul>
    </td>
  </tr>
</tbody>
</table>
<!-- Put a horizontal rule under the table. -->
<hr/>
<!-- A regular paragraph of text -->
<p>This is the first paragraph. This is the first paragraph.
This is the first paragraph. This is the first paragraph.
This is the first paragraph. This is the first paragraph.
This is the first paragraph. This is the first paragraph.
This is the first paragraph. This is the first paragraph. </p>
<table frame="border" align="center">
<tr>
  <td>
  This paragraph is put in a single cell table in order to draw
  a border around the paragraph.
  </td>
</tr>
</table>
<!--Insert a blank line-->
<br/>
<!-- The following image is placed inside a paragraph element
  to permit it to be centered on the page.-->
<p align="center">
<img src="http://www.pgacon.com/images/dcdg/oldphoto.jpg"
```

```
    width="138" height="200" alt="My great-grandfather">
  </p>
  <p><a href="http://www.microsoft.com">This</a> is a link to
     the Microsoft home page.</p>
  <p><a href="#top">This</a> is a link to the top of the document.
  </p>
  </body>
</html>
```

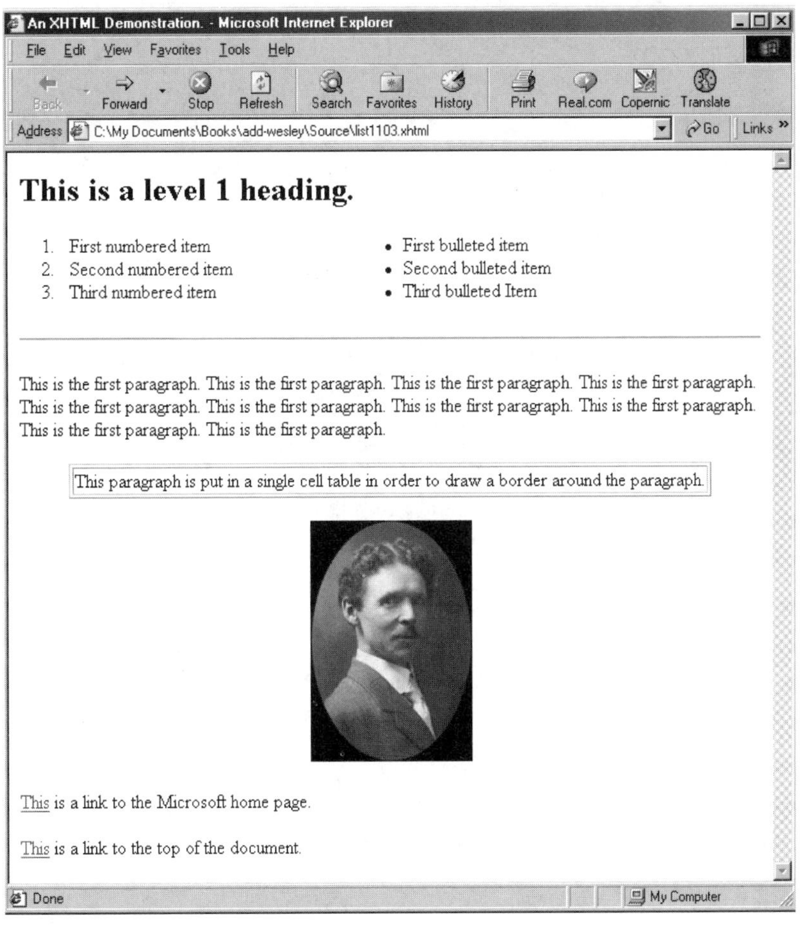

Figure 14.3 Displaying the XHTML file from Listing 14.3

Summary

Extensible Hypertext Markup Language (XHTML) was designed to be the next "language of the Web," improving upon the Hypertext Markup Language (HTML) specification. XHTML is an XML vocabulary, and as such it offers the advantages of XML while retaining most of the syntax and elements that have proven so successful with HTML. The current HTML specification remains perfectly adequate for many applications, and it is not likely to be replaced in the near future. As Web publishing becomes more sophisticated, however, you are likely to see a gradual shift from HTML to XHTML, particularly for new projects.

CHAPTER 15

Visual Basic and XML

Visual Basic is an extremely popular programming language used by hundreds of thousands of developers around the world. With its ease of designing visual interfaces, excellent text-handling capabilities, and wide array of plug-in tools, Visual Basic is certainly a good choice for a developer who needs to work with XML. This chapter presents several Visual Basic projects that work with XML in various ways. You can examine these projects to see how a number of tasks can be accomplished in Visual Basic, and you can also use them as starting points for your own development efforts.

This chapter assumes that the MSXML Parser version 4.0 is installed on your system, and that you are using Visual Basic version 6.0, Professional Edition. At the time this chapter was written, version 6.0 was the latest release of Visual Basic. A new Visual Basic, called Visual Basic .NET, is in development and may be released by the time you read this. Chapter 13 explains how Microsoft's new .NET programming tools provide XML support.

You should have some familiarity with Visual Basic to get the most from this chapter. I assume that readers have a basic knowledge of Visual Basic programming, and therefore I do not provide detailed step-by-step instructions for creating the projects.

Verifying Well-Formedness and Validity of an XML Document: DTD and XDR

An important step in many XML processing tasks is to verify that the document is well-formed, meeting XML syntax requirements, and that it is valid, adhering to the data model defined in a DTD or a schema. The techniques presented in this section provide validation against a DTD or an XDR Schema. Validation against an XSD Schema is covered in the next section.

The MSXML Parser always checks a document for well-formedness when it is loaded. It can also validate the document against its DTD or XDR Schema (as referenced in the XML file itself), depending on the setting of the `validateOnParse` property. Errors of XML syntax are reported, as are validity errors (where the document does not adhere to its model) and miscellaneous errors, such as if the DTD referenced in the document cannot be found. A limitation of the MSXML Parser is that it halts and reports at the first error that it finds, which means that finding and fixing errors is unavoidably a one-at-a-time process.

The program developed in this section is a utility that lets the user load an XML file, checking it for well-formedness only or for validity as well. The basic steps involved are:

1. Create an instance of the `DOMDocument` class.
2. Set its `validateOnParse` property to True if you want to check validity or to False if you want to check only well-formedness.
3. Load the XML document.
4. If an error occurs, report it to the user so he or she can correct it. If no error occurs, report success.

There is a potential problem, however. If the user requests validation, but the XML document does not contain a reference to a DTD or a schema, the program will report success. This could be misleading because technically, the document was not validated. Perhaps the user would know this ahead of time, but you cannot count on this. What is needed is a way to determine whether the document contains a reference to a DTD or schema. If so, and no errors occur, there is no problem. If not, it can be reported to the user that the document could not be validated because the document does not contain a reference to a DTD or a schema.

MSXML Class Names

When you install the MSXML Parser version 4.0, it is installed in side-by-side mode. This means that if you have any earlier versions of the parser on your system, they are not replaced. To enable you to use the older parser when and if desired, Microsoft provides version-dependent and version-independent names for the various classes that MSXML provides. The version-independent name, which is the qualified class name, always refers to the latest version of the class that is available. Thus, `MSXML2.DomDocument` *will refer to version 4.0 of the* `DomDocument` *class if available, and if not, an earlier available version such as 3.0. The version-dependent names are the qualified class name with a suffix indicating the version.* `MSXML2.DomDocument40`, *for example, refers specifically to version 4.0 of the class, and it will not work if this version is not installed regardless of any other installed versions.*

How, then, can you determine whether an XML document contains a DTD or an XDR Schema reference? You could look for the reference using the Document Object Model to access the individual elements of the document. This would not be all that easy to do, however, particularly because a DTD reference is in a different type of element than an XDR Schema reference. (XSD Schemas are not referenced within an XML file, as explained in Chapter 5.)

There is an easier way to determine whether an XML document contains a DTD or an XDR Schema reference that makes use of the `DOMDocument` object's `validate()` method. If you call this method, and the document does not contain a DTD/schema reference, the method returns a nonzero error code. If a DTD/schema reference is present, the method returns 0. In the latter case, the document will be verified twice—once when it is loaded and once when the `validate()` method is called—but this does no harm beyond wasting a few milliseconds of processor time.

The program is created as a standard EXE project. It has only a single form, which contains two command buttons and one frame. The frame contains two option buttons. The form requires a Common Dialog control as well. Don't forget to add references to the MSXML Parser and the Common Dialog control to the project. The program's form is shown in Figure 15.1, and its source code appears in Listing 15.1.

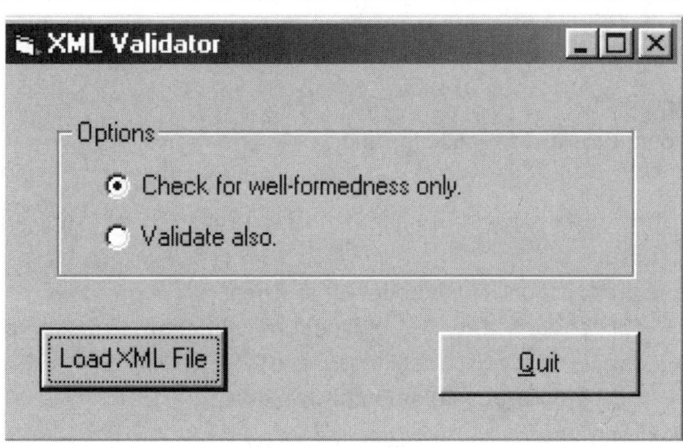

Figure 15.1 The XML Validator program

Listing 15.1 Code for the XML Validator Program for DTDs and XDR

```
Option Explicit

Dim xmlDoc As MSXML2.DOMDocument
```

```
Private Sub cmdLoadFile_Click()
' Lets the user select an XML file for validation.
Dim filename As String
Dim msg As String
Dim retval As Long

' Use the common dialog control to permit the user
' to select an XML file to open.
CommonDialog1.Filter = "XML files | *.xml"
CommonDialog1.ShowOpen

If CommonDialog1.filename = "" Then Exit Sub

' Set for synchronous processing so execution will not return
' from the load method until the entire file has been loaded.
xmlDoc.async = False

' Instruct parser to validate document or not
' depending on option settings.
If optWellFormedOnly.Value = True Then
    xmlDoc.validateOnParse = False
Else
    xmlDoc.validateOnParse = True
End If

' Load the file.
xmlDoc.Load CommonDialog1.filename

' Check for an error. If present, display information
' and exit sub.
If xmlDoc.parseError.errorCode <> 0 Then
    msg = "Error on line " & xmlDoc.parseError.Line & vbCrLf
    msg = msg & xmlDoc.parseError.srcText & vbCrLf
    msg = msg & xmlDoc.parseError.reason
    MsgBox msg
    Exit Sub
End If

' If the user requested validation, try to validate the document.
' If there is no DTD or schema specified this returns nonzero.
If optValidateAlso.Value = True Then
    retval = xmlDoc.Validate
    If retval <> 0 Then
```

```
        msg = CommonDialog1.filename & " is well formed." & vbCrLf
        msg = msg & "However it contains no DTD or schema reference" &
vbCrLf
        msg = msg & "and so cannot be validated."
    Else
        msg = CommonDialog1.filename & " is well formed and valid." &
vbCrLf
    End If
Else
    msg = CommonDialog1.filename & " is well formed." & vbCrLf
End If

MsgBox msg

End Sub

Private Sub cmdQuit_Click()

Unload Me

End Sub

Private Sub Form_Load()

Dim msg As String

On Error Resume Next

' Create the DOMDocument object.
Set xmlDoc = New DOMDocument
' Check for error.
If Err Then
    msg = "DOMDocument object could not be created." & vbCrLf
    msg = msg & "Program will terminate."
    MsgBox msg
    Unload Me
End If

End Sub
```

Verifying Well-Formedness and Validity of an XML Document: XSD

The MSXML Parser version 4.0 has the capability to validate an XML document against an XSD Schema. The procedure is a bit different from the one you learned earlier in this chapter for validating against a DTD or an XDR Schema. Because an XSD Schema is not referenced directly in the XML file, it must be loaded separately. The link between the XML file and its schema is provided by one or more namespaces, as you learned in Chapter 5. Here are the steps required in your program:

1. Create an instance of the `MSXML2.XMLSchemaCache` class.
2. Use the `Add()` method to load the XSD Schema file. At the same time the schema file is loaded, it is associated with the namespace that will link it to the XML file.
3. Create an instance of the `MSXML2.DomDocument` class.
4. Assign the `XMLSchemaCache` object to the `DomDocument` object's schemas property.
5. Call the `DomDocument` object's `Load()` method to load the XML file. The document is checked for well-formedness and validated automatically when it is loaded. Errors are reported by the `parseError` object, as described in an earlier chapter.

Step 2 may need further elaboration. In Chapter 5, you learned that the association between an XML file and an XSD Schema is made indirectly by means of a namespace. For example, an XML file could define a namespace and use the associated prefix as follows:

```
<?xml version="1.0" encoding="UTF-8"?>
<x:recordings xmlns:x="urn:recordings">
...
</x:recordings>
```

The root element of this XML document is now in the "urn:recordings" namespace. Next, suppose that the XSD Schema you want to validate this file against is in the file MySchema.xsd. The connection between the schema and the namespace is made when you add the schema to the `XMLSchemaCache` object, as follows:

```
Dim xmlSchema As New MSXML2.XMLSchemaCache
xmlSchema.Add "urn:recordings", "MySchema.xsd"
```

Then, load the XML document (steps 3–5):

```
Dim xmlDoc As New MSXML2.DomDocument
xmlDoc.schemas = xmlSchema
xmlDoc.Load "recordings.xml"
```

At this point, the parser sees the namespace in the XML document, matches it against the namespace associated with the schema file, and knows to validate the XML file against that schema.

Listing 15.2 presents the code for ValidateXSD, a program to validate an XML file against an XSD Schema. This program is similar to the DTD/XDR validator presented earlier, with the only differences being in the code, so I will not go into the details of creating it. When you run the program, the user has a choice of checking for well-formedness only, or validating as well. The user then selects the XML file, and if the validation option was chosen, the user selects the XSD file as well. The program reports any parse or validation errors that are encountered.

Listing 15.2 Code for the XML Validator Program for XSD

```
Option Explicit

Dim xmlDoc As MSXML2.DOMDocument
Dim xmlSchema As MSXML2.XMLSchemaCache

Private Sub cmdLoadFile_Click()

' Lets the user select an XML file for validation, and an
' XSD file containing the schema.
Dim msg As String
Dim retval As Long
Dim XMLFile As String

On Error Resume Next

' Use the common dialog control to permit the user
' to select an XML file to open.
CommonDialog1.Filter = "XML files | *.xml"
CommonDialog1.ShowOpen
If CommonDialog1.filename = "" Then Exit Sub
XMLFile = CommonDialog1.filename
```

```
' Get schema file only if validation has been requested.
If optWellFormedOnly.Value = False Then
    CommonDialog1.Filter = "XSD files | *.xsd"
    CommonDialog1.filename = ""
    CommonDialog1.ShowOpen
    If CommonDialog1.filename = "" Then Exit Sub
    xmlSchema.Add "urn:recordings", CommonDialog1.filename
    If Err <> 0 Then
        msg = "Error loading schema: " & Err.Description
        MsgBox msg
        Exit Sub
    End If
    Set xmlDoc.schemas = xmlSchema
End If

' Instruct parser to validate document or not
' depending on option settings.
If optWellFormedOnly.Value = True Then
    xmlDoc.validateOnParse = False
Else
    xmlDoc.validateOnParse = True
End If

' Set for synchronous processing so execution will not return
' from the load method until the entire file has been loaded.
xmlDoc.async = False
' Load the file.
xmlDoc.Load XMLFile

' Check for an error. If present, display information.
If xmlDoc.parseError.errorCode <> 0 Then
    msg = "Error on line " & xmlDoc.parseError.Line & vbCrLf
    msg = msg & xmlDoc.parseError.srcText & vbCrLf
    msg = msg & xmlDoc.parseError.reason
Else
    msg = "No errors."
End If

MsgBox msg

End Sub

Private Sub cmdQuit_Click()
```

```
Unload Me

End Sub

Private Sub Form_Load()

Dim msg As String

On Error Resume Next

' Create the DOMDocument object.
Set xmlDoc = New DOMDocument
Set xmlSchema = New MSXML2.XMLSchemaCache

' Check for error.
If Err Then
    msg = "DOMDocument object could not be created." & vbCrLf
    msg = msg & "Program will terminate."
    MsgBox msg
    Unload Me
End If

End Sub
```

Processing Raw XML

Given that XML files are plain text, there is no reason why a program cannot read and manipulate the XML directly, without using the intermediary of the MSXML Parser or a similar tool. There may not be many times that you'll need or want to access the XML directly—after all, the MSXML Parser makes most XML-related tasks a lot easier. Some special situations, however, may be better served by direct access. If you need only to get at specific information in the file, you may find significant time savings using direct access because all of the MSXML Parser's overhead is avoided. For instance, if all you need to do is see if the file contains an element named "partnumber" with a value of "12Q-0098," you may find that not only is direct access faster but the programming is easier, too.

In my experience, there are four factors that argue against using direct access in a specific situation.

- You want to check the document for well-formedness.
- You want to validate the document against its DTD or schema.

- The document contains entities that must be resolved.
- You do not know the details of the document's logical structure.

If none of these conditions hold, your situation *may* be a good candidate for direct access.

For the present demonstration, the task is to read and edit an XML file that contains contact information, as shown in Listing 15.3. While the logical structure of this file is relatively simple, the principles that will be applied are applicable to XML files of any complexity.

Listing 15.3: The XML "Contacts" Data File

```
<?xml version="1.0" encoding="UTF-8"?>
<contacts>
<person category="business">
  <lastname>Smith</lastname>
  <firstname>Adrian</firstname>
  <email>asmith@somewhere.com</email>
  <phone>555-555-1212</phone>
</person>
<person category="family">
  <lastname>Baker</lastname>
  <firstname>Alex</firstname>
  <email>alex123@somemailserver.com</email>
  <phone>555-666-7777</phone>
</person>
<person category="personal">
  <lastname>Chang</lastname>
  <firstname>Lee</firstname>
  <email>lee.chang@overthere.net</email>
  <phone>999-888-1111</phone>
</person>
<person category="personal">
  <lastname>Alexander</lastname>
  <firstname>Jane</firstname>
  <email>jane@alexander.org</email>
  <phone>919-555-1212</phone>
</person>
</contacts>
```

The program needs to perform the following tasks.

- Read the XML file from disk and parse it. For the current purposes, the term "parse" means to extract the data from the XML and store it in program variables.
- Display the first data record onscreen for the user to view and optionally edit.
- Permit the user to move through the records one at a time or to move to the first or last record directly.
- Permit the user to enter one or more new records. With each new record, the user should have the option to accept the new record or to cancel the operation.
- When the user quits the program, the data should be written back to the XML file.

Visual Basic offers several options for storing data that could be used for this project. I decided to use a dynamic array of user-defined types (UDTs). A UDT permits a data type to be custom tailored for the XML data, with a member for each XML element or attribute. By using a dynamic array, the array size is not fixed, and it can be increased as needed if the user adds more records to the data.

This Visual Basic project has two modules: a Basic module that contains the UDT definition and a constant that specifies the data file, and a standard form module that contains the remainder of the program code as well as its visual interface elements. The code in these two modules is presented in Listings 15.4 and 15.5.

The project's visual interface is shown in Figure 15.2. It uses the following controls to provide for user input:

- Four text boxes for viewing and editing of data
- A set of three option buttons for displaying and selecting the value of the "category" attribute
- A control array of four command buttons for the movement buttons
- Additional individual command buttons for other functions

The program is written to expect a certain logical structure in the XML file—namely, the structure shown in Listing 15.2. If there are any deviations from this structure, the program will not operate properly. This is a clear example of how knowing the logical structure of an XML file greatly simplifies the task of writing a program to manipulate the raw XML.

Listing 15.4 Module1.bas

```
' Module1.bas
' For the RawXML project.

' The name of the XML data file.
Public Const DATAFILE = "c:\my documents\data\list1503.xml"

' A user-defined type for each record.
Public Type person
    category As String
    lastname As String
    firstname As String
    email As String
    phone As String
End Type
```

Listing 15.5 Source Code in frmMain.frm

```
' frmMain.frm
' For the RawXML project.

Option Explicit

' Dynamic array to hold the data records.
Dim data() As person

' Number of records in the array.
Dim num As Long

' Pointer to current record in the array.
Dim current As Long

' Flag to indicate whether current record
' has been changed by the user.
Dim CurrentRecordChanged As Boolean

' Flag that is true when a new record is being entered.
Dim EnteringNewRecord As Boolean

'*****************
Private Sub cmdCancel_Click()
```

```
' Cancels the entering of a new record.

Dim retval As Integer

' Verify cancel request.
retval = MsgBox("cancel - are you sure?", vbYesNo, "Cancel New Record")
If retval = vbNo Then Exit Sub

' Cancel has been verified. Display the record
' that was displayed previously.
showdata (current)

' Enable move buttons as needed.
EnableMoveButtons
UpdateFormCaption

' Change caption on "New" button.
cmdNew.Caption = "New"

' Toggle flag.
EnteringNewRecord = False

' Hide this button.
cmdCancel.Visible = False

' Enable Quit button.
cmdQuit.Enabled = True

End Sub

'*****************
Private Sub cmdNew_Click()

' When the New/Save button has been clicked.

Dim i As Integer

' If we are entering a new record, this is the Save button.
If EnteringNewRecord Then
    ' Extend the array by one element.
    num = num + 1
    ReDim Preserve data(num)
```

```
        ' Hide the Cancel button.
        cmdCancel.Visible = False
        ' Restore the caption on this button to "New"
        cmdNew.Caption = "New"

        ' Toggle flag.
        EnteringNewRecord = False
        ' Current record is the newly entered one.
        current = num
        SaveCurrentRecord
        UpdateFormCaption
        ' Enable movement buttons.
        EnableMoveButtons
        ' Enable Quit button.
        cmdQuit.Enabled = True
    ' Otherwise it is the New button.
    Else
        ' Change form caption to reflect new record.
        frmMain.Caption = "Contacts - entering new record."
        ' Disable the movement and quit buttons.
        For i = 0 To 3
            cmdMove(i).Enabled = False
        Next i
        cmdQuit.Enabled = False
        EnteringNewRecord = True
        ' Show the Cancel button.
        cmdCancel.Visible = True
        ' Change the caption on this button.
        cmdNew.Caption = "Save"
        ' Save the current record if needed.
        If CurrentRecordChanged Then SaveCurrentRecord
        ' Blank the text boxes.
        txtFirstName.Text = ""
        txtLastName.Text = ""
        txtPhone.Text = ""
        txtEmail.Text = ""
        ' Set focus to the first text box.
        txtFirstName.SetFocus
    End If

    End Sub

    '*****************
    Private Sub cmdMove_Click(Index As Integer)
```

```
' This is the control array of movement buttons.
' Index = 0 for first
'         1 for previous
'         2 for next
'         3 for last

' Save the current record if it has changed.
If CurrentRecordChanged Then
    SaveCurrentRecord
End If

Select Case Index
    Case 0
        ' Make first record current.
        current = 1
    Case 1
        ' Make previous record current.
        current = current - 1
    Case 2
        ' Make next record current.
        current = current + 1
    Case 3
        ' Make last record current.
        current = num
End Select

' Display the record.
showdata (current)
' Update the title bar display.
UpdateFormCaption

' Disable/enable movement buttons.
EnableMoveButtons

End Sub
'*****************
Private Sub cmdQuit_Click()

' When the Quit button is clicked.
SaveDataToDisk
Unload Me

End Sub
```

```
'*****************
Private Sub Form_Load()

' Initiaize record count.
num = 0

' Load the data file.
If Not LoadDataFile Then
    MsgBox "The data file could not be loaded - program will terminate."
    Unload Me
End If

' Display the first record.
current = 1
showdata (current)
' Disable the "first" and "previous" buttons.
cmdMove(0).Enabled = False
cmdMove(1).Enabled = False

CurrentRecordChanged = False
EnteringNewRecord = False

' Update title bar display.
UpdateFormCaption

End Sub

'*****************
Public Function LoadDataFile() As Boolean

' Loads the data file into the array. Returns True
' on success, False on failure.

Dim fso As New Scripting.FileSystemObject
Dim ts As Scripting.TextStream
Dim buf As String

On Error Resume Next
Set ts = fso.OpenTextFile(DATAFILE)
If Err Then
    LoadDataFile = False
    Set fso = Nothing
```

```
    Exit Function
End If

Err.Clear

' Read the entire file into a variable, then
' close the file.
buf = ts.ReadAll
ts.Close
Set ts = Nothing

' Load the array with the data.
LoadArrayWithData (buf)

Set fso = Nothing
LoadDataFile = True

'*****************
End Function

Public Sub LoadArrayWithData(s As String)

' Passed a string containing the contents of the XML file,
' loads the array data() with the records.

Dim p1 As Long
Dim p2 As Long

' Find the start of the first "person" element.
p1 = InStr(s, "<person")

' Set up a repeating loop. Each time this loop starts,
' p1 should be pointing at the start of the next
' <person> element.
Do While True
    ' Add another element to the array.
    num = num + 1
    ReDim Preserve data(num)
    ' Find the beginning of the "category" attribute.
    p1 = InStr(p1, s, "category=") + 10
    ' Find the end of the "category" attribute.
    p2 = InStr(p1, s, Chr(34))
```

```
        ' Extract the value.
        data(num).category = Mid(s, p1, p2 - p1)

        ' Locate the end of the <lastname> tag.
        p1 = InStr(p1, s, "<lastname>") + Len("<lastname>")
        ' Locate the start of the </lastname> tag.
        p2 = InStr(p1, s, "</lastname>")
        ' Extract the value.
        data(num).lastname = Mid(s, p1, p2 - p1)

        ' Locate the end of the <firstname> tag.
        p1 = InStr(p1, s, "<firstname>") + Len("<firstname>")
        ' Locate the start of the </firstname> tag.
        p2 = InStr(p1, s, "</firstname>")
        ' Extract the value.
        data(num).firstname = Mid(s, p1, p2 - p1)

        ' Locate the end of the <email> tag.
        p1 = InStr(p1, s, "<email>") + Len("<email>")
        ' Locate the start of the </email> tag.
        p2 = InStr(p1, s, "</email>")
        ' Extract the value.
        data(num).email = Mid(s, p1, p2 - p1)

        ' Locate the end of the <phone> tag.
        p1 = InStr(p1, s, "<phone>") + Len("<phone>")
        ' Locate the start of the </phone> tag.
        p2 = InStr(p1, s, "</phone>")
        ' Extract the value.
        data(num).phone = Mid(s, p1, p2 - p1)

        ' Look for the next <person> element.
        ' If it cannot be found we are done so can exit loop.
        p1 = InStr(p1, s, "<person")
        If p1 = 0 Then Exit Do
    Loop

    End Sub

    '****************
    Public Sub showdata(idx As Long)
```

```
' Displays record idx.

 txtFirstName.Text = data(idx).firstname
 txtLastName.Text = data(idx).lastname
 txtPhone.Text = data(idx).phone
 txtEmail.Text = data(idx).email

 Select Case data(idx).category
    Case "personal"
        optPersonal.Value = True
    Case "family"
        optFamily.Value = True
    Case "business"
        optBusiness.Value = True
 End Select

End Sub

'*****************
Private Sub txtEmail_Change()

CurrentRecordChanged = True

End Sub

'*****************
Private Sub txtFirstName_Change()

CurrentRecordChanged = True

End Sub

'*****************
Private Sub txtLastName_Change()

CurrentRecordChanged = True

End Sub

'*****************
Private Sub txtPhone_Change()
```

```
CurrentRecordChanged = True

End Sub

'*****************
Public Sub SaveCurrentRecord()

' Writes the current record back into the array.

data(current).firstname = txtFirstName.Text
data(current).lastname = txtLastName.Text
data(current).phone = txtPhone.Text
data(current).email = txtEmail.Text
If optPersonal.Value Then data(current).category = "personal"
If optFamily.Value Then data(current).category = "family"
If optBusiness.Value Then data(current).category = "business"
CurrentRecordChanged = False

End Sub

'*****************
Public Sub SaveDataToDisk()

' Writes the data back to the XML file.

Dim fso As New Scripting.FileSystemObject
Dim ts As Scripting.TextStream
Dim i As Long
Dim buf As String

On Error GoTo Errorhandler

Set ts = fso.CreateTextFile(DATAFILE, True)

' Write the XML header.
ts.WriteLine ("<?xml version=" & Chr(34) & "1.0" & Chr(34) & "
encoding=" _
    & Chr(34) & "UTF-8" & Chr(34) & "?>")
' Write the root element start tag.
ts.WriteLine ("<contacts>")

' Loop for each record (each <contact> element).
For i = 1 To num
```

```
    ' The <person> element with its one attribute.
    buf = "<person category=" & Chr(34) & data(i).category & Chr(34) &
">"
    ts.WriteLine buf
    ' The <lastname> element.
    buf = "<lastname>" & data(i).lastname & "</lastname>"
    ts.WriteLine buf
    ' The <firstname> element.
    buf = "<firstname>" & data(i).firstname & "</firstname>"
    ts.WriteLine buf
    ' The <email> element.
    buf = "<email>" & data(i).email & "</email>"
    ts.WriteLine buf
    ' The <phone> element.
    buf = "<phone>" & data(i).phone & "</phone>"
    ts.WriteLine buf
    ' The </person> end tag.
    ts.WriteLine "</person>"
Next i

' Write the root element's closing tag.
ts.WriteLine "</contacts>"

ts.Close
Set ts = Nothing
Set fso = Nothing
Exit Sub

Errorhandler:
    MsgBox "There was an error writing the data file."

End Sub

'*****************
Public Sub EnableMoveButtons()

' Disable/enable movement buttons as needed.
If current = 1 Then
    cmdMove(0).Enabled = False
    cmdMove(1).Enabled = False
    cmdMove(2).Enabled = True
    cmdMove(3).Enabled = True
ElseIf current = num Then
```

```
    cmdMove(0).Enabled = True
    cmdMove(1).Enabled = True
    cmdMove(2).Enabled = False
    cmdMove(3).Enabled = False
Else
    cmdMove(0).Enabled = True
    cmdMove(1).Enabled = True
    cmdMove(2).Enabled = True
    cmdMove(3).Enabled = True
End If

End Sub

'*****************
Public Sub UpdateFormCaption()

' Updates the form's caption to reflect the current record number.
frmMain.Caption = "Contacts - record " & current & " of " & num

End Sub
```

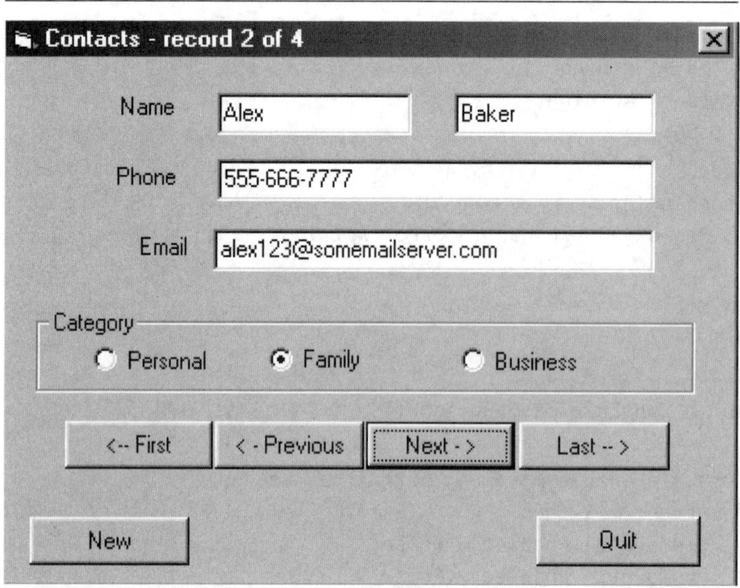

Figure 15.2: The Raw XML project's form

Using SAX to Extract XML Data

Many XML applications do not require that the entire XML file be processed. Rather than needing access to all the data, such applications need only to extract a specific subset of the data from the XML file. The Simple API for XML, or SAX, is ideal for such tasks. Unlike DOM, SAX does not construct a complete logical document tree in memory, which is a processor- and memory-intensive task. Rather, SAX goes through the XML document from start to finish and calls methods as it encounters elements and data in the document. By responding to these methods and gathering only the specific data that is needed, a program can efficiently extract specific data from an XML file. Chapter 11 covers the details of SAX. This section presents a complete Visual Basic program that uses SAX to locate and process specific data in an XML file.

The target XML file is shown in Listing 15.6. It is a database of sales information, with each "sale" element containing the data for an individual sale. The item that was sold is identified in the "item" attribute, and the quantity and total amount data are located in the "quantity" and "price" elements, respectively. The goal of the program is to produce a summary that shows for each item the total number sold and the total amount.

Listing 15.6 XML File Containing Sales Information

```
<?xml version="1.0" encoding="UTF-8"?>
<sales>
  <sale item="hammer">
    <quantity>12</quantity>
    <price>44.50</price>
  </sale>
  <sale item="wrench">
    <quantity>6</quantity>
    <price>72.25</price>
  </sale>
  <sale item="hammer">
    <quantity>24</quantity>
    <price>84.25</price>
  </sale>
  <sale item="chisel">
    <quantity>9</quantity>
    <price>27.75</price>
  </sale>
```

```
  <sale item="wrench">
    <quantity>48</quantity>
    <price>509.95</price>
  </sale>
  <sale item="chisel">
    <quantity>18</quantity>
    <price>48.05</price>
  </sale>
  <sale item="hammer">
    <quantity>4</quantity>
    <price>15.20</price>
  </sale>
</sales>
```

The design of the program is based on the concept of a *state machine.* This term means that the program keeps track of its current state as it processes the XML file. For the current task, there are two states that need keeping track of: which item (hammer, chisel, or wrench) is being processed and which data (quantity or price) is being read. This information can be kept in two state variables, and the events, or methods, provided by the SAX interface can be used to manage these variables. The following is an outline of the steps involved.

1. The `startElement()` method at the beginning of a "sale" element. The value of the "item" attribute can be retrieved at this time and an item state variable set accordingly to identify the item being processed.
2. The `startElement()` method at the beginning of a "quantity" element or a "price" element. The name of the element can be used to set another state variable, this one identifying the element being processed (quantity or price).
3. The `characters()` method when the data inside a "quantity" or "price" element is read. This data will be added to the appropriate program total based on the values of the state variables that were set in steps 1 and 2.
4. The `endElement()` method at the close of a "quantity" element or a "price" element. At this time the element state variable will be cleared.
5. The `endElement()` method at the end of a "sale" element. At this time the item state variable will be cleared.

You can see that four of these five methods are used to manage the program's state variables, and only step 3 actually involves processing the numerical data of interest. There is one final method, `endDocument()`, that is called

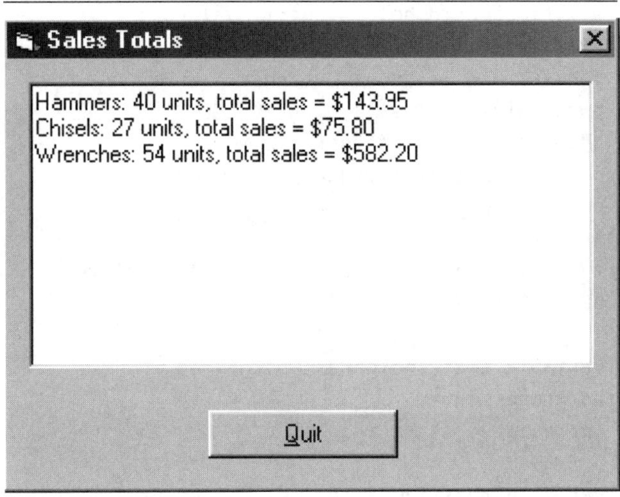

Figure 15.3: The SAX demonstration program

when the document processing is complete. This method will be used to set a flag that tells the program when the summary is ready to be displayed.

The program's visual interface is extremely simple, consisting of a form with only two controls on it: a text box (with the `MultiLine` property set to True) for display of the results and a command button to quit the program. The program's form is shown, with results displayed, in Figure 15.3.

Any program that uses MSXML's SAX Reader must implement the `IVBSAXContentHandler` and `IVBSAXErrorHandler` classes. Chapter 11 covers the details of implementing these classes. Briefly, you must create a Visual Basic class module for each class, and then implement each class' methods. In the current project, these classes are implemented as the modules SAXContentHandler.cls and SAXErrorHandler.cls. Code in the error handler takes care of reporting errors that the SAX parser encounters, and code in the content handler does the program's main task of managing the state variables and processing the data. The content handler class also implements a variety of read-only properties that are used to hold the calculated totals as well as the "parsing complete" flag. The code for the content handler and error handler classes is presented in Listing 15.7 and Listing 15.8.

Listing 15.7 The `SAXContentHandler` Class

```
Option Explicit
Implements IVBSAXContentHandler
```

```
' Private variables to hold property values.
Private pHammerTotalSales As Currency
Private pChiselTotalSales As Currency
Private pWrenchTotalSales As Currency
Private pHammerCount As Integer
Private pChiselCount As Integer
Private pWrenchCount As Integer

' Property to indicate whether parsing is complete.
Private pParseComplete As Boolean

' State variable that indicates which item
' is being processed.
Private CurrentItem As String

' State variable that indicates which element
' is currently being processed.
Private CurrentElement As String

'***********
Private Sub Class_Initialize()

' Initialize property and state variables.
CurrentItem = ""
CurrentItem = ""
pHammerTotalSales = 0
pChiselTotalSales = 0
pWrenchTotalSales = 0
pHammerCount = 0
pChiselCount = 0
pWrenchCount = 0
pParseComplete = False

End Sub

'***********
Private Sub IVBSAXContentHandler_characters(strChars As String)

' If we receive characters while processing
' a "quantity" or "price" element, the value should
' be added to the total for the item being processed.

If CurrentElement = "price" Then
    Select Case CurrentItem
```

```
        Case "hammer"
            pHammerTotalSales = pHammerTotalSales + strChars
        Case "chisel"
            pChiselTotalSales = pChiselTotalSales + strChars
        Case "wrench"
            pWrenchTotalSales = pWrenchTotalSales + strChars
    End Select
ElseIf CurrentElement = "quantity" Then
    Select Case CurrentItem
        Case "hammer"
            pHammerCount = pHammerCount + strChars
        Case "chisel"
            pChiselCount = pChiselCount + strChars
        Case "wrench"
            pWrenchCount = pWrenchCount + strChars
    End Select
End If

End Sub

'***********
Private Property Set IVBSAXContentHandler_documentLocator _
    (ByVal RHS As MSXML2.IVBSAXLocator)

End Property

'***********
Private Sub IVBSAXContentHandler_endDocument()

pParseComplete = True

End Sub

'***********
Private Sub IVBSAXContentHandler_endElement(strNamespaceURI _
    As String, strLocalName As String, strQName As String)

' Reset element state variable.
CurrentElement = ""

' If a "sale" element ends, reset item state variable.
If strLocalName = "sale" Then
```

```
    CurrentItem = ""
End If

End Sub

'***********
Private Sub IVBSAXContentHandler_endPrefixMapping(strPrefix As String)

End Sub

'***********
Private Sub IVBSAXContentHandler_ignorableWhitespace _
    (strChars As String)

End Sub

'***********
Private Sub IVBSAXContentHandler_processingInstruction(strTarget _
    As String, strData As String)

End Sub

'***********
Private Sub IVBSAXContentHandler_skippedEntity(strName As String)

End Sub

'***********
Private Sub IVBSAXContentHandler_startDocument()

End Sub

'***********
Private Sub IVBSAXContentHandler_startElement(strNamespaceURI _
    As String, strLocalName As String, strQName As String, _
    ByVal oAttributes As MSXML2.IVBSAXAttributes)

Dim item As String
' Set element state variable.
CurrentElement = strLocalName

' If this is a "sale" element, get the value of the "item" attribute.
If strLocalName = "sale" Then
```

```
    ' Set the item state variable
    CurrentItem = oAttributes.getValueFromName("", "item")
'    Debug.Print CurrentItem
End If

End Sub

'***********
Private Sub IVBSAXContentHandler_startPrefixMapping(strPrefix _
    As String, strURI As String)

End Sub

'***********
Public Property Get HammerTotalSales() As Currency

HammerTotalSales = pHammerTotalSales

End Property

'***********
Public Property Get ChiselTotalSales() As Currency

ChiselTotalSales = pChiselTotalSales

End Property

'***********
Public Property Get WrenchTotalSales() As Currency

WrenchTotalSales = pWrenchTotalSales

End Property

'***********
Public Property Get WrenchCount() As Long

WrenchCount = pWrenchCount

End Property

'***********
Public Property Get HammerCount() As Long
```

```
HammerCount = pHammerCount

End Property

'***********
Public Property Get ChiselCount() As Long

ChiselCount = pChiselCount

End Property

'***********
Public Property Get ParseComplete() As Boolean

ParseComplete = pParseComplete

End Property
```

Listing 15.8 The `SAXErrorHandler` **Class**

```
Implements IVBSAXErrorHandler

Private Sub IVBSAXErrorHandler_error(ByVal oLocator _
    As MSXML2.IVBSAXLocator, strErrorMessage As String, _
    ByVal nErrorCode As Long)

End Sub

Private Sub IVBSAXErrorHandler_fatalError(ByVal oLocator _
    As MSXML2.IVBSAXLocator, strErrorMessage As String, _
    ByVal nErrorCode As Long)

' Handles SAX parser errors by displaying
' information to the user.
Dim msg As String

msg = "The parser encountered an error: " & vbCrLf
msg = msg & "  Error code: " & nErrorCode & vbCrLf
msg = msg & "  Description: " & strErrorMessage
msg = msg & "  Location: just before line "
msg = msg & oLocator.lineNumber & " column " & oLocator.columnNumber

MsgBox msg

End Sub
```

```
Private Sub IVBSAXErrorHandler_ignorableWarning(ByVal _
    oLocator As MSXML2.IVBSAXLocator, _
    strErrorMessage As String, ByVal nErrorCode As Long)

End Sub
```

Code in the program's form module is placed in the `Form_Load()` event procedure so it will execute automatically when the program starts. The code performs these tasks:

1. It creates an instance of the `SAXXMLReader` class.
2. It creates instances of the content handler and error handler classes.
3. It connects the content handler and error handler classes with the SAX Reader by assigning references to its `contentHandler` and `errorHandler` properties.
4. It calls the SAX Reader's `parseURL` method to parse the XML file.
5. It waits until the content handler's "done" flag indicates that parsing is complete.
6. It retrieves the summary results from the content handler's properties and displays them for the user to view.

The code in the program's main form (frmMain.frm) is shown in Listing 15.9.

Listing 15.9 Code in the Program's Main Form Module

```
Option Explicit

' The name of the file to process.
Const FILENAME = "c:\my documents\xml\list1506.xml"

'***********
Private Sub cmdQuit_Click()

Unload Me

End Sub

'***********
Private Sub Form_Load()

Dim reader As New SAXXMLReader
Dim contentHandler As New SAXContentHandler
```

```
Dim errorHandler As New SAXErrorHandler
Dim msg As String

Set reader.contentHandler = contentHandler
Set reader.errorHandler = errorHandler

On Error Resume Next
reader.parseURL FILENAME
' Check for parser errors.
If Err Then
    MsgBox "The parser reported an error."
    Unload Me
End If

' Construct the summary message.
msg = "Hammers: " & contentHandler.HammerCount
msg = msg & " units, total sales = "
msg = msg & FormatCurrency(contentHandler.HammerTotalSales) & vbCrLf

msg = msg & "Chisels: " & contentHandler.ChiselCount
msg = msg & " units, total sales = "
msg = msg & FormatCurrency(contentHandler.ChiselTotalSales) & vbCrLf

msg = msg & "Wrenches: " & contentHandler.WrenchCount
msg = msg & " units, total sales = "
msg = msg & FormatCurrency(contentHandler.WrenchTotalSales) & vbCrLf

' Loop until parsing is complete.
Do Until contentHandler.ParseComplete
    DoEvents
Loop

' Display the results.
Text1.Text = msg

End Sub
```

Using DOM to Modify Document Structure

The processing of XML documents is not limited to accessing the data in the document. There are times when the document structure needs to be modified, and for these situations using DOM is the best approach. When DOM parses an XML document, it creates a node tree representing the entire document and makes it available to a program. By accessing this tree, changes to the document structure and content are straightforward. Chapter 10 covers the details of DOM. In this section, I present a complete demonstration program showing how to use DOM to modify a document's structure.

This project uses the XML data file that was presented earlier in this chapter, in Listing 15.6. This XML file contains a set of "sale" elements, each containing data for an individual sale. The item sold is identified by the "sale" element's "item" attribute, as shown here:

```
<sale item="hammer">
  <quantity>12</quantity>
  <price>44.50</price>
</sale>
```

The task at hand is to modify the XML file structure so that each sale is also identified by the item's part number. This information is to be contained in an element named "partnumber" that will be a sibling of the "quantity" and "price" elements. Thus, after the modification, the previous element would look like this:

```
<sale item="hammer">
  <quantity>12</quantity>
  <price>44.50</price>
  <partnumber>QC1132</partnumber>
</sale>
```

The procedure to use DOM to make these modifications is as follows:

1. Create an instance of the `DOMDocument` class.
2. Load the input file and check for errors.
3. Obtain a reference to the root element, which is named "sales."
4. Loop through all children of the root element. These will be the "sale" elements.
5. For each "sale" element, determine the value of the "item" attribute.
6. Create a new `IXMLDOMElement` node named "partnumber."
7. Based on the value of the "item" attribute obtained in step 5, set the value of the new node to the appropriate part number.
8. Insert the new node as a child of the current "sale" element.
9. When all "sale" elements have been processed, save the modified XML in a new file.

The code for this project, which contains only a single form, is shown in Listing 15.10. The project's form is very simple, containing only two command buttons as shown in Figure 15.4. The modified XML is shown in Listing 15.11. You'll note that this XML is not formatted as nicely as the input file. That's a result of the way that the `DOMDocument` object's `save()` method writes XML to a file.

Listing 15.10 DOM Demo Source Code

```
Option Explicit

Const INFILE = "c:\my documents\xml\list1506.xml"
Const OUTFILE = "c:\my documents\xml\list1511.xml"

'***********
Private Sub cmdGo_Click()

Dim xmlDoc As New DOMDocument
Dim anyNode As IXMLDOMNode
Dim rootElement As IXMLDOMNode
Dim newNode As IXMLDOMElement
Dim item As String
Dim s As String

' Load the source document.
xmlDoc.Load INFILE

' Check for parse errors.
If xmlDoc.parseError.errorCode <> 0 Then
    s = "Error on line " & xmlDoc.parseError.Line & vbCrLf
    s = s & xmlDoc.parseError.srcText & vbCrLf
    s = s & Space(xmlDoc.parseError.linepos)
    s = s & "^-- " & xmlDoc.parseError.reason
    MsgBox s
    Exit Sub
End If

' Locate the document root element named "sales".
Set rootElement = Nothing
For Each anyNode In xmlDoc.childNodes
    If anyNode.nodeName = "sales" Then
        Set rootElement = anyNode
        Exit For
```

```
    End If
Next anyNode

' If rootElement is nothing then the "sales" node was not found.
If rootElement Is Nothing Then
    MsgBox "Root 'sales' element not found."
    Unload Me
End If

' Loop for all children of the root "sales"
' element (for all "sale" elements).
For Each anyNode In rootElement.childNodes
    ' Get the value of the "item" attribute.
    item = anyNode.Attributes.getNamedItem("item").Text
    ' Create a new element node named "partnumber"
    Set newNode = xmlDoc.createElement("partnumber")
    ' Set the new attribute's value based
    ' on the value of "item".
    Select Case item
        Case "hammer"
            newNode.Text = "QC1132"
        Case "wrench"
            newNode.Text = "JH665"
        Case "chisel"
            newNode.Text = "KA6612"
    End Select
    ' Add the new node as a child
    ' of the current "sale" element.
    anyNode.appendChild newNode
    Set newNode = Nothing
Next anyNode

' Save the modified document
xmlDoc.save OUTFILE

' Display "done" message.
MsgBox "File converted successfully."

End Sub

'***********
Private Sub cmdQuit_Click()

Unload Me

End Sub
```

Listing 15.11 Modified XML File

```
<?xml version="1.0" encoding="UTF-8"?>
<sales>
<sale item="hammer">
    <quantity>12</quantity>
    <price>44.50</price>
    <partnumber>QC1132</partnumber></sale>
<sale item="wrench">
    <quantity>6</quantity>
    <price>72.25</price>
    <partnumber>JH665</partnumber></sale>
<sale item="hammer">
    <quantity>24</quantity>
    <price>84.25</price>
    <partnumber>QC1132</partnumber></sale>
<sale item="chisel">
    <quantity>9</quantity>
    <price>27.75</price>
    <partnumber>KA6612</partnumber></sale>
<sale item="wrench">
    <quantity>48</quantity>
    <price>509.95</price>
    <partnumber>JH665</partnumber></sale>
<sale item="chisel">
    <quantity>18</quantity>
    <price>48.05</price>
    <partnumber>KA6612</partnumber></sale>
<sale item="hammer">
    <quantity>4</quantity>
    <price>15.20</price>
    <partnumber>QC1132</partnumber></sale>
</sales>
```

Figure 15.4 The DOM Demo program

Summary

Microsoft's Visual Basic programming language is the preferred tool of many developers. With its speed of development and excellent text-handling capabilities, it provides a powerful platform for developing XML applications. This chapter demonstrated how to perform several important XML-related programming tasks in Visual Basic, including document validation, processing raw XML, and modifying document structure. These example programs should provide you with a good starting point for your own projects.

CHAPTER 16

Visual C++ and XML

by T.E. Rajagopal

With the introduction of smart pointers, programming in Visual C++ has become a lot easier—especially COM programming. You can now follow Visual Basic code and repeat it line for line, in Visual C++, without using the enormous amounts of code for performing the same task that used to be required. In this chapter, you'll see how various tasks can be accomplished in Visual C++ and how Visual C++ works with XML in various ways. The projects presented in this chapter outline a variety of activities, such as loading XML into a DOM document, transforming XML using XSLT, and applying schemas to an XML document to validate it.

This chapter assumes that you are using Visual C++ version 6.0, Professional Edition. This chapter also assumes that the MSXML Parser version 4.0 is installed on your system. Please see the note that Microsoft has included in the latest release of the MSXML Parser:

> **Note:** *Beginning with the current release of the MSXML 4.0, version-independent GUIDs and ProgIDs are no longer supported. After you install MSXML 4.0, applications that use version independent ProgIDs continue to run using the latest version of MSXML prior to version 4.0. To use version 4.0, applications must be written to use the appropriate version-dependent class IDs (CLSIDs) and ProgIDs that reference Msxml4.dll.*

Due to this statement, you'll see that the examples in this chapter use the version-dependent ProgIDs.

The reader is assumed to have some level of familiarity with Visual C++ and ATL COM programming. The samples in this chapter require some fundamental knowledge of the creation of ATL projects and Active Server Pages (ASP). The client is a browser-based client and the ATL objects run under COM+. The samples have not been tested with the Netscape browser.

Outline of the Samples in This Chapter

XML is being used for several different purposes today. Just as there was an explosion of the usage of the Internet when people realized its potential, there is an explosion in the use of XML today. In this chapter, the samples presented relate to data being stored in and retrieved from an XML document, which serves as a database. The XML database contains a list of families, their members, addresses, and the like. Any information that has an associated hierarchical structure can be stored in an XML document–based database.

Figure 16.1 shows a sample of the database. A count of the families is kept at the root. The database has families. Each family may have parents, children, an address, and a phone number. There can be two parents per family (up for philosophical discussion) and any number of children. The information stored per member and the address and phone number are also shown. Later on, you will see how the type of parent or child is being validated, as well as the data format for the phone number and the like.

Figure 16.2 shows the two primary operations permitted in this sample application: You can search for a member or you can maintain the members. The "searching" section of the samples illustrates loading an XML document and applying a transformation to display the outcome of a search. The "maintenance" section of the samples illustrates using a schema to validate an XML document and adding, updating, and removing data from the XML document.

The ATL objects written for this chapter have Message Boxes that pop up. For this reason, when you drop the objects inside of a package under COM+, please make sure that the package runs under the identity of the "interactive user."

Even though the title of this chapter states that it is to demonstrate the usage of XML from within a Visual C++ project, it also demonstrates how XML can be generated from the client side and posted to the server. In addition, you'll see how to use XSLT to transform XML from the XML document for display on the client side. The information is submitted by the client using the traditional form-posting mechanism and is loaded into an XML template and posted to the ATL objects for processing. This can also be done by using client-side XML data islands that would be used to send data to the server via the `Msxml2.XMLHTTP` interface.

```
family.xml - Notepad
File Edit Format Help
<?xml version="1.0"?>
<x:family_db xmlns:x="urn:samples">
        <families count="1">
                <family id="1" name="Smith">
                        <parents status="married">
                                <parent type="father">
                                        <fname>John</fname>
                                        <minitial/>
                                        <lname>Smith</lname>
                                        <dob>01/01/1960</dob>
                                        <mobile>317-555-1212</mobile>
                                        <email>johnsmith@myemail.com</email>
                                </parent>
                                <parent type="mother">
                                        <fname>Mary</fname>
                                        <minitial>J</minitial>
                                        <lname>Smith</lname>
                                        <dob>1962-02-02</dob>
                                        <mobile>317-555-1313</mobile>
                                        <email>marysmith@myemail.com</email>
                                </parent>
                        </parents>
                        <children>
                                <child type="son">
                                        <fname>Dave</fname>
                                        <minitial/>
                                        <lname>Smith</lname>
                                        <dob>12/14/1995</dob>
                                        <email/>
                                </child>
                                <child type="daughter">
                                        <fname>Jane</fname>
                                        <minitial/>
                                        <lname>Smith</lname>
                                        <dob>07/24/1998</dob>
                                        <email/>
                                </child>
                        </children>
                        <address>
                                <line1>1234, Main St.</line1>
                                <line2/>
                                <city>Beautiful City</city>
                                <state>IN</state>
                                <zip>46000</zip>
                        </address>
                        <phoneno>317-555-1414</phoneno>
                </family>
        </families>
```

Figure 16.1 The sample XML database used in this chapter

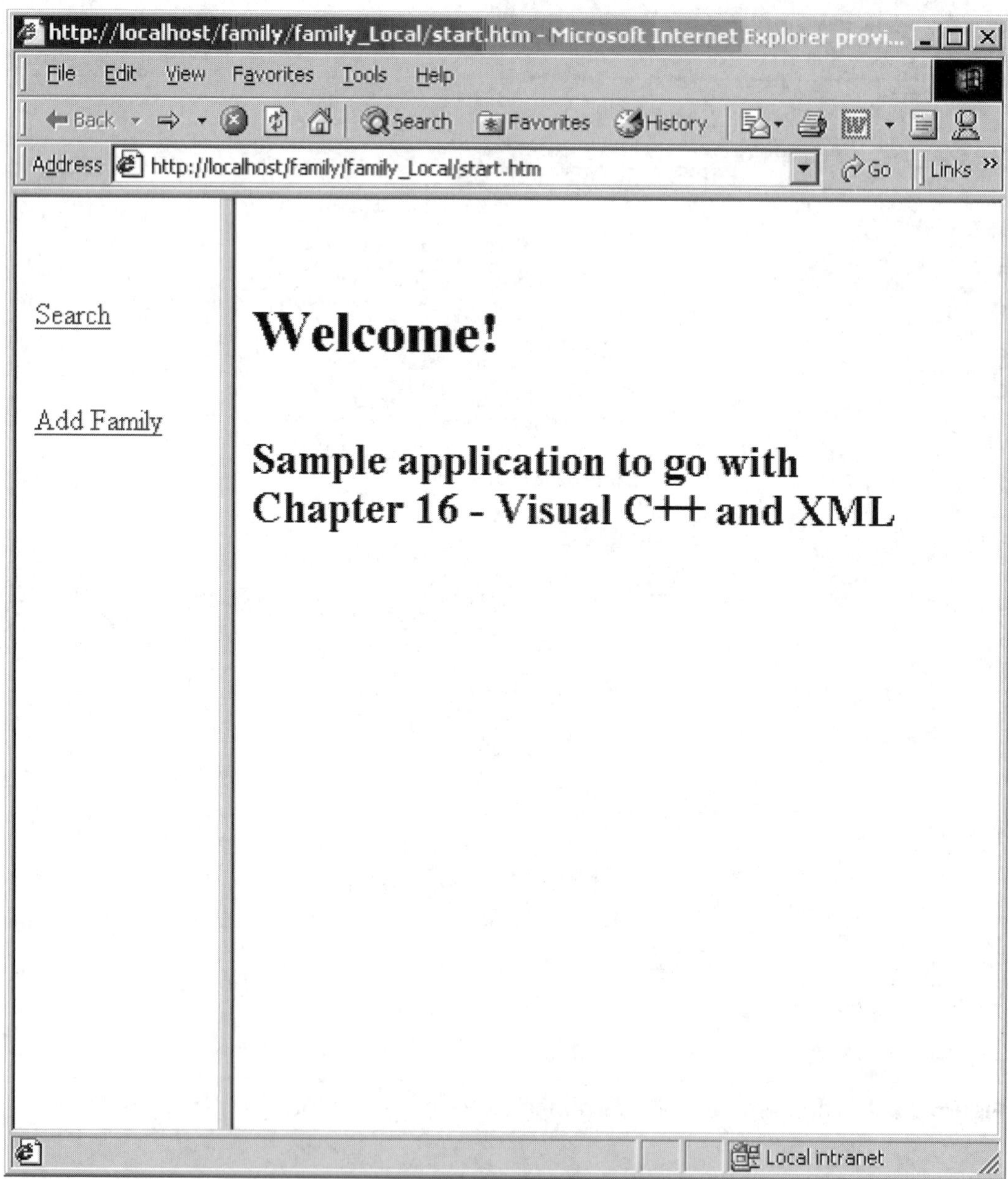

Figure 16.2 Starting page of the sample application

To outline the different operations that this sample permits, you will

- Search for a family by family name (case-sensitive)
- Search for a parent by last name (case-sensitive)
- Search for a child by last name (case-sensitive)
- Add a family
- Add a parent
- Add a child
- Remove a family

You'll now look at how the samples work. For a search, the following steps are performed:

1. The user inputs data in the browser.
2. The request is passed to an ASP page.
3. The ASP page instantiates an object.
4. The ASP page invokes a method within that object and passes the data.
5. The COM object loads the XML database.
6. The COM object uses the input data to do a lookup.
7. The COM object transforms the result of the lookup.
8. The transformed data is sent to the ASP page.
9. The ASP page passes the response back to the browser for display.

For an add, the following steps are performed:

1. The user inputs data in the browser.
2. The request is passed to an ASP page.
3. The ASP page loads an XML template for the data.
4. The ASP page loads the input data into the template.
5. The ASP page instantiates an object.
6. The ASP page invokes a method within that object and passes the data.
7. The COM object validates the input data using a schema.
8. The COM object loads the XML database.
9. The COM object adds the data to the XML database.
10. The COM object persists the modified XML document.
11. The COM object sends a response back to the ASP page.
12. The ASP page passes the response back to the browser.

Following the Search

Let's now look at what happens when the user requests for a search to be performed for a family. The outcome of the results for the search is shown in Figure 16.3. The ASP page that makes the request for the search is as follows:

```
set objSearch = server.CreateObject("CFamily.Family.1")
strRet = objSearch.DoSearch(Request.Form("searchText"),
Request.Form("searchType"))
set objsearch = nothing
if Len(strRet) = 0 then
Response.Write "No match found!"
else
Response.Write strRet
end if
```

CFamily is the object with the interface being IFamily. The `DoSearch` method within the interface is shown in Listing 16.2. The XML database is loaded into DOM using a helper function called `LoadDom`, which is shown in Listing 16.1. This function also checks for any errors that might occur during loading. As you can see, the samples all use the version-dependent ProgIDs for the MSXML Parser 4.0.

Listing 16.1: Method `LoadDom` from family.cpp

```
// helper function to load a file into an XML DOM Document
bool LoadDom (IXMLDOMDocument2Ptr pDom, const char* pszFileName)
{
  // set the flag to load the DOM synchronously
  pDom->Putasync(VARIANT_FALSE);
  // set the flag to validate the document while loading
  pDom->PutvalidateOnParse(VARIANT_TRUE);
  // load the xml document from a file
  pDom->load (pszFileName);
  // check for any errors during parsing
  if ( pDom->parseError->errorCode != 0 )
  {
    CComBSTR bstrMsg = _T("Error on line ");
    bstrMsg += CComBSTR(pDom->parseError->line);
    bstrMsg += _T("\n");
    bstrMsg.AppendBSTR(pDom->parseError->srcText);
    bstrMsg += _T("\n");
    bstrMsg.AppendBSTR(pDom->parseError->reason);
```

```
    MessageBox (NULL, _bstr_t(bstrMsg), _T("Loading DOM"), MB_OK);
    return false;
  }
  return true;
}
```

Listing 16.2 Method DoSearch from family.cpp

```
// this is the method that is used to perform one of three searches
// a) search for a family by last name - type = 'F'
// b) search for a parent by last name - type = 'P'
// c) search for a child by last name - type = 'C'
// the result is returned as an xml document.
STDMETHODIMP CFamily::DoSearch(
BSTR bstrName, BSTR bstrType, BSTR *xmlSearch)
{
  HRESULT hr;
  char cType;
  CComBSTR  bstrMsg         = L"";
  CComBSTR  bstrMatch       = L"";
  IXMLDOMDocument2Ptr       pDom;
  IXMLDOMDocument2Ptr       pDomRet;
  IXMLDOMDocument2Ptr       pDomTemp;
  IXMLDOMDocument2Ptr       pXslDom;
  IXMLDOMNodePtr            pNode;
  IXMLDOMNodePtr            pNodeAdd;
  IXSLTemplatePtr           pXslT;
  IXSLProcessorPtr          pXslP;

  strcpy (&cType, (const char*)bstrType);

  hr = pDom.CreateInstance(L"Msxml2.DOMDocument.4.0");
  if (FAILED(hr)) _com_raise_error(hr);

  // load the family database
  if (!LoadDom(pDom, "c:\\family\\family.xml")) return E_FAIL;

  if ( SysStringLen(bstrName) > 0 )
  {
    // please note: under 4.0, a freethreadeddomdocument is needed
    // for performing this transformation
    hr = pXslDom.CreateInstance(L"Msxml2.FreeThreadedDOMDocument.4.0");
    if (FAILED(hr)) _com_raise_error(hr);
```

```
    // build the string for the pattern match
    // and load the xsl that will
    // be used to transform the results for display
    switch (cType)
    {
      case 'F':
        // here, the match is on an attribute
        bstrMatch = _T("x:family_db/families/family[@name='");
        bstrMatch.AppendBSTR(bstrName);
        bstrMatch += _T("']");
        if (!LoadDom(pXslDom, "c:\\family\\family_d.xsl"))
          return E_FAIL;
          break;
      case 'P':
        // here, the match is on an element text
        bstrMatch =
    _T("x:family_db/families/family/parents/parent[lname='");
        bstrMatch.AppendBSTR(bstrName);
        bstrMatch += _T("']");
        if (!LoadDom(pXslDom, "c:\\family\\parent_d.xsl"))
return E_FAIL;
        break;
      case 'C':
        bstrMatch =
 _T("x:family_db/families/family/children/child[lname='");
        bstrMatch.AppendBSTR(bstrName);
        bstrMatch += _T("']");
        if (!LoadDom(pXslDom, "c:\\family\\child_d.xsl"))
return E_FAIL;
        break;
    }

    MSXML2::IXMLDOMNodeListPtr pNL;
    pNL = pDom->selectNodes(_bstr_t(bstrMatch));

    // if we found any matches, then proceed
    if ( pNL->Getlength() > 0 )
    {
      IXMLDOMNodePtr           pClone;
      IXMLDOMElementPtr        pElem;
      CComBSTR                      bstrID;
      CComBSTR                      bstrFamilyName;
      hr = pDomRet.CreateInstance(L"Msxml2.DOMDocument.4.0");
      if (FAILED(hr)) _com_raise_error(hr);
```

```
      // set the base for the return structure
      pDomRet->loadXML(
_T("<x:results xmlns:x=\"urn:samples\"></x:results>"));
      // loop through each match and add it to the result
      for (int i = 0; i < pNL->Getlength(); i++)
      {
        pNodeAdd = NULL;
        bstrID.Empty();
        bstrFamilyName.Empty();
        switch (cType)
        {
          case 'F':             // family
            // add the entire node for a family
            pNodeAdd =
pDomRet->firstChild->appendChild(pNL->Getitem(i));
            break;
          case 'P':             // parent
            // for a parent, save the id of the family that the parent
            // belongs to so that it can used to subsequent operations
            hr = pNL->Getitem(i)->parentNode->parentNode->
QueryInterface( MSXML2::IID_IXMLDOMElement,
   (void**)&pElem);
            if (FAILED(hr)) _com_raise_error(hr);
            bstrID.AppendBSTR(_bstr_t(pElem->getAttribute(_T("id"))));
            bstrFamilyName.AppendBSTR(
_bstr_t(pElem->getAttribute(_T("name"))));
            // add the node for the parent to the result
            pNodeAdd = pDomRet->firstChild->appendChild(
pNL->Getitem(i));
            hr = pNodeAdd->QueryInterface(MSXML2::IID_IXMLDOMElement,
(void**)&pElem);
            if (FAILED(hr)) _com_raise_error(hr);
            // set the family information for the parent
            pElem->setAttribute(_T("id"), _bstr_t(bstrID));
            pElem->setAttribute(_T("name"), _bstr_t(bstrFamilyName));
            break;
          case 'C':             // child
            // for a child, the information of the
// first parent is saved within the node for the child
            pDomTemp.CreateInstance(L"Msxml2.DOMDocument.4.0");
            pDomTemp->loadXML (
pNL->Getitem(i)->parentNode->parentNode->xml);
            // the node is being cloned here just to show a
// different approach to copy the data from the original
```

```
// xml. also, if a direct appendchild is used, it removes // it from the
original xml, with the result that if we
// come through here the second time, there is no
            // 'parent' node.
            pClone = pDomTemp->
selectSingleNode(_T("family/parents/parent"))
->cloneNode(VARIANT_TRUE);
            pNodeAdd = pDomRet->firstChild->
appendChild(pNL->Getitem(i));
            // add the node for the child to the result
            pNodeAdd->appendChild (pClone);
            break;
        }
      }

      // create an xsl template to do the transformation
      hr = pXslT.CreateInstance(L"Msxml2.XSLTemplate.4.0");
      if (FAILED(hr)) _com_raise_error(hr);
      // reference the dom that has the xsl loaded
      pXslT->PutRefstylesheet(pXslDom);
      // create a processor that will do the transformation
      pXslP = pXslT->createProcessor();
      if (FAILED(hr)) _com_raise_error(hr);
      VARIANT varDisp;
      varDisp.vt = VT_DISPATCH;
      varDisp.pdispVal = pDomRet;
      // reference the dom that has the xml to be transformed
      pXslP->Putinput(&varDisp);
      // perform the transformation
      pXslP->transform();
      // the processor has the output xml
      *xmlSearch = _bstr_t(pXslP->Getoutput());
    }
  }

  return S_OK;
}
```

The key to this search is the ability to use XPath syntax to do a pattern match. The name of the family is an attribute on which a pattern match is used to do a lookup. For the other searches, the pattern match is against the element text. The search could return multiple nodes within the database. A root node called "results" is set up to return the results. For a family search, the results are straightforward. You add the family to the result. For a parent search, the family ID and name are also added to the search and for a child search, the information about the first parent is added to the result. These help in making the display more meaningful and also tag the information with a family ID, which can then be used as a key for future operations.

It is surprising to see how the object model has been created for DOM. The DOM Node and the DOM Element both represent the same piece of information—however, the DOM Element is derived from the DOM Node. Attributes are not defined as child nodes of an element and attributes are not considered to be part of the document tree. Because the DOM Nodes provide access to parts of the tree, the DOM Element provides easier access to the attributes. For this reason, you'll see that the QueryInterface is used to get to the DOM Element interface from the DOM Node interface.

Once the information is retrieved from the database, you need to transform the information so that it can be displayed in a well-formatted manner. This is an operation that could either be performed in the COM+ layer or at the ASP layer. It is being included in the COM+ layer in these samples for demonstration purposes. So far, you have been doing all your operations within the context of a DOM document. When you perform the transformation, you'll use a Free Threaded DOM document for loading the XSL to be used for the translation. Listing 16.3 shows the XSL that is used to transform the results of a family search.

The translation piece has been designed to perform well under a multithreaded environment. Also, because the translation piece has been moved to outside the DOM document, there are some key benefits that you derive through this design:

- Scalability, because the processor can be cached and used by multiple threads at the same time
- Performance, because the XSL script can be compiled and cached
- Parameterization support within the compiled code

The different components that participate in the translation are as follows:

- A DOM document to hold the XSL for translation
- An XSLTemplate object that holds a compiled version of the script in memory
- An XSLT Processor object that processes the template rules and applies them to the input source
- A DOM document that holds the input data that needs to be transformed

The outcome of the translation is available as output from the XSLT Processor object. It appears that the output is available for retrieval only once. If you try to access the output a second time, it is not available for output anymore.

As the results were being built, for a child search, because the first parent was being included in the result, you cannot do an "appendChild" of the node of the corresponding "parent" of the "child." An appendChild removes the node from the original XML and appends it to the new node. As a result, if more than one child of the same parent appear in the result, the appendChild approach will show a different parent for each child in the family or error out because there would be no more nodes of "parents" in the tree. To avoid this, the node of the first parent is cloned and used.

Let's look at Listing 16.3 briefly. It is the XSL that is used for performing the transformation. It states that the output being generated is HTML, because the output is for display at the client. There is a loop over all the families and the data for each family being formatted for display. The interesting part comes at the end, where for each family, a set of buttons is included for performing certain actions. If you look at Figure 16.3, you'll see these buttons at the bottom. They are for performing the following tasks:

- Removing the family from the tree
- Adding a parent
- Adding a child

Listing 16.3 XSL for Display of Results for Family Search

```
<?xml version="1.0"?>
<xsl:stylesheet version="1.0"
  xmlns:xsl="http://www.w3.org/1999/XSL/Transform"
                                        xmlns:x="urn:samples">
  <xsl:output method="html"/>
  <xsl:template match="/">
    <html>
      <head>
        <title>Family details</title>
      </head>
      <body>
        <xsl:for-each select="x:results/family">
          <h1>Family Name: <xsl:value-of select="@name"/></h1>
          <xsl:variable name="familyId" select="@id"/>
          <h2>Members</h2>
          <table border="1">
            <tr>
```

```
        <th>First Name</th>
        <th>Last Name</th>
        <th>Relationship</th>
      </tr>
      <xsl:for-each select="parents/parent">
        <tr>
          <td><xsl:value-of select="fname"/></td>
          <td><xsl:value-of select="lname"/></td>
          <td><xsl:value-of select="@type"/></td>
        </tr>
      </xsl:for-each>
      <xsl:for-each select="children/child">
        <tr>
          <td><xsl:value-of select="fname"/></td>
          <td><xsl:value-of select="lname"/></td>
          <td><xsl:value-of select="@type"/></td>
        </tr>
      </xsl:for-each>
    </table>
    <h2>Contact Information</h2>
    <table border="1">
      <tr><td><xsl:value-of select="address/line1"/></td></tr>
      <tr><td><xsl:value-of select="address/line2"/></td></tr>
      <tr><td><xsl:value-of select="address/city"/></td></tr>
      <tr><td><xsl:value-of select="address/state"/> -
                  <xsl:value-of select="address/zip"/></td></tr>
      <tr><td>Phone: <xsl:value-of select="phoneno"/></td></tr>
    </table>
    <br/>
    <table>
      <tr>
        <td><form name="formFamily" action="doDel.asp?delType=F"
             method="post">
        <input type="hidden" name="familyId"
             value="{$familyId}"/>
        <input type="submit" value="Remove Family"/>
        </form></td>
        <td><form name="formParent" action="Add.asp?addType=P"
             method="post">
        <input type="hidden" name="familyId"
             value="{$familyId}"/>
        <input type="submit" value="Add Parent"/>
        </form></td>
        <td><form name="formChild" action="Add.asp?addType=C"
             method="post">
```

```
                <input type="hidden" name="familyId"
                     value="{$familyId}"/>
                <input type="submit" value="Add Child"/>
                </form></td>
              </tr>
            </table>
          </xsl:for-each>
        </body>
      </html>
  </xsl:template>
</xsl:stylesheet>
```

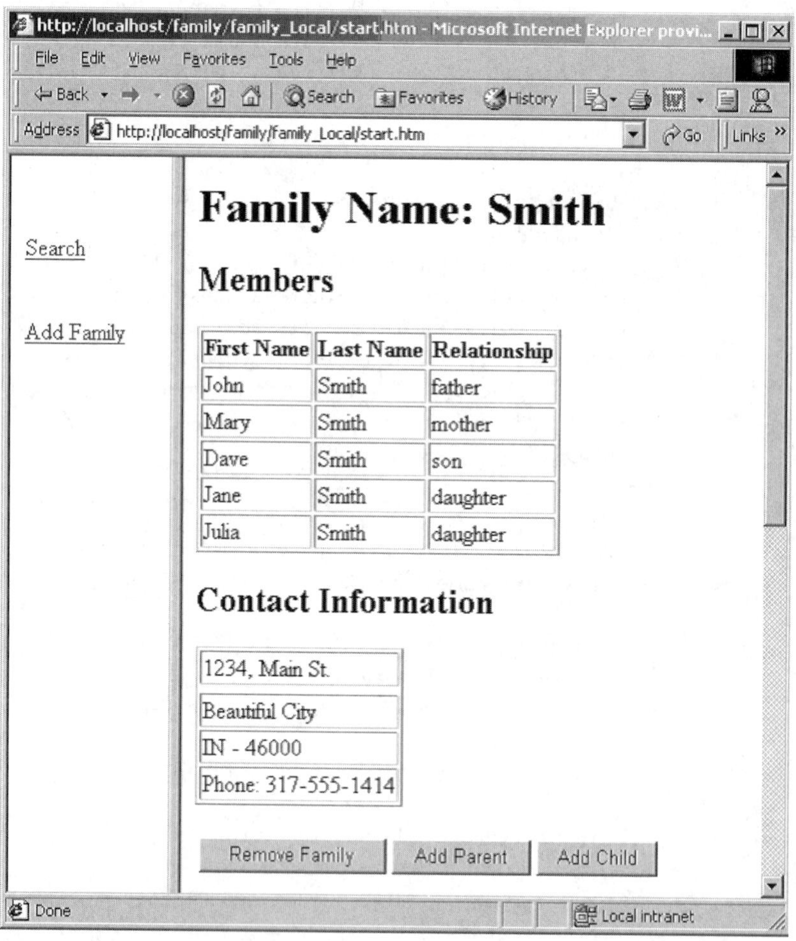

Figure 16.3 Output of a family search

Setting up the buttons is the easy part. Trying to set up the action that occurs when one of these buttons is clicked is where it gets interesting. The question is, How do you generate a dynamic link from within XSL? The answer is easy: Use XSL variables. When you process a family, save the family ID because it is the key and use it later on when the buttons are set up. However, there is no documentation currently available that tells you how to do that. If you use the documented feature of `<xsl:variable select = "$variable_name">` for setting the actions dynamically, the scripts won't compile, because you cannot say `<input type="hidden" name="familyId" value="<xsl:variable....>`. So, how do you generate a dynamic value? You do it by using the following format:

```
<xsl:variable name="familyId" select="@id"/>
<input type="hidden" name="familyId" value="{$familyId}">
```

Line 1 shows how to set up the variable and line 2 shows how to use it. A search for a parent brings up a list of parents with a hyperlink to their families.

Listing 16.4 shows the call that is used to get details of a family when a user clicks the hyperlink for that family.

Listing 16.4 Method `GetFamily` from family.cpp

```
// this method returns the xml for a family identified by the id
STDMETHODIMP CFamily::GetFamily(BSTR bstrFamilyId, BSTR *xmlFamily)
{
  HRESULT   hr;
  CComBSTR  bstrMsg    = L"";
  CComBSTR  bstrMatch       = L"";

  IXMLDOMDocument2Ptr        pDom;
  IXMLDOMDocument2Ptr        pDomRet;
  IXMLDOMDocument2Ptr        pXslDom;
  IXMLDOMNodePtr             pNode;
  IXSLTemplatePtr            pXslT;
  IXSLProcessorPtr           pXslP;

  hr = pDom.CreateInstance(L"Msxml2.DOMDocument.4.0");
  if (FAILED(hr)) _com_raise_error(hr);

  // load the family database
  if (!LoadDom(pDom, "c:\\family\\family.xml")) return E_FAIL;
```

```
  if ( SysStringLen(bstrFamilyId) > 0 )
  {
    // match the family with the id passed in
    bstrMatch = _T("x:family_db/families/family[@id='");
    bstrMatch.AppendBSTR(bstrFamilyId);
    bstrMatch += _T("']");
    pNode = pDom->selectSingleNode(_bstr_t(bstrMatch));

    // get ready for the transformation
    hr = pXslDom.CreateInstance(L"Msxml2.FreeThreadedDOMDocument.4.0");
    if (FAILED(hr)) _com_raise_error(hr);

    if (!LoadDom(pXslDom, "c:\\family\\family_d.xsl")) return E_FAIL;

    hr = pDomRet.CreateInstance(L"Msxml2.DOMDocument.4.0");
    if (FAILED(hr)) _com_raise_error(hr);
    pDomRet->loadXML(_T("<x:results xmlns:x=
              \"urn:samples\"></x:results>"));

    // append the family node to the result
    pDomRet->firstChild->appendChild(pNode);

    // do the transformation
    hr = pXslT.CreateInstance(L"Msxml2.XSLTemplate.4.0");
    if (FAILED(hr)) _com_raise_error(hr);
    pXslT->PutRefstylesheet(pXslDom);
    pXslP = pXslT->createProcessor();
    if (FAILED(hr)) _com_raise_error(hr);
    VARIANT varDisp;
    varDisp.vt = VT_DISPATCH;
    varDisp.pdispVal = pDomRet;
    pXslP->Putinput(&varDisp);
    pXslP->transform();

    *xmlFamily = _bstr_t(pXslP->Getoutput());
  }

  return S_OK;
}
```

Maintaining the XML Database

The maintenance activities demonstrated here show how to manipulate an XML document in memory. The links for the maintenance activities are available from the start page or from the results screen of a family search. It could have been more complete or available at other places, but this works for demonstration purposes.

The key things to do when maintaining a database are to make sure that the data stored in the database adheres to certain structures, is formatted the right way, contains valid data, and follows the business rules. Any database that is not organized in this fashion is waiting for a disaster to happen. However, when all these rules are applied to data, the maintenance becomes a headache and retrieval and storage operations become complicated. Structured storage has been around for a long time, and even though the required programming has become easier with the development of consistent access mechanisms, the appearance of XML as potential data storage on the horizon felt like a relief valve for developers. Every developer jumped on the XML bandwagon to use it for unstructured storage—unstructured because there was no rule that said you could not create whatever you wanted. It was file-based, so it was easy to code for. There were tools available to manipulate the data easily and so it became a popular storage medium, so much so that developers would store data in an XML format inside a database.

DBAs all around the world probably watched with consternation as data was being pumped into their databases with all kinds of primary keys embedded in them; columns with foreign key constraints were now part of an XML document with values that would have triggered a constraint violation error if it had been stored in a database. And then, when the developer felt that he or she didn't like the current XML format—poof!—there was a new one. Sure enough, XSLs popped up to handle the issues that a normal data conversion script would have handled in a database if a database structure had changed.

To enforce some kind of method to this madness, you have XML Schemas. The main benefits of using schemas are as follows:

- To define the structure of an XML document
- To define the vocabulary that the XML document must follow
- To define the validation rules that the data in the XML document must follow

Let's look at the path that adding a family in our sample takes. Figure 16.4 shows the screen that captures data from the user for adding a family. Once

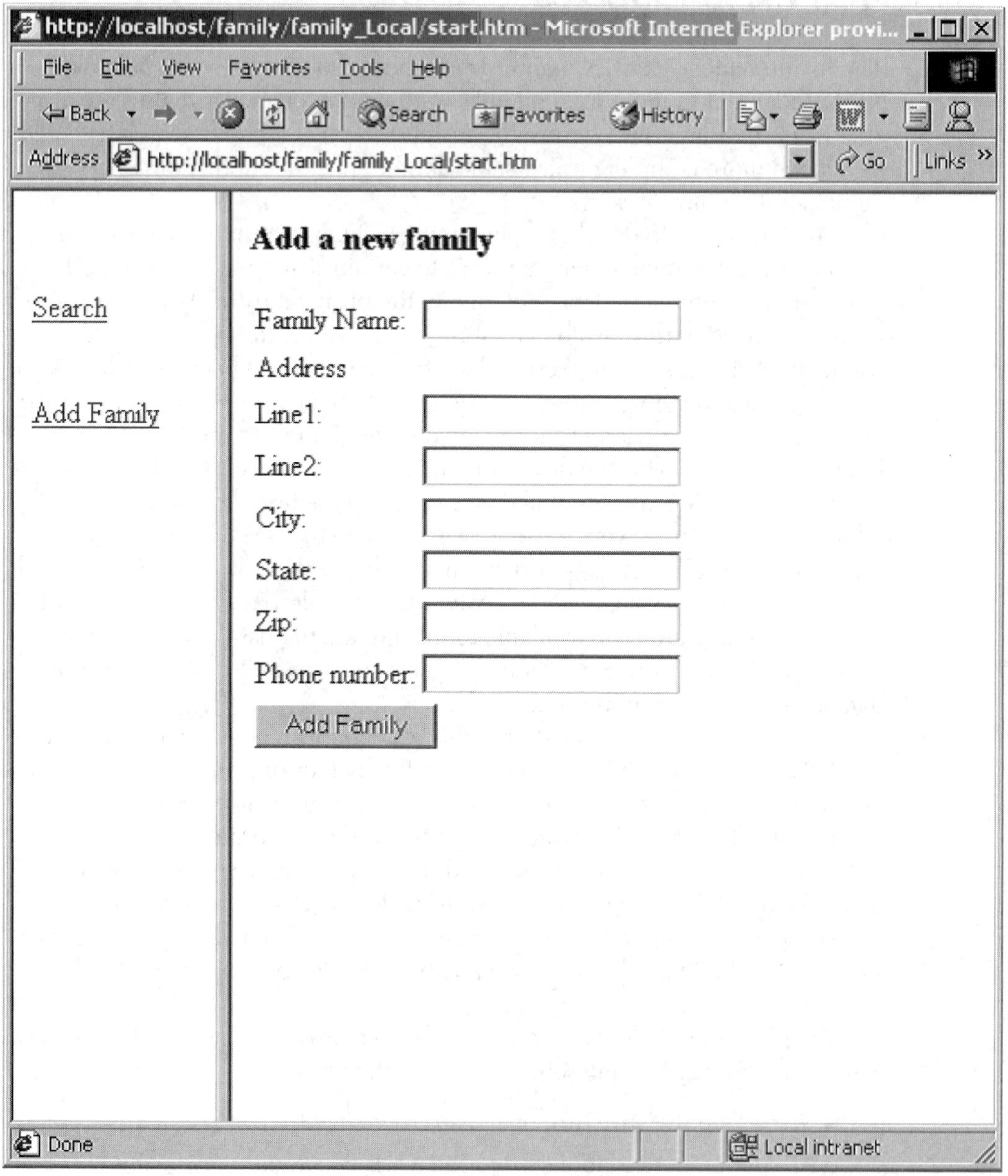

Figure 16.4 Screen for adding a new family

the user keys in all the information and clicks the Add Family button, the request to add comes to an ASP page. Listing 16.5 shows the ASP page that handles this request. The page first loads the template, shown in Listing 16.6, for a new family into a DOM document. It then loads the values that the user keyed in into the corresponding nodes/elements and also sets the attributes that will be used to load the data into the appropriate locations within the database. A call is then made into the object that performs the addition of the data to the database.

Listing 16.5 ASP Page for Adding a New Family

```
set xdom = Server.CreateObject("MSXML2.DOMDocument")
   xdom.async = false
   xdom.validateOnParse = true
   xdom.load Server.MapPath("new_family.xml")
xdom.selectSingleNode("/x:new_family/family").setAttribute "name",
Request.Form("nameText")
xdom.selectSingleNode("/x:new_family/family/address/line1").Text =
Request.Form("line1Text")
xdom.selectSingleNode("/x:new_family/family/address/line2").Text =
Request.Form("line2Text")
xdom.selectSingleNode("/x:new_family/family/address/city").Text =
Request.Form("cityText")
xdom.selectSingleNode("/x:new_family/family/address/state").Text =
Request.Form("stateText")
xdom.selectSingleNode("/x:new_family/family/address/zip").Text =
Request.Form("zipText")
xdom.selectSingleNode("/x:new_family/family/phoneno").Text =
Request.Form("phoneText")

   set objAdd = server.CreateObject("CFamily.Family.1")
   strRet = ""
   on error resume next
   strRet = objAdd.DoAdd(CStr(xdom.xml), CStr(strType))
   set objAdd = nothing
   if err.number <> 0 then
   Response.Write err.description
   else
   Response.Redirect "getfamily.asp?familyId=" & strRet
   end if
```

Listing 16.6 XML Template Used for a New Family

```
<?xml version="1.0"?>
<x:new_family xmlns:x="urn:samples">
```

```
    <family name="">
        <address>
            <line1/>
            <line2/>
            <city/>
            <state/>
            <zip/>
        </address>
        <phoneno/>
    </family>
</x:new_family>
```

Listing 16.7 shows the method DoAdd that does the addition of a family, parent, or child. There is no IXMLSchemaCache interface available to use. So far, there has been a one-to-one correspondence, for the most part, between the interface name and the ProgID. There is a remarkable deviation from that standard as far as the XML Schemas are concerned. The IXMLDOMSchemaCollection2 is the interface that is used, but it is instantiated as Msxml2.XMLSchemaCache.4.0. A single schema document can belong to multiple schema collections, and a single schema collection can contain multiple schema documents. The association of the namespace URI is what triggers which schema within a collection will be used for validation.

Once a schema has been loaded into a schema collection, the schema is added as a reference to the DOM document into which the XML data that needs to be validated will be loaded. Next, the XML is loaded into the DOM document. Any validation errors that occur will prevent the loading from progressing. Figure 16.5 displays a validation error that shows the outcome of having an unexpected node in the data—"line0" was not expected, "line1" was. Figure 16.6 shows a validation error that shows the outcome of having invalid

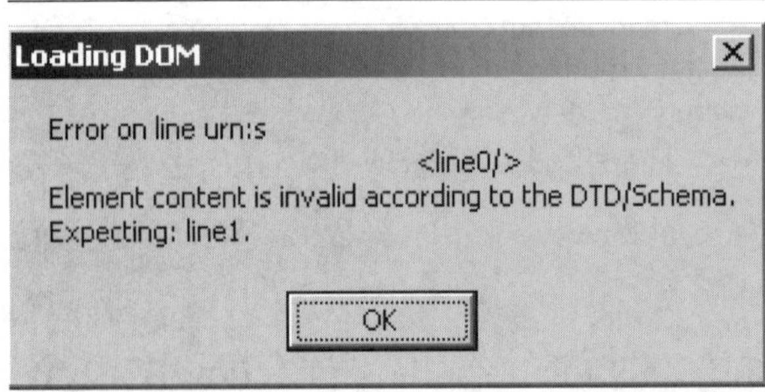

Figure 16.5 Error when adding a family with unexpected information

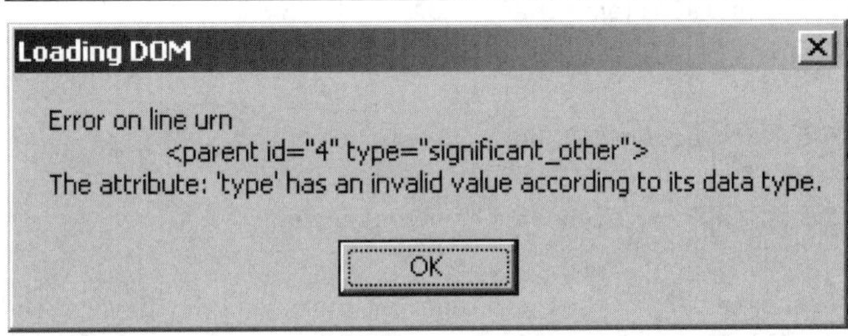

Figure 16.6 Error when adding a family with invalid information

information in the data—in this case, the recommended values for this attribute were "father" and "mother," and hence "significant_other" was causing the error. Obviously, this sample will have to be modified if it is going to be used for real-world purposes. Listing 16.8 shows the XSD that was used for this validation.

Listing 16.7: Method DoAdd from family.cpp

```
// this method adds either a family, a parent or a child
// it returns the id of the family that was affected
STDMETHODIMP CFamily::DoAdd(BSTR xmlAdd, BSTR bstrType, BSTR *bstrID)
{
  HRESULT hr;

  char cType;
  char cID[25] = {0};

  CComBSTR  bstrMsg      = L"";
  CComBSTR  bstrMatch    = L"";
  CComBSTR  bstrCurID    = L"";

  IXMLDOMDocument2Ptr           pDom;
  IXMLDOMDocument2Ptr           pDomRet;
  IXMLDOMDocument2Ptr           pDomOld;
  IXMLDOMDocument2Ptr           pDomNew;
  IXMLDOMDocument2Ptr           pXslDom;
  IXMLDOMNodePtr                pNode;
  IXMLDOMNodePtr                pNodeAdd;
  IXMLDOMNodePtr                pNodeColl;
```

```
    IXMLDOMSchemaCollection2Ptr pXsch;
    IXMLDOMElementPtr           pElem;

    if ( SysStringLen(xmlAdd) > 0 )
    {
      strcpy (&cType, (const char*)bstrType);

      // create the schema collection that will hold the schemas that
      // will be used to validate the input
      hr = pXsch.CreateInstance(L"Msxml2.XMLSchemaCache.4.0");
      if (FAILED(hr)) _com_raise_error(hr);

      hr = pDom.CreateInstance(L"Msxml2.DOMDocument.4.0");
      if (FAILED(hr)) _com_raise_error(hr);

      // load the appropriate schema documents
      switch (cType)
      {
        case 'F':
          pXsch->add (_T("urn:samples"),
  _T("c:\\family\\schFamily.xsd"));
          break;
        case 'P':
          pXsch->add (_T("urn:samples"),
  _T("c:\\family\\schParent.xsd"));
          break;
        case 'C':
          pXsch->add (_T("urn:samples"),
  _T("c:\\family\\schChild.xsd"));
          break;
      }

      VARIANT varDisp;
      varDisp.vt          = VT_DISPATCH;
      varDisp.pdispVal    = pXsch;

      pDom->Putasync(VARIANT_FALSE);
      pDom->PutvalidateOnParse(VARIANT_TRUE);
      // add a reference to the schema that will be used to validate
      pDom->PutRefschemas(&varDisp);
      pDom->loadXML (xmlAdd);
      // if there are any validation errors, they will be shown here.
      if (!DomLoaded(pDom)) return E_FAIL;
```

```
    hr = pDomOld.CreateInstance(L"Msxml2.DOMDocument.4.0");
    if (FAILED(hr)) _com_raise_error(hr);

    // load the family database
    if (!LoadDom(pDomOld, "c:\\family\\family.xml")) return E_FAIL;

    long          l = 0;
    CComBSTR      bstrMatch = L"";

    // once the validation of the input data is successful,
    // add the data to the family database.
    switch (cType)
    {
      case 'F':         // family
        pNode = pDomOld->selectSingleNode(_T("x:family_db/families"));
        // increment the count of families in the database
        hr = pNode->QueryInterface(
MSXML2::IID_IXMLDOMElement, (void**)&pElem);
        if (FAILED(hr)) _com_raise_error(hr);
        bstrCurID.AppendBSTR(
_bstr_t(pElem->getAttribute(_T("count"))));
        sprintf(cID, "%s", bstrCurID);
        l = atol(cID)+1;
        sprintf(cID, "%ld", l);
        pElem->setAttribute (_T("count"), cID);

        // add the new family
        pNodeAdd = pNode->appendChild (
pDom->documentElement->firstChild);
        hr = pNodeAdd->QueryInterface(
  MSXML2::IID_IXMLDOMElement, (void**)&pElem);
        if (FAILED(hr)) _com_raise_error(hr);
        pElem->setAttribute (_T("id"), cID);

        // persist the updated document
        pDomOld->save (_T("c:\\family\\family.xml"));
        break;
      case 'P':         // parent
        // extract the id of the family to which
  // this parent needs to be added to
        hr = pDom->documentElement->
firstChild->QueryInterface(
  MSXML2::IID_IXMLDOMElement, (void**)&pElem);
        if (FAILED(hr)) _com_raise_error(hr);
```

```
        bstrCurID.AppendBSTR(_bstr_t(pElem->getAttribute(_T("id"))));
        sprintf(cID, "%s", bstrCurID);
        pElem->removeAttribute (_T("id"));

        // lookup the family
        bstrMatch = _T("x:family_db/families/family[@id='");
        bstrMatch.Append(cID);
        bstrMatch += _T("']");
        pNode = pDomOld->selectSingleNode(_bstr_t(bstrMatch));
        // if the family does not have the "parents" node yet, add one
        pNodeColl = pNode->selectSingleNode(_T("parents"));
        if ( pNodeColl == NULL )
        {
          pDomNew.CreateInstance(L"Msxml2.DOMDocument.4.0");
          pDomNew->Putasync(VARIANT_FALSE);
          pDomNew->PutvalidateOnParse(VARIANT_FALSE);
          pDomNew->loadXML (_T("<parents></parents>"));
          if (!DomLoaded(pDomNew)) return E_FAIL;
          pNodeColl = pNode->appendChild(pDomNew->documentElement);
        }

        // some basic validation - open to philosophical discussions
        if ( pNodeColl->selectNodes(_T("parent"))->Getlength() >= 2 )
        {
          MessageBox (NULL,
_T("Too many parents exist already!"),
_T("add parent"),
MB_OK);
          return S_OK;
        }

        // add the new parent to the family
        pNodeColl->appendChild (pDom->documentElement->firstChild);
        // persist the updated document
        pDomOld->save (_T("c:\\family\\family.xml"));

        break;
      case 'C':          // child
        // extract the id of the family to which
  // this child needs to be added to
        hr = pDom->documentElement->
    firstChild->QueryInterface(
MSXML2::IID_IXMLDOMElement,
```

```
(void**)&pElem);
        if (FAILED(hr)) _com_raise_error(hr);

        bstrCurID.AppendBSTR(_bstr_t(pElem->getAttribute(_T("id"))));
        sprintf(cID, "%s", bstrCurID);
        pElem->removeAttribute (_T("id"));

        // lookup the family
        bstrMatch = _T("x:family_db/families/family[@id='");
        bstrMatch.Append(cID);
        bstrMatch += _T("']");
        pNode = pDomOld->selectSingleNode(_bstr_t(bstrMatch));
        // if the family does not have the "children" node yet, add one
        pNodeColl = pNode->selectSingleNode(_T("children"));
        if ( pNodeColl == NULL )
        {
          pDomNew.CreateInstance(L"Msxml2.DOMDocument.4.0");
          pDomNew->Putasync(VARIANT_FALSE);
          pDomNew->PutvalidateOnParse(VARIANT_FALSE);
          pDomNew->loadXML (_T("<children></children>"));
          if (!DomLoaded(pDomNew)) return E_FAIL;
          pNodeColl = pNode->appendChild(pDomNew->documentElement);
        }

        // add the new child to the family
        pNodeColl->appendChild (pDom->documentElement->firstChild);
        // persist the updated document
        hr = pDomOld->save (_T("c:\\family\\family.xml"));
        break;
    }

  }

  *bstrID = _bstr_t(cID);

  return S_OK;
}
```

Listing 16.8 XSD for Validating Data for a New Family

```
<?xml version="1.0"?>
<xsd:schema xmlns:xsd="http://www.w3.org/2001/XMLSchema">
```

```
  <xsd:element name="new_family">
    <xsd:complexType>
      <xsd:sequence>
        <xsd:element name="family">
          <xsd:complexType>
            <xsd:sequence>
              <xsd:element name="address"
type="addressType" maxOccurs="1"/>
              <xsd:element name="phoneno" minOccurs="0" maxOccurs="1">
                <xsd:simpleType>
                  <xsd:restriction base="xsd:string">
                    <xsd:pattern value="[0-9](3)-[0-9](3)-[0-9](4)"/>
                  </xsd:restriction>
                </xsd:simpleType>
              </xsd:element>
            </xsd:sequence>
            <xsd:attribute name="name"
type="xsd:string" use="required"/>
          </xsd:complexType>
        </xsd:element>
      </xsd:sequence>
    </xsd:complexType>
  </xsd:element>

  <xsd:complexType name="addressType">
    <xsd:sequence>
      <xsd:element name="line1"
type="xsd:string" minOccurs="1" maxOccurs="1"/>
      <xsd:element name="line2"
type="xsd:string" minOccurs="0" maxOccurs="1"/>
      <xsd:element name="city"
type="xsd:string" minOccurs="1" maxOccurs="1"/>
      <xsd:element name="state"
minOccurs="1" maxOccurs="1">
        <xsd:simpleType>
          <xsd:restriction base="xsd:string">
            <xsd:pattern value="[A-Z](2)"/>
          </xsd:restriction>
        </xsd:simpleType>
      </xsd:element>
      <xsd:element name="zip" minOccurs="0" maxOccurs="1">
        <xsd:simpleType>
          <xsd:restriction base="xsd:string">
            <xsd:pattern value="[0-9](5)-[0-9](4)"/>
```

```
          </xsd:restriction>
        </xsd:simpleType>
      </xsd:element>
    </xsd:sequence>
  </xsd:complexType>

</xsd:schema>
```

Passing the validation test is good news—the DBAs are now happy that they don't have to worry that the data in the database could be corrupt or invalid. You now have to get the data into the database. The database is loaded into memory. The location the data will go needs to be identified. In the case of a new family, all you have to do is increment the count of families by one and insert the new node for the family. For a new parent or a new child, you have to first check to see if a "parent" or "child" node exists, add one if it doesn't, and then insert the new node for the parent or child. After these operations, the database is persisted back to disk.

Listing 16.9 shows the details of removing a family from the database. The node to be removed is identified using the input information. The node is then removed and the count of families in the database is updated.

Listing 16.9 Method RemoveFamily from `family.cpp`

```
// this method is to remove a family from the database
// this is the lowest level in this mode - there is no 'remove parent'
// or 'remove child' functionality available in this sample.
STDMETHODIMP CFamily::RemoveFamily(BSTR bstrFamilyID)
{
  HRESULT hr;
  long    l = 0;
  char    cID[25] = {0};
  CComBSTR              bstrMatch   = L"";
  CComBSTR              bstrCurID   = L"";
  IXMLDOMDocument2Ptr   pDom;
  IXMLDOMNodePtr        pNode;
  IXMLDOMElementPtr     pElem;


  hr = pDom.CreateInstance(_T("Msxml2.DOMDocument.4.0"));
  if (FAILED(hr)) _com_raise_error(hr);
```

```
  // load the family database
  if (!LoadDom(pDom, "c:\\family\\family.xml")) return E_FAIL;

  if ( SysStringLen(bstrFamilyID) > 0 )
  {
    // lookup the family that we need to remove
    bstrMatch = _T("x:family_db/families/family[@id='");
    bstrMatch.AppendBSTR(bstrFamilyID);
    bstrMatch += _T("']");
    pNode = pDom->selectSingleNode(_bstr_t(bstrMatch));
    if ( pNode != NULL )
    {
      // remove the family
      pDom->selectSingleNode(
_T("x:family_db/families"))->removeChild(pNode);

      // update the count of the families in the database
      hr = pDom->selectSingleNode(
 _T("x:family_db/families"))->
   QueryInterface(MSXML2::IID_IXMLDOMElement,
(void**)&pElem);
      if (FAILED(hr)) _com_raise_error(hr);

      bstrCurID.AppendBSTR(_bstr_t(pElem->getAttribute(_T("count"))));
      sprintf(cID, "%s", bstrCurID);
      l = atol(cID)-1;
      sprintf(cID, "%ld", l);
      pElem->setAttribute (_T("count"), cID);

      // persist the updated document
      pDom->save (_T("c:\\family\\family.xml"));
    }
    else
    {
      MessageBox (NULL,
_T("Family not found!"),
_T("remove family"),
MB_OK);
    }
  }

  return S_OK;
}
```

The disadvantage of using an XML database is that it is fairly new and does not have the sophisticated features of a relational database, such as transaction support, recovery features, concurrency support, design tools, knowledge and expertise levels, and so on. However, database vendors are realizing the need for XML support within their database environment. When accessing data served by SQL Server, you can use the FOR XML addition to the `SELECT` statement to retrieve data in an XML format. Also, data in the database can be updated using an XML-based update gram. However, these are features that are wrapped around SQL Server using ADO. When .NET is released, SQL Server will have native support for stored procedures that are written in any language, which means that the usage of XML could increase significantly. Oracle is also very proactive in this space by adding XML as a native data type that can be stored and indexed upon.

Summary

This chapter provided an outline of how to manipulate XML using Visual C++. The samples provided in this chapter demonstrate how to do various XML operations using Visual C++. You learned how to load an XML file into a DOM document, use an XSD Schema to enforce data structure, and how to detect parse errors. You also saw how to use XPath for pattern matches and XSLT for transformations. These are perhaps the most important XML-related tools available to the Visual C++ programmer.

CHAPTER 17

Internet Explorer: Client-Side Scripting and Dynamic HTML

The Web is a means for delivering information to users. Given the power of XML as a technique for storing structured data, it is a logical step for Web developers to want to leverage XML as storage for data to be delivered on the Web. Because of the way the Web works, this means that the XML data must be integrated into an HTML document and presented in a browser. Several techniques have been developed for making XML data available on the Web. One of these techniques, using an XSLT style sheet to transform an XML document into an HTML document, is covered in Chapter 7. Other techniques that make use of client-side scripting and dynamic HTML technologies are covered in this chapter. The use of server-side scripting with XML is covered in Chapter 18.

Scripting

When dealing with the topic of XML and the Web, it is impossible to avoid talking about scripting. Scripting is a fairly involved topic, and a detailed treatment is well beyond the scope of this book. In this section I provide a brief introduction to scripting, particularly as it relates to XML.

A *script* is programming code that is placed inside a Web page. Some script code is executed when the Web page is accessed, and some code is executed in response to user actions, such as clicking a button on the page. Scripts perform many functions, and these functions for the most part are in the area of creating dynamic Web pages—pages that interact with the user and provide automatically updated information.

Scripts can be divided into two types: client side and server side. A client-side script is part of an HTML or XHTML page that is downloaded and displayed in the user's browser. The script code is executed on the user's, or client's, computer, hence the name "client side." A server-side script is located in a file on the server computer. When it is accessed by a user, the server computer executes the script code and the results are sent to the user for viewing in the browser. Some applications combine server-side and client-side scripting.

Microsoft supports two languages for scripting: VBScript and JScript. VBScript is based on the Visual Basic language, whereas JScript is Microsoft's version of the widely used JavaScript language. For client-side scripting, the browser must support the script language, and for server-side scripting, the Web server must provide support. Both client-side and server-side scripting are relevant to XML.

Within an HTML document, script code is enclosed in `<SCRIPT>` tags. The tags identify the script as code, so the browser does not try to render the script as part of the document display. The tag also identifies the language of the script using the `LANGUAGE` property:

```
<SCRIPT LANGUAGE="JavaScript">
...
script code here
...
</SCRIPT>

<SCRIPT LANGUAGE="VBScript">
...
script code here
...
</SCRIPT>
```

Because Internet Explorer supports both scripting languages, a given HTML document can contain script in JScript and VBScript, as long as each type of script is enclosed in its own `<SCRIPT>` tag with the `LANGUAGE` property set appropriately. Note that the quotes around the script language name, while technically required by the HTML 4.01 standard, can be omitted without problem in most browsers.

Dynamic HTML

Dynamic HTML, or DHTML, is one of the tools you will use when you work with XML in Internet Explorer. A complete treatment of the subject is beyond the scope of this book, but this section provides a sufficient introduction to

DHTML to get you started using it with your XML projects. You can find complete DHTML documentation on the Microsoft Developer Network Web site (`http://msdn.microsoft.com/`).

The original HTML model was static—a browser could download an HTML page and display it, but that was all. No changes to the style, structure, or content of the page were possible without making a request to the server and downloading the revised page. As developers tried to create more sophisticated Web pages, particularly pages that could interact dynamically with the user, this static model soon became a serious obstacle. DHTML was developed, primarily by Netscape and Microsoft working separately, in response to this need. Based on a document object model developed by W3C, DHTML uses standard HTML tags not only to display document content, but also to permit manipulation of that content within the browser without requiring any requests to the server. DHTML is particularly powerful when used in conjunction with scripting.

At the heart of DHTML is its Document Object Model, or DOM. The DHTML DOM provides access to all of the elements, or tags, within the HTML document. This is similar in concept to the way the XML DOM (covered in Chapter 10) exposes the elements of an XML document; however, the DHTML DOM and the XML DOM are separate entities. At the top of the DHTML DOM hierarchy is the `document` object, which represents the entire HTML document. Elements within the document are represented by objects in the DOM. For example, the `DIV` object represents a `<DIV>` tag, the `FONT` object represents a `<FONT>` tag, and the `P` object represents a `<P>` tag. To enable a DOM object that represents a tag to be referenced in script, the tag must be assigned an ID property, as in this HTML fragment:

```
<P ID=FIRST>This is the first paragraph</P>
<P ID=SECOND>This is the second paragraph</P>
```

Two DHTML elements of particular interest when you work with XML are `<SPAN>` and `<DIV>`. These elements serve as containers into which your script code can insert HTML. The two elements are essentially identical except that `<SPAN>` is an inline element while `<DIV>` is a block element. You can include an empty `<SPAN>` or `<DIV>` element in the HTML document at a location where you may want to display some dynamic content:

```
<DIV ID=output></DIV>
```

The empty element has no effect on document display, but when your script code, using the element's ID property, inserts some content into the element it will immediately be displayed. You'll see examples of this technique later in the chapter in Listing 17.2 and Listing 17.3.

Objects in the DHTML DOM can detect events, such as mouse clicks and keystrokes. You can write script code that responds to these events, so that the page responds to user input. DHTML supports *event bubbling*, which means that an event can be handled directly by the object that receives the event, or the event can be passed, or bubbled, up to objects that are higher in the hierarchy and be handled there. Thus, each `Paragraph` element in a document could handle its own `Click` events, or the events could be allowed to bubble up to be handled by the `Body` element.

Objects in the DHTML DOM also have properties and methods that are used to control the element's data and appearance. There are a few properties and methods that are particularly relevant to the present chapter and apply to both the `SPAN` and `DIV` objects.

The `innerText` property specifies the text inside the element tags. When you set this property, the new text completely replaces the existing text in the element, except for the `<html>`, `<head>`, and `<title>` tags (although these are rarely found within a `<DIV>` or `<SPAN>` element).

The `outerText` property specifies the text of the entire element, including its start and end tags.

The `insertAdjacentHTML` and `insertAdjacentText` methods insert text into the document. The syntax is the same for both methods:

```
insertAdjacentText(where, text)
insertAdjacentHTML(where, text)
```

`Text` is the text to insert, and `where` is a string value specifying where the text is to be inserted in relation to the element. Values for this argument are described in Table 17.1. These two methods are identical except that the

Table 17.1 Values of the `where` Argument for the `insertAdjacentText` and `insertAdjacentHTML` Methods

Argument	Where the Text Is Inserted
`BeforeBegin`	Immediately before the element's start tag
`AfterBegin`	After the element's start tag but before any element content
`BeforeEnd`	After any element content but before the element's end tag
`AfterEnd`	Immediately after the element's end tag

insertAdjacentHTML method treats the text as HTML and parses it. If the text includes invalid HTML, the method fails. In contrast, insertAdjacentText treats the text as plain text and does not parse it.

Client-Side Scripting and Data Islands

The concept of a *data island* is a result of the increasing need to embed XML data in HTML (or XHTML) documents. A data island is a section of XML that is enclosed in special tags within an HTML document. When the HTML is loaded into Internet Explorer, the content of the data island receives special treatment: It is not displayed in the browser, but it is made available for access by means of the MSXML Parser or Internet Explorer's DATASRC object. The use of the Microsoft parser is covered in this section, and the DATASRC object is covered in the next section.

A data island is defined by <XML> tags, as follows:

```
<xml ID="identifier">
...
</xml>
```

Identifier is a name that identifies the data island. This name is used to refer to the island in your script code. The XML can be placed within the XML tag, but more often the XML will be located in an external file and specified by the src attribute. You can specify this attribute as part of the tag, as shown here:

```
<xml ID="XMLIsland1" src="http://www.somewhere.com/data.xml">
</xml>
```

You can also set the src attribute in script code. This example sets the src attribute of the data island with the ID "MyXML":

```
MyXML.src = "somedata.xml"
```

You will note from these two examples that the XML file can be retrieved over the Web by specifying a URL, or it can be retrieved from a local file.

Another way of creating a data island is by using the <SCRIPT> tag, as shown here:

```
<SCRIPT LANGUAGE="XML" ID="MyXML">
...
```

```
XML goes here
...
</SCRIPT>
```

This format has been deprecated, however, and while you may see it in old HTML documents you should not use it in new work.

The Two DOMs

When you work with Internet Explorer and XML, there are two Document Object Models that come into play. One is the DOM exposed by the XML parser, which you learned about in Chapter 10. The other is the DOM that Internet Explorer uses to access and manipulate the content of HTML documents as part of dynamic HTML. The overlapping terminology can be confusing, and sometimes the two object models are referred to as the XML DOM and the HTML DOM to avoid misunderstanding.

There are two ways to access an XML data island by means of a parser. The first method uses a parser that is automatically associated with any XML data island loaded into Internet Explorer and that can be accessed without any special steps. The second method explicitly creates an instance of the MSXML Parser. If you installed the MSXML Parser in replace mode, the two methods access the same parser. If you installed the MSXML Parser in side-by-side mode, the first method uses whatever parser version was originally installed with Internet Explorer, while the second method accesses the (probably newer) parser that was installed separately. By explicitly creating a parser instance, you ensure that your script is using the most recent parser version installed on your system.

Using Internet Explorer's Parser

When an HTML document contains an XML data island, the built-in parser is available simply by referring to the `ID` attribute of the data island. For example, suppose an HTML file contains a data island with the ID "MyDataIsland." The following JScript code sets the variable "count" to the number of "sale" elements in the XML data:

```
count = MyDataIsland.selectNodes("//sale").length
```

To demonstrate using an XML data island with Internet Explorer's internal parser, I have created a Web page to display XML data to the user. The data, which consists of information on contact people at a company's three regional offices, is maintained in three separate XML files, one for each office. Listing 17.1 shows one of the XML files; the other two are identical in structure but with different data.

Listing 17.1 Mainoffice.xml (One of the XML Data Files)

```
<?xml version="1.0" encoding="UTF-8"?>
<!-- Contact list - main office -->
<contacts>
  <contact>
    <name>Alexandra Knowles</name>
    <title>Director of Media Relations</title>
    <phone>555-555-6666</phone>
  </contact>
  <contact>
    <name>Helen Hanson</name>
    <title>Assistant to the CEO</title>
    <phone>999-888-1111</phone>
  </contact>
  <contact>
    <name>Jackson Smith</name>
    <title>VP for Corporate Affairs</title>
    <phone>555-444-3333</phone>
  </contact>
</contacts>
```

The goal of the project is to present the user with a Web page that displays three buttons, one for each regional office. When the user clicks one of the buttons, script code accesses the XML data and generates HTML that displays the data as a table. The following points describe how the HTML was designed.

- The three button elements are placed inside a single `SPAN` element. This enables click events for all three buttons to be handled by the same event procedure. Each button includes properties that identify the associated XML file and provide information for the title of the table.
- An empty `DIV` element is included. This element will receive the generated HTML.

The complete HTML for this project is shown in Listing 17.2. Figure 17.1 shows the page displayed in a browser after one of the buttons was clicked.

Listing 17.2 DataIsland1.html Uses Internet Explorer's Internal Parser to Access a Data Island

```
<HTML>
<HEAD>
<TITLE>Using Internet Explorer Data Islands</TITLE>
</HEAD>
<BODY >
<H1>Using XML Data Islands in Internet Explorer</H1>
<HR>

<p>Click a button to display a list of contacts for the specified
office.</p>

<!-- XML data island that is used to retrieve the data -->
<XML ID="xmlDataIsland"></XML>

<SCRIPT LANGUAGE="JavaScript">
// This function generates an HTML table
// containing the list of contacts.
function createHTML( objParser, title ) {

    // Put title in variable to hold the html that will be output.
    var strOutput = "<H2>";
    strOutput += title;
    strOutput += "</H2>";

    // The table headings.
    strOutput += "<HR><TABLE cellpadding=8><THEAD><TH>Name</TH>";
    strOutput += "<TH>Title</TH><TH>Phone</TH></THEAD><TBODY>";

    // Retrieve the list of <contact> nodes from the XML Parser
    var collContacts = objParser.selectNodes( "//contact" );

    // Iterate the list of <contact> nodes, extracting data and
    // creating the HTML for output.
    for( var idx = 0; idx < collContacts.length; idx++ ) {
        strOutput += "<TR>";
        strOutput += "<TD>" + collContacts.item(idx).
           selectSingleNode( "name" ).text + "</TD>";
```

```
            strOutput += "<TD>" + collContacts.item(idx).
                selectSingleNode( "title" ).text + "</TD>";
            strOutput += "<TD>" + collContacts.item(idx).
                selectSingleNode( "phone" ).text + "</TD>";
            strOutput += "</TR>";
        }
        // Finish off the table elements.
        strOutput += "</TBODY></TABLE>";
        return strOutput;
}

// This event handler is for the click events of the INPUT
// elements in the theButtons SPAN element.
function theButtons_onclick() {
    // If the event was on an INPUT element.
    if( event.srcElement.tagName == "INPUT" ) {

        // Retrieve the button that was clicked.
        var objButton = event.srcElement;

        // The XML data island should use synchronous data transfer
        xmlDataIsland.async = false;

        // Set the XML data island's src property to the path
        // property of the button that was clicked.
        xmlDataIsland.src = objButton.path;

        // Create the table title.
        var tableTitle = "Contacts at the ";
        tableTitle += objButton.title;

        // Call the createHTML function to convert the contents
        // of the XML parser object into HTML.
        // Pass the title information as well. The HTML returned
        // by the function is placed in the DIV element for display.
        divOutput.innerHTML = createHTML( xmlDataIsland, tableTitle );
    }
}
</SCRIPT>

<!-- By putting the button elements inside a SPAN element, the events
     from all three can be handled in the same procedure. -->
<SPAN ID=theButtons LANGUAGE="JavaScript" onclick=
   "return theButtons_onclick()">
```

```
<!-- For each button, the "path" property points to the corresponding
     XML file, and the "title" property provides information that
     will be used to construct the table's title. -->

<INPUT TYPE=button VALUE="Main Office" path="mainoffice.xml"
   title="main office">
<INPUT TYPE=button VALUE="West Office" path="westoffice.xml"
   title="west office">
<INPUT TYPE=button VALUE="East Office" path="eastoffice.xml"
   title="east office">

</SPAN>

<!-- The generated HTML will be placed in this DIV element -->
<DIV ID=divOutput></DIV>
<HR>
<A href="#" onclick='self.close()'>Close demo</A>
</BODY>
</HTML>
```

Using the External Parser

The second option for script access to XML data islands is to explicitly create an instance of the Microsoft parser. The identifier for this component is "MSXML2.DOMDocument" (although you'll sometimes see the identifier "Microsoft.XMLDOM" used as well), and you create an instance of it using the `ActiveXObject()` function in JScript or the `CreateObject()` function in VBScript. Once you have a reference to an instance of this parser, you use it in the same way you use the internal parser. The HTML document in Listing 17.3 illustrates this technique. This is essentially the same application that was presented in the previous section, but it uses the external rather than the internal parser. The code differences are all located in the `theButtons_onclick()` function.

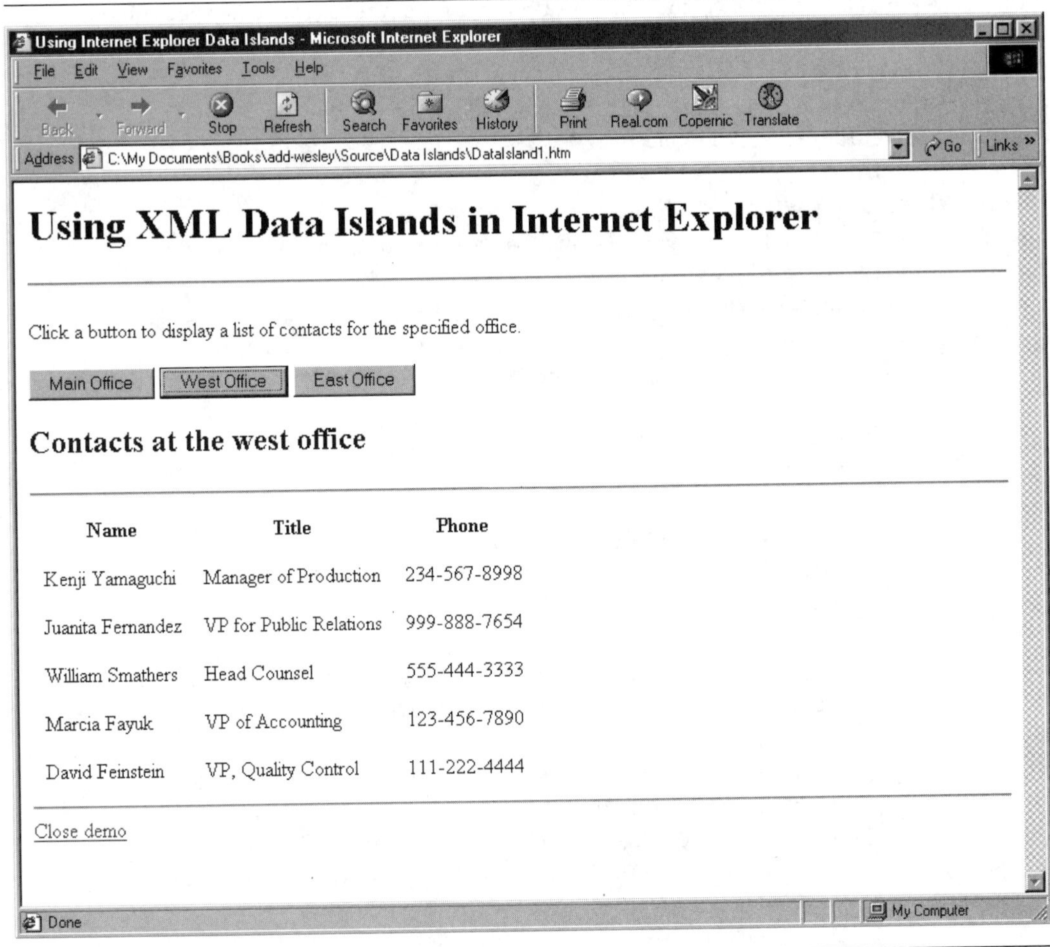

Figure 17.1 The HTML page displaying XML data in Internet Explorer

Listing 17.3 DataIsland2.html Uses the External Parser to Access a Data Island

```
<HTML>
<HEAD>
<TITLE>Using Internet Explorer Data Islands</TITLE>
</HEAD>
<BODY >
<H1>Using XML Data Islands in Internet Explorer</H1>
<HR>
```

```
<p>Click a button to display a list of contacts for the specified
office.</p>

<!-- XML data island that is used to retrieve the data -->
<XML ID="xmlDataIsland"></XML>

<SCRIPT LANGUAGE="JavaScript">
// This function generates an HTML table containing
// the list of contacts.
function createHTML( objParser, title ) {

    // Put title in variable to hold the html that will be output.
    var strOutput = "<H2>";
    strOutput += title;
    strOutput += "</H2>";

    // The table headings.
    strOutput += "<HR><TABLE cellpadding=8><THEAD><TH>Name</TH>";
    strOutput += "<TH>Title</TH><TH>Phone</TH></THEAD><TBODY>";

    // Retrieve the list of <contact> nodes from the XML Parser
    var collContacts = objParser.selectNodes( "//contact" );

    // Iterate the list of <contact> nodes, extracting data and
    // creating the HTML for output.
    for( var idx = 0; idx < collContacts.length; idx++ ) {
        strOutput += "<TR>";
        strOutput += "<TD>" + collContacts.item
           ( idx ).selectSingleNode( "name" ).text + "</TD>";
        strOutput += "<TD>" + collContacts.item
           ( idx ).selectSingleNode( "title" ).text + "</TD>";
        strOutput += "<TD>" + collContacts.item
           ( idx ).selectSingleNode( "phone" ).text + "</TD>";
        strOutput += "</TR>";
    }
    // Finish off the table elements.
    strOutput += "</TBODY></TABLE>";
    return strOutput;
}

// This event handler is for the click events of the INPUT
// elements in the theButtons SPAN element.
function theButtons_onclick() {
```

```
    // If the event was on an INPUT element.
    if( event.srcElement.tagName == "INPUT" ) {

        // Retrieve the button that was clicked.
        var objButton = event.srcElement;

        // Create a new instance of the external parser.
        var objParser = new ActiveXObject( "MSXML2.DOMDocument" );

       // The parser should use synchronous data transfer.
        objParser.async = false;

        // Load the parser with the XML file, based on.
        // the path property of the button that was clicked.
        objParser.load( objButton.path );

        // Create the table title.
        var tableTitle = "Contacts at the ";
        tableTitle += objButton.title;

        // Call the createHTML helper function to convert the
        // contents of the XML parser object into HTML that we
        // will use for display.
        // Pass the title information as well.
        divOutput.innerHTML = createHTML( objParser, tableTitle );
    }
}
</SCRIPT>

<!-- By putting the button elements inside a SPAN element, the events
     from all three can be handled in the same procedure. -->
<SPAN ID=theButtons LANGUAGE="JavaScript" onclick=
  "return theButtons_onclick()">

<!-- For each button, the "path" property points to the corresponding
     XML file, and the "title" property provides information that
     will be used to construct the table's title. -->

<INPUT TYPE=button VALUE="Main Office" path="mainoffice.xml"
   title="main office">
<INPUT TYPE=button VALUE="West Office" path="westoffice.xml"
   title="west office">
<INPUT TYPE=button VALUE="East Office" path="eastoffice.xml"
   title="east office">
```

```
</SPAN>

<!-- The generated HTML will be placed in this DIV element -->
<DIV ID=divOutput></DIV>
<HR>
<A href="#" onclick='self.close()'>Close demo</A>
</BODY>
</HTML>
```

The Data Source Object

The Data Source Object (DSO) is a DHTML component that is used to connect, or bind, an HTML page to a data source. The term “data source” is used generically to refer to any source of data that could be displayed on a page, and the DSO component has the capability of binding to a variety of sources, but for the present purposes it is the capability to bind to an XML data island that is of interest.

Using a DSO to access a data island is not as powerful or flexible as using a parser from script (the technique that was demonstrated in the previous section). Why, then, would a developer ever turn to this technique? First of all, it is relatively simple, and for certain tasks, the DSO is more than adequate. More important, users will sometimes disable scripting in their browsers for security reasons. Unless you are sure that your users have scripting enabled, you may want to use the DSO whenever possible to ensure the widest compatibility.

Displaying XML data with a DSO always involves an HTML table. The connection between the table and the XML data island is created in the `<TABLE>` start tag using this syntax:

```
<TABLE DATASRC=#DataIslandID>
...
</TABLE>
```

`DataIslandID` is the ID property of the XML data island. Within the table, the XML data is accessed using the `<DIV>` tag with the `datafld` property set to the name of the XML element whose data is to be retrieved. For example, this tag will retrieve the contents of the “firstname” element in the XML data island:

```
<DIV datafld="firstname"></DIV>
```

To create the table, you write the HTML table elements to display a single row of data, using the <DIV> tags to specify what data is to be displayed in what column. For example, suppose the XML data is composed of elements like this:

```
<book>
  <title>War and Peace</title>
  <author>Leo Tolstoy</author>
  <category>fiction</category>
</book>
```

The HTML to display all the XML data in the table will look like this (assuming the data island's ID is "bookdata"):

```
<TABLE DATASRC=#bookdata>
<TR>
<td><div datafld="title"></div></td>
<td><div datafld="author"></div></td>
<td><div datafld="category"></div></td>
</TR>
</TABLE>
```

Attributes are displayed in the same way as elements: by referring to their name. When Internet Explorer loads the HTML page, it connects the DSO to the data island and then iterates through the XML. For each element in the XML, it creates a separate row in the output table. For example, using the preceding example, if the XML file contained 12 <book> elements, the resulting table would have 12 rows.

Listings 17.4 and 17.5 present a simple example of using the DSO with an XML data island. The XML data is shown is Listing 17.4 and consists of a books database with information contained in both elements and attributes. The output of this HTML page is shown in Figure 17.2.

Listing 17.4 XML Data Used by the HTML Document in Listing 17.5

```
<?xml version="1.0"?>
<?xml-stylesheet type="text/xsl" href="list0602.xsl"?>
<books>
<book category="reference">
  <title>The Cambridge Biographical Encyclopedia</title>
  <author>David Crystal</author>
```

```
    <publisher>Cambridge University Press</publisher>
  </book>
  <book category="fiction">
    <title>Travels with Charley</title>
    <author>John Steinbeck</author>
    <publisher>Putnam</publisher>
  </book>
  <book category="fiction">
    <title>Crime and Punishment</title>
    <author>Fyodor Dostoyevsky</author>
    <publisher>Oxford</publisher>
  </book>
  </books>
```

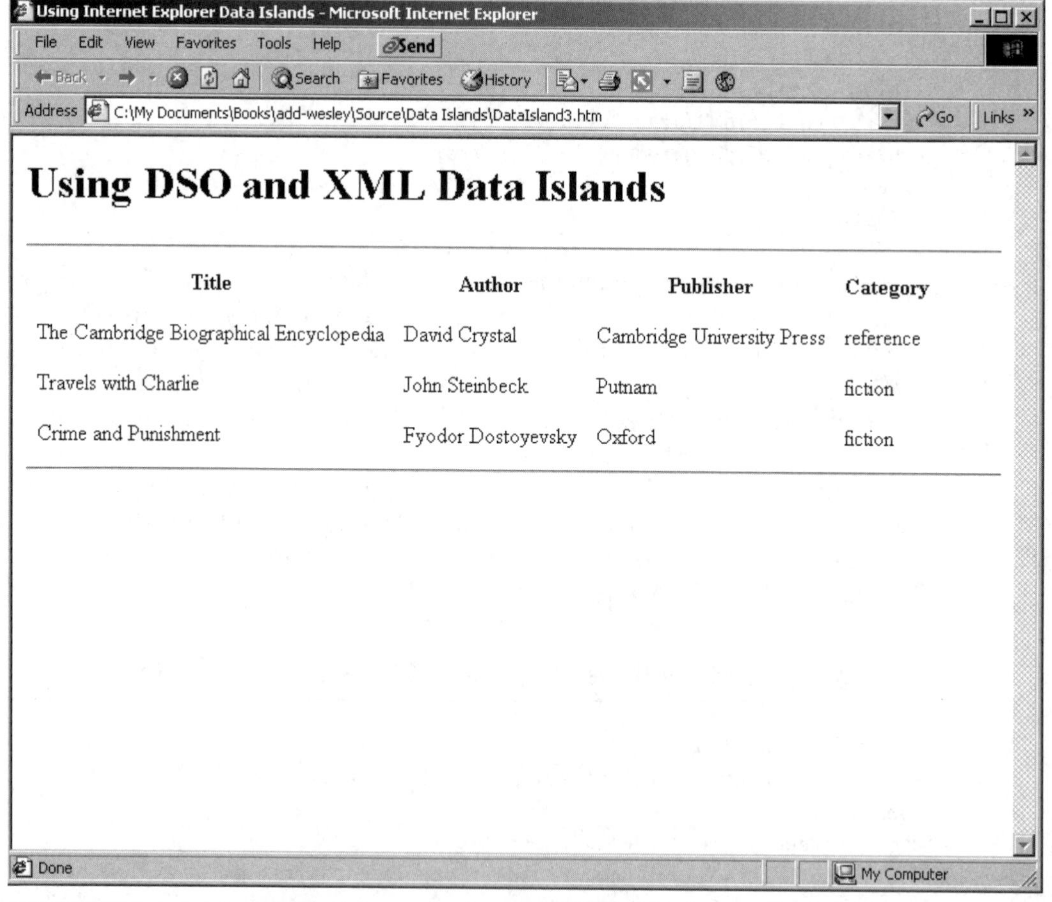

Figure 17.2 The DSO demonstration from Listing 17.4

Listing 17.5 DataIsland3.html Demonstrates Using DSO with an XML Data Island

```
<HTML>
<HEAD>
<TITLE>Using Internet Explorer Data Islands</TITLE>
</HEAD>
<BODY>

<H1>Using DSO and XML Data Islands</H1>
<hr>
<!-- XML data island that is used to retrieve the data -->
<XML ID=XMLDataIsland src="list1704.xml"></XML>

<table datasrc="#xmlDataIsland" cellpadding=6>
<tr>
<thead>
<tr>
<th>Title</th>
<th>Author</th>
<th>Publisher</th>
<th>Category</th>
</tr>
</thead>
<td><div datafld="title"></div></td>
<td><div datafld="author"></div></td>
<td><div datafld="publisher"></div></td>
<td><div datafld="category"></div></td>
</tr>
</table>
<hr>


</BODY>
</HTML>
```

Viewing Partial Data

In the previous examples, the DSO was used to display the entire contents of the XML data island at one time. This is practical for short data sets, but if the XML contains dozens or hundreds of records it would result in a very long table that would be difficult to view. DSO provides the option of displaying only a specified number of rows at a time, and then letting the user move forward and backward through the data to display different rows.

To specify the number of rows that are displayed in the table, set the DATAPAGESIZE property in the <TABLE> element. This example specifies that the table will display four rows at a time:

```
<table ID=table1 datasrc="#xmlDataIsland" datapagesize=4>
```

Note that this tag also has the ID property set. This is required to enable the user to move through the rows. When a DSO with a DATAPAGESIZE value of *n* is displayed, the first *n* rows will be displayed initially. To move through the rows, you use the following DSO methods:

```
firstPage()
lastPage()
nextPage()
previousPage()
```

Most often, these methods are associated with buttons that the user can click to move through the rows. You use the table's ID value followed by the method name, as shown in this HTML example that creates a button that when clicked will cause the DSO table with the ID property "table1" to display the first set of rows:

```
<INPUT TYPE="button" VALUE="First Page" ONCLICK="table1.firstPage();">
```

The HTML document in Listing 17.6 demonstrates this technique. It uses the XML data that was presented in Listing 17.4. On this page, the book data is displayed one row at a time, and the user can move from row to row using the button. The page is shown in Figure 17.3.

Listing 17.6 DataIsland4.html Shows How to Use DSO to Display Part of a Data Set

```
<HTML>
<HEAD>
<TITLE>Using Internet Explorer Data Islands</TITLE>
</HEAD>
<BODY>

<H1>Using DSO and XML Data Islands</H1>
<hr>
<!-- XML data island that is used to retrieve the data -->
<XML ID=XMLDataIsland src="list1704.xml"></XML>

<table ID=table1 datasrc="#xmlDataIsland" datapagesize=1 cellpadding=6>
<tr>
```

```
<thead>
<tr>
<th>Title</th>
<th>Author</th>
<th>Publisher</th>
<th>Category</th>
</tr>
</thead>
<td><div datafld="title"></div></td>
<td><div datafld="author"></div></td>
<td><div datafld="publisher"></div></td>
<td><div datafld="category"></div></td>
</tr>
</table>
<hr>
<INPUT TYPE="button" VALUE="First" ONCLICK="table1.firstPage();">
<INPUT TYPE="button" VALUE="Next" ONCLICK="table1.nextPage();">
<INPUT TYPE="button" VALUE="Previous" ONCLICK="table1.previousPage();">
<INPUT TYPE="button" VALUE="Last"" ONCLICK="table1.lastPage();">

</BODY>
</HTML>
```

The $Text Data Field

The DSO automatically creates a data field called `$Text` when it binds to data in an XML data island. This data field contains the data from all the elements in the current record concatenated into one string. Look at this example:

```
<person>
  <name>Jack Kornfield</name>
  <position>Writer</position>
  <employeenumber>16253</employeenumber>
</person>
```

When the DSO processes this element, the `$Text` field will contain the following:

```
Jack Kornfield Writer 16253
```

If you want to display the concatenated data in your table, refer to the `$Text` data field in a `<div>` element, as shown here:

```
<td><div datafld="$Text"></div></td>
```

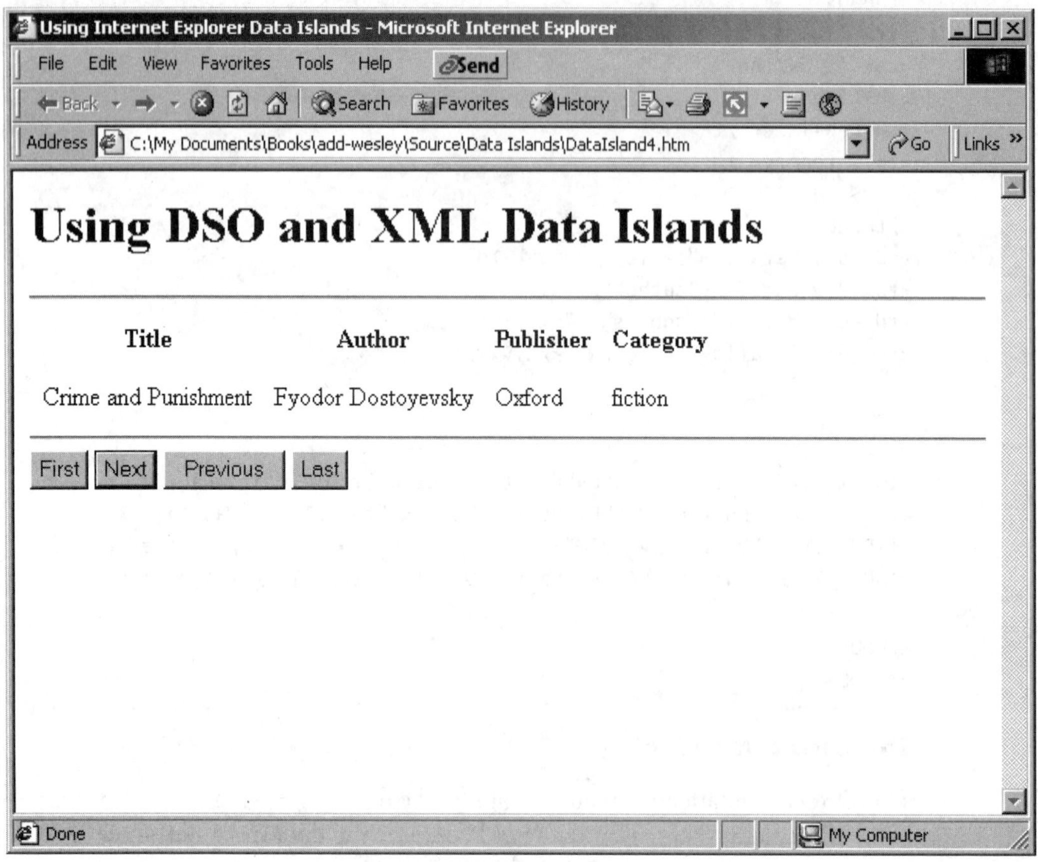

Figure 17.3 DataIsland4.htm displays one row of data at a time.

Summary

Client-side scripting allows for the embedding of VBScript or JScript code in HTML Web pages. The script is executed in the browser when the page is loaded or in response to user actions. The script code has access to the page's contents through the dynamic HTML model. Scripting can be used in conjunction with data islands, which contain XML data embedded in the HTML document or located in an external file and references from the HTML document. This combination permits dynamic, interactive access to XML data in a Web page. Using a Data Source Object adds additional flexibility to an HTML/XML combination.

CHAPTER 18

Server-Side Scripting and XML

The term "server-side scripting" refers to scripts that are executed on the Web server, rather than on the client computer. Server-side scripting is implemented by Microsoft using Active Server Pages (ASP). This technology has a wide variety of uses, and it is certainly not limited to working with XML. However, it offers developers a great deal of flexibility and power for XML-related tasks.

ASP Fundamentals

An ASP page, identified by the .asp extension, contains script code (VBScript and/or JavaScript) and, in most cases, some HTML as well. When an ASP page is accessed, it is loaded by the Web server software and the script it contains is executed. The script can perform a variety of tasks, such as opening and accessing databases, but the end result of the script is always some HTML output. The Web server takes this script output and combines it with any HTML in the ASP page. The result is sent to and displayed in the client browser that requested the ASP page.

ASP Syntax

An ASP page begins with a processing directive tag identifying the script language that the page uses. This tag identifies a page as using VBScript:

```
<%@ Language="VBScript" %>
```

A processing directive tag can include additional directives as well, but they will not be mentioned here. The remainder of an ASP page consists of script code, which is contained in `<% ... %>` tags, and HTML, which is not contained in any special tags.

When the script code in a page executes, there are two methods it can use to generate output. One method uses the `Write` method of the `Response` object. The `Response` object is implicitly available in any ASP script—you do not have to create an instance of it. The `Write` method sends data to the client browser. The syntax is as follows:

```
Response.Write data
```

`Data` is the data to be sent to the client. It can be a literal string, a variable, or any expression. The following statement sends the text "<TR><TD>" to the client:

```
Response.Write "<TR><TD>"
```

This statement sends the contents of the variable "total" to the client:

```
Response.Write total
```

The following statement sends the current date to the client. Note that `Date()` is a VBScript function that returns the current system date.

```
Response.Write Date()
```

The second way to send output to the client is to use the `<%= ... %>` tag. Any expression inside this tag is evaluated and the result sent to the client. This tag must appear outside other script tags. For example, this tag causes the value of the variable "total" to be sent to the client:

```
<%= total %>
```

Both of these methods are demonstrated by the simple ASP page in Listing 18.1. The HTML output of this ASP page is shown in Listing 18.2, and the result displayed in a browser is shown in Figure 18.1.

Listing 18.1 A Very Simple ASP Document

```
<%@ LANGUAGE="VBScript" %>
<HTML>
<BODY>
<% Response.Write "<H1>Simple ASP Demo</H1><HR/>"
```

```
msg = "The time at the server is " & Time()
%>
<%= msg %>
</BODY>
</HTML>
```

Listing 18.2 HTML Returned by the ASP Page in Listing 18.1

```
<HTML>
<BODY>
<H1>Simple ASP Demo</H1><HR/>The time at the server is 1:58:23 PM
</BODY>
</HTML>
```

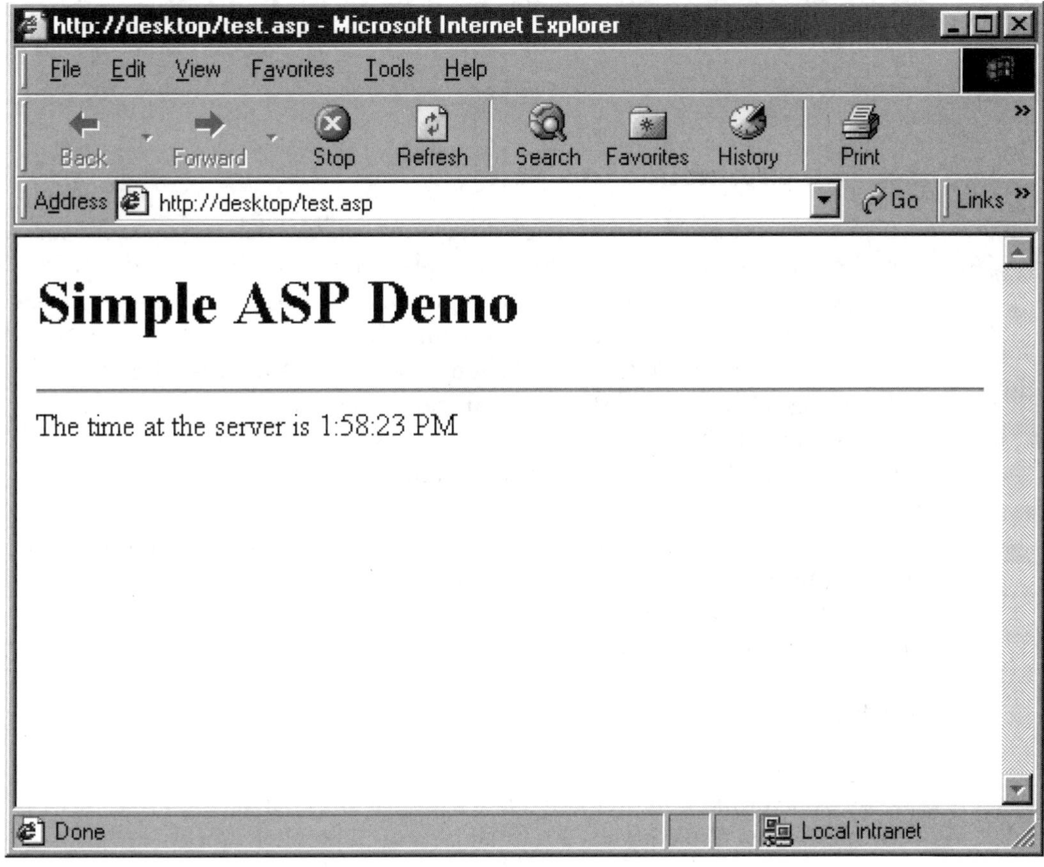

Figure 18.1: The output of Listing 18.1 displayed in Internet Explorer

> ***Viewing Local ASP Pages***
>
> *Because an ASP page must be processed by a Web server, you cannot open the page by double-clicking the filename or by using Internet Explorer's Open command to browse for the file. If you want to test ASP pages on a single machine, you must have a Web server running. This can be Microsoft Internet Information Server on Windows NT/2000, or the Microsoft Personal Web Server on Windows 98/ME (third-party products are available that permit running ASP pages on other types of Web servers). Then, you access the page using the HTTP protocol and either the Web server's local IP address (which is 127.0.0.1 by default) or the name that was assigned to your local Web folder. For example, on my system the name "localhost" is used for my Web folder. To view the page TEST.ASP located in my root folder, I open Internet Explorer, press Ctrl-O to display the Open dialog box, and then enter either http://localhost/test.asp or http://127.0.0.1/test.asp.*

Sending Information to a Script

A browser can request an ASP page directly, as explained in the previous section. Frequently, however, an ASP page will be requested from another Web page, permitting custom information to be sent to the ASP page. For example, a search Web site might first display a regular HTML page to the user, who enters search criteria on the page. When the user clicks the Search button, the HTML page sends a request to the ASP page, including the details of the search criteria in the request. Script code in the ASP page can retrieve this information, perform the appropriate search, and return the customized results to the user.

HTML provides several page elements that are used to input information from the user and send it to the server. In an ASP script, the `Response` object is used to retrieve the information sent as part of the page request. These topics are covered in the next sections.

HTML Forms

An HTML page can accept user input by means of a form element. A form contains one or more input elements (covered soon) that accept input from the user. A form also contains a Submit button. When the user clicks this button, the information entered by the user is sent to the server, and the response returned by the server is displayed in the browser. A form element has the following syntax:

```
<FORM NAME=Name ACTION=action METHOD=method>
...
Input elements are placed here.
...
</FORM>
```

Name is an optional attribute specifying the form name. *Action* is the URL of the script file that the response is to be sent to. *Method* is either GET or POST, specifying the method used to send the request. I'll explain the differences between these methods soon. Inside the <FORM> element you can place regular HTML elements as well as the special INPUT elements. The general syntax for all INPUT elements is as follows:

```
<INPUT TYPE=type NAME=name VALUE=value />
```

Type specifies the type of INPUT element. *Name* is a unique name for the element; your ASP script will use this name when retrieving the data from the element. *Value* specifies the initial value, or data, for the element. There are seven types of input elements (plus one special type that is covered later).

A text field is used for entry of text. The length attribute specifies the width of the field in characters, and the maxlength attribute specifies the maximum length of the text the field will accept. The following HTML creates a Text input element that is 20 characters wide and is initially blank:

```
<INPUT TYPE="text" NAME="color" length="20" value="" />
```

A password field (TYPE="password") is identical to a text field except that text the user types is displayed as asterisks (*).

A hidden field is not displayed and cannot accept user input directly. Hidden fields can be used to send static information to the server. If your HTML page contains multiple forms, you can use a hidden input element to identify the form to the server:

```
<INPUT TYPE="hidden" NAME="form3" VALUE="main" />
```

A check box field displays a box that the user can select (check) or deselect (uncheck). The value attribute of the element is returned to the server if the box is checked. If the box is not checked, no value is returned to the server. To specify that a box be checked initially, set the `checked` attribute to "yes." You can have more than one check box element with the same name as long as the `value` attributes are different. Here's an example:

```
<INPUT TYPE="checkbox" NAME="search" CHECKED="yes" VALUE="all" />
<INPUT TYPE="checkbox" NAME="search" value="recent" />
```

A radio button field is like a check box in that it provides an on/off option for the user. The difference is that radio buttons always come in groups of two or more, and only one button in a group can be on at a time. To create a group of radio buttons, give each button the same `NAME` attribute and a unique `VALUE` attribute. By default, no button in a group is initially selected. To specify one button to be selected initially, set its `checked` attribute to "yes." When the form is submitted, the `VALUE` attribute of the one selected button will be sent to the server. This HTML creates a group of three radio buttons with the "red" button initially selected:

```
<INPUT TYPE="radio" NAME="color" VALUE="blue" />
<INPUT TYPE="radio" NAME="color" VALUE="red" CHECKED="yes" />
<INPUT TYPE="radio" NAME="color" VALUE="green" />
```

Every form requires a way to submit it (send its data to the server). Usually this is accomplished with a Submit button, although it can also be done in script code. When a Submit button is clicked, the form is submitted (using the parameters specified in the `<FORM>` tag). A Submit button's `VALUE` attribute specifies the text to display on the button, and its `NAME` attribute serves to identify the button. Here is an example:

```
<INPUT TYPE="submit" VALUE="Search Now" NAME="button1" />
```

A reset button clears all user data from the form, resetting all form elements to their initial values. It provides the user with an easy way to start over from scratch. Here is a reset button tag:

```
<INPUT TYPE="reset" VALUE="Clear Form" />
```

There is one additional input element that has its own syntax. It is the select element, and it displays a list of choices from which the user can select. The syntax is as follows:

```
<SELECT NAME=name SIZE=size>
  <OPTION VALUE=value>text</OPTION>
```

```
  <OPTION VALUE=value>text</OPTION>
  ...
  <OPTION VALUE=value>text</OPTION>
</SELECT>
```

Name is the unique name of the element, and *size* specifies the number of options to display. If the select element contains more options than `size`, the element functions as a drop-down list. Each option is represented by an `<option>` element. For each option, *value* is the data sent to the server if that option is selected, and *text* is the text that is displayed in the option list. Here is an example of a select element that lets the user select a month and then returns the corresponding number to the server:

```
<SELECT NAME="month" SIZE="1">
  <OPTION VALUE="1">January</OPTION>
  <OPTION VALUE="2">February</OPTION>
  <OPTION VALUE="3">March</OPTION>
  <OPTION VALUE="4">April</OPTION>
  <OPTION VALUE="5">May</OPTION>
  <OPTION VALUE="6">June</OPTION>
  <OPTION VALUE="7">July</OPTION>
  <OPTION VALUE="8">August</OPTION>
  <OPTION VALUE="9">September</OPTION>
  <OPTION VALUE="10">October</OPTION>
  <OPTION VALUE="11">November</OPTION>
  <OPTION VALUE="12">December</OPTION>
</SELECT>
```

The HTML document in Listing 18.3 demonstrates how to use these form and input elements. The page created by this HTML is shown in Figure 18.2.

Listing 18.3 Demonstrating the HTML Form and Input Elements

```
<html>
<head>
<title>HTML INPUT elements</title>
</head>
<body>
<h2>Demonstrating the HTML INPUT elements.</h2>
<hr/>
<form action="www.pgacon.com/links.asp" method="GET">
<input type="hidden" value="test form" />
<p>Your name: <input type="text" name="name" length="20" value=""/></p>
```

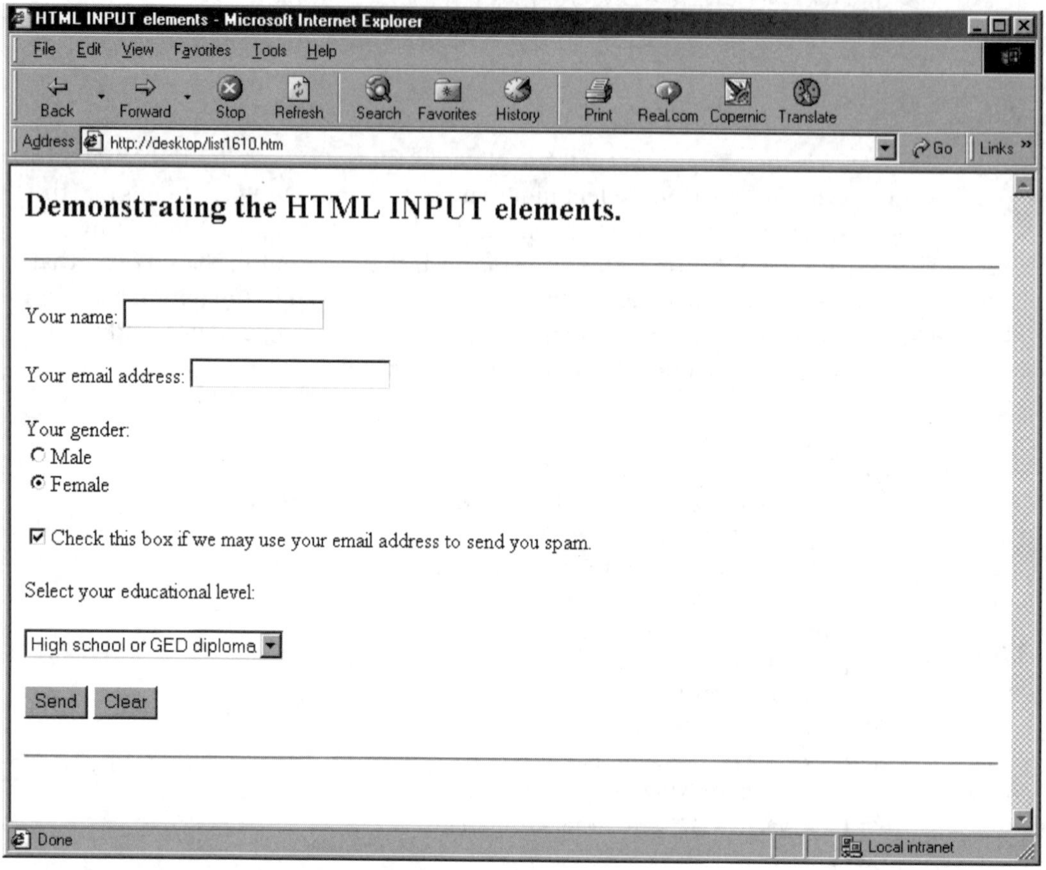

Figure 18.2 The HTML form created by Listing 18.3

```
<p>Your email address: <input type="text" name="email" length="20"
value=""/></p>
<p>Your gender:<br/>
<INPUT type="radio" name="gender" value="male"/>Male<br/>
<INPUT type="radio" name="gender" value="female"
checked="yes"/>Female</p>
<p><input type="checkbox" name="emailOK" value="spam_ok"
checked="yes"/>Check this box if we may
use your email address to send you spam.</p>
<p>Select your educational level:</p>
<p><select name="education" size="1">
  <option value="highschool">High school or GED diploma</option>
  <option value="bachelor">Bachelor's degree</option>
```

```
  <option value="graduate">Graduate degree</option>
</select></p>
<INPUT type="submit" value="Send" />
<INPUT type="reset" value="Clear" />
</form>
<hr/>
</body>
</html>
```

Using GET versus POST

When you create an HTML `<form>` element, you need to decide whether the form will use the `GET` or the `POST` method to send the form data to the server. When you use `GET`

- The amount of data submitted is limited. The precise limit depends on the server in use, but is typically about 1,000 characters.
- The submitted data is appended at the end of the URL to which the data is being submitted.

The 1,000-character limit is not a problem is many situations. The way the data is sent may be a concern, however. The `GET` method encodes the form data as a set of *`element=value`* pairs separated by an ampersand (&). The form data is then appended to the end of the submission URL and separated by a question mark (?). For example, a form that uses `GET` might submit its data by navigating to a URL like this one:

```
http://www.myserver.com/scripts/myscript.asp?Name=Peter&Age=29
```

This `GET` submission tells us that the originating form has an element named "Name" where the user entered "Peter," and an element named "Age" where the user entered "29." Some other encoding rules are followed by `GET`: Spaces in the data are replaced by the plus sign (+), and special symbols are replaced by a percent sign (%) followed by the hexadecimal code of the symbol. For example, the forward slash is encoded as %2F, the plus sign is encoded as %2B, and the dollar sign is encoded as %24.

The `POST` method differs from `GET` in two ways.

- The amount of data that can be sent is greater. The exact limit on a `POST` submission is determined by the server software, but it is always much greater than the roughly 1,000-character limit of `GET`.
- The form data is sent in the HTTP headers, where it is hidden from view.

When you decide whether to use GET or POST, the amount of data being submitted in the chief concern. If there is any chance it will come close to the approximately 1,000-character limit, you must use POST. Otherwise, your choice depends on if you want the data visible in the submission URL (which the user will be able to see in the browser's Address bar). Note also that if you design your ASP script to read data from a GET method, you will be able to link directly to your ASP page without using a form by including the data in the link URL. For example, the following link in an HTML page mimics a GET submission where the "searchfor" element has the value "igloos":

```
<a href="http://www.myserver.com/scripts/search.asp?searchfor=igloos">
Click here to search for information on igloos</a>
```

Accessing Submitted Data in an ASP Script

An ASP page that uses data submitted by a GET or POST method must access that data in order to make use of it. Both types of data are accessed using the Request object, but in different ways: the QueryString collection for GET data and the Form collection for POST data. Note that the Request object provides access to other information, such as client-side cookies, but they are not covered here.

The Form collection contains one member for each element on the form that submitted the data. You can access the values of the individual items by name (the name attribute of the control) or by index, with the first item having index=1. The syntax is as follows:

```
Request.Form(name)
Request.Form(index)
```

For example, if your ASP page is expecting data to be submitted from an element named "UserName," it could read the value of that element into a script variable as follows:

```
Uname = Request.Form("UserName")
```

The Form collection has the Count property, which returns the number of items in the collection. If you try to access the Form collection when data was not submitted by the POST method (or GET was used, or no data was submitted at all), the collection will be empty. In addition to retrieving the value of an element using the syntax previously provided, you can reference an item in the collection directly to get the element's name, and you can also refer to the

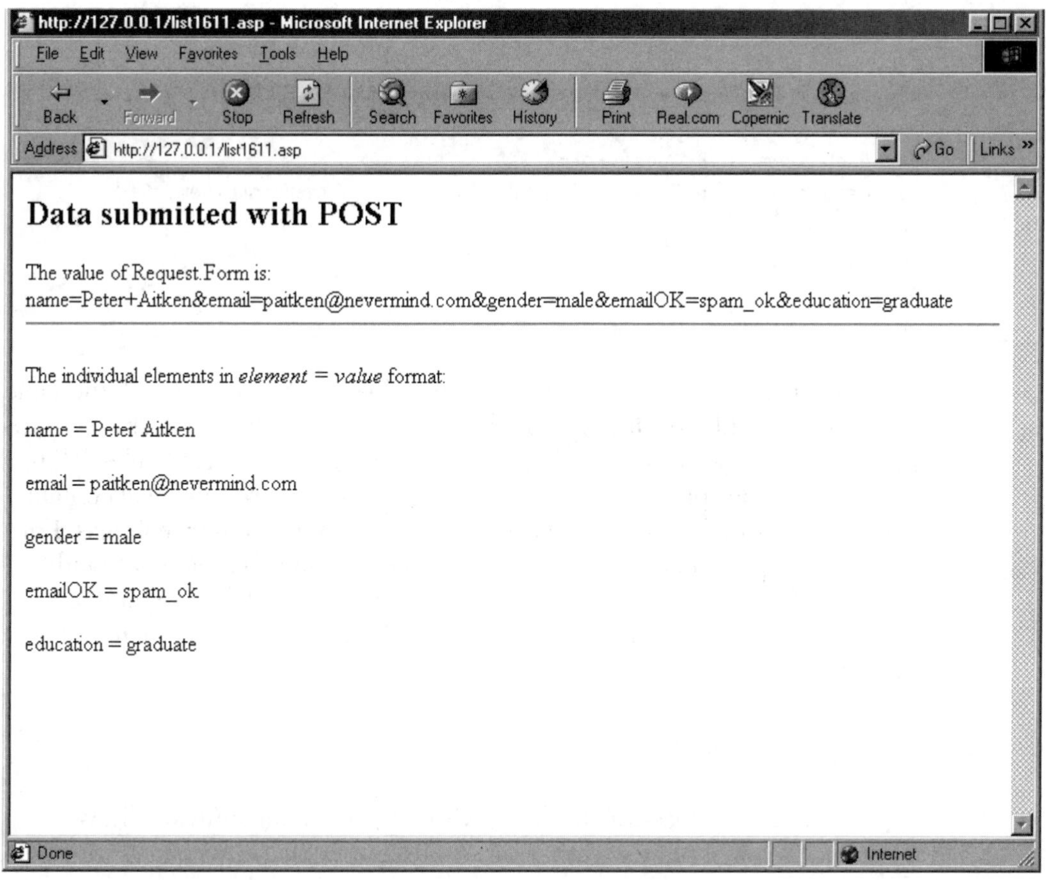

Figure 18.3 Data submitted with the POST method displayed by an ASP page

`Request.Form` collection without a name or index argument to retrieve a string containing all the *name=value* pairs that were sent by the POST method. The ASP page in Listing 18.4 shows how to retrieve and display data submitted by a POST method. The output when the ASP page is called by the HTML document in Listing 18.3 is shown in Figure 18.3.

Listing 18.4 ASP Page That Displays Data Submitted with POST

```
<%@ LANGUAGE="VBScript" %>
<HTML>
<BODY>
<h2>Data submitted with POST</h2>
```

```
<%
Response.Write "<p>The value of Request.Form is: " & Request.Form &
"<hr/>"
Response.Write "<p>The individual elements in <i>element = value</i>
format:</p>"
for each item in Request.Form
    Response.write "<p>" & item & " = " & Request.Form(item) & "</p>"
next
%>
</BODY>
</HTML>
```

If an HTML form contains two or more check box elements with the same name, it is possible for the user to select more than one of the check boxes. In this case, the `Form` collection will contain an item for each selected check box. If you access the collection by the shared name, the return value will contain the values of all selected check boxes of that name separated by commas. For example, suppose that the form contains multiple check box elements with the name “Foods,” and two check boxes with the values “Chinese” and “Mexican” are selected. The following expression will return the string “Chinese, Mexican”:

```
Request.Form("Foods")
```

If you need to access a check box with a shared name individually, you must add an index value to the syntax. For example, this expression returns the value of the second check box with the name “Foods”:

```
Request.Form(“Foods”)(2)
```

When data is submitted using the `GET` method, you use the `QueryString` collection instead of the `Form` collection. The syntax for using this collection is exactly the same as for using the Form collection. If data was submitted with `POST`, or no data was submitted, the `QueryString` collection will be empty.

ASP Demonstration Programs

The remainder of this chapter is devoted to several demonstration programs that show you various ways to use server-side scripting to integrate XML data into your Web pages.

Using the MSXML Parser in a Script

An ASP script running on the server can create an instance of the MSXML Parser, then load an XML file into the parser, extract data from the XML file, and generate HTML to be returned to the user. This is a very powerful technique that permits "live" data to be displayed, meaning that the user always sees the latest information. The assumption in this technique is that the XML data file is maintained on the server and is updated as needed with new data. How the XML file is updated is not a concern for this project.

The aim of this project is to demonstrate a "search" function that permits the user to search the XML data for specific information. The XML data consists of a list of books, with each book categorized as biography, fiction, or reference. The category information is kept in an attribute, while the remaining book information is kept in child elements. Listing 18.5 shows the XML data file.

Listing 18.5 XML Data File for the Server-Side Search Project

```
<?xml version="1.0"?>
<books>
<book category="reference">
  <title>The Cambridge Biographical Encyclopedia</title>
  <author>David Crystal</author>
  <publisher>Cambridge University Press</publisher>
</book>
<book category="fiction">
  <title>Travels with Charley</title>
  <author>John Steinbeck</author>
  <publisher>Putnam</publisher>
</book>
<book category="biography">
  <title>Darwin</title>
  <author>Adrian Desmond, James Moore</author>
  <publisher>Warner Books</publisher>
</book>
<book category="fiction">
  <title>Crime and Punishment</title>
  <author>Fyodor Dostoyevsky</author>
  <publisher>Oxford</publisher>
</book>
<book category="reference">
  <title>Bartlett's Familiar Quotations</title>
  <author>John Bartlett</author>
```

```
  <publisher>Little, Brown</publisher>
</book>
<book category="fiction">
  <title>Death in Venice</title>
  <author>Thomas Mann</author>
  <publisher>Norton</publisher>
</book>
<book category="fiction">
  <title>Under the Volcano</title>
  <author>Malcolm Lowry</author>
  <publisher>Plume</publisher>
</book>
<book category="biography">
  <title>Thomas Jefferson: A Life</title>
  <author>Willard Sterne Randall</author>
  <publisher>Henry Holt</publisher>
</book>
</books>
```

The project is designed so that the user enters his or her search criteria on an HTML page. This page uses a `<form>` element containing one `<select>` element to permit the user to select a category of book to search for. The form uses the `GET` method to submit the search request to the server. The HTML document code is presented in Listing 18.6, and the page is shown in Figure 18.4.

Listing 18.6 HTML Document for Submitting a Search Request

```
<html>
<head>
<title>Book search</title>
</head>
<body>
<h2>Find books by category.</h2>
<hr/>
<form method="GET" action="list1807.asp">
<p>Select your category, then press Submit.</p>
<p>Category:
<select name="category" size="1">
  <option value="biography">Biography</option>
  <option value="fiction">Fiction</option>
  <option value="reference">Reference</option>
<select>
```

```
</p>
<p><input type="submit" value="Submit"/>
</p><hr/>
</form>
</body>
</html>
```

When the user selects a book category and then clicks Submit, the search request is submitted to the server-side script that is shown in Listing 18.7. The script performs the following tasks:

1. It retrieves the search category from the `Request.QueryString` collection.
2. It verifies that the requested category is one of the three permitted values.

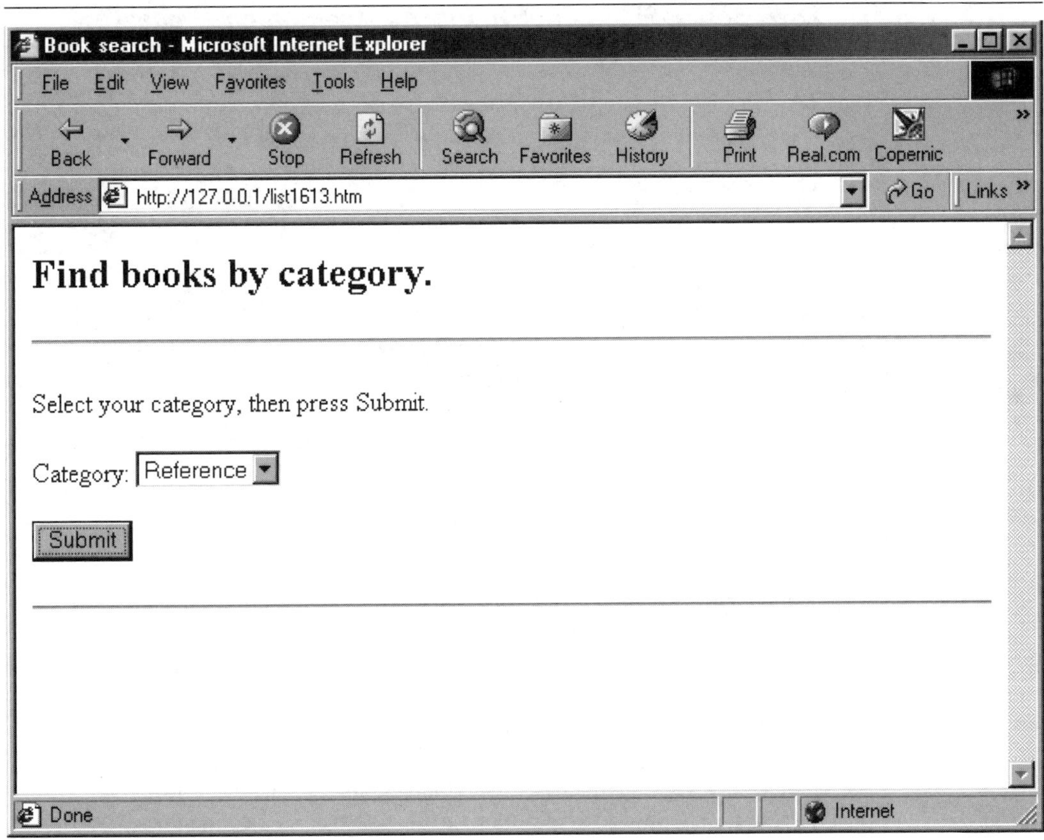

Figure 18.4 The user selects a search criterion on this page.

3. It creates an instance of the parser using the `Server` object's `CreateObject` method (provided by the Web server as part of ASP).
4. It loads the XML file into the parser, using the `Server.MapPath` method to obtain a path to the file.
5. It outputs the elements to define the start of an HTML table and the table heading.
6. It creates a node list containing all the `<book>` elements in the file.
7. For each `<book>` element, it checks to see if it matches the requested category. If so, the element's data is output to the HTML table.
8. It completes the table.
9. It displays a link back to the search page.

The result of a search as displayed by this script is shown in Figure 18.5.

Listing 18.7 Server-Side Script to Process the Search Request

```
<%@ LANGUAGE="VBScript" %>
<HTML>
<BODY>
<h2>Search results</h2>
<hr/>
<%
' Get the category submitted.
category = Request.QueryString("category")
 ' Make sure it is valid. While the HTML page cannot send an
' invalid category, it is possible that this script will be
' accessed from another source.
if category <> "biography" and category <> "fiction" and _
     category <> "reference" then
  Response.Write "<hr/>Invalid category.<hr/>"
else
  ' Create the parser.
  set parser = Server.CreateObject("MSXML2.DOMDocument")

  ' Load the XML file.
  parser.async=false
  parser.load(Server.MapPath("list1805.xml"))

  ' At this point we could check for parser errors using the
  ' following code, but we will assume that this is not necessary.
  'if parser.parseError.errorCode <> 0 Then
```

```
  '  s = "Error on line " & parser.parseError.Line & vbCrLf
  '  s = s & parser.parseError.srcText & vbCrLf
  '  s = s & Space(parser.parseError.linepos)
  '  s = s & " -- " & parser.parseError.reason
  '  Response.Write s
  'end if


  Response.Write "<p>Books in the '" & category & "' category:</p>"
  ' Start the table.
  Response.Write "<table cellpadding=4>"
  Response.Write "<thead>"
  Response.Write "<td><b>Author</b></td>"
  Response.Write "<td><b>Title</b></td>"
  Response.Write "<td><b>Publisher</b></td>"
  Response.Write "</tr></thead>"
  ' Get a node list containing all the <book> elements.
  set nl = parser.selectNodes("//book")
  ' Loop through the list.
  for i = 0 to nl.length - 1
    ' Get the category attribute. We know that it is
    ' the first (and only) attribute of the <book> element.
    cat = nl.item(i).attributes.item(0).text
    ' Is this the requested category? If so, output the data.
    if cat = category then
      Response.Write "<tr><td>"
      Response.Write nl.item(i).selectSingleNode("author").text
      Response.Write "</td><td>"
      Response.Write nl.item(i).selectSingleNode("title").text
      Response.Write "</td><td>"
      Response.Write nl.item(i).selectSingleNode("publisher").text
      Response.Write "</td></tr>""
    end if
  next
  ' End the table.
  Response.Write "</table>"
end if
%>
<hr/>
<a href="list1813.htm">New search</a>


</BODY>
</HTML>
```

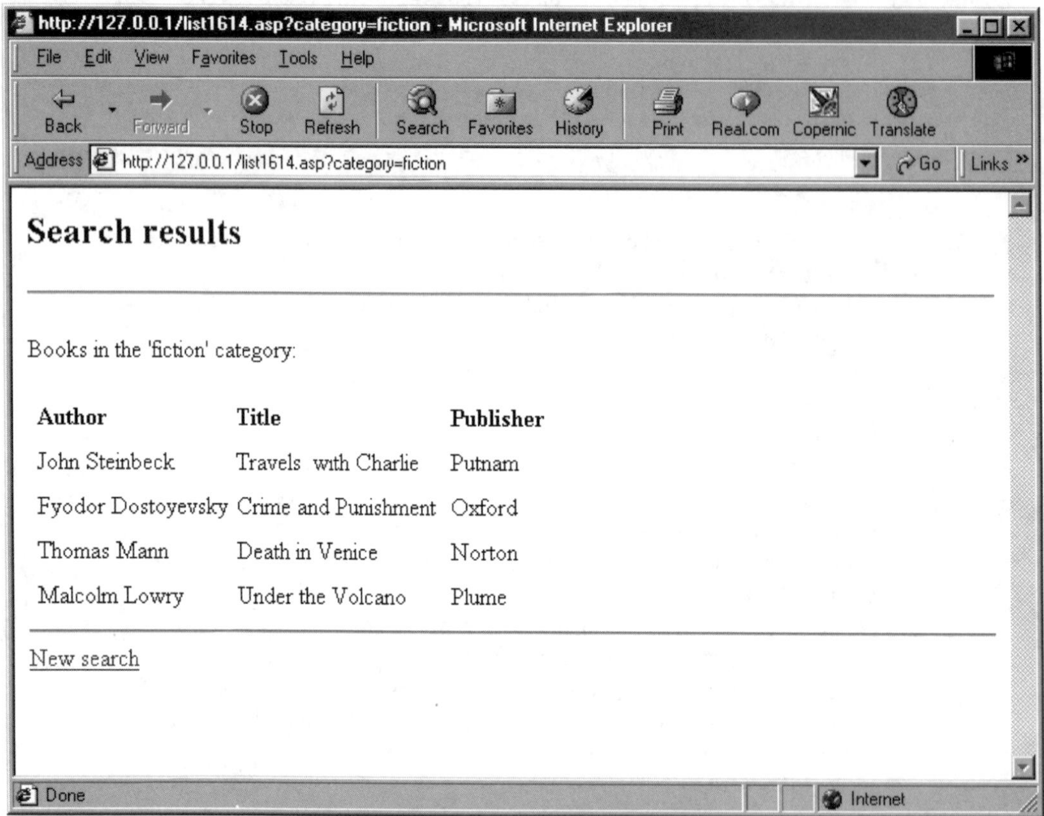

Figure 18.5 The search results displayed by Listing 18.7

Using Server-Side Transformations

The XSLT language is a powerful tool for transforming XML documents. By applying a style sheet to an XML document, you can create output to meet just about any need. Perhaps the most popular use of XSLT is to transform XML into HTML for display in a browser—you saw some examples of this in Chapter 7. Using the MSXSL.EXE command-line utility (also covered in Chapter 7), you can apply an XSL style sheet to an XML document to create an HTML document, and then place the HTML document on your Web server. While this technique works well in some situations, its shortcoming is that the HTML document is static—it is not updated automatically if the XML data changes. To ensure that the HTML document reflects the latest data, you want the transform to be applied automatically each time the page is accessed. Server-side scripting makes this possible.

When an XML document that contains a reference to an XSL style sheet is loaded into the MSXML Parser, the style sheet is not applied automatically. While this may seem like a design flaw, it actually increases flexibility by letting you apply any style sheet to the XML document, not just the one it references. In order to apply a style sheet to an XML document, you must load both documents and then call the parser's `transformNode()` method. The return value of this method is the result of the transformation.

The first example in this section shows how to generate an HTML page "live" based on an XSLT transform. The XML data that the example uses is the file containing book data that was presented earlier in the chapter in Listing 18.5. The objective is to display all of the book data in tabular format sorted by title. The XSL style sheet that performs the transformation is shown in Listing 18.8. If you are not clear as to how this style sheet works, please refer to Chapter 7 for the details on XSTL transforms.

The ASP page that performs the transform is surprisingly simple, as shown in Listing 18.9. All it needs to do is create two instances of the parser and load the XML document into one and the XSL style sheet into the other. Then, calling the `transformNode()` method and outputting the result is all that's required. The results of the transformation are shown in Figure 18.6.

Listing 18.8 XSL Style Sheet to Transform the Book Data into HTML

```
<?xml version="1.0"?>
<xsl:stylesheet xmlns:xsl="http://www.w3.org/1999/XSL/Transform"
version="1.0">
<xsl:template match="/">
  <html><body>
  <h2>The Complete Book List</h2>
  <table border="2" cellpadding="4">
  <thead><tr>
  <th>Title</th>
  <th>Author</th>
  <th>Publisher</th></tr></thead>
  <xsl:apply-templates select="/books/book">
    <xsl:sort select="title"/>
  </xsl:apply-templates>
  </table>
  </body></html>
</xsl:template>

<xsl:template match="book">
<tr>
```

```
    <xsl:apply-templates/>
</tr>
</xsl:template>

<xsl:template match="title | author | publisher">
<td>
    <xsl:value-of select='.'/>
</td>
</xsl:template>
</xsl:stylesheet>
```

Listing 18.9 The ASP Page to Display "Live" Book Data

```
<%@ LANGUAGE="VBScript" %>
<%
' Create the 2 parser objects.
set parserXML = Server.CreateObject("MSXML2.DOMDocument")
set parserXSL = Server.CreateObject("MSXML2.DOMDocument")
' Load the XML file.
parserXML.async=false
parserXML.load(Server.MapPath("list1805.xml"))

' Load the XSL file.
parserXSL.async=false
parserXSL.load(Server.MapPath("list1808.xsl"))

' Generate and output the transform.
Response.Write parserXML.transformNode(parserXSL)
%>
```

The use of "live" transforms demonstrated in Listing 18.9 is useful in many situations. Note that the page viewed by the user reflects not only changes to the XML data file, but also changes to the XSL style sheet.

With the flexibility of ASP, even more elaborate scenarios are possible. For example, in addition to providing live data, you could offer the user a choice of formatting options. The user could choose to have the data displayed in tabular format or as a list. Based on the user's choice, the script would apply the appropriate XSL style sheet to the XML data.

This is the approach taken in this chapter's final example program. This demonstration builds on the previous example in this section. It uses the same XML data file (Listing 18.5) and the XSL style sheet for presenting the data in tabular format (Listing 18.8). It adds a second style sheet, presented in Listing

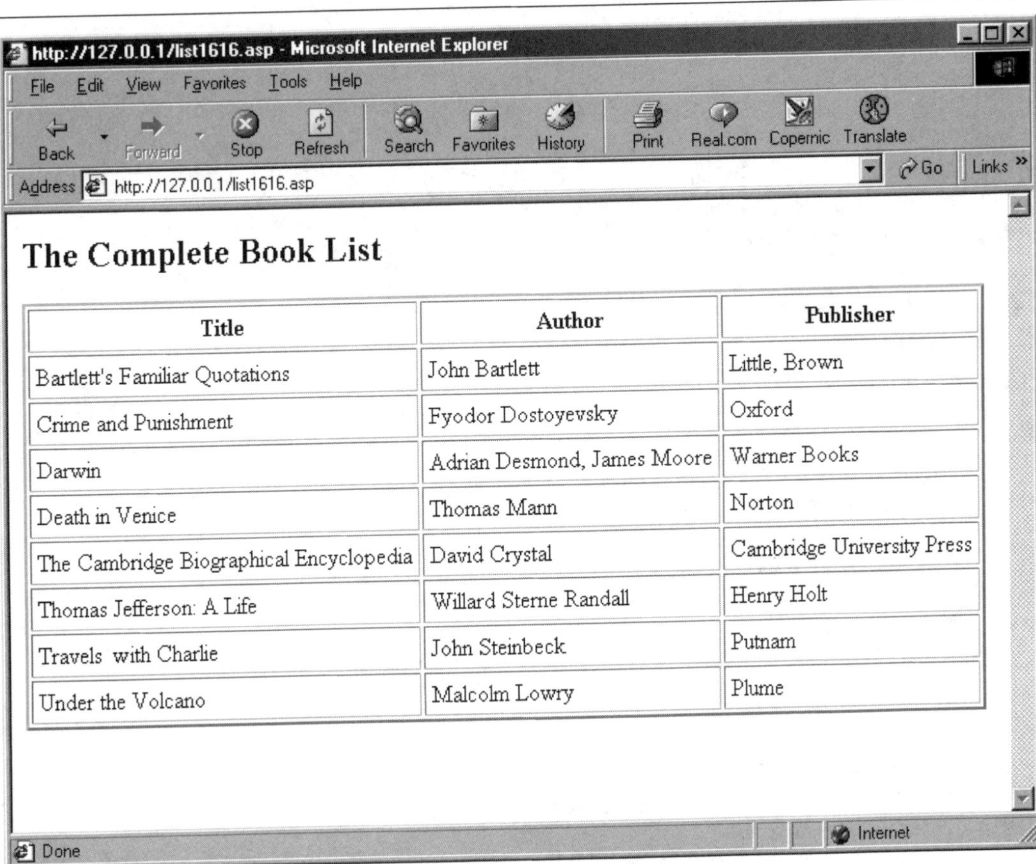

The Complete Book List

Title	Author	Publisher
Bartlett's Familiar Quotations	John Bartlett	Little, Brown
Crime and Punishment	Fyodor Dostoyevsky	Oxford
Darwin	Adrian Desmond, James Moore	Warner Books
Death in Venice	Thomas Mann	Norton
The Cambridge Biographical Encyclopedia	David Crystal	Cambridge University Press
Thomas Jefferson: A Life	Willard Sterne Randall	Henry Holt
Travels with Charlie	John Steinbeck	Putnam
Under the Volcano	Malcolm Lowry	Plume

Figure 18.6 Displaying the results of a server-side transformation

18.10, that transforms the XML data to display in a list format rather than in a table. The user first navigates to an HTML document (Listing 18.11 and Figure 18.7) and selects the desired formatting. When the request is submitted, the ASP script (Listing 18.12) performs the transformation using the appropriate style sheet and returns the result to the client. The data displayed in list format is shown in Figure 18.8.

Listing 18.10 XSL Style Sheet to Display the Book Data in List Format

```
<?xml version="1.0"?>
<xsl:stylesheet xmlns:xsl="http://www.w3.org/1999/XSL/Transform"
version="1.0">
```

```
<xsl:template match="/">
  <html><body>
  <h2>The Complete Book List</h2><hr/>
  <xsl:apply-templates select="/books/book">
    <xsl:sort select="title"/>
  </xsl:apply-templates>
  <hr/></body></html>
</xsl:template>

<xsl:template match="book">
<p>
   <xsl:apply-templates/>
</p>
</xsl:template>

<xsl:template match="author">
Author:
   <xsl:value-of select='.'/>
<br/>
</xsl:template>

<xsl:template match="title">
Title:
   <xsl:value-of select='.'/>
<br/>
</xsl:template>

<xsl:template match="publisher">
Publisher:
   <xsl:value-of select='.'/>
<br/>
</xsl:template>

</xsl:stylesheet>
```

Listing 18.11 HTML File to Permit the User to Display the Book List in Different Formats

```
<html>
<head>
<title>Selecting a display format.</title>
</head>
<body>
```

```
<h2>The book list:</h2>
<form action="list1812.asp" method="GET">
<p>Please select a display format:
<input type="radio" name="format" value="table">Table format
<input type="radio" name="format" checked="yes" value="list">List format
<p>
<input type="submit" value="Display" />
<form>
<hr/>
</body>
</html>
```

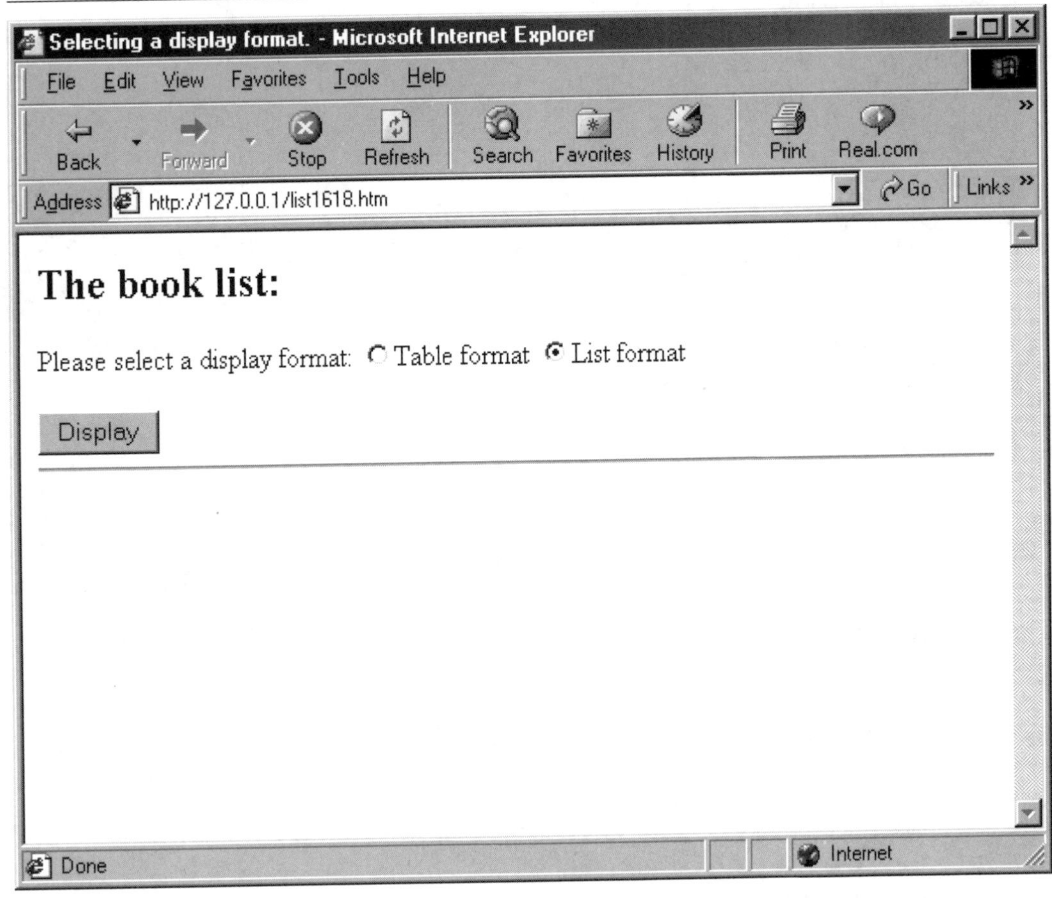

Figure 18.7 The HTML document that lets the user select a display format

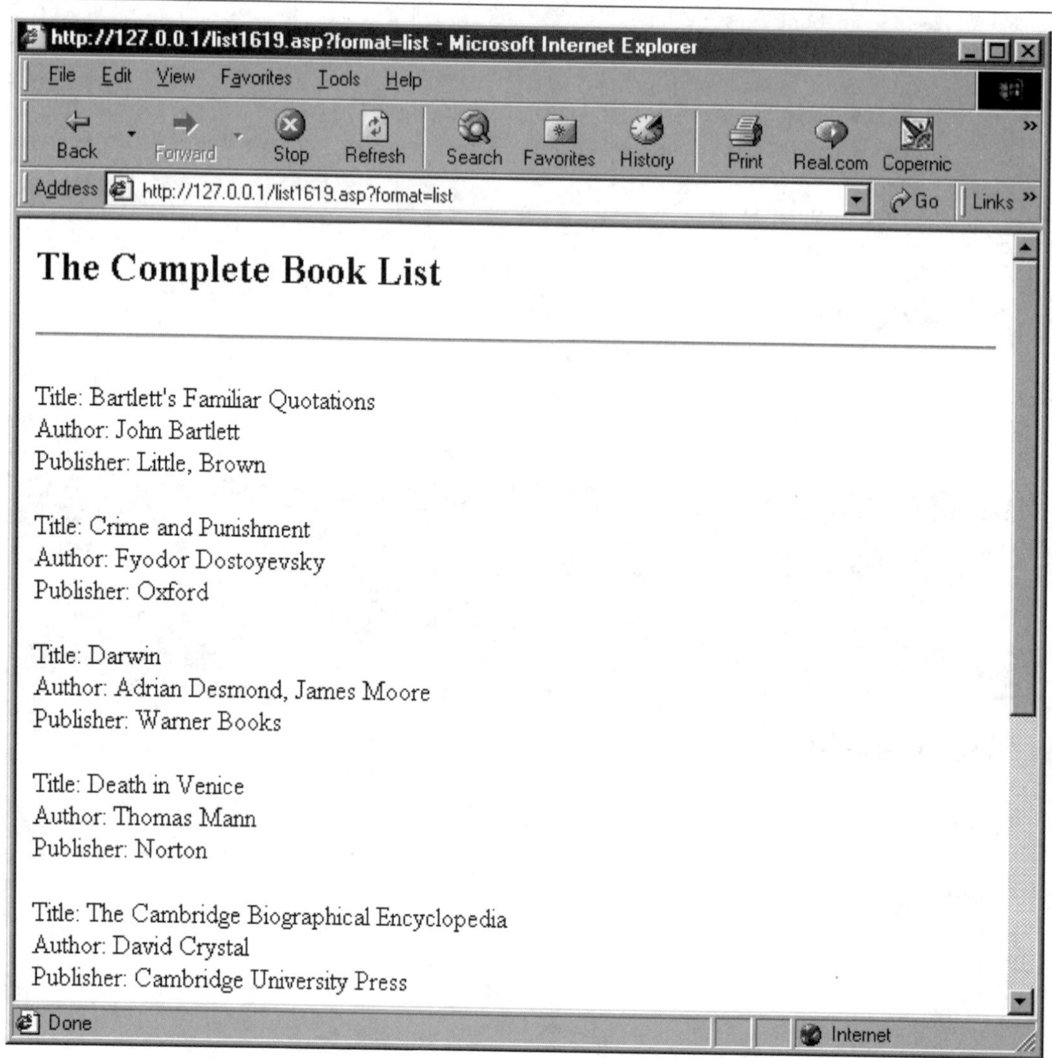

Figure 18.8 The XML data displayed in list format

Listing 18.12 ASP File Called by the HTML Document in Listing 18.11

```
<%@ LANGUAGE="VBScript" %>
<%
' Create the 2 parser objects.
set parserXML = Server.CreateObject("MSXML2.DOMDocument")
set parserXSL = Server.CreateObject("MSXML2.DOMDocument")
```

```
' Load the XML file.
parserXML.async=false
parserXML.load(Server.MapPath("list1805.xml"))

' Get the user's choice of formats.
format=Request.QueryString("format")

' Load the XSL file based on the user's choice.
parserXSL.async=false
if format="list" then
    parserXSL.load(Server.MapPath("list1810.xsl"))
else
    parserXSL.load(Server.MapPath("list1808.xsl"))
end if

' Generate and output the transform.
Response.Write parserXML.transformNode(parserXSL)
%>
```

Summary

An Active Server Pages script is located at, and executed on, the server. A user navigates to an ASP page in the usual manner. Then, the script page is loaded by the server, the script is executed, and the output of the script is returned to the user for viewing in his or her browser. Script code can use the MSXML Parser to access and process XML data located on the server. The combination of ASP and XML provides a powerful and flexible means for providing live, customizable views of data.

CHAPTER 19

The BizTalk Framework

The BizTalk framework is an initiative started by Microsoft in collaboration with some other companies. Its name, short for "business talk," describes its main purpose: to provide a framework for electronic communication between businesses. The BizTalk framework is XML based, and as such it is one of many attempts to define XML vocabularies for different purposes. Because BizTalk is a Microsoft initiative, and because it has been gaining acceptance in the business world, it merits a chapter in a book on Microsoft's XML technologies.

BizTalk Background

The power and flexibility of XML are undisputed but are not themselves sufficient to ensure reliable, secure communication between businesses. There is no doubt that XML can be used to describe essentially any business document, such as a purchase order. Hire any competent XML developer and in short order he or she will create a purchase order schema that defines tags for purchase order number, date, ship to address, and all the other pieces of information that make up a purchase order.

At the same time, all over the world, a thousand other companies are also developing XML-based purchase orders. The schemas that they develop will likely contain most or all of the same information as your purchase order schema, but will surely be different in some of the details, such as tag names or default values. Clearly, it will be very difficult to share such documents between companies. A firm that wanted to use electronic processing for incoming purchase orders would have to deal with hundreds of different schemas. Things would be a lot simpler if everyone used the same purchase order schema. While getting every company in the world to agree on one purchase order format is certainly an impossible task, standardization on a smaller scale, such as across all branches of a large company, is a lot more realistic.

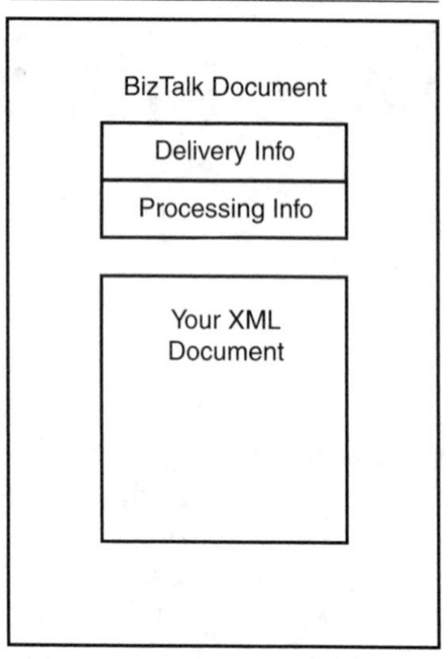

Figure 19.1 BizTalk provides a wrapper for your XML document.

The goal of the BizTalk framework is to make this possible. BizTalk provides a set of rules and guidelines for using XML to encode business data (or any other kind of data for that matter). BizTalk places essentially no restrictions on how your data is structured, but it does provide rules as to how the overall BizTalk document must be structured. Put another way, BizTalk provides a wrapper to enclose your XML document, permitting it to be processed by BizTalk-compliant software. The BizTalk wrapper contains information about how the document should be delivered and processed. This is illustrated in Figure 19.1.

The delivery and processing information in the document are contained in BizTalk-specific tags, called *BizTags*. At the center of BizTalk is this document specification, which will be covered in more detail later in the chapter. The other parts to the picture are as follows:

- A BizTalk server: A BizTalk server is software that reads BizTalk documents and processes them. What exactly that processing consists of will depend on the specific document, but common functionality will likely include the ability to forward a document to a different destination if needed and to send a receipt indicating that a document has been received. A BizTalk server can be created for any platform, and in many cases it will need to integrate with corporate back-end systems. Some companies will write their own in-house servers, while others will reply on commercially available products.

- Microsoft BizTalk Server 2000: This product is Microsoft's entry in the BizTalk server market. It runs only on Windows 2000 Server, and in addition to reading and writing BizTalk documents it provides a sophisticated business-to-business (B2B) environment for communication using XML. You can find more information at `http://www.microsoft.com/biztalk/`.
- BizTalk.org: This Web site (`http://www.biztalk.org/`) serves as a central clearinghouse for BizTalk-related information. There is a library of downloadable user-submitted schemas for various purposes, a community of BizTalk discussion groups, and the latest news and information.

BizTalk Standards

As of this writing, the current version of BizTalk is 2.0. The BizTalk "standard" is what Microsoft says it is. In and of itself this is no problem, but it is also the case that because BizTalk relies so heavily on XML, the question of XML standards comes into play. Specifically, which of the XML-related recommendations of W3C does BizTalk follow?

In this area, BizTalk becomes somewhat problematic. There is no blame to assign, in my opinion, because some of the XML technologies that BizTalk uses had not reached recommendation status at the time BizTalk was being developed. Microsoft decided to go ahead with BizTalk even though some of the relevant XML technology was still in flux. Most important is the fact that BizTalk was developed using an early and Microsoft-specific version of XML Schema known as XML Data Reduced, or XDR (see Chapter 4). In other words, the schemas that define BizTalk vocabularies are created using XDR. XDR is supported only by the Microsoft MSXML Parser.

Since BizTalk was developed, the W3C process on XML Schemas has progressed quite a bit. XML Schemas Part 1 (Structures) and Part 2 (Data Types) achieved Recommendation status in May 2001. As of this writing, however, BizTalk has not moved to embrace these recommendations, although it is promised that this change will be made eventually. It is also promised that the current XDR implementation will be supported for some period, and that software tools will be provided to assist with the transition from XDR to XML Schema. The fact remains that, for the present, you are tied to Microsoft tools if you want to use BizTalk.

The BizTalk Document

A BizTalk document is transported inside a Simple Object Access Protocol (SOAP) wrapper. SOAP is covered in Chapter 12, and you can return there for review if needed. A SOAP message has two parts: a header and a body. They relate to the BizTalk document content as follows:

- The SOAP header contains BizTalk-specific elements (BizTags) that provide information about the delivery and handling of the document. The semantics, namespaces, and schema for these tags are defined in the BizTalk specification.
- The SOAP body contains one or more business documents, such as an invoice or purchase order. The elements and namespace of the business documents are defined by the specific application and not by BizTalk.

Listing 19.1 shows an example of a simple BizTalk document. Most of the elements of this document will not be clear to you until you read the remainder of this chapter, but it may be helpful for you to see a complete, if simple, document.

Listing 19.1: A Simple BizTalk Document

```
<SOAP-ENV:Envelope
      xmlns:SOAP-ENV="http://schemas.xmlsoap.org/soap/envelope/"
      xmlns:xsi="http://www.w3.org/1999/XMLSchema-instance">
  <SOAP-ENV:Header>
     <eps:endpoints SOAP-ENV:mustUnderstand="1"
           xmlns:eps="http://schemas.biztalk.org/btf-2-0/endpoints"
           xmlns:agr="http://www.trading-agreements.org/types/">
        <eps:to>
            <eps:address xsi:type="agr:department">
               Accounts Payable
            </eps:address>
        </eps:to>
        <eps:from>
            <eps:address xsi:type="agr:organization">
              Acme Corp.
            </eps:address>
        </eps:from>
     </eps:endpoints>
     <prop:properties SOAP-ENV:mustUnderstand="1"
           xmlns:prop="http://schemas.biztalk.org/btf-2-0/properties">
```

```
            <prop:identity>
                uuid:44c9g5n7-56hu-1z55-x12g-4bp56709d1p9
            </prop:identity>
            <prop:sentAt>2001-06-12T14:30:00+07:00</prop:sentAt>
            <prop:expiresAt>2001-06-15T12:00:00+05:00</prop:expiresAt>
            <prop:topic>http://whatever.org/invoice/</prop:topic>
        </prop:properties>
    </SOAP-ENV:Header>
    <SOAP-ENV:Body>
            <inv:invoice xmlns:po="http://whatever.org/invoice/">
                <inv:amount>199.50</inv:amount>
            </inv:invoice>
        </SOAP-ENV:Body>
</SOAP-ENV:Envelope>
```

The Document Header

The header of a BizTalk document—the part the goes in the SOAP header—contains two required and two optional elements that provide information about the document. These BizTags are described in this section.

Document Delivery

Information about the document delivery is contained in the required `<endpoint>` tag. As you might expect, proper understanding of the information in this section is essential, so the tag is marked with the `SOAP-ENV:mustUnderstand="1"` attribute (this attribute is explained in the chapter on SOAP). Within the `<endpoint>` tag are one optional and two required child elements, as follows:

- `<to>` element: Required. Holds information about the document recipient.
- `<from>` element: Required. Holds information about the document sender.
- `<reliability>` element: Optional. Contains information required to send a receipt for the document.

The `<to>` and `<from>` elements each hold exactly one `<address>` element. The data in this element identifies a business entity. The `<address>` element has the required `xsi:type` attribute, whose value identifies the category of the address information. The `<to>` and `<from>` elements from the sample BizTalk document are reproduced here:

```
<eps:endpoints SOAP-ENV:mustUnderstand="1"
      xmlns:eps="http://schemas.biztalk.org/btf-2-0/endpoints"
      xmlns:agr="http://www.trading-agreements.org/types/">
   <eps:to>
      <eps:address xsi:type="agr:department">
         Accounts Payable
      </eps:address>
   </eps:to>
   <eps:from>
      <eps:address xsi:type="agr:organization">
         Acme Corp.
      </eps:address>
   </eps:from>
</eps:endpoints>
```

The `<reliability>` element is optional. When present, it contains two child elements. The `<sendReceiptTo>` element contains a URL specifying where the receipt should be sent. The `<receiptRequiredBy>` element contains a time instant (as a `dateTime` value) specifying the time by which the receipt must be received. The following is an example `<reliability>` element:

```
<eps:reliability>
   <eps:sendReceiptTo>
      www.acme.com/bt/receipts
   </eps:sendReceiptTo>
   <eps:receiptRequiredBy>
      2001-06-05T15:45:00-5:00
   </eps:receiptRequiredBy>
</eps:reliability>
```

DateTime Values

The `dateTime` *data type is one of the types of data that are defined in the XML Schema Part 2 Recommendation (*`http://www.w3.org/TR/xmlschema-2/`*). This format identifies a time and date in three parts, as follows:*

- *A date in the format yyyy-mm-dd, such as 2001-06-21.*
- *The letter* T *followed by the 24-hour time in the format hh:mm:ss. For example, 13:35:00 for 1:35 PM.*

> - *The relationship of the time to Coordinated Universal Time (UTC). This can be the letter Z if the time is UTC or the difference between the time and UCT expressed as a plus (+) or minus (-) sign followed by hh:mm.*
>
> *For example, Eastern Standard Time is 5 hours behind (earlier than) UTC. To represent 3:45 PM in that time zone on June 5, 2001, you would write 2001-06-05T15:45:00-5:00.*

Document Properties

Information about the document, including its identity, is contained in the required `<properties>` element. As with the `<endpoints>` element, the `<properties>` element is marked with the `SOAP-ENV:mustUnderstand="1"` attribute. This element contains four child elements, all of which are required.

- `<identity>`: A `uriReference` that uniquely identifies the document. This reference must be universally unique, and it may be a Universally Unique Identifier (UUID) as in the previous example, or it may be generated with a cryptographic hash algorithm. The details of generating the unique identifier are implementation-specific.
- `<sentAt>`: A `dateTime` value specifying when the document was sent.
- `<expiresAt>`: A `dateTime` value specifying when the document expires. The recipient of the document must not process the document after this time.
- `<topic>`: A `uriReference` that uniquely identifies the nature of the BizTalk document. The details of identifying the topic are implementation-specific.

The `<properties>` element from the previous example is reproduced here for you to examine:

```
<prop:properties SOAP-ENV:mustUnderstand="1"
    xmlns:prop="http://schemas.biztalk.org/btf-2-0/properties">
  <prop:identity>
     uuid:44c9g5n7-56hu-1z55-x12g-4bp56709d1p9
  </prop:identity>
  <prop:sentAt>2001-06-12T14:30:00+07:00</prop:sentAt>
  <prop:expiresAt>2001-06-15T12:00:00+05:00</prop:expiresAt>
  <prop:topic>http://whatever.org/invoice/</prop:topic>
</prop:properties>
```

Document Manifest

The optional <manifest> element provides a manifest, or catalog, of the business documents that are contained in the body of the BizTalk document. It can also reference attachments—files such as binary data that accompany the BizTalk document but are not contained in it. If present, the manifest must reference all of the business documents and attachments associated with the BizTalk document.

A manifest is useful primarily when a single BizTalk document contains more than one business document. The <manifest> element can contain one or more <reference> child elements, one for each document or attachment being catalogued. Each <reference> element must contain a <description> child element that contains a text description (optionally containing XML markup) of the referenced document and a uri attribute that is a URI resolving to the references document. This URI can take several forms, including the following:

- A URL that resolves to a resource containing the document (for example, a binary file containing an image).
- A Content-ID URL identifying an attachment carried as a MIME part in the message.
- A fragment identifier in the form #id that resolves to an ID attribute of the referenced document that is part of the message.

The following example of a <manifest> element demonstrates these three forms of the uri attribute:

```
<fst:manifest xmlns:fst="http://schemas.biztalk.org/btf-2-0/manifest">
    <fst:reference fst:uri="http://www.mysite.com/widget.jpg">
        <fst:description>Picture of a widget</fst:description>
    </fst:reference>
    <fst:reference fst:uri="#purchase_order">
        <fst:description>Purchase order</fst:description>
    </fst:reference>
    <fst:reference fst:uri="CID:specs@mysite.com">
        <fst:description>Specs of widget</fst:description>
    </fst:reference>
</fst:manifest>
```

Document Processing

The optional <process> element contains process management information. This element contains one optional and two required child elements:

- <type>: Required. A URI reference that identifies the type of business process involved, such as paying an invoice.
- <instance>: Required. A URI reference that identifies a specific instance of the business process. This URI is often constructed as an extension of the <type> URI, by adding a sequence number, for example.
- <handle>: Optional. A URI reference that provides additional application-specific information.

The following shows an example of a <process> element:

```
<prc:process SOAP-END:mustUnderstand="1"
    xmlns:SOAP-ENV="http://schemas.xmlsoap.org/soap/envelope"
    xmlns:prc="http://schemas.biztalk.org/btf-2-0/process">
  <prc:type>accounts_payable:invoice</prc:type>
  <prc:instance>accounts_payable:invoice#09123</prc:instance>
</prc:process>
```

The Document Body

The business documents that are part of a BizTalk document are carried in the body of the SOAP message. The details of these documents will depend on the specific application. It is not uncommon for multiple business documents to be part of one BizTalk document. Sometimes the information that you might normally think of as being contained in one document is broken up among several documents. For example, when a purchase is being made, the shipping information may be in a separate document from the order information. However, these related documents may share content. Where can this shared content be placed?

By default, every element that is an immediate child of the <SOAP-ENV:Body> element is considered to be a separate business document. You can include an element that is not a document, but rather contains shared information, by using the SOAP-ENC:root attribute with a value of 0. This is illustrated in Listing 19.2, where this technique is used to include some shared information in the <body> element. Note that the business documents reference the shared information using standard XML ID attributes and relative URIs.

Listing 19.2 Including Shared Information in the SOAP <body> Element

```
<SOAP-ENV:Envelope
      xmlns:SOAP-ENV="http://schemas.xmlsoap.org/soap/envelope/"
```

```
        xmlns:SOAP-ENC="http://schemas.xmlsoap.org/soap/encoding/"
        xmlns:xsi="http://www.w3.org/1999/XMLSchema-instance">
<SOAP-ENV:Header>
  <!-- headers here -->
</SOAP-ENV:Header>
<SOAP-ENV:Body>

  <po:purchaseOrder xmlns:po="http://whatever.org/purchaseorder/">
    <po:item href="#item1"/>
    <po:item href="#item2"/>
    <!-- other information -->
  </po:purchaseOrder>

  <shp:shippingInfo xmlns:shp="http://whatever.org/shippinginfo/">
    <shp:item href="#item1"/>
    <shp:item href="#item2"/>
    <shp:address>
      Acme Corporation
      123 Main Street
      New York, NY 10001
    </shp:address>
  </shp:shippingInfo>

  <item xmlns:itm="http://whatever.org/items/" ID="item1"
             SOAP-ENC:Root="0">
    <itm:name>Left handed widget</itm:name>
    <itm:partno>QZ998</itm:partno>
  </item>

  <item xmlns:itm="http://whatever.org/items/" ID="item2"
             SOAP-ENC:Root="0">
    <itm:name>Electric banana</itm:name>
    <itm:partno>WA2111</itm:partno>
  </item>

</SOAP-ENV:Body>
</SOAP-ENV:Envelope>
```

Summary

BizTalk is an XML-based framework for electronic communication between businesses and other organizations. It is a strictly Microsoft initiative, and it relies on some proprietary XML technology. Even so, BizTalk has been gaining acceptance in the business world and may continue to increase in importance.

CHAPTER 20

Microsoft Office and XML

Office XP is the latest version of Microsoft's suite of business productivity applications. It includes programs for word processing, spreadsheets, databases, presentations, e-mail, and more. Office also provides a full-featured programming language, Visual Basic for Applications (VBA), that can be combined with the Office object model to create sophisticated business applications. XML is not a large player in Office, primarily because each application has its own specialized file formats. Because of the increasing importance of XML, however, several of the Office applications include XML-related capabilities that can be used to work with XML within Office. In addition, the VBA language enables developers to create custom XML solutions in Office. This chapter covers both of these topics.

Programming in VBA

Visual Basic for Applications (VBA) is a full-featured programming language that is an integral part of the Office suite. In any Office application, you can open the VBA Editor by pressing Alt-F11 or by selecting Macros from the Tools menu then selecting Visual Basic Editor. In terms of its syntax, VBA is essentially identical to Microsoft's stand-alone Visual Basic language (version 6.0). Much of what was presented about using Visual Basic to work with XML in Chapter 15 can be applied to programming in Office as well.

When you are programming in Office, you also have the full Office object model at your disposal. Each Office application exposes a hierarchy of objects that represents the data the program works with and the tasks it can perform. For example, a document in Word is represented by the `Document` object. Parts of a document, such as paragraphs and sentences, are represented by objects as well. A treatment of the Office object model is well beyond the scope of this book, but you can find more information in the Office online Help material.

To use the MSXML Parser in a VBA program, you must add a reference to "MSXML v4.0" to your project. You do this by selecting References from the VBA Editor's Tools menu, then selecting from the list of available references in the dialog box. Then you must create an instance of the parser using the same techniques covered in Chapter 15. To review briefly, this consists of declaring a variable of the proper type and then instantiating the parser, as shown in this code fragment:

```
Dim xmlDoc As MSXML2.DOMDocument
Set xmlDoc = New DOMDocument
```

Once you have done this, all the tools of the MSXML Parser will be available to your VBA code. The VBA procedure in Listing 20.2 presents a simple example of how you might use the parser. This procedure, which is intended to be run in Word, loads an XML file (Listing 20.1), places the data in a new document, and then saves the document. The resulting document is shown in Figure 20.1.

I'll present some additional examples of VBA XML programming in this chapter.

Listing 20.1: XML File Used by the VBA Procedure in Listing 20.2

```
<?xml version="1.0" encoding="UTF-8"?>
<!-- Contact list - west office -->
<contacts>
  <contact>
    <name>Kenji Yamaguchi</name>
    <title>Manager of Production</title>
    <phone>234-567-8998</phone>
  </contact>
  <contact>
    <name>Juanita Fernandez</name>
    <title>VP for Public Relations</title>
    <phone>999-888-7654</phone>
  </contact>
  <contact>
    <name>William Smathers</name>
    <title>Head Counsel</title>
    <phone>555-444-3333</phone>
  </contact>
```

```
  <contact>
    <name>Marcia Fayuk</name>
    <title>VP of Accounting</title>
    <phone>123-456-7890</phone>
  </contact>
  <contact>
    <name>David Feinstein</name>
    <title>VP, Quality Control</title>
    <phone>111-222-4444</phone>
  </contact>
</contacts>
```

Listing 20.2 VBA Procedure to Read XML Data into a Word Document

```
Public Sub LoadXML()

Dim xmlDoc As MSXML2.DOMDocument
Dim contacts As MSXML2.IXMLDOMNodeList
Dim idx As Integer
Dim newDoc As Document
Dim s As String

Set xmlDoc = New DOMDocument
xmlDoc.async = False

' Load the XML file.
xmlDoc.Load "c:\data\list2001.xml"
' Get a node list containing all "contact" elements.
Set contacts = xmlDoc.selectNodes("//contact")

' Create a new Word document.
Set newDoc = Documents.Add

' Loop through the contact elements.
For idx = 0 To contacts.Length - 1
    s = contacts.Item(idx).selectSingleNode("name").Text
    Selection.TypeText s & vbCrLf
    s = contacts.Item(idx).selectSingleNode("title").Text
    Selection.TypeText s & vbCrLf
    s = contacts.Item(idx).selectSingleNode("phone").Text
    Selection.TypeText s & vbCrLf & vbCrLf
Next
```

```
' Save the document.
newDoc.SaveAs "Contacts.doc"

End Sub
```

Excel

The Excel spreadsheet program provides excellent support for XML files, both for opening XML files in a spreadsheet and for saving spreadsheet data in XML format.

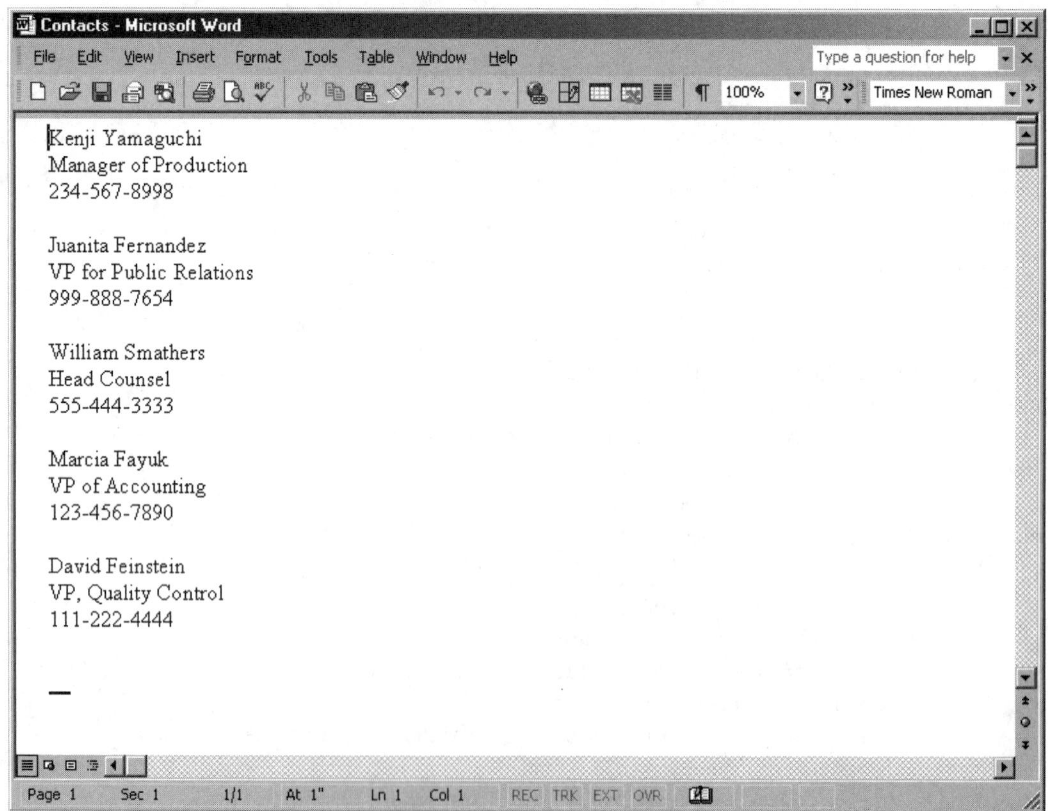

Figure 20.1 The Word document created by the VBA procedure in Listing 20.2

Opening XML Files in Excel

Support for opening XML files is built into Excel. When you display Excel's Open dialog box, you can select XML from the Files of Type list. When you select an XML file to open, what happens depends on whether the XML file references a style sheet.

If the XML file does not reference a style sheet, it is opened directly and placed in the Excel spreadsheet as follows:

- The first cell contains the name of the root element.
- Each child element and attribute gets its own column. The first cell in each column contains the element or attribute name, including the names of parent elements. Attribute names are preceded by the at sign (@).
- The remainder of each column contains the data for that element or attribute.

Figure 20.2 shows an example of the spreadsheet that results when the XML file in Listing 20.1 is opened in Excel.

	A	B	C
1	/contacts		
2	/contact/name	/contact/phone	/contact/title
3	Kenji Yamaguchi	234-567-8998	Manager of Production
4	Juanita Fernandez	999-888-7654	VP for Public Relations
5	William Smathers	555-444-3333	Head Counsel
6	Marcia Fayuk	123-456-7890	VP of Accounting
7	David Feinstein	111-222-4444	VP, Quality Control

Figure 20.2 The spreadsheet that results from opening the XML file in Listing 20.1

When the XML file references a style sheet, you have more options. You can elect to open the XML file without using the style sheet, in which case the XML file is read into the spreadsheet as described previously. If the XML file references a style sheet, you can also apply the style sheet when opening the file. If the XML file references more than one style sheet, you can select which style sheet to apply. Excel "understands" HTML, so if you have an XSL style sheet designed to render your XML data in HTML, it will display properly in Excel.

To illustrate, I use the XML data in Listing 20.3 and the style sheet in Listing 20.4. The style sheet formats the data in the XML file as an HTML table, and it also performs some summary calculations on the data and displays the results. When the XML file is opened in Excel with the style sheet applied, the result is as shown in Figure 20.3.

Listing 20.3 XML Data File That References a Style Sheet

```
<?xml version="1.0"?>
<?xml-stylesheet type="text/xsl" href="list2004.xsl"?>
<salesinfo>
<item numbersold="26">
  <name>Hammer</name>
  <sales>543.25</sales>
</item>
<item numbersold="12">
  <name>Wrench</name>
  <sales>901.15</sales>
</item>
<item numbersold="31">
  <name>Screwdriver</name>
  <sales>255.00</sales>
</item>
<item numbersold="6">
  <name>Chisel</name>
  <sales>99.95</sales>
</item>
</salesinfo>
```

Listing 20.4 XSL Style Sheet for the XML File in Listing 20.3

```
<?xml version="1.0"?>
<xsl:stylesheet xmlns:xsl="http://www.w3.org/1999/XSL/Transform"
version="1.0">

<xsl:variable name="items" select="/salesinfo/item"/>

<xsl:template match="/">

  <!-- Get the sum of all "sales" elements -->
  <xsl:variable name="totalsales"
    select="sum(/salesinfo/item/sales)"/>
  <!-- Get the sum of all "numbersold" attributes -->
  <xsl:variable name="numitemssold"
    select="sum(/salesinfo/item/@numbersold)"/>
  <!-- Get the average sale per item by dividing the total sales
  by the count of "item" elements -->
  <xsl:variable name="averagesale"
    select="$totalsales div count(/salesinfo/item)"/>

  <html><body>
  <h1>Sales Figures</h1>
  <table cellpadding="6" border="2">
  <tr>
  <td><b>Item</b></td>
  <td><b>Sales</b></td>
  <td><b>Number sold</b></td>
  </tr>

  <xsl:for-each select="$items">
    <tr>
    <td><xsl:value-of select="name"/></td>
    <td><xsl:value-of select="format-number(sales, '$#.00')"/></td>
    <td><xsl:value-of select="@numbersold"/></td>
    </tr>
  </xsl:for-each>

  </table>
  <p>Total sales =
  <xsl:value-of select="format-number($totalsales, '$#.00')"/>
  </p>
  <p>Number items sold =
  <xsl:value-of select="$numitemssold"/>
  </p>
```

```
  <p>Average sales =
  <xsl:value-of select="format-number($averagesale, '$#.00')"/>
  per item.</p>
  </body></html>
</xsl:template>

</xsl:stylesheet>
```

Saving XML Spreadsheets

Microsoft has defined an XML vocabulary for saving spreadsheet information. This vocabulary contains elements for not only the spreadsheet data, but also for all other worksheet information including the data; document properties, such as the author's name and company; workbook settings, such as the

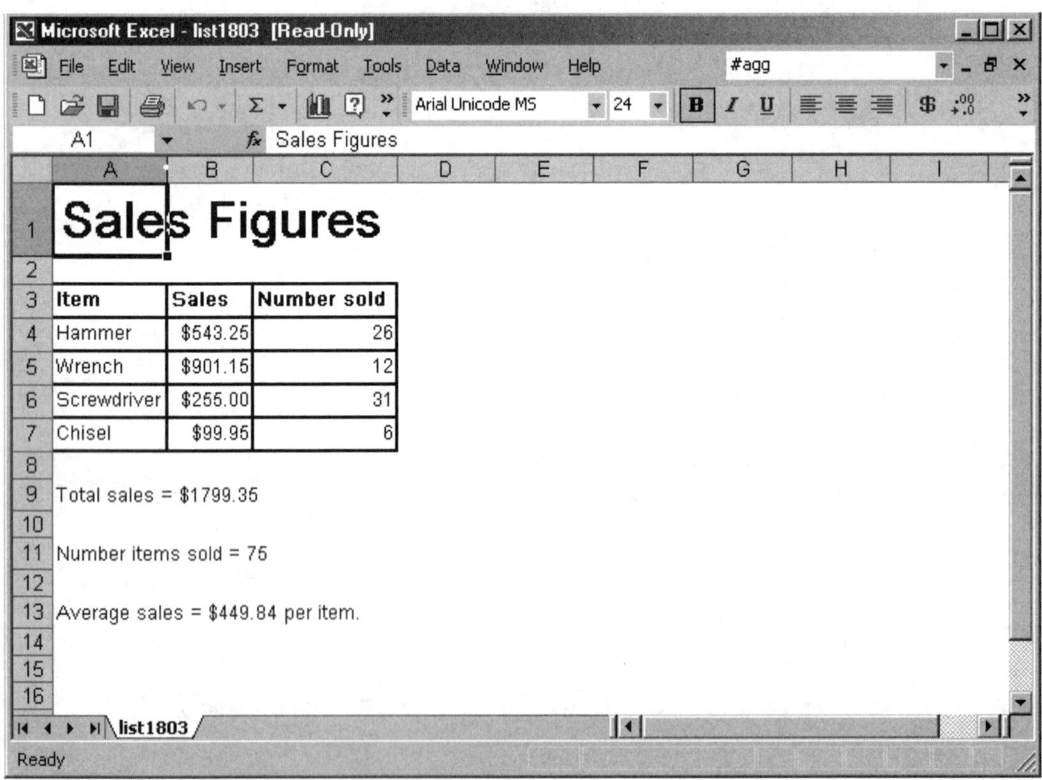

Figure 20.3 An XML file with a style sheet applied opened in Excel

window size and protection status; style definitions; and column widths and row heights. The following parts of an Excel workbook are not saved in XML format:

- Charts and other graphic objects
- Macro sheets and dialog sheets
- Custom views
- Drawing object layers
- Outlining
- Scenarios
- Shared workbook information
- VBA projects

Note that you cannot save a password-protected workbook in XML format. The purpose of saving a workbook in XML format in not, of course, for opening again in Excel, as Excel's own data file format works perfectly well for that. Rather, by making the information available in the widely supported XML format, it becomes accessible for many uses. For example, you could use XSLT to transform the Excel/XML data into another format for reading by a specialized data analysis program, or you could use a style sheet to format the data for Web presentation.

To get an idea of how Excel saves workbook information in XML format, look at the worksheet shown in Figure 20.4. When this worksheet is saved in XML format, the resulting XML file is shown in Listing 20.5.

Listing 20.5 XML File Created When the Worksheet Shown in Figure 20.4 Is Saved in XML Format

```
<?xml version="1.0"?>
<Workbook xmlns="urn:schemas-microsoft-com:office:spreadsheet"
 xmlns:o="urn:schemas-microsoft-com:office:office"
 xmlns:x="urn:schemas-microsoft-com:office:excel"
 xmlns:ss="urn:schemas-microsoft-com:office:spreadsheet"
 xmlns:html="http://www.w3.org/TR/REC-html40">
 <DocumentProperties xmlns="urn:schemas-microsoft-com:office:office">
  <Author>Peter G. Aitken</Author>
  <LastAuthor>Peter G. Aitken</LastAuthor>
  <Created>2001-04-06T14:21:57Z</Created>
  <LastSaved>2001-04-06T14:26:01Z</LastSaved>
  <Company>PGA Consulting</Company>
  <Version>10.2511</Version>
```

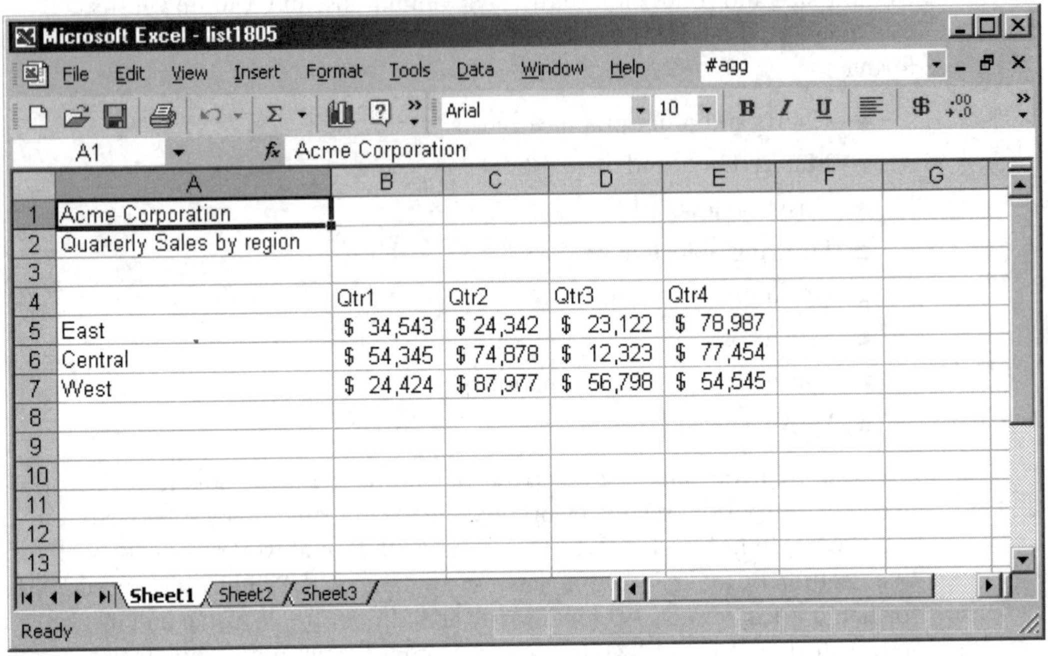

Microsoft Excel - list1805

	A	B	C	D	E	F	G
1	Acme Corporation						
2	Quarterly Sales by region						
3							
4		Qtr1	Qtr2	Qtr3	Qtr4		
5	East	$ 34,543	$ 24,342	$ 23,122	$ 78,987		
6	Central	$ 54,345	$ 74,878	$ 12,323	$ 77,454		
7	West	$ 24,424	$ 87,977	$ 56,798	$ 54,545		

Figure 20.4 A worksheet to be saved in XML format

```
 </DocumentProperties>
 <OfficeDocumentSettings xmlns="urn:schemas-microsoft-
com:office:office">
  <DownloadComponents/>
  <LocationOfComponents HRef="file:///E:\"/>
 </OfficeDocumentSettings>
 <ExcelWorkbook xmlns="urn:schemas-microsoft-com:office:excel">
  <WindowHeight>5265</WindowHeight>
  <WindowWidth>9420</WindowWidth>
  <WindowTopX>240</WindowTopX>
  <WindowTopY>105</WindowTopY>
  <ProtectStructure>False</ProtectStructure>
  <ProtectWindows>False</ProtectWindows>
 </ExcelWorkbook>
 <Styles>
  <Style ss:ID="Default" ss:Name="Normal">
   <Alignment ss:Vertical="Bottom"/>
   <Borders/>
   <Font/>
```

```
    <Interior/>
    <NumberFormat/>
    <Protection/>
   </Style>
   <Style ss:ID="s18" ss:Name="Currency">
    <NumberFormat
     ss:Format="_(&quot;$&quot;* #,##0.00_);_(&quot;$&quot;*
\(#,##0.00\);_(&quot;$&quot;* &quot;-&quot;??_);_(@_)"/>
   </Style>
   <Style ss:ID="s23" ss:Parent="s18">
    <NumberFormat ss:Format="_(&quot;$&quot;* #,##0_);_(&quot;$&quot;*
\(#,##0\);_(&quot;$&quot;* &quot;-&quot;??_);_(@_)"/>
   </Style>
  </Styles>
  <Worksheet ss:Name="Sheet1">
   <Table ss:ExpandedColumnCount="5" ss:ExpandedRowCount="7"
x:FullColumns="1"
    x:FullRows="1">
    <Column ss:AutoFitWidth="0" ss:Width="126"/>
    <Column ss:AutoFitWidth="0" ss:Width="51"/>
    <Column ss:Index="4" ss:AutoFitWidth="0" ss:Width="51.75"/>
    <Column ss:AutoFitWidth="0" ss:Width="51"/>
    <Row>
     <Cell><Data ss:Type="String">Acme Corporation</Data></Cell>
    </Row>
    <Row>
     <Cell><Data ss:Type="String">Quarterly Sales by region</Data></Cell>
    </Row>
    <Row ss:Index="4">
     <Cell ss:Index="2"><Data ss:Type="String">Qtr1</Data></Cell>
     <Cell><Data ss:Type="String">Qtr2</Data></Cell>
     <Cell><Data ss:Type="String">Qtr3</Data></Cell>
     <Cell><Data ss:Type="String">Qtr4</Data></Cell>
    </Row>
    <Row>
     <Cell><Data ss:Type="String">East</Data></Cell>
     <Cell ss:StyleID="s23"><Data ss:Type="Number">34543</Data></Cell>
     <Cell ss:StyleID="s23"><Data ss:Type="Number">24342</Data></Cell>
     <Cell ss:StyleID="s23"><Data ss:Type="Number">23122</Data></Cell>
     <Cell ss:StyleID="s23"><Data ss:Type="Number">78987</Data></Cell>
    </Row>
    <Row>
     <Cell><Data ss:Type="String">Central</Data></Cell>
     <Cell ss:StyleID="s23"><Data ss:Type="Number">54345</Data></Cell>
```

```
   <Cell ss:StyleID="s23"><Data ss:Type="Number">74878</Data></Cell>
   <Cell ss:StyleID="s23"><Data ss:Type="Number">12323</Data></Cell>
   <Cell ss:StyleID="s23"><Data ss:Type="Number">77454</Data></Cell>
  </Row>
  <Row>
   <Cell><Data ss:Type="String">West</Data></Cell>
   <Cell ss:StyleID="s23"><Data ss:Type="Number">24424</Data></Cell>
   <Cell ss:StyleID="s23"><Data ss:Type="Number">87977</Data></Cell>
   <Cell ss:StyleID="s23"><Data ss:Type="Number">56798</Data></Cell>
   <Cell ss:StyleID="s23"><Data ss:Type="Number">54545</Data></Cell>
  </Row>
 </Table>
 <WorksheetOptions xmlns="urn:schemas-microsoft-com:office:excel">
  <Selected/>
  <Panes>
   <Pane>
    <Number>3</Number>
    <ActiveRow>4</ActiveRow>
    <ActiveCol>2</ActiveCol>
   </Pane>
  </Panes>
  <ProtectObjects>False</ProtectObjects>
  <ProtectScenarios>False</ProtectScenarios>
 </WorksheetOptions>
</Worksheet>
<Worksheet ss:Name="Sheet2">
 <WorksheetOptions xmlns="urn:schemas-microsoft-com:office:excel">
  <ProtectObjects>False</ProtectObjects>
  <ProtectScenarios>False</ProtectScenarios>
 </WorksheetOptions>
</Worksheet>
<Worksheet ss:Name="Sheet3">
 <WorksheetOptions xmlns="urn:schemas-microsoft-com:office:excel">
  <ProtectObjects>False</ProtectObjects>
  <ProtectScenarios>False</ProtectScenarios>
 </WorksheetOptions>
</Worksheet>
</Workbook>
```

Word

The word processing component of Office, Microsoft Word, does not provide any specialized XML tools. You do have the option of saving a Word document as a Web page (an HTML document), and the resulting HTML document will use XML data islands to hold some information about the document. Otherwise, however, the Word user must turn to VBA programming in order to work with XML. You saw an example of using a VBA procedure to read XML into a Word document earlier in this chapter. In this section I show you how to use VBA to save a Word document as XML.

When you save a Word document as XML, you may want to make use of a namespace that has been defined by Microsoft as pertaining to Word: "urn: schemas-microsoft-com:office:word." This namespace is used with Word-related tags in the XML data islands that are included when a Word document is saved as HTML. Whether or not you use this namespace depends on your specific needs.

The VBA project presented in this section shows how you can save a Word document in XML format. The XML format used is based on the fact that a Word document is made up of paragraphs. Each paragraph contains text (at least in most cases—in theory, a paragraph could be empty), and it also has a style associated with it that determines how the paragraph is formatted in Word. A document also has a name, which is the filename it is saved under. Therefore, the XML format to be used is as follows:

- A `<docname>` element containing the document's name.
- A `<para>` element for each paragraph in the document. The `<para>` element will contain the paragraph text and will have a "style" attribute specifying the paragraph's style.

This is a very simple way of looking at a Word document, but it will serve for demonstration. A real-world VBA program to save the complete contents of a Word document as XML would have to take many more document components into consideration, such as footnotes, headers, and comments. While this would be an involved process, the Word object model provides easy access to all parts of the document.

The VBA procedure is shown in Listing 20.6. You can paste this procedure into the Word VBA Editor and run it. The code is fully commented, so its operation should be clear. Note that this procedure creates the XML file as a Word document and then saves it in text format. It would also be possible to use VBA's file access commands to open and write a text file directly.

Figure 20.5 shows a short Word document that was used to test this procedure. Listing 20.7 displays the resulting XML.

Listing 20.6 VBA Procedure to Save the Current Word Document in XML Format

```
Public Sub SaveCurrentDocAsXML()

Dim p As Paragraph
Dim OutputFile As String
Dim newDoc As Document
Dim currentDoc As Document
Dim s As String

' Get the output file name.
OutputFile = InputBox("Enter XML file name, without extension:", _
    "Save as XML", "Sample")
OutputFile = OutputFile & ".xml"

' Get a reference to the active document.
Set currentDoc = ActiveDocument

' Create a new, blank document and activate it.
Set newDoc = Documents.Add
newDoc.Activate

' Add the basic XML info.
Selection.TypeText "<?xml version='1.0'?>" & vbCrLf

' Save the document name.
s = "<docname>" & currentDoc.Name & "</docname>" & vbCrLf
Selection.TypeText s

' Save each paragraph.
For Each p In currentDoc.Paragraphs
    s = "<para style='" & p.Style & "'>"
    s = s & vbCrLf & p.Range.Text & "</para>" & vbCrLf
    Selection.TypeText s
Next

' Save the new document as text format.
newDoc.SaveAs OutputFile, wdFormatDOSText
' Close the new document.
newDoc.Close
' Activate the original document.
currentDoc.Activate
```

```
' Display a "done" message"
s = currentDoc.Name & " has been saved as " & OutputFile
MsgBox s

End Sub
```

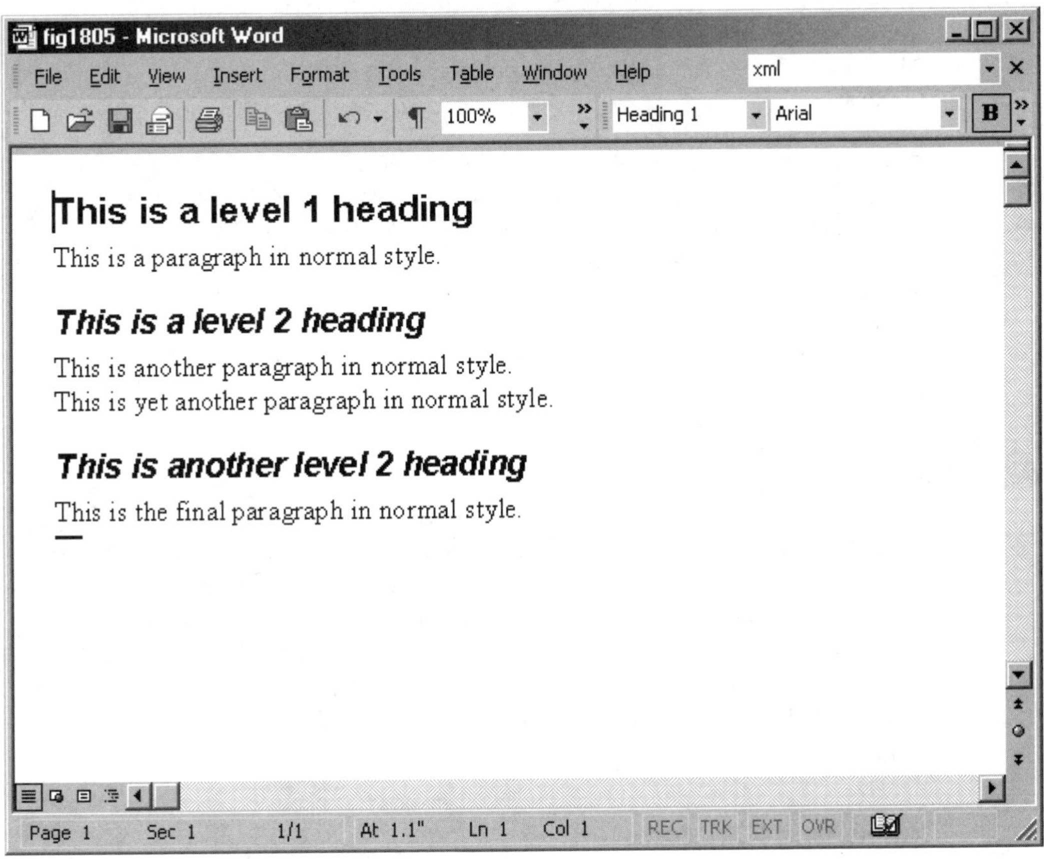

Figure 20.5 A simple Word document for testing the document-to-XML conversion

Listing 20.7 XML File Created When the Word Document in Figure 20.5 Is Converted into XML

```
<?xml version='1.0'?>
<docname>fig2005.doc</docname>
<para style='Heading 1'>
```

```
This is a level 1 heading
</para>
<para style='Normal'>
This is a paragraph in normal style.
</para>
<para style='Heading 2'>
This is a level 2 heading
</para>
<para style='Normal'>
This is another paragraph in normal style.
</para>
<para style='Normal'>
This is yet another paragraph in normal style.
</para>
<para style='Heading 2'>
This is another level 2 heading
</para>
<para style='Normal'>
This is the final paragraph in normal style.
</para>
```

Access

It makes sense that Access would provide the most XML support of all the Office applications. After all, both Access and XML are designed for data storage. XML data can be imported into an Access data table, and data as well as database schemas can be exported from Access to XML. When you export to XML from Access, the resulting XML files make use of a special XML vocabulary called ReportML, which is designed specifically to describe various aspects of a database.

Importing XML Data

To import XML data into an Access table, the XML must be well-formed. You can import XML data into a Jet, SQL Server, or SQL Server 2000 Desktop Edition (formerly called MSDE) database. You can import the structure of the XML file alone or along with its data. If you select the former option, Access creates an empty data table with a field for each element in the XML file.

Before importing XML data, you need to understand how Access imports nested elements. In the simplest situation, the XML data will consist of one level of child elements under the main elements, as in this example:

```
<addresslist>
  <person>
    <name>Ann Smith</name>
    <address>35 Oak Street</address>
    <city>Albany</city>
    <state>NY</state>
    <zipcode>12345</zipcode>
  </person>
</addresslist>
```

Thus, under the `<person>` element there is only one level of child elements. When Access imports an XML file with this structure, it creates a table with the same name as the top-level child element ("person" in this case), and the table contains one field for each second-level child element ("name," "address," "city," "state," and "zipcode").

More complex XML structures are handled differently. Consider this XML example, in which there are two levels of children under the main elements:

```
<addressbook>
    <person>
        <firstname>Arthur</firstname>
        <lastname>Williams</lastname>
        <address>
            <street>5 Oak Street</street>
            <apartment>3B</apartment>
            <city>Anytown</city>
            <state>NC</state>
            <postalcode>23456</postalcode>
            <country>US</country>
        </address>
    </person>]
</addressbook>
```

In this case, Access will make two tables:

- A table named "person" with two fields: "firstname" and "lastname"
- A table named "address" with six fields: "street," "apartment," "city," "state," "postalcode," and "country"

After importing a complex XML file such as this, you can use tools in Access to combine the resulting tables if you like.

> ***No Attributes***
>
> *When you import XML files into Access, the application ignores attributes and their data will be lost. It is difficult to believe that this is intentional, and it may be an oversight in the prerelease Office XP software I'm using to write this chapter. Perhaps the problem will be fixed in the final release version.*

Here are the steps required to import an XML file into Access:

1. Select Get External Data from the Access File menu, and then select Import.
2. In the Import dialog box, select XML Documents from the Files of Type list. Select the desired XML file, and then click Import.
3. The Import XML dialog box (see Figure 20.6) lists the table(s) that will be created. If you want to import structure and data, click OK. To import structure only or to append to an existing table, click the

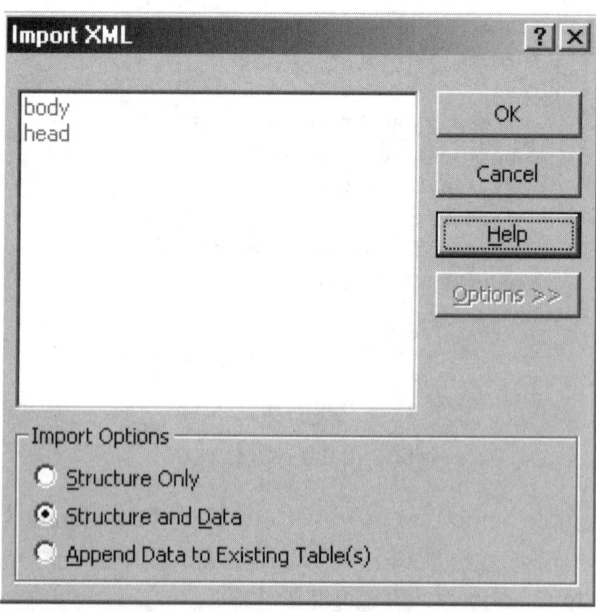

Figure 20.6 The Import XML dialog box in Access

Options button to display the Import Options, as shown in Figure 20.6, and then select the desired option before clicking OK.

Note that the Append Data to Existing Tables option is applicable only if your database table already contains one or more tables with the same name and structure as the XML data being imported.

Exporting Data and Schemas

Access provides a great deal of flexibility when it comes to exporting data tables to XML and other database components to XML. To export a data table, select the table in Table view, and then select Export from the File menu to display the Export Table dialog box. In this dialog box, select XML Documents from the Save as Type box, enter a name for the export file (if the default is not acceptable), and then click Export. Access displays the Export XML dialog box, as shown in Figure 20.7. In this dialog box, select one or more options as follows:

- Select the "Data (XML)" option to export the table data to an XML file with the .xml extension.
- Select the "Schema of the data" option to export the table schema in a format compatible with the W3C standard, as a XSD file.
- Select the "Presentation of your data" option to export a presentation consisting of two files: an XSL (*.xsl) style sheet containing XSLT commands to transform the XML file into HTML for display, and an HTML document that uses the MSXML Parser to apply the style sheet to the

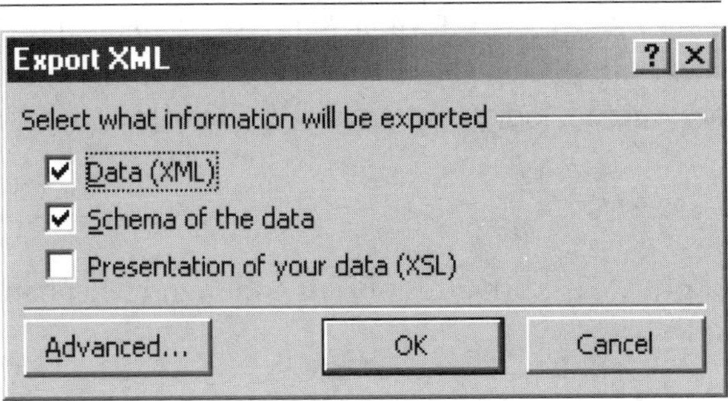

Figure 20.7 The Export XML dialog box enables you to select options when you export a table.

XML file and display the results. You cannot select this option unless the “Data (XML)” option is selected also.

The Export XML dialog box has an Advanced button that enables you to select some additional export options. For example, you can decide whether an exported schema is embedded in the XML document or output as a separate file (the default). You can also select whether a presentation is exported as a client-side HTML document (the default) or as a server-side ASP page.

Other Access database components, such as forms and reports, can be exported to XML as well. The procedure is essentially the same as described previously for tables, although the exact steps and available options differ. Data access pages, however, cannot be exported in this format.

FrontPage

FrontPage is the Office application for creating and managing Web sites. As such, it is designed to work primarily with HTML. Somewhat surprisingly, the latest version of FrontPage offers no special features for creating pages in XHTML, and it offers almost no support for XML. If you want to create a data island, you must insert XML into an HTML document manually or by using the FrontPage Insert command.

FrontPage offers only one XML-specific feature, a command called Apply XML Formatting Rules. If you display a Web page in HTML view and right-click in the document, this command becomes available on the pop-up menu that appears. This command goes through the HTML code in the document looking for incomplete or missing tags, and it inserts corrections as needed so the document follows XML formatting rules. Specifically, this means that closing tags will be added and stand-alone tags will have the forward slash (/) added. For example, look at the following HTML:

```
<p>My Web Page<hr>
```

The Apply XML Formatting Rules command will change this HTML to the following:

```
<p>My Web Page</p><hr />
```

The primary use for this command is when you are converting an HTML document into XHTML.

Summary

Microsoft Office is a highly customizable suite of office productivity applications. It includes a full-featured programming language, Visual Basic for Applications (VBA), that can be used to create custom solutions for specific data manipulation and presentation needs. A VBA program can make use of the MSXML Parser and all of its XML processing capabilities, permitting any Office application to be integrated into an XML-centric environment. In addition, the Access database program provides its own commands for importing and exporting XML data.

APPENDIX A

XDR Schema Data Types

This list includes all of the data types supported for the `dt:type` attribute of the `datatype` element in the XDR Schema (Microsoft implementation). Types marked with an asterisk (*) are the primitive data types that correspond to the data types supported in DTDs.

`dt:type` **Setting**	**Data Type**
`bin.base64`	MIME-style Base64 encoded binary BLOB.
`bin.hex`	Hexadecimal digits representing octets.
`boolean`	0 or 1, where 0 = "false" and 1 = "true."
`char`	String, one character long.
`date`	Date in a subset ISO 8601 format, without the time data. For example, 1999-10-09.
`dateTime`	Date in a subset of ISO 8601 format, with optional time and no optional zone. Fractional seconds can be as precise as nanoseconds. For example, 1999-05-06T17:19:29.
`dateTime.tz`	Date in a subset ISO 8601 format, with optional time and optional zone. Fractional seconds can be as precise as nanoseconds. For example, 1999-05-06T17:19:19-09:00.
`entities*`	References to multiple entities.
`entity*`	A reference to an entity.

(continued)

dt:type Setting	Data Type
enumeration*	An enumeration (attributes only).
fixed.14.4	Same as "number" but no more than 14 digits to the left of the decimal point, and no more than 4 to the right.
float	Real number, with no limit on digits; can have a leading sign, fractional digits, and optionally an exponent. Punctuation as in U.S. English. Values range from 1.7976931348623157E+308 to 2.2250738585072014E-308.
i1	Integer represented in 1 byte. A number, with optional sign, no fractions, no exponent. Range from –128 to 127. For example, 1, –120, 100.
i2	Integer represented in 2 bytes. A number, with optional sign, no fractions, no exponent. Range from –32,768 to 32,767.
i4	Integer represented in 4 bytes. A number, with optional sign, no fractions, no exponent. Range +/– 2.15 billion (approximately).
id*	A unique identifier (DTD ID type)
idref*	A reference to an "id" type (DTD idref type).
idrefs*	Multiple references to "id" types (DTD idrefs type).
int	Number, with optional sign, no fractions, and no exponent.
nmtoken*	A name consisting of XML token characters (DTD NMTOKEN type).
nmtokens*	Multiple names consisting of XML token characters (DTD NMTOKENS type).
notation*	Reference to a notation (DTD NOTATION type).
number	Number, with no limit on digits; can potentially have a leading sign, fractional digits, and optionally an exponent. Punctuation as in U.S. English. (Values have same range as most significant number, R8, 1.7976931348623157E+308 to 2.2250738585072014E-308.)

(continued)

dt:type Setting	Data Type
r4	Real number, with 7-digit precision; can potentially have a leading sign, fractional digits, and optionally an exponent. Punctuation as in U.S. English. Values range from 3.40282347E+38F to 1.17549435E-38F.
r8	Real number, with 15-digit precision; can potentially have a leading sign, fractional digits, and optionally an exponent. Punctuation as in U.S. English. Values range from 1.7976931348623157E+308 to 2.2250738585072014E-308.
string*	Text (DTD #PCDATA).
time	Time in a subset ISO 8601 format, with no date and no time zone. For example, 06:19:47.
time.tz	Time in a subset ISO 8601 format, with no date but optional time zone. For example, 09:1416-06:00.
ui1	Unsigned integer stored in 1 byte. A number, unsigned, no fractions, no exponent. Range from 0 to 255.
ui2	Unsigned integer stored in 2 bytes. A number, unsigned, no fractions, no exponent. Range from 0 to 65,535.
ui4	Unsigned integer stored in 4 bytes. A number, unsigned, no fractions, no exponent. Range from 0 to approximately 4.29 billion.
uri	Universal Resource Identifier (URI). For example, "urn:schemas-microsoft-com:Office9."
uuid	Hexadecimal digits representing octets, optional embedded hyphens that are ignored. For example, 333C7BC4-460F-11D0-BC04-0080C7055A83.

Bibliography

Web Resources

http://www.w3.org/XML/1999/XML-in-10-points. A clear, brief introduction to XML and related technologies.

http://www.w3.org/XML/. The W3C's main page for XML, providing links to many other XML resources.

http://www.w3.org/TR/2000/REC-xml-20001006. The complete W3C Recommendation for XML version 1.0.

http://www.w3.org/XML/Schema. The W3C's main page for XML Schemas (XSD Schemas).

http://www.w3.org/TR/xmlschema-0/, http://www.w3.org/TR/xmlschema-1/, and http://www.w3.org/TR/xmlschema-2/. A three-part instructional presentation on XML Schemas.

http://www.xfront.com/. An XML Schema tutorial by Roger L. Costello.

http://www.xfront.com/BestPracticesHomepage.html. XML Schema's best practices page.

http://www.w3.org/TR/xpath. W3C's main page for XML Path Language (XPath).

http://www.w3.org/TR/1999/REC-xpath-19991116. The complete W3C Recommendation for XPath.

http://www.w3.org/Style/XSL/. The W3C's main page for Extensible Stylesheet Language (XSL).

http://www.w3.org/TR/xslt11/. The complete W3C Recommendation for XSL Transformations (XSLT) version 1.1.

http://www.nwalsh.com/docs/tutorials/xsl/. An XSL tutorial by Paul Grosso and Normal Walsh.

http://www.w3.org/MarkUp/. The W3C's main page for Extensible HTML (XHTML).

http://www.w3.org/TR/xhtml11/. The complete W3C Recommendation for XHTML version 1.1.

http://www.w3.org/MarkUp/Guide/. A tutorial on HTML by Dave Raggett.

http://msdn.microsoft.com/library/default.asp?url=/library/en-us/xmlsdk30/ htm/xmmscxmlreference.asp. Microsoft's reference material on XML and DOM.

http://www.xml.org/xml/xmlfaq.shtml. FAQs for XML and related technologies.

Books

Bob DuCharme, *XML the Annotated Specification* (Upper Saddle River, NJ: Prentice Hall PTR, 1999).

Elliotte Rusty Harold and W. Scott Means, *XML in a Nutshell* (Sebastopol, CA: O'Reilly, 2001).

Michael Kay, *XSLT Programmer's Reference* (Chicago: WROX Press, 2000).

Didier Martin et al., *Professional XML* (Chicago: WROX Press, 2000).

Ann Navarro, *XHTML by Example* (Indianapolis: Que, 2001).

Natanya Pitts, *XML Black Book, 2nd Edition* (Scottsdale, AZ: Coriolis, 2001).

Index

F

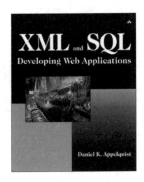

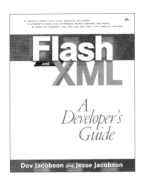